D0508446

Science in the Multicultural Classroom

A Guide to Teaching and Learning

SECOND EDITION

Robertta H. Barba

San Jose State University

Allyn and Bacon

Boston ■ London ■ Toronto ■ Sydney ■ Tokyo ■ Singapore

Series Editor: Frances Helland
Marketing Manager: Kathy Hunter
Production Administrator: Deborah Brown
Editorial-Production Service: P. M. Gordon Associates, Inc.
Text Design and Electronic Composition: Denise Hoffman
Composition Buyer: Linda Cox
Manufacturing Buyer: Suzanne Lareau
Cover Administrator: Suzanne Harbison
Photo Researcher: Susan Duane

Copyright © 1998, 1995 by Allyn & Bacon
A Pearson Education Company
160 Gould Street
Needham Heights, MA 02194
Internet: www.abacon.com
America Online: keyword: College Online

Library of Congress Cataloging-in-Publication Data

Barba, Robertta H.
    Science in the multicultural classroom : a guide to teaching and
learning / Robertta H. Barba. — 2nd ed.
        p.   cm.
    Includes bibliographical references (p.   ) and index.
    ISBN 0–205–26737–8
    1. Science—Study and teaching (Elementary)   2. Multicultural
education.   I. Title.
LB1585.B27   1998
372.3'5'044—dc21   97–10531
                                                                CIP

Printed in the United States of America
10 9 8 7 6 5 4 3   02 01 00 99 98 97

Photo Credits: Will Hart (pp. 17, 35, 57, 107, 108, 131, 167, 170, 201, 299, 321, 344, 376);
Stephen Marks (pp. 19, 33, 99, 311); North Wind Picture Archive (p. 59); The Bettmann Archive
(p. 62); Lyrl Ahern (p. 66); Robert Harbison (p. 80); Alon Reininger/Woodfin Camp & Associates
(p. 83); Jim Pickerell (p. 199); Brian Smith (pp. 229, 317); Will Faller (pp. 280, 368).

Contents

CHAPTER 3
The History of Science: A Culturally Affirming Perspective   54

PART TWO   ■   **Constructing a Knowledge of Science**

 CHAPTER 4
Ways of Knowing Science   74

CHAPTER 5
Groups in the Science Classroom   102

CHAPTER 6
Assessing Knowledge in the
Science Classroom   126

PART THREE ■ **Developing Pedagogical Content Knowledge**

 CHAPTER 7

Instructional Strategies for Culturally Diverse Learners   162

 CHAPTER 8

Constructing a Knowledge of Science and Language   190

CHAPTER 9
**Constructing a Knowledge of
Science Processes   224**

CHAPTER 10
Technology in the Multicultural Classroom   268

PART FOUR ■ **Teaching through Thematic Units**

CHAPTER 11
Math/Science Integration in the
Multicultural Classroom   294

CHAPTER 12
Constructing a Knowledge of Science from Text in the Multicultural Science Classroom **314**

◢ Preface

Some Thoughts on Karaoke

As I have written this second edition, I have considered the words of my university colleagues and the voices from the field, those teacher-practitioners who, in real classrooms with real kids, try to implement that which we say. While some of my colleagues have advocated some intriguing ideas about translating theory into practice, I have balanced their words with the thoughts and ideas from classroom teachers who wrestle with ways to teach science to every child, every school day. In that process I have learned that great and wonderful theories sometimes don't pan out in the science classroom. If I have erred in presenting ideas about ways of teaching science to children in this book, it is on the side of the practical, on the side of teachers striving to make science come alive in their classrooms.

Sometimes, as university faculty, we have wonderful ideas about teaching and learning that simply don't work in the classroom. I recently suggested to a group of inservice teachers that karaoke was a wonderful technique for encouraging second language learners to improve their English language skills and to showcase their conceptual understandings of science. I had rigged up a karaoke demonstration in a graduate-level class at the university. I played some sappy love songs and asked the students to compose new science lyrics to accompany the music. At the appropriate time, I handed the microphone to the students and allowed them to sing their new science lyrics for the class. We had a wonderful evening in class. Then the teachers went to their own classrooms and tried out the idea. The feedback was enlightening.

While I was able to set up a karaoke demonstration in a university classroom, I forgot that most teachers don't have access to the sound mixers, amplifiers, and microphones necessary to do karaoke in a public school setting. My students reported that they were lucky to have even one or two laser disc players in each school; sound mixers and amplifiers were beyond their schools' budgets. My students chastened me for my lack of understanding about the realities of public school life. Justifiably so. I had forgotten the lessons that I learned in 21 years of public-school teaching. My students were the voices from the field that brought me back in touch with classroom practice.

While I acknowledge my colleagues' great and wonderful ideas about teaching and learning science, sometimes those ideas just aren't practical for everyday use. This does not mean that we should not dream dreams of what could or should be, it only means that we need to temper those dreams with a good dose of reality. As I reviewed, corrected, and proofed this manuscript, I sought to keep teachers and children at the center of my writing. If I could not personally do something in a classroom with children, then I did not advocate it for others. Likewise, if teachers with whom I work found something to be cumbersome or impractical, I substituted a "working" idea. The purpose of this reflection was to establish an appropriate balance between theory and practice.

Acknowledgments

I am deeply indebted to my sons P. Javier and Aaron Miguel Barba for their support and patience during the writing of this manuscript. Thank you, gentlemen, for being so understanding and so considerate, for making do a thousand times in the past years in order to allow me time to write and reflect.

Professionally, I am grateful for the encouragement and expertise of my colleagues, who have counseled, coached, supported, and mentored me during the writing of the first and second editions of this book, including Dr. Karen E. Reynolds (professor at San Jose State University); Dr. Margie Kitano (associate dean of the College of Education at San Diego State University), who served as mentor and guide for the research; Dr. Judith Sowder (Mathematics Department at San Diego State University), for her insights into mathematical problem solving and the sociocultural construction of knowledge and for her expertise in editing the manuscript; Dr. Sandra Marshall (director, Center for Research in Mathematics and Science Education at San Diego State University), who provided encouragement for the work and space for the research; Dr. Patricia Grinager (retired from the University of Wisconsin), who guided the conceptual framing of the text; and Dr. Patricia Keig (California State University–Fullerton), who served as a personal coach and encourager during the years of writing. Additionally, I am deeply appreciative of Nancy Forsyth, my editor at Allyn and Bacon, for her counsel and expertise during the writing of this manuscript.

Robertta Barba

CHAPTER

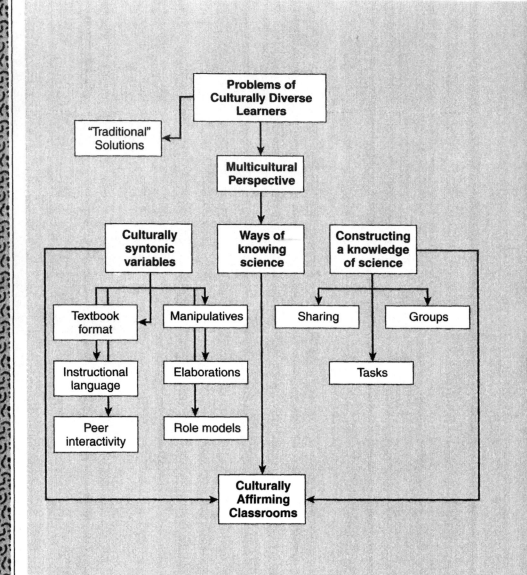

Science in the Multicultural Classroom: An Introduction

The evening that I returned home from teaching a science methods class at the university to find Javier, my number two son, preparing for high school registration, will remain fixed in my memory for many years. According to Javier, he and his father had spent several hours pouring over the high school course brochure and discussing his future aspirations. The two of them had diligently filled out the schedule request forms, which were to be taken back to the high school guidance counselor the next morning. Being more than a little curious about the product of their labors, I picked up one of the completed forms and began to read. "Javier, you forgot to take a science class," I yelled. Like many parents I sometimes have to compete with music videos. "Mom," responded Javier, "I don't have to take science next year."

"What do you mean you don't have to take science next year?" I said in my growling, motherly voice. "We only have to take two years of science in high

school, and so I'll take it my sophomore and junior years," answered Javier. For a mother who has spent her entire professional career in science educa- tion, this was not the preferred pronouncement. "But, Javier," I protested, "I thought you'd want to take science every year in high school." "Oh, Mom, get real!" answered Javier. "I don't like science." "Why don't you like science?" I queried. "Science is dull and boring, and besides, Mom, everyone knows sci- ence is for snowflakes," Javier answered.

Javier's words have haunted me every day since that conversation. They haunt me as a parent and as a professional science educator. Certainly, I found Javier's reference to Anglos as "snowflakes" (an expression commonly used in the West Coast inner-city schools that Javier attended at that time) an intolera- ble racist remark, worthy of a parental tongue lashing. But while Javier's Anglo teachers would have found his remark highly offensive, a 40 to 50% drop-out rate among Hispanic teenagers is equally offensive to the Hispanic/Latino com- munity of this nation. I have come to realize both as a parent and as a science educator that his remarks reflect the feelings of many children of color and white females who perceive the study of science and the pursuit of science-related careers as they might view an exclusive country club that they may observe but not enter. For too long, our children have come to regard science as a white male domain.

The purpose of this book is to present ways of science teaching that will help you as a science educator meet the needs of all of our culturally diverse learners. This text is divided into four main parts:

- *Addressing Diversity*
- *Constructing a Knowledge of Science*
- *Developing Pedagogical Content Knowledge*
- *Teaching through Thematic Units*

The first part, "Addressing Diversity," deals with issues germane to the science education needs of culturally diverse learners. This section contains discus- sions of equity issues, the nature of science, motivational strategies, and the history of science from the viewpoint of culturally diverse children. The second part, "Constructing a Knowledge of Science," contains a discussion of ways in which children learn and means for facilitating the academic growth of chil- dren of color and white females. "Developing Pedagogical Content Knowledge" deals with content area–specific knowledge necessary for effective science teaching. Finally, the part on "Teaching through Thematic Units" presents models for integrating content areas, for presenting science as part of a unified whole.

SCIENCE EDUCATION AND
DIVERSE LEARNERS

Perhaps it is best to begin our discussion of science education and culturally diverse children by looking at national trends in science education. Hart (1977) states that "despite the faith of under-represented minorities in the American educational system as a means for social and economic advancement, equal education has not assured culturally diverse individuals equal access to opportunity" (p. 2), especially in science, mathematics, and related computer technology fields. African American, Hispanic/Latino, Native American, and other culturally diverse individuals comprise approximately 18% of our U.S. population, but only 2.2% of our technical work force. The numbers of culturally diverse students enrolled in mathematics, science, computer science, and computer engineering studies remain low, despite the removal of many social and legal barriers to the full participation of these students in science careers. Colleges and universities in our country are still experiencing an underrepresentation of culturally diverse applicants capable of meeting entry standards in science and mathematics majors. Many high-ability and culturally or linguistically diverse students and many of those with high potential face not only educational but also economic barriers in their pursuit of training for high-tech jobs. The gap between socioeconomic levels is widening as the upward mobility rate remains less than 3% per generation in this country. It is important to realize that this problem of underrepresentation of culturally diverse students in science careers does not begin at the university level but rather in the elementary schools.

As Table 1.1 clearly illustrates, socioeconomic status is strongly related to educational level. Additionally, race, ethnic origin, or both are also strongly related to educational level.

Equity in Science Education

Culturally diverse students, especially those who speak a first language other than English, consistently perform less well on standard measures of academic achievement (e.g., SAT, GRE, MAT) than do their English-speaking peers. High school attrition (drop-out) rates at all socioeconomic levels in this nation are higher for culturally diverse students than for white students (see Table 1.1). Since the passage of the Civil Rights Act in 1965, the high school graduation rate for African American students in this nation has gradually improved, but the graduation rate for Hispanic/Latino students has actually declined (see Figure 1.1).

The African American "drop-out" rate, shown in Figure 1.1, is rapidly approaching the white "drop-out" rate. The attrition rate for Hispanic/Latino students, declining a decade ago, has risen rapidly in recent years. The reasons for this phenomenon are not clearly understood.

TABLE 1.1 ■ Highest Level of Education Attained by 1995 High School Seniors, by Socioeconomic Status and Race/Ethnicity

Socioeconomic Status and Ethnicity	No High School	High School Diploma	License	Associate Degree	Bachelor's Degree	Graduate Degree
Lower 30%						
White	0.9%	75.1%	12.2%	5.0%	6.6%	0.3%
Black	1.4%	73.0%	12.7%	5.1%	7.7%	0.1%
Hispanic	1.6%	73.9%	11.8%	7.8%	4.9%	<0.05%
Asian	<0.05%	53.4%	17.3%	15.7%	12.0%	1.6%
Middle 50%						
White	0.3%	62.0%	13.0%	8.0%	16.3%	0.4%
Black	0.3%	67.5%	14.7%	6.5%	10.7%	0.3%
Hispanic	1.0%	67.0%	14.7%	6.5%	10.7%	0.2%
Asian	<0.05%	51.1%	11.7%	11.1%	26.1%	<0.05%
Upper 30%						
White	<0.05%	44.9%	8.6%	6.2%	38.2%	2.2%
Black	<0.05%	56.3%	12.4%	5.4%	30.5%	0.4%
Hispanic	0.3%	60.0%	11.4%	9.6%	18.0%	0.7%
Asian	<0.05%	42.9%	6.5%	4.8%	40.0%	5.9%

Source: National Center for Education Statistics, *Digest of Education Statistics, 1995.* U.S. Department of Education, Office of Educational Research and Improvement, Washington, D.C.: 1996.

Proportionally few culturally diverse students choose to attend and graduate from four-year degree-granting institutions, a condition that limits the potential of these students, their communities, and society in general. University participation rates among culturally diverse and low-income students provide good indicators of progress in educational equity. In 1988 only 28% of African American high school graduates and 20% of Hispanic/Latino high school graduates enrolled in colleges or universities (*Statistical Abstract of the United States,* 1990). Historically, most culturally diverse students have enrolled in two-year community colleges rather than at four-year degree-granting institutions. Although many states have made strides to improve the participation, persistence, and graduation rates of their culturally diverse students, the number of these students enrolled in mathematics and science-related careers lags far behind white student enrollments. Statistics from states such as California (home of the nation's largest population of culturally diverse students) provide an image of a nation in which culturally diverse individuals are not preparing for jobs in mathematics, sciences, or related com-

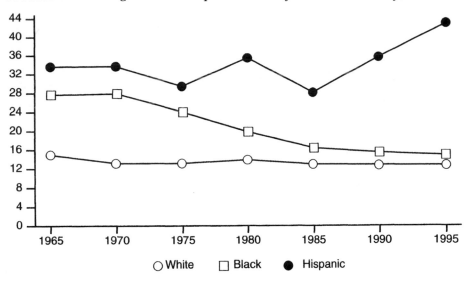

FIGURE 1.1 ■ High School "Drop-Out" Rates by Race and Ethnicity, 1965–1995.

○ White ☐ Black ● Hispanic

puter technology fields (see Table 1.2). Within a decade, nearly every state in this nation will face a situation similar to that of California. We are becoming a nation of racial and ethnic "unmeltables," a nation in which "minorities" are becoming the majority population.

Table 1.2 reflects mathematics, science, and related technology degrees awarded in a recent two-year period in the state of California in terms of race and ethnic origin. From these data it is apparent that few are awarded to culturally diverse individuals, a problem not only of California, but of the entire nation.

TABLE 1.2 ■ Distribution of Bachelor's Degrees by Race and Ethnicity in Selected Math and Science Fields of Study

	White	African American	Hispanic/ Latino	Asian American	Native American	Total
Computer Science	685	35	72	471	1	1,264
Engineering	2,056	68	274	1,096	23	3,517
Mathematics	368	8	38	82	8	504
Physics	423	15	30	63	2	533
Total Degrees	3,532	126	414	1,712	34	5,818

Source: CSU Office of the Chancellor, Division of Analytical Studies, "Undergraduate and Graduate Degrees Granted," *1992–1994 Statistical Report,* June 1994.

Factors of race, gender, and socioeconomic status continue to play a major role in the education of culturally diverse students, especially in science, mathematics, and related technology careers that require high levels of specialized or technical training. While race, class, and gender have tremendous impact on the education of white females and culturally diverse individuals in all disciplines, participation rates of culturally diverse individuals in science fields do not seem to follow the patterns of other disciplines. Culturally diverse individuals have made significant gains in their participation rates in business and industry sectors during the past three decades in this nation, but they have not made gains in science and related technology fields. Why haven't white females and culturally diverse individuals significantly increased their participation rates in science disciplines?

Elementary Science Instruction

Numerous studies have shown that many elementary teachers rely heavily on expository teaching methods and textbooks as the primary means for instructing children in science. On an average, across this nation, elementary students spend less than 20 minutes a day studying science (Weiss, 1987). When science is taught in the elementary school, it is taught from textbooks rather than as a hands-on, inquiry-based learning experience. Surveys indicate that 75% of lower elementary (K–3) and 90% of upper elementary (4–6) science instruction involves lecture and discussion teaching methods. Elementary science is taught by many teachers as if science learning consists of memorizing facts, definitions, and rules. In most elementary classrooms, children are expected to assume a passive role when science is taught. It is little wonder that many children find science dull and boring.

THE NATURE OF SCIENCE

Too often, science is taught not as a way of knowing, as a way of responding to curious questions about the natural world, but as a body of facts and vocabulary words to be memorized and recited. "School science," or science as it is practiced in many U.S. elementary school classrooms, has little to do with real science. In writing of the nature of science, Rubba and Anderson (1978) have identified six **characteristics of scientific knowledge:**

- *Amoral:* Scientific knowledge itself cannot be judged as morally good or bad.
- *Creative:* Scientific knowledge is the product of human creativity.
- *Developmental:* Scientific knowledge is tentative, the best possible explanation of phenomena, based on what is currently known.
- *Parsimonious:* Scientists explain phenomena in terms of simplicity rather than complexity.

- *Testable:* Scientific knowledge is capable of being tested.
- *Unified:* Scientific laws, theories, and concepts are interrelated.

Scientific knowledge in and of itself is neither good nor bad; rather it is our use of scientific knowledge that causes moral dilemmas. Technology is the application of science. Contrary to popular belief, scientific knowledge of the structure of the atom is neither harmful nor helpful; it is simply knowledge. Weapons of war, a military technology, or the application of the knowledge of atomic structure represent humankind's misapplication of scientific knowledge. Likewise, a knowledge of the mechanism of mammalian reproduction is neither benevolent nor injurious; it is simply knowledge. Technological applications of that knowledge have been developed in many different arenas. As a child growing up on a farm, I remember the visits of the agent from the artificial breeders' association. He appeared periodically and artificially inseminated our dairy herd. My father and mother thought that artificial insemination of the herd was a good idea; it saved us the expense and trouble of keeping a bull on the farm. When this same technology is applied to humans, the result is a plethora of lawsuits regarding surrogate parents, children's rights, and parental rights. Knowledge is amoral—without value.

Science is a creative enterprise. Science is not a discipline that urges us to read, memorize, and recite; rather it is an enterprise that encourages us to use our intellect to solve real world problems—to create, to invent, to build, and to develop new ideas and ways of thinking. Children actively engaged in learning science should be engaged in problem solving. Our society needs creative thinkers who look at natural phenomena for new solutions to problems. How will we get to work when our petroleum resources are used up? What is the cure for the current Hantavirus epidemic? A multitude of real world problems await a new generation of creative thinkers, the children who are in your classroom today.

Scientific knowledge is developmental. It is in process, never fully completed. Each new generation adds to the knowledge of the previous generations. Albert Einstein, in developing his theory of relativity, said that he was "standing on the shoulders of giants." His "new" scientific knowledge was built on the knowledge of previous scientists. As a young child, I remember noticing that as Claude, our neighbor, plowed he would periodically stop his tractor and pick up field stones. He would carry the newly unearthed stones to one of the walls surrounding his fields and add them to the top of the walls. One day I asked him about the practice; he told me that generations of farmers in his family had been adding stones to those walls, that the walls were works in progress. Thus it is with science; science is like a wall of knowledge in progress. Each new generation of scientists adds to the knowledge of previous women and men of science, yet there is still more knowledge to add.

Science is parsimonious. Scientists seek simple, comprehensible explanations for natural phenomena, not complicated, complex, contorted explanations. As a child, I often walked through the woods with my father. On a particularly beautiful autumn day, I asked him why the leaves changed color in the fall. In his usual quiet and gentle manner, he said, "They don't." When pressed for an explanation, my father said simply that the reds, oranges, yellows, and browns had been there all along. I couldn't see them because they were masked by the green chlorophyll. As the chlorophyll was destroyed by the lower autumn temperatures, the other colors became visible to my eye. Good scientific explanations are simple; they are comprehensible explanations for real world phenomena.

Scientific knowledge is testable. When a scientific discovery is made, other scientists throughout the world are able to duplicate the experiment and achieve the same results. Recently, a friend gave me a recipe for banana bread. No matter how carefully I followed his instructions, I couldn't duplicate the flavor and texture of his bread. When I asked him about this, he remembered that he had forgotten to list several key ingredients. Scientific knowledge is testable; folk practice isn't. Replicability is a cornerstone of science. This ability to verify new discoveries through experimental replication differentiates scientific knowledge from folklore and quackery.

Scientific knowledge is unified, in that scientific laws, theories, and concepts are interrelated. The transfer of energy from potential energy (stored energy) into kinetic energy (energy of motion) illustrates this concept. In the physical sciences we learn that a rock sitting atop a cliff is an illustration of potential or stored energy. When the rock falls from the cliff, it exhibits kinetic energy. In the human body, as food is burned in the process of respiration, potential energy (stored in the food) is converted into kinetic energy (muscle movement). In the geological sciences, earthquakes illustrate the conversion of potential energy into kinetic energy. The concept of energy transfer occurs in physical, life, and earth and space sciences. Laws, theories, and concepts associated with energy are interrelated and apply to all sciences. Scientific knowledge and methods are gender and ethnicity free. All members of our society ought to be encouraged to pursue the study of science.

Ways of Knowing Science

The study of science and related technology often requires students to adapt to a white male culture, to an **androcentric/Eurocentric** worldview. The basic assumptions of science, as it is taught to U.S. children in textbooks, focus on male as opposed to female, and European as opposed to Eastern or African or South American ways of viewing the world. The axiological and epistemological beliefs of textbook science are tied to a European or white male way of viewing the world. This culture values competitiveness and individual achievement. Most modern science instruction is based on principles of realism. This value system holds that there is an ultimate truth and that humans can discover this truth in the natural world. The Eurocentric foundation of science focuses on European (and European descendants') values, attitudes, and ways of "knowing things."

Androcentric instructional models focus on male or individual ways of knowing and doing things. Teachers often emphasize famous "men of science" to children, while ignoring females and group contributions to the history of science. Our public schools typically teach mathematics, science, and computer technologies from this Eurocentric/androcentric perspective. In order for the educational process to be successful in these content areas, children must assimilate to this instructional model, that is, they must accept a white/European male–dominated instructional model and value system.

Culturally diverse children, those who are **bilingual/bicultural** and **bidialectic** (who speak a dialect of English other than that used in mainstream middle-class America), often do not share many of the values, beliefs, and attitudes inherent in Eurocentric/androcentric science instruction. Additionally, white females, even though they are linguistically assimilated in mainstream U.S. culture, are often not culturally assimilated to male ways of learning science. The use of Eurocentric/androcentric instructional models precludes the participation of culturally diverse individuals and white females (see Figure 1.2).

FIGURE 1.2
Culturally Syntonic Variables

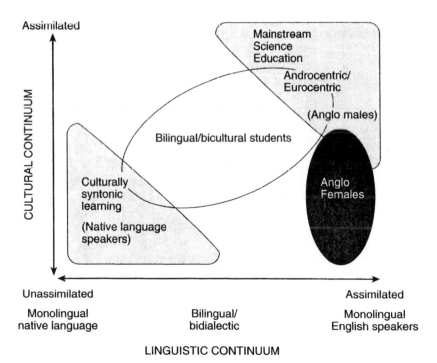

White male students find it relatively easy to become engaged in science activities, for science is presented in a language and in a cultural manner familiar to them. While white females may be fully assimilated linguistically into mainstream U.S. culture, they may not be assimilated into male ways of "knowing" and "doing" things. Many females find careers in science unappealing, because accommodation to "male ways" of interacting and learning are unfamiliar. Many culturally diverse students—even those whose families have lived in the United States for generations—are not from middle-class communities. Indeed, many of these students exhibit the same characteristics as bilingual/bicultural students who have recently arrived in this country. Students from lower socioeconomic backgrounds and those who are bidialectic (e.g., who speak a dialect of English such as Appalachian English or the language of the "hood" or barrio) or bicultural, find assimilation to the "white male" science model very difficult, both academically and culturally. Changing the ways that we teach science and related technology courses involves changing the ways that we view knowledge and the ways we view the teaching and learning process.

MINORITY PARTICIPATION IN SCIENCE CAREERS

Recent literature has attributed the underrepresentation of minority students and white females in science fields to a variety of variables, including (1) lack of student interest in science, (2) science anxiety, (3) personality factors, (4) white male–dominated images of science, (5) lack of minority role models in science and related technology careers, (6) socioeconomic barriers, (7) improper counseling regarding academic track coursework at the high school level, (8) teacher attitudes and expectations, and (9) lack of proper academic preparation. Although all of these variables are salient in the education of culturally diverse individuals and white females, each is part of an encompassing cultural history that extends from children's earliest years of schooling through their final years of schooling.

Looking at Elephants

Science education researchers working on identifying variables that impact the participation of culturally diverse individuals and white females in science careers each see part of the problem, but none seems to have the big picture. Helen Keller is credited in modern folklore with telling the story of blind children visiting the circus for the first time. When the children arrived at the elephant compound, each child was assigned by their teacher to stand at a different portion of the elephant. The blind child assigned to stand by the ear described an elephant as a giant piece of warm paper. The child assigned by the teacher to stand by the leg described the elephant as like a tree trunk. The child assigned to stand by the tail described the elephant as like a rope. Finally, the child assigned to the trunk described the elephant as like a giant snake. Each child correctly described part of the elephant, yet no child was correct in that none had the total picture. Perhaps this is the situation with researchers dealing with culturally diverse individuals and science careers. Each researcher description is right, yet none seems to have integrated all of the parts and pieces into a unified whole.

Pipeline Theory

During recent years, the National Science Foundation has been publishing a pipeline chart based on the numbers of individuals who at various ages declare an interest in a career in mathematics and science (National Science Foundation, 1987). The chart begins on the right-hand side with a vast "supply" of some four or five million high school sophomores who are potential scientists, mathematicians, computer programmers, and so forth. "Drips" and "leaks" in the pipeline, in the form of attrition at various stages of the educational process, gradually constrict the flow until at the end of the educational process (or the left-hand side of the pipeline chart) only about 10,000 individuals emerge with a Ph.D. degree in a science or mathematics discipline.

Extrapolating from this model, one could increase the numbers of culturally diverse individuals and females receiving degrees in science and mathematics simply by plugging up the leaks. Indeed, vast amounts of money are currently spent in this country to identify white females and culturally diverse students who show an interest in mathematics and science careers at the elementary, middle school, and high school level and to treat these children with the "right stuff." The underlying philosophy of these programs is that once these students are identified and given some remediation and a little mentoring, they will stay in the pipeline and will emerge as successful scientists, mathematicians, or computer programmers. The major flaw inherent in this pipeline model is the assumption that females and culturally diverse students are deficient and that "correction of their deficiencies" will repair the problem.

Remember my son Javier? He opted out of science in eighth grade and elected not to pursue a rigorous program of science studies in high school. Two years before the National Science Foundation study begins to keep track of him, Javier has already left the pipeline. His elementary and middle school science experiences influenced him not to continue his study of science. Calling the plumber to fix the leaks may not be a viable educational solution. For a very long time science educators have been asking the question, What's wrong with the children? Perhaps they should have been asking, What's wrong with the system?

WHAT'S WRONG WITH THE SYSTEM?

A hint as to what's wrong with the system comes from Sheila Tobias, who in *They're Not Dumb, They're Different* (1990) has pointed out that mathematics and science instruction is frequently "distasteful" even for mainstream accomplished scholars. For her study, Tobias recruited graduate students and professors (from disciplines other than science) to audit science courses at the university level and to keep journals and diaries of their experiences. Her recruits described science instruction as "user unfriendly" in three specific areas: (1) student/teacher interactions, (2) physical environment, and (3) content presentation.

The subjects in Tobias's study pointed out that science is presented primarily through the use of expository teaching techniques with very little student/teacher interaction. Additionally, a well-established hierarchy within the classroom placed students in the lowest caste, teaching assistants in the middle caste, and professors in the upper caste. Interactions between students and teachers rarely occurred in the classroom. When students had difficulty with the course content they were referred to the middle-level managers or teaching assistants instead of being allowed to interact directly with the professor, the implication being that only a select group of individuals had a sufficient knowledge base to interact with the professor. Participants in this study described the university-level science classes as devoid of human contact, environments in which each student works alone without the support and guidance of a mentor or human interaction. The textbooks presented factual information without explanatory narrative sections. The professors occasionally talked of famous men of science, but the exemplary models they used came from the domain of Western science (i.e., Eurocentric science) and the examples focused on androcentric (male-centered as opposed to female-centered or human-centered) models.

The physical environment of science classrooms and laboratories was hostile, according to the subjects in Tobias's study. In addition to being isolated from each other by the nature of the work, the students in science classes were physically isolated from each other by the seating arrangements in the classrooms. Students sat in rows in large lecture halls, usually with an empty seat on either side of them. The "sage-on-stage" (the teacher standing in the front of the room lecturing to the class) learning model used so commonly for introductory courses in mathematics and sciences did not lend itself to social interactions among students.

Finally, the subjects in Tobias's study found science courses dull, dry, factual, and computationally oriented. The instructors observed by Tobias in her study emphasized computation before concepts. "How" questions rather than "why" questions seemed to be the benchmarks of the science classes observed. The insistence on performance before competence combined with a rapid instructional rate and a lack of explanations resulted in high anxiety and reduced class attendance among students. The problems of science in-struction that Tobias described in her study have been reported previously by other researchers and are typical of elementary and secondary schools as well as university science classrooms.

ADDRESSING EQUITY ISSUES

You may well ask, How does one address equity issues? How do schools re-spond to the needs of culturally diverse students? Many teachers believe that culturally diverse children come from culturally deficient communities and environments. In the United States, where cultural assimilation has been an important movement, people who speak a language other than English or who have different patterns of interacting are sometimes considered less "ad-vanced" than those who possess mainstream culture (Pang, 1988). Sometimes teachers believe that culturally diverse children do not excel because they come from families and communities that do not properly prepare students for learning. Teachers occasionally believe that some students do not care whether they do well in school, that these students are not properly prepared to succeed in an academic environment, that they are not motivated to learn. The cultural deficit model as described by Sleeter and Grant (1987) assumes that schools should change learners, should help them assimilate to main-stream culture, including the "culture of science." From this viewpoint, chil-dren need remedial work to compensate for their lack of knowledge, skills, and attitudes in the sciences and mathematics. Those who advocate this worldview regard students as being "at risk" when they do not share U.S. mainstream language and culture. The National Science Foundation pipeline approach typifies this worldview. If we just call the plumber, if we just plug the leaks, then we can "fix the students."

Multicultural Approach

In contrast to the deficit model, those who adhere to a multicultural model (Sleeter & Grant, 1987) see the cultural and linguistic backgrounds of diverse students as valuable educational resources. A "multicultural approach to ed-ucation promotes cultural pluralism and social equality by reforming the school program for all students to make it reflect diversity" (Sleeter & Grant, 1987, p. 139). If one adopts this worldview, then children who speak a pri-mary language other than English are an asset because they have constructed a knowledge of science in a different sociocultural context than have others in the class and thus they bring added resources to the classroom. Those who advocate the use of a multicultural approach to education see diversity as a strength in the classroom, as a vehicle for increasing the learning of all students.

Culturally Syntonic Variables

Mastery of content knowledge has been shown to include an interplay between culture (which includes language) and concept formation. Historically, many culturally diverse children have encountered school science taught in a culturally unfamiliar manner as well as in an unfamiliar language. As a result these students never acquire the desired level of language proficiency, nor do they "understand" the science and mathematics concepts taught in the classroom.

In a study of the learning patterns of Hmong students, Hvitfeldt (1986) found that cultural variables influenced verbal interaction patterns in the classroom, students' preferred learning modes, and students' concept acquisition. Studies with Hawaiian American (Au, 1980; Spring, 1950; Weisner, Gallimore & Jordan, 1988), Asian American (Cheng, 1992), African American (Stewart & Benson, 1988), and Native American (Harris, 1985) children indicated that children's culture influences the ways they interact with teachers and the ways they construct knowledge in the classroom. Many Native American children have been socialized to divert their gaze, as a mark of respect, when they speak to an elder. Teachers who are unaware of this habit may tend to regard these children as inattentive or impolite, rather than as extremely courteous and respectful. As children grow into adults, their ways of interacting become ingrained. Culturally diverse learners sometimes find that their ways of thinking, knowing, and interacting are unacceptable in the elementary science classroom. For many culturally diverse children, the rules of social interaction and the patterns of learning acquired at home become impediments as they struggle to make sense of school learning.

Culturally syntonic stimuli were first defined in the medical literature nearly a hundred years ago as "stimuli which oscillate in harmony with one's culture" (Spitler, 1889, p. 2). The existence of culturally syntonic variables that impact the education of Hispanic/Latino adults was delineated by Valle (1978) in a neuropsychological context. Valle has since redefined culturally syntonic variables to be "those factors or influences which are in harmony with normative behaviors, values and attitudes of a particular ethnic or cultural group" (1986, p. 30). Ensuing research has shown that these variables impact not only the learning, but also the teaching and testing of students. Elementary science teachers should view culturally syntonic or culturally harmonious variables as those culture-of-origin beliefs, attitudes, and practices that influence (both positively and negatively, functionally and dysfunctionally) the teaching/learning process.

In the science classroom, culturally syntonic or culturally harmonious variables for diverse learners would include variables such as the format of printed materials, preferred instructional mode, instructional language, level of peer interaction, use of culturally familiar role models, culturally familiar elaboration and context, and level of interactivity with manipulative materials. In identifying culturally syntonic variables, we must be careful to recognize that culturally diverse students represent many different cultures and belief systems. Mexican American, Puerto Rican American, Central American, South American, and Cuban American students may share a common language; but beliefs, values, attitudes, and cultural histories differ from one individual to another. Additionally, we need to be cautious to avoid stereotyping all members of a particular ethnic group as having the same attributes. For example, although most culturally and linguistically unassimilated Hispanic/Latino children prefer a *fotonovela* format for reading materials (that is, a highly visualized presentation of declarative knowledge), not all Hispanic/Latino students share this preference. Country of origin, level of assimilation with mainstream culture, degree of acculturation, socioeconomic status, and individual differences need to be taken into account when identifying culturally syntonic variables.

Format of Printed Materials

Research involving the format of printed materials has shown that the fotonovela or photonovel (a highly visual storybook format) is the most effective means for conveying verbal information to most unassimilated Hispanic/Latino and certain Southeast Asian learners (Comes-Diaz, 1984; Costantino, Malgady, & Rogler, 1988; Flora, 1980; Hill and Browner, 1982; Horn, 1983; le Boterf, 1984). These studies have shown that unassimilated students learn more declarative knowledge (knowledge that can be stated) from textual materials printed in a fotonovela format than from traditional textbooks. Additionally, culturally unassimilated Hispanic/Latino and Southeast Asian learners have been shown to prefer the fotonovela format, which is commonly used in third-world literacy campaigns, over the text format used in traditional Eurocentric textbooks.

While elementary science textbooks used in the United States include many pictures, charts, and diagrams, the books are not structured in a way that tells a story through those pictures. Children used to constructing meaning from a sequence of photographs, sketches, or drawings find the format used in U.S. science textbooks unfamiliar and difficult to understand. *The Popcorn Book* (DePaolo, 1978) is probably the best-known example of a fotonovela format in U.S. children's literature. This book tells the story of popcorn through colored line drawings, "balloons" containing information about popcorn written at an early elementary reading level, and script boxes with additional information written at an upper elementary reading level. *The Popcorn Book* allows for the use of a linguistic scaffolding technique for learning. The teacher or parent encourages the child to talk about the pictures showing the history of popcorn and the uses of popcorn. Older children and those who can read at an early elementary school level glean more information about popcorn by reading the words in the balloon. Finally, the teacher or the parent reads the detailed information about popcorn, from the script boxes at the bottom of the page. This format, in which knowledge is constructed from a sequence of pictures, simple reading words, and complicated textual passages, is common in fotonovelas and is widely used in third-world literacy campaigns. Elementary science textbooks used in the United States do not incorporate this type of text format.

Instructional Language

For content area concept acquisition, access to instruction in the home language for purposes of cued recall benefits students who are not fully assimilated linguistically into mainstream culture (Cortes, 1986; Cummins, 1979; Ehindero, 1980; Olson, 1986; Ortiz & Maldonado-Colon, 1986; Watts, 1986). Research shows that the use of native language in the classroom (1) builds students' self-esteem, (2) improves students' attitudes toward schooling, (3) facilitates content area acquisition of declarative knowledge, and (4) aids in mainstream English language development. New knowledge can be integrated with existing knowledge only when existing knowledge (which may have been constructed in the student's native language) is restructured and when students elaborate on what they already know. Allowing students to use their home language in small group settings for purposes of cued recall is rarely encouraged in traditional elementary classrooms. Additionally, the use of multimedia courseware that contains multiple language tracks also benefits second language learners. Culturally syntonic classrooms are those in which students are encouraged to bring their home learning to class and to combine that with their school learning.

Level of Peer Interactivity

Peer tutoring, especially when new concepts or vocabulary are introduced in a class, improves students' concept acquisition (Cohen & Lotan, 1990; Cohen, Knight, & Kagan, 1977; Cohen, Lotan, & Catanzarite, 1990; Ortiz, 1988; Watson, 1991). Negotiating meaning by building a personal rendition of knowledge through social interactions is foundational in the learning process. All of us have had the experience of sharing the meaning of a word in a group setting, of contributing our ideas to the collective body of knowledge, and of finally reaching agreement about a new expanded definition for a term. Research with unassimilated culturally diverse students has shown that many such children prefer peer tutoring environments to large group instructional situations. Peer tutoring appears to be an effective means of bridging linguistic barriers for bilingual/bicultural students and for conferring status on unassimilated students. Previous research indicates that most culturally diverse learners profit from cooperative group work and peer tutoring in terms of cognitive growth, attitude change, and self-esteem.

Many culturally diverse learners prefer group environments.

The works of Cohen, Lotan, and Catanzarite (1990), Ramirez and Castaneda (1974), Rodriguez and Bethel (1983), Valle (1978, 1986), and Watson (1991) indicate that use of cooperative learning or familia (cross-age tutoring) groups increases students' science concept acquisition. When culturally diverse students are allowed to work in cooperative groups, their attitudes toward science and school in general improve. Finally, students' self-esteem is increased through use of cooperative activities. Although research has shown that cooperative learning is highly effective in meeting the educational needs of culturally diverse learners, studies have found that cooperative learning is rarely used in practice in elementary schools. Likewise peer tutoring, if it occurs at all, is seen as the domain of the student—to be accomplished outside of class settings, not as part of the regular instructional program.

Role Models

The presence of culturally familiar role models or significant others, both in person and in printed materials or textbooks, constitutes an important variable that impacts the cognitive learning of all students, including culturally diverse students (Bandura, 1962; Cicourel, 1974; Kahle, 1985; Pearson & Bechtel, 1989; Shade, 1982; Tanner & Lindgren, 1971; Van Sertima, 1986). I remember as a child reading the life story of Marie Curie. For years, I aspired to be like Curie, to win a Nobel Prize for the discovery of a new element. Children need successful role models to emulate.

Marie Curie has served as a role model for generations of women in science.

Studies by Cicourel (1974), Healy (1990), Pitman (1989), and Tanner and Lindgren (1971) demonstrated that the presence of culturally familiar role models in textual materials significantly increases students' self-esteem, concept acquisition, and motivation to pursue science careers. Few if any culturally diverse role models are presented to students in elementary science classrooms (a discussion of culturally diverse scientists is presented in Chapter 3 of this book).

Elaboration and Context

Culturally familiar elaborations, which employ culturally familiar objects, environments or contexts, examples, and analogies, function as powerful variables in terms of culturally diverse students' concept acquisition. Culturally familiar contexts significantly increase students' acquisition of declarative knowledge (Halpern, Hansen, & Riefer, 1990; Kessler & Quinn, 1980; Rodriguez & Bethel, 1983). Previous research has shown that culturally familiar examples proportionally benefit students who are not yet culturally or linguistically assimilated into mainstream U.S. culture. Additionally, research supports the notion that culturally familiar objects, contexts, examples, and analogies increase students' self-esteem and increase the rate at which stu-

dents master content area concepts. Culturally familiar examples and elaborations append new learning to existing schema. Cued recall serves to activate prior knowledge and to allow students to connect new knowledge to existing schema.

As teachers, we tend to use examples and analogies from our own mainstream U.S. experience. Sometimes, when students do not share our frame of
reference, the examples we use are not part of the child's milieu; thus children don't understand our explanations. When we use cultural objects and
examples familiar to students we help them connect their home learning to
school learning. Recently, I observed a kindergarten teacher present a lesson

*Culturally familiar contexts
increase learning.*

on seeds. The teacher had asked students to bring seeds from home. Each child came to class with seeds that their family ate. Some children proudly exhibited pinto beans, while others displayed sesame seeds, long-grained rice, and black-eyed peas gathered from their families' gardens and pantries. Each child contributed to the class's knowledge of seeds by bringing objects familiar to their families.

Interactivity with Manipulative Materials

Finally, interaction with laboratory equipment and/or manipulative materials increases the learning of conceptual or declarative knowledge among students. Interaction with manipulative materials positively impacts students' attitudes toward science. Research by Brown, Fournier, and Moyer (1977), Comes-Diaz (1984), Kessler and Quinn (1980), and Ornstein-Galicia & Penfield (1981), indicates that use of laboratory and/or manipulative materials significantly increases the speed with which students master concepts and assists students in developing problem-solving skills. While many teachers know the value of laboratory investigations, these activities are rarely seen as part of the main instructional program. Research has shown that using multiple means of knowledge representation benefits all learners, yet teachers rarely hold hands-on manipulative activities in the same regard with which they view textbook-based activities.

Other culturally syntonic variables identified as salient for the education of culturally diverse learners include the talk story (Au & Jordan, 1977), holistic learning (Rhodes, 1988), students' geocentric perspectives (Van Otten & Tsutsui, 1983), bidialectic expression (Cronnel, 1981; Hochel, 1983; Levine & Hanes, 1976), and stage-setting behaviors (Longstreet, 1987; Shade, 1979).

Constructing a Knowledge of Science

Constructivists hold that knowledge is constructed, not transmitted. From a **constructivist** viewpoint, conceptual knowledge of science is constructed (1) gradually over time, (2) by the learners within a social context, (3) through a series of interactions with the content, (4) when new information is integrated with old information, and (5) so that the result is an awareness of what is being learned. Learning occurs within a social context as students share their ideas with peers, both in small groups and within the total society of the classroom. From a multicultural perspective, schools, rather than students, are seen as being "at risk," especially when they do not capitalize on the richness of experience that culturally diverse learners bring to classroom social interactions.

For many students, especially culturally diverse students, mathematics and science classes are hostile environments. Making these instructional environments user friendly requires changes in three areas: teacher/student interactions, instructional methods, and curriculum content. Improving the teacher/student interactions in a classroom requires awareness on the part of the teacher of the ways in which students learn. For many culturally diverse students, "mugs and jugs" or purely expository teaching models, which have their origins in the essentialist theories of education, are culturally unfamiliar learning models. Personal interactions with teachers are vital in the learning process for many students. The instructional methods used in classrooms with culturally diverse learners need to be models in which students are free to interact with others in ways that are culturally familiar and comfortable. Large group interactions in which students are expected to receive information are highly ineffective pedagogical strategies for many culturally diverse learners. Personalized instruction, small group interactions, and opportunities for hands-on/minds-on experiences are vitally needed in science classrooms. Finally, the science curriculum and the ways that knowledge is presented to students need to be addressed in science and related technology content areas. In order for students to actualize an interest in science, they must feel that its content relates to their lives. For science instruction to be effective, it must be personalized to meet the needs of the students.

Constructivist learning models (Cobern, 1991; Driver & Bell, 1986; Driver & Oldham, 1986; Roth, 1990; Wheatley, 1991), which use problem-solving thematic approaches to learning, appear to be highly appropriate pedagogical approaches for use with culturally diverse learners because they (1) provide multiple means of data representation, (2) allow for peer tutoring, (3) provide for the use of home language in small groups, (4) allow students to bring culturally familiar examples and elaborations into the classroom, (5) permit students to interact with manipulative materials, (6) encourage students to work cooperatively in constructing new knowledge, and (7) "fit" with what is known of the learning/teaching process (from research in cognitive psychology).

CLASSROOM PRACTICE

The lack of achievement of culturally diverse learners in science- and technology-related content areas is of grave concern to all of us. In making culturally affirming schools, our ways of viewing students and the teaching/learning process itself need to change dramatically. Students can't be "fixed" in the way that flat tires are fixed on automobiles. Rather, what is needed is a view of students and schools that affirms us all. First, we need to begin with an assumption that students are not deficient, but rather that they bring a wealth of knowledge of the world around them to the classroom and to their academic endeavors. Second, we need to allow students to bring their culture and experiences to each new learning experience. We need to affirm our students, to assist them in appending new knowledge to that which they already possess. Third, our teaching models need to be changed from teacher-centered to student-centered learning models, especially in the science content area. Problem-solving or problem-centered learning needs to form the core of our instructional program. Doing science, rather than hearing about science or reading about science, needs to be central to our educational process.

If elementary science instruction is to become culturally affirming instruction, then we need to understand that often our schools are deficient in the ways that they present knowledge to students, rather than to assume that our students are deficient. The *National Science Education Standards* (National Research Council, 1996) state that one content standard for all students is the concept that humans depend on their natural and constructed environments (p. 129). Achieving this standard requires that students develop an environmental ethic, a belief that we need to conserve our natural resources. As a nation, our students are our most valuable resource. It is imperative that we preserve and protect our children with even more vigor than we protect our planet. If we are to prevent culturally diverse men and women from becoming endangered species in science, mathematics, and related technology careers, then we must make the instruction of these subjects user-friendly.

CHAPTER SUMMARY

Culturally diverse students participate in science, mathematics, and related technology careers in proportionally fewer numbers than do other individuals in U.S. society. Traditionally, schools have viewed bilingual/bicultural and bidialectic students as deficient, as needing remediation in order to fully participate in mainstream science instruction. The purpose of this book is to propose culturally affirming instructional strategies; that is, ways of viewing children and schools and science curricula that affirm all children.

▓ TOPICS TO REVIEW

- Characteristics of science
- Eurocentric/androcentric viewpoint
- Bilingual/bicultural and bidialectic students
- Barriers to minority participation in science
- Pipeline theory
- Multicultural model
- Culturally syntonic variables
- Constructivism

REFLECTIVE PRACTICE

1. From the perspective of culturally diverse learners, what are some of the problems of "traditional" science instruction? What might be done to "correct" these problems?

2. In your opinion, how might classrooms be modified so that they are culturally affirming places of learning?

3. What type(s) of instructional materials might be best for use with culturally diverse learners? Justify your answers.

4. Has your perception of the needs of culturally diverse learners changed as a result of reading this chapter? If so, how? If not, why?

5. In your opinion, why have most schools failed to reach culturally diverse learners?

6. Assume that you are in charge of purchasing instructional materials, supplies, and so forth for a school with a large population of culturally diverse learners. What types of science materials would you purchase? Why?

7. Based on what you have read so far, how might elementary science instruction be modified to meet the needs of culturally diverse learners?

8. Based on your prior knowledge and what you have read in this chapter, how might a child's language and/or culture influence how that child constructs a knowledge of science?

CHAPTER 2

Views of Motivational Factors

Behavioral
Psychology

Status
Success
Interest
Feeling Tone
Level of Concern
Knowledge of Results

Humanistic
Psychology

Cognitive
Psychology

Motivation in the Multicultural Science Classroom

 POINTS TO PONDER

- What factors motivate children to learn science?
- How can you encourage children to learn science?
- What strategies can you use to encourage children to develop an interest in science?

Some students stand out in our memories in spite of the passage of years. Carolyn was one of those students in my life. I met Carolyn during my second year of teaching. A beautiful 17-year-old African American woman who had been placed in the eighth grade, Carolyn was a daily topic of discussion among the lounge lizards, the teachers who spent a considerable portion of each day sitting in the faculty lounge. This group perceived her to be short tempered, foul mouthed, and feisty. I met Carolyn because she was assigned to me by the principal as a teacher's helper during my planning period. Apparently most of the teachers in the building had prior experience working with Carolyn and didn't care to have her in their classes a second time. Ignoring the advice of these peers, I accepted Carolyn as a teacher's helper and agreed to provide her a quasi-supervised work experience in the science lab.

During the year that I knew Carolyn, I found her to be polite, considerate, dependable, and very personable. In the course of our year together, I came to respect and trust her. One day in particular sticks in my memory. A parent of another student had come unexpectedly to the office seeking a conference re-

25

garding the child's academic progress. I had to leave Carolyn unsupervised while I met with the parent. As I left the room, I directed Carolyn to get out supplies and materials for the next class, and I asked the teacher next door to look in on her from time to time. The conference lasted longer than expected, and by the time I returned to my classroom, the bell had rung and Carolyn had gone on to her next class.

About an hour after the conference, I began to smell an overpowering odor of rotten eggs in my classroom. At first, I suspected that the school cafeteria had served pork and beans for lunch and that some student had expelled gas. Unobtrusively, I opened the windows of the classroom, one after another. The odor grew in intensity. Soon all of the children were holding their noses and pointing accusing fingers at each other. Finally, mercifully, class ended, and yet the odor lingered. As I walked around the room, I noticed that the stench seemed to be coming from the back corner of the classroom, in the lab prep area. When I opened the acid cabinet under the sink, I noticed that all of the acid bottles were empty and that a large portion of my drainpipe was missing.

At about that time, Carolyn came bounding in the door of my classroom. "Hey, Ms. B.," she called, "I forgot to tell you, while I was getting out the equipment, I emptied out those old bottles under your sink. I'll wash 'em for you tomorrow." She ran out the door, pleased with the job she had done. Voluntarily cleaning out my storage cabinets was Carolyn's way of showing her friendship; she was internally motivated to clean out my acid cabinet. Unfortunately, she had worked without adult supervision and had disposed of the acids improperly; my drainpipe was eaten away. As I stood in the office after school explaining why I wanted to requisition a new drainpipe, I thought about children and motivation.

Carolyn wonderfully illustrates some ideas about motivation and culturally diverse children. First, she performed the task of helping me on that particular day, not because she had to, but because she wanted to be helpful. Her results surprised both of us. Many children are internally motivated to learn, to share, and to help; sometimes we don't allow them the opportunity. Second, we need to remember to avoid prejudging students, or judging them based on what others have told us. Carolyn had a reputation for being unmotivated and a troublemaker. In reality, she was a kind and sensitive person who had great difficulty learning in school and who covered up her educational difficulties with acting-out behaviors. Finally, what motivates one child may not motivate another child. From all that I could learn of her, Carolyn found school learning difficult. While she was motivated to work and learn in an informal setting, she had great difficulty in a formal class setting.

ENCOURAGING CHILDREN TO LEARN

In stating its position regarding the education of children in the multicultural science classroom, the National Science Teachers Association's board of directors wrote that "culturally diverse children must have access to quality science education experiences that enhance success and provide the knowledge and opportunities required for them to become successful participants in our democratic society" (1991). Implementation of this goal requires that children be motivated to learn science, to participate in activities that will enable them to fully participate in science and related technology careers. A student's motivation to learn science is therefore critical in the science classroom.

We can broadly define **motivation** in this context as being a student's intent or desire to learn. Gagné has stated that motivation includes a consideration of the motives that make students want to seek knowledge, to utilize their talents, to desire self-fulfillment as human beings, to relate to other people in a satisfying manner, and to become effective members of society (1987, p. 207). In writing of the role of motivation among culturally diverse students, Gay states that variables associated with learning, such as ability, motivation, interest, and classroom climate, must be understood and applied within the contexts of culture and ethnicity (1988, p. 329). Ogbu (1992) echoes those sentiments when he writes that teachers often do not recognize the meaning and value that culturally diverse students associate with school learning and achievement. Motivation plays a significant role in all children's learning, particularly minority students' learning. A knowledge of motivational factors is vital for elementary science teachers who work with culturally diverse students. Unless students are motivated to learn science, the pattern of underrepresentation of culturally diverse students in science and related technology fields will persist.

Perspectives on Motivation

At one time, students' motivation to learn was considered to be almost totally dependent on individual personality or disposition. This viewpoint arose from the notion that the responsibility for academic involvement and achievement rested primarily with the individual student. From this perspective, if students were unwilling to learn, there was little that teachers, parents, or the community could do. In challenging this belief system, Maehr points out that if one assumes that motivational change only comes through personality change, one accepts a certain fatalistic outlook as a teacher (1978, p. 223). There are many ways to view motivation; each viewpoint depends on our basic assumptions about the ways that children learn science.

Behavioral Psychology View of Motivation

If we hold a behavioral psychology view of teaching and learning, we see motivation to learn science or any subject as closely aligned with stimulus-response learning theories. Within this framework, motivation is thought to be based on a system of extrinsic or external rewards (teacher praise, grades, points, prizes, special privileges). The experiments of B. F. Skinner demonstrated that organisms tend to repeat actions that are reinforced and that behavior can be shaped by reinforcement (Biehler & Snowman, 1986, p. 469). Advocates of stimulus-response learning theories have developed behavior modification plans for motivating students to complete a task by promising them a reward.

Within the strict behavioral framework, to motivate students is really to apply the principles of contiguity, reinforcement, punishment, and modeling in order to increase, decrease, or develop behaviors. Behavioral psychologists rely on tangible rewards as the primary means for motivating students. Premack's (1965) principle is an example of a behaviorist worldview concerning motivation. Premack stated that a high-frequency behavior (a preferred activity) may be an effective reinforcer for a low-frequency behavior (a less preferred activity). In other words, First do what I want you to do; then you may do what you want to do. In my role as a parent, there are times when I have used this principle of motivation with great success. When my children were teenagers and wanted to go out on a date, I would frequently step in and say, "Not until your room is clean." It's amazing how quickly teenaged boys can clean a bedroom when teenaged girls are expecting their companionship. Cleaning is a less preferred activity for most teenagers, and dating is a preferred activity.

Behaviorist principles of motivation are normally founded on dangling carrots, that is, providing external rewards that students are expected to internalize. Behaviorists hold that the teacher should supply rewards in response to students' "appropriate" behaviors. Teachers who provide students with stars, lollipops, smiley faces, and extra time on the playground are practicing behaviorist motivational principles. For example, if you wanted to encourage sixth-grade students to learn the symbols and spellings for the 20 most common elements of the periodic table of elements, you could set up a star chart system and give students colored stars for each element they learned. You would be applying behaviorist learning principles in a classroom setting.

Humanistic Psychology View of Motivation

Humanistic psychologists such as Abraham Maslow, Carl Rogers, and Arthur Combs, in contrast, have stressed that teachers should trust pupils enough to permit them to make choices about their own learning. Humanistic psychologists, especially Maslow, view motivation as arising from a hierarchy of needs within the student. A **need,** according to Kolesnik (1978, p. 149), is any type of deficiency in the human organism or the absence of anything individuals require, or think they require, for their overall well-being. In Maslow's theory of human motivation, referred to as growth motivation or need gratification, human needs are arranged in order from physiological needs to aesthetic needs. Physiological needs (food, clothing, and shelter) are on the bottom rung of Maslow's hierarchy. Personal needs for safety, belonging, esteem, intellectual achievement, aesthetic appreciation, and self-fulfillment complete this hierarchy.

Within Maslow's hierarchy, students' desires to fill low-level needs could supersede their higher-level educational needs. If, for instance, a student comes to school hungry, the student is motivated to fill that need before engaging in academic work. Likewise, belonging to a social group and maintaining esteem within that group are important to students. If doing what the teacher says conflicts with group rules, students may choose to ignore or even defy the teacher. This type of behavior is most commonly found among prepubescent middle school or junior high school students. Occasionally, small groups of students in this age group begin to take pride in failure rather than in success. The flirtation with the failure fad is short-lived in most children's lives.

TABLE 2.1 ▓ Maslow's Hierarchy of Needs

Need	Description
Self-fulfillment	Self-actualization and the realization of all that a person is capable of being.
Aesthetic appreciation	The search for structure, order, and beauty.
Intellectual achievement	The need to know, to explore, and to understand.
Self-esteem	The desire to gain recognition and approval from others.
Belonging	The need to be loved and to be accepted among one's peers or family.
Safety	The need to feel psychologically and physically secure, free from danger.
Physiological	Survival needs—food, water, air, and shelter.

Source: Adapted from Maslow, A. M. (1970). *Motivation and Personality.*

Cognitive Psychology View of Motivation

Cognitive psychologists often highlight intrinsic or internal motivation. One central assumption of cognitive psychology is that people do not respond automatically to external events or to physical conditions; rather, they respond to their perceptions of these events. Those who adhere to a cognitive psychology paradigm emphasize that motivation is intrinsic and as such is activated by an internal satisfaction with learning as a form of self-achievement. Cognitivists see the student as active and curious, searching for information to solve personally relevant problems, and sometimes ignoring personal discomfort in order to achieve self-selected goals. Motivation, from a cognitive psychology viewpoint, is based on choices, decisions, plans, interests, goals, and calculations of likely success or failure.

Attribution theory (Weiner, 1980) and social learning theory (Bandura, 1977), theories derived from the cognitive psychology tradition, offer insights into factors that impact students' learning in the classroom. In observing students' ability to handle stress associated with success and failure, Weiner asked students to identify the reasons for their success or lack of success in the classroom. Students attributed their success or failure to four common variables: ability, effort, task difficulty, and luck.

Children with long histories of academic failure routinely attribute their success to easy questions or luck, and their failures to lack of ability. Because low-achieving students attribute failure to their own low ability, future failure is seen by these children as more likely than future success. High achievers, on the other hand, attribute their success to their ability and effort, and their failures to their lack of effort. When high achievers fail, they view the failure as a temporary setback and resolve to try harder in the future. From the viewpoint of attribution theory, external rewards will probably not be effective with low-achieving students because these children tend to view success as attributable to factors (namely their perceived lack of ability) beyond their personal control.

Bandura's social learning theory (1977) suggests that personal goal setting is a critical variable in a student's motivation or desire to learn. In the first part of his theory, Bandura states that we evaluate tasks in terms our perceptions of future outcomes. Am I likely to be successful or to fail at this? How will my peers perceive me if I am successful (or a failure) at this? According to Bandura, the goals we set become our standards for evaluating our own performance. Individuals tend to persist in their endeavors until they meet the standards or goals that they have set for themselves. As we work toward our self-selected goals, we evaluate our performance in terms of the positive things that will occur when we achieve the goal and in terms of the negative consequences of not reaching our goals. When we have achieved a goal, we tend to be satisfied for a short time and then begin the process of setting new goals, thus raising our level of aspiration. Within the context of Bandura's social learning theory, the teacher assists students in setting goals, in reflecting on performance, and in self-reinforcement.

Motivating Students

Based on what is known of student characteristics, how can we best "motivate" students to learn science? In truth, it is probably impossible for one person to motivate another. Research indicates that motivation is intrinsic or internal, not extrinsic or external. However, it is possible to change the ways things are done in the elementary science classroom to make our classroom environments more appealing to students, to encourage students to set goals, and to increase their effort and intent to learn science. Six factors have been shown to increase students' effort and desire to learn: (1) level of concern, (2) feeling tone, (3) success, (4) interest, (5) status, and (6) knowledge of results.

Level of Concern

Level of concern, the first factor shown to impact culturally diverse students' motivation to learn science, may be broadly defined as a student's level of concern about achieving in the classroom. The concept is based on Weiner's (1980) attribution theory and on Bandura's (1977) social learning theory. When a teacher presents a task, or new learning, students evaluate the task for themselves in order to determine their ability to "do the work." If a task is viewed by a child as being too easy and unchallenging, the child may begin to engage in "off-task" behaviors. Teachers are encouragers. We use persuasive communication to encourage children to attempt tasks, to try new learnings. For example, the child who is asked to plant a couple of bean seeds in a paper cup and to adjust the variables that control plant growth would probably regard this task as a fun and challenging learning activity. However, if we asked children to plant an acre of bean seeds by hand, most children would regard such a chore as dull, boring, repetitious, and devoid of new learning.

Ideal learning environments are those that offer tasks that students can accomplish. A moderate level of concern stimulates the effort to learn, but anxiety interferes with students' performance. As you attend to the needs of culturally diverse learners, remember to present tasks that are "do-able," tasks that children can accomplish with a moderate amount of effort. In writing of the characteristics of a "good task," Wheatley states that teachers should select tasks that have a high probability of being problematic for students—tasks that may cause students to find a problem (1991, p. 15). According to Wheatley, **rich educational activities** or tasks should (1) be accessible to everyone at the start, (2) invite students to make decisions, (3) encourage "what if" questions, (4) encourage students to use their own methods, (5) promote discussion and communication, (6) lead somewhere, (7) have an element of surprise, (8) be enjoyable, and (9) be extendable (1991, p. 16).

Educational researchers (Gonzales, 1989; Sieber, O'Neill, & Tobias, 1977) and sociologists (Gay, 1988; Ogbu, 1992; Suzuki, 1984) who work with culturally diverse learners point out that all children want to learn. Success in school depends not only on what schools and teachers do, but also on what students do. Students' level of concern about learning science determines their desire to learn. An excellent example of this principle is illustrated by the life of Jaime Escalante, a Los Angeles mathematics teacher whose life is depicted in the movie *Stand and Deliver*. Escalante's students were among the weakest in the city of Los Angeles in terms of their academic abilities, yet Escalante encouraged them to learn calculus by making it seem "learnable." In the movie and in real life, Escalante states that students need to have the *ganas* (a concept that entails self-concept, self-efficacy, and motivation) to learn.

Feeling Tone

Feeling tone is another motivating factor in the elementary science classroom. Hunter has defined feeling tone as the way a student feels in a particular situation that affects the amount of effort that student is willing to put forth to achieve learning (1982, p. 12). She goes on to say that feeling tones exist on a continuum that extends from pleasant through neutral to unpleasant. The overall classroom climate, the environment a teacher establishes for culturally diverse children, greatly impacts the learning that occurs in the classroom. The establishment of a positive feeling tone, the development of a motivating learning environment for children, requires a sensitivity to children's home culture and home learning. Culturally diverse students view schools as places of learning when they are allowed to bring their home culture to school and to append new learning to existing learning.

In writing of the motivational principle of feeling tone, Gay states that research in sociopsychology, learning theory, ethnicity, and educational anthropology informs us that students differ both individually and by social, ethnic, and cultural group membership (1988, p. 331). Gay also writes that efforts to incorporate ethnic and cultural diversity in the core of all school curricula and to make instructional programs more responsive to the unique needs of diverse learners historically have been neither impressive nor comprehensive. How do teachers bring children's home learning and/or home culture into a school environment? How can science classrooms be modified so that they are culturally affirming (i.e., exhibit positive feeling tones for culturally diverse learners)?

Culturally diverse learners (indeed all children) come to schools with a wealth of prior knowledge or a fund of knowledge, ready to negotiate meaning from the educational environment. Teachers can facilitate children's motivation to learn science by providing positive feeling tone in the forms of culturally affirming content and contexts. Geneva Gay has pointed out that the means appropriate for teaching poor, urban black students differ from those appropriate for teaching other students because teaching and learning are sociocultural processes that take place within given social systems. Feeling tone is a multifaceted construct that is encouraged by culturally familiar instructional strategies and content including (1) interactional patterns, (2) group processes, (3) analogies, (4) materials, and (5) the physical environment. Some culturally diverse children may be more comfortable observing demonstration lessons and modeling their performance after the teacher, while others are more attentive when they engage in hands-on exploratory learning. Still, other children may prefer interacting in a group setting rather than answering teacher-directed questions during expository teaching sessions.

In creating culturally affirming classrooms, classrooms with positive feeling tones, teachers need to incorporate culturally familiar analogies, themes, and curricular materials as part of the instructional program. The use of these elaborative strategies builds bridges between the student's prior knowledge and new knowledge. Culturally familiar analogies may be examples or stories used to illustrate concepts taught in the classroom. A teacher introducing the concept of a myelin sheath to a group of Chicano students could say that a myelin sheath surrounds the nerve cell in the way that a corn husk surrounds a tamale. The use of this analogy validates the child's home learning and assists the child in appending new learning to existing knowledge structures.

Culturally familiar materials can help students make linkages between their real world experiences and abstract science concepts. A teacher who brings culturally based materials into the classroom, whether pinto beans, origami paper, bagels, milk cartons, automobile tires, or paper kites, is valuing the child's real world learning experiences while providing conceptual

Culturally familiar analogies and elaborations increase student learning.

bridges to link the child's prior knowledge to new learning. Assuredly, all new learning does not have to be culturally relevant or linked to culturally familiar objects and events. However, children are motivated to learn when classroom environments establish a positive feeling tone.

Success

Success is the third motivational factor that has been shown to improve the learning of culturally diverse students in the elementary science classroom. A popular adage states that "success breeds success." Within the context of children's learning, this adage could be worded as follows: the more success students have experienced in the past, the more optimistic they are about their future academic performance. The corollary to this statement reads: the more children have failed in the past, the less willing they are to expose themselves to risk, because their prediction is that they won't be successful.

Success as a motivational principle is grounded in the affiliative drive and ego-enhancement components of achievement motivation theory. Ausubel, Novak, and Hanesian point out that children need to do well in school to retain the approval of the superordinate figure (i.e., a significant other) with whom the child emotionally identifies (1978, p. 398). Success in school contributes to a child's ego enhancement, another component of achievement motivation theory. McClelland (1965) and Atkinson (1964) in formulating achievement motivation theories stated that achievement behavior is based on two competing needs—the need to achieve success versus the need to avoid failure. The desire to achieve adult approval (including the approval of their teacher) is very strong in young children. Toward the end of elementary school, the approval of a superordinate figure diminishes in most children's lives, to be gradually replaced by peer approval in middle school years.

Studies show that children with high expectations of success generally persist longer in attempting new learning than those with lower expectancies of success. Highly motivated students, those who anticipate being successful, are rarely a problem in the classroom. These students typically enjoy challenging assignments and corrective feedback from the teacher and respond with greater effort and enthusiasm when they meet with temporary failure. Students concerned with avoiding failure present teachers with their greatest challenge. Typically, these students prefer to work in cooperative learning groups, thus avoiding individual failure. Assistance in goal setting is also vital for the success of students with low expectancy states. Teachers can help students break the cycle of academic failure by (1) breaking large tasks down into bite-sized pieces, (2) restating tasks in terms of subtasks, (3) helping students to set reasonable goals, (4) providing ample reinforcement for success, (5) avoiding public recognition of children's mistakes or failures, and (6) providing supportive instructional environments (e.g., cooperative or familial learning groups).

Teachers are frequently significant others in the lives of children.

Closely related to personal success is the concept of successful role models. Ausubel's writings regarding significant others and Bandura's writings regarding role models speak to the need for culturally diverse role models in the elementary science classroom. All children need successful role models they may emulate in life. Sometimes teachers become significant others in the lives of students; at other times parents or other adults in the community become role models for young children. Role models are vital in actualizing a child's interest in science. If students see that other culturally diverse men and women have been successful in science careers, then they are able to imagine themselves in those same careers (see Activity 2.8 and Chapter 3, "The History of Science"). Success in the elementary science classroom is highly related to other motivational factors, including level of concern and feeling tone. Learning is maximized when these three motivational factors work in concert.

Interest

Interest or curiosity is the fourth factor shown to improve students' motivation to learn science. Interest is a multifaceted motivational construct that includes real-world connections of learning, novelty, surprise, ego-enhancement, personal preferences, curiosity, and intellectual needs. Maehr (1978) points out that some tasks or topics are by their very nature more interesting and inherently motivating than other tasks. Most children would rather learn about the life and times of dinosaurs than about regrouping numbers. This is not to say that both are not equally good learnings, but that children tend to be motivated to learn some things more readily than others. Children's interests can be inventoried with interest surveys (see Activity 2.1).

From the perspective of cognitive psychology, interest as a motivational factor is grounded in theories of cognitive dissonance or cognitive disequilibrium. Wadsworth (1978) states that children of all ages need to have opportunities to select activities that interest them. He goes on to point out that what is desirable is that children experience disequilibrium; to put it another way, they must come to realize that their conception is no longer adequate in some sense (Wadsworth, 1978, p. 79). Disequilibrium is an intrinsic motivation. Piaget states that equilibrium can be thought of as a more or less temporary state of balance or stability between the processes of assimilation and accommodation in the child's cognitive system (Wadsworth, 1978, p. 79). Equilibrium may be thought of as a self-regulating factor in the development of a child's knowledge. Assimilation (taking new knowledge into an existing knowledge structure without altering that schema) and accommodation (taking new knowledge into a knowledge structure with minor modifications of the knowledge structure) allow the child to remain in a state of cognitive equilibrium.

A child raised on a dairy farm who is used to seeing brown Swiss cows every day would probably not be upset at the sight of a black-and-white Holstein cow. In other words, the child takes in the information that cows come in more than one color and incorporates that information into his or her knowledge structure regarding cows. The child accommodates new information and remains in a state of cognitive equilibrium. When, on the other hand, a young inner-city child used to seeing dogs and cats encounters a live cow for the first time, the child might be thrown into a state of cognitive disequilibrium. The inner-city child would not have an existing schema to accommodate the concept of "cows." In this instance, the child would move from a state of cognitive equilibrium to a state of cognitive disequilibrium. Interest and curiosity are aroused when we encounter new phenomena. We are motivated to learn when we are presented with information that we cannot assimilate or accommodate with our existing knowledge structures.

A knowledge of relationships between classroom learning and real world experiences increases our interest or motivation to learn. We become interested or reinterested in something when we see its utility or practical applications. Most of us, as children, were interested in learning about electricity, in constructing circuits from bulbs, batteries, and wire. As adults, our interest in electricity may be rekindled each year when we are faced with replacing burned-out bulbs on strings of lights associated with the celebration of Christmas or Chanukah. As we realize that our prior knowledge of parallel and series circuits is useful in solving the problem of which bulb is the bad bulb, our interest in or appreciation of our knowledge of electrical circuits increases. Relevancy or usefulness of learning increases our interest and our motivation to learn.

Science educators have come to rely on discrepant events as motivational tools in the science classroom. A discrepant event is a "phenomenon which occurs that seems to run contrary to our first line of reasoning; it is a device to stimulate student's interest in learning science concepts and principles" (Wright, 1981, p. 575). The "Kung Fu" demonstration Wright (1981) developed illustrates the concept of a discrepant event. In this activity, the teacher places a slat of wood extending over the edge of a desk, then places two pieces of newspaper smoothly over the portion of the slat that is resting on the desk. The teacher hits the overhanging portion of the slat with the side of one hand, and the slat snaps. This activity illustrates the concept of air pressure, or, as Wright says, "the tremendous pressure exerted on the newspaper and transmitted to the slat by atmospheric pressure" (1981, p. 579). The "Kung Fu" activity also illustrates the concept of a discrepant event. As the teacher hits the slat, students expect the paper to fly up in the air; however, the unexpected happens: the slat breaks. Discrepant events move students from a state of cognitive equilibrium to a state of cognitive dissonance or disequilibrium, that is, they motivate students (see Activity 2.4 and Activity 2.5).

Status

Status is a fifth factor vital in motivating culturally diverse students to learn science in the elementary classroom. Status may be defined within a humanistic psychology tradition as the need to belong or the need for self-esteem.

FIGURE 2.1 ■ "Kung Fu" Discrepant Event

Within Maslow's hierarchy of needs, belonging involves being loved and accepted in one's peer group or family. The need for self-esteem is closely related to the need for belonging, in that self-esteem involves the desire to gain recognition and approval from others. Status may be broadly defined as one's social position or rank within a group.

In writing from a cognitive psychology viewpoint of a student's status within the peer group, Ausubel says an adolescent's exaggerated need to conform to peer group values is a function of the student's marginal and prolonged interim status in our culture (Ausubel, Novak, & Hanesian, 1978, p. 463). He further points out that adolescents are highly dependent on their peers for much of their social status. Status is a function of a child's social class, ethnicity, peer acceptance, and academic role in the classroom.

Cohen (1991) explains the motivational aspects of status in terms of expectation states theory. She points out that academic status characteristics are the most powerful of the status characteristics in the classroom because of their relevance to classroom activities. Cohen and her associates have investigated the effect of teacher intervention in the motivational process through a series of experiments in which teachers orally "confer status" on students through the use of praise. Findings from her study support the notion that teachers can increase the participation of low-status students in classroom activities through the verbal feedback that they provide to students. Improving students' status in the classroom increases their motivation to learn science (see Activity 2.6).

Knowledge of Results

A knowledge of results is the final motivational factor that has been shown to impact students' learning of science. A knowledge of results may also be thought of as feedback. As a rule of thumb, when teachers give students knowledge of results (for instance, of test results), they give them the correct answer with the reason it is correct (Hunter, 1982, p. 22). Research from cognitive psychology demonstrates that students are very logical and intelligent in making errors—few errors are made at random (Woolfolk & McCune-Nicolich, 1984, p. 560). Feedback assists students to restructure their schemata, their perceptions of the world around them.

Schimmel (1988) points out that feedback is a powerful force with both motivational and cognitive effects on students' learning. He writes that three types of feedback are commonly used in the classroom: (1) confirmatory feedback, (2) corrective feedback, and (3) explanatory feedback.

Confirmatory Feedback.   Confirmatory feedback provides students with information as to the correctness of an answer. Confirmatory feedback answers the question, Is the answer correct? The response to corrective feedback is a simple yes or no answer. An "x" marked on a spelling paper next to a word indicates to the student that the word is incorrectly spelled.

Corrective Feedback.   Corrective feedback provides the student not only with a knowledge of whether an answer is right or wrong but also with the correct answer. Assume that a teacher has asked students to identify the parts of a plant cell on a quiz. The teacher could provide corrective feedback by writing a statement such as "No, that's not the nucleus, it's the chloroplast" on the child's paper.

Explanatory Feedback.   Explanatory feedback is the most reflective and corrective type of feedback. Explanatory feedback is usually provided to students when higher-order thinking skills are being taught in the classroom. This type of feedback provides students with a knowledge of the accuracy of their answer, of the correct answer, and of where they went wrong. For example, assume a teacher has asked students to compare (which also implies contrast) monocot and dicot plants in terms of their leaves and seeds. In writing a journal entry to contrast the two types of plants, a student missed some of the salient information about the differences between the plants. The teacher might write the following comment:

> "Your answer is good, but you need to spend some more time looking at the leaves of the plant. Why not go back and compare the monocot leaf with the dicot leaf? Pay particular attention to the veins in the leaves of the plants."

Explanatory feedback provides students with a knowledge that their answer was incomplete and that they need to reflect more on what they have learned and what they need to learn. In the example, the teacher has focused the attention of the student on the critical attribute, the vein structure of the leaf. The feedback is motivating, since the student is challenged to go back and look at the leaves and determine the difference(s) between them.

CLASSROOM PRACTICE

Sometimes, as a teacher, you will introduce activities in your classroom for their motivational value as well as for their educational value. Discrepant events, games, and activity corners capitalize on the motivational factors of level of concern, feeling tone, success, interest, status, and knowledge of results. In this section of the chapter, examples of some field-tested motivational devices are presented to give you ideas of activities that you can replicate in the elementary science classroom. When using motivational devices, remember to first inventory your students to determine their interests (see Activity 2.1).

A knowledge of your students and the community that they come from is vital in assisting students to acquire a knowledge of science. Some students have been socialized to enjoy games and competition, while other children have been socialized to enjoy cooperative group work. This section of the chapter focuses on practical everyday suggestions for activities that may encourage children to acquire or build a knowledge of science. The activities include (1) games for individuals, small groups, and large groups; (2) interest and esteem-building activities; (3) discrepant events; (4) role model building; and (5) parental involvement.

ACTIVITY 2.1   ■   Student Interest Inventory

Grade Level: Any grade level

Purpose: To motivate student interest in science topics

Type of Activity: Motivational (individual survey)

Student Directions: Read the list of science topics. Rank the topics from the one that you would most like to learn about (1) to the one that you would least like to learn about (10).

____ Dinosaurs

____ Plants

____ Human body

____ Animals without backbones

____ Environment

____ Oceans

____ Weather

____ Magnetism and electricity

____ Space travel

____ Solar system

ACTIVITY 2.2   ■   Chemistry Bingo

Grade Level: Upper elementary

Purpose: To review chemical symbols

Type of Activity: Motivational (large group)

Teacher Preparation: Prepare blank "Chemo" (chemistry bingo cards with a 5 by 5 grid) cards for the students as shown. Make a set of chemical symbol cards by placing the name of the element on one side of the card and the symbol on the other. On the day of the game, place a list of chemical symbols for elements on the chalkboard and ask the students to select 24 symbols from the list and place them randomly on their cards.

"Chemo" card

Ca	H	Na	Fe	N
Ag	Au	K	Ni	Cl
O	Al	Chemo	Br	Zn
Cu	I	S	P	U
Mg	Mn	F	Cd	He

Conducting the Activity: When students have marked the symbols for 24 elements on their playing cards, have them tear markers from a sheet of scrap paper. Conduct the game as a bingo game, except that you call off the name of the element and the student is to cover the symbol. Prizes for the game would typically include edible rewards such as granola bars and small prizes such as balloons or pencils.

ACTIVITY 2.3 ▨ Life in the Estuary

Grade Level: Intermediate to upper elementary

Type of Activity: Motivational (small group)

Materials: Paper clip, pencil, playing board, and spinner for each group; 1 marker per student (coin, piece of colored paper, etc.)

Teacher Preparation: Duplicate the "Life in the Estuary" game board and the paper spinners.

Life in the estuary game

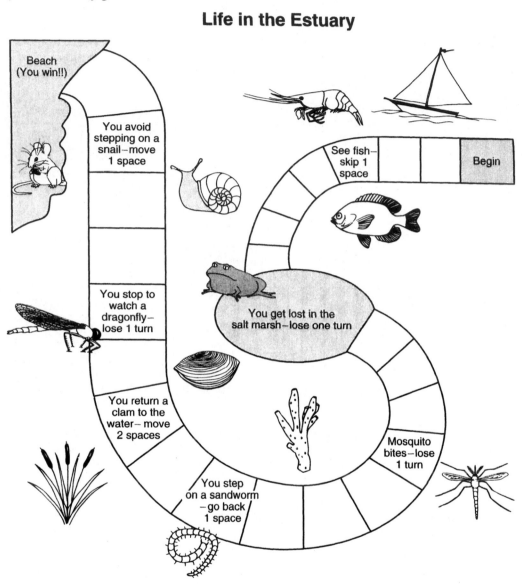

Life in the Estuary

Beach (You win!!)

You avoid stepping on a snail—move 1 space

See fish—skip 1 space

Begin

You stop to watch a dragonfly—lose 1 turn

You get lost in the salt marsh—lose one turn

You return a clam to the water—move 2 spaces

Mosquito bites—lose 1 turn

You step on a sandworm—go back 1 space

Student Directions: The object of the game is to be the first one in your group (place 3–4 students in each group) to travel through the estuary. On your journey you will travel from a boat offshore to the beach. To move across the board, spin the paper clip and move the number of spaces directed on the playing board. The first person to successfully touch the flag on the beach wins.

ACTIVITIES

Spinner for estuary game

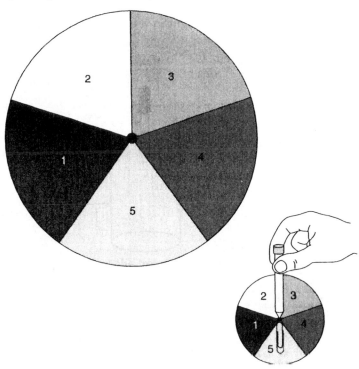

Notes: 1. For durability, tape the game board and spinner inside a manila file folder.

2. If students do not have access to game boards at home, run extra copies and allow students to color and take home a copy to play with parents or siblings. This affords students the opportunity to share what they are learning and provides a board game for the home.

ACTIVITY 2.4 ■ Cartesian Diver

Grade Level: Primary to upper elementary

Purpose: Discrepant event

Type of Activity: Motivational (group)

Materials: 1 plastic soda bottle and 1 eye dropper per group of students

Student Directions: Fill the plastic soda bottle completely full of water. Squeeze the bulb of the eye dropper and suck up half a dropper full of water. Lightly place the dropper upright in the soda bottle and tightly cap the bottle.

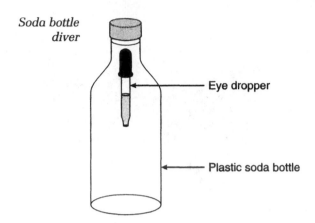

Soda bottle diver

Eye dropper

Plastic soda bottle

Operational Questions: (teacher-directed questions to guide students' investigations)

1. What happens when you squeeze the bottle?
2. What happens with a one-handed squeeze?
3. What happens with a two-handed squeeze?
4. Can you make the diver stay on the bottom of the container?
5. As you squeeze the bottle, what happens to the level of water in the eye dropper?
6. Can you make the diver rise and sink faster? If so, how?
7. What happens to the diver if you loosen the cap on the bottle?

Note: This apparatus demonstrates the concept of the Cartesian diver.

ACTIVITY 2.5 ■ Standing Vortex

Grade Level: Intermediate to upper elementary

Purpose: Discrepant event

Type of Activity: Motivational (group)

Materials: 2 plastic soda bottles and 1 piece of rubber tubing per group (heavy duct tape may be substituted for the tubing)

Teacher Preparation: Fill one soda bottle completely full of tap water and stand it on a table. Invert the second bottle on top of the first one. Connect the bottles with rubber tubing or heavy duct tape.

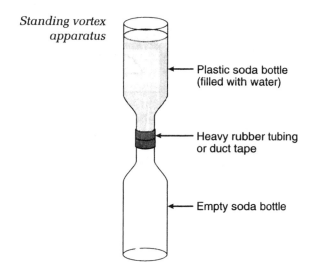

*Standing vortex
apparatus*

← Plastic soda bottle
(filled with water)

← Heavy rubber tubing
or duct tape

← Empty soda bottle

ACTIVITIES

**Student
Directions:**   Turn the bottles so that the one full of water is on top.

**Operational
Questions:**   1. What happens when the bottle full of water is placed on top?
2. What happens if you gently swirl the bottle?
3. Can you make the vortex move faster? How?
4. How can you make the vortex move slower?

Note: This activity illustrates the principle of a standing vortex or a Coriolis effect.

ACTIVITY 2.6 ▦ Mini Museum

Grade Level: Primary to upper elementary

Purpose: To arouse interest and curiosity

**Type of
Activity:**   Motivational (individual)

Materials: Plain index cards, marking pen, science field guides

**Teacher
Preparation:**   Set aside a corner of the classroom for a mini museum, a student-centered motivational device used to build students' self-esteem and to involve parents in children's education. At the beginning of each unit of study, clean out existing displays and explain the next unit of study to students. Encourage students to bring realia associated with the new unit of study to the classroom. Exhibits should be marked with their

Combined mini museum and activity corner

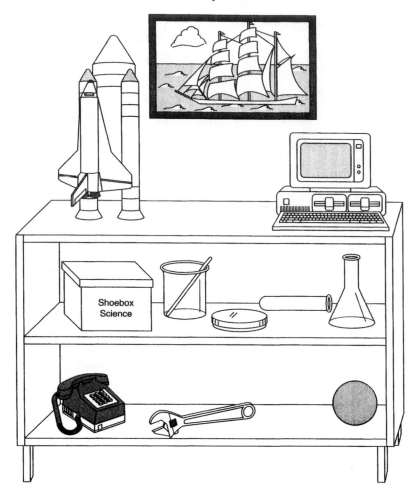

name and the name of the contributing student. Exhibits involve students in identifying objects in the natural world. Additionally, a mini museum involves parents in children's education.

ACTIVITY 2.7 ■ Activity Corner

Grade Level: Primary to upper elementary

Purpose: To arouse interest and curiosity

Type of Activity: Motivational (individual)

Materials: Shoebox science kits (see Chapter 7 on instructional strategies), teacher-provided realia, computer software, learning stations, library books, and so forth

Teacher Preparation: Set aside a corner of the classroom as an activity center. Prior to beginning a unit of study, round up filmstrips, library books, computer software, posters, models, and realia associated with the new unit of study. The purpose of these materials is to provide the opportunity for students to pursue their own interests when time permits. An activity corner is a teaching resource, a place where students can go during transitional time periods and unassigned time to engage in independent learning.

ACTIVITY 2.8 ■ Grand Prix

Grade Level: Primary to upper elementary

Type of Activity: Motivational (large group)

Materials: 1 grand prix race car for each group in the classroom (cut from colored construction paper), masking tape, and 1 grand prix racecourse drawn on the chalkboard.

Grand prix cars

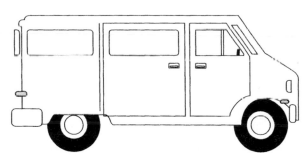

Grand prix racecourse

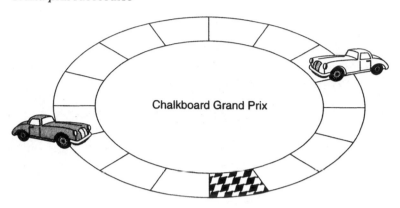

Chalkboard Grand Prix

Teacher Preparation: This is a large group board game designed to involve all students in the class. Before the students begin the activity, draw the racecourse on the chalkboard and cut out race cars, one for each group of students. This activity works well as a unit review of low-level knowledge.

Conducting the Activity: Divide the students into groups of 4 to 8. Select or allow the students to select a captain for each group (official answers must come from the group captain). Ask the students questions derived from the current unit of study. When a group gets a correct response, its car moves forward 1 space on the racecourse. The first car across the finish line wins.

ACTIVITY 2.9   ■   Concentration

Grade Level: Primary to upper elementary

Purpose: To review scientists and contributions

Type of Activity: Instructional (large or small group)

Materials: 1 concentration game board (a 5 by 6 grid of numbers) with detachable numbers and questions behind each number.

Older Students: This version of concentration uses famous culturally diverse scientists and their contributions. The object is for students to match each scientist with the contribution. The student calls off two numbers; if the

Concentration game board

1	2	3	4	5
6	7	8	9	10
11	12	13	14	15
16	17	18	19	20
21	22	23	24	25
26	27	28	29	30

Concentration—famous scientists board game

Value of pi	Al Khwarizmi	Beta disintegration	Semiconductors	Ramón y Cajal
Smallpox inoculation	Synthesized RNA	Plant genetics	Invented paper	Invented algebra
Burbank	Ochoa	Filament for light bulb	Chang Heng	Jumping genes
D'Elhuyar	Discovered tungsten	Esaki	Wu	Discovered neuron
Tsai Lun	Discovered radium & polonium	Latimer	Heavy metal poisoning	Shen Kua
McClintock	Discovered magnetic compass	Ishimure	Onesimus	M. Curie

name under the number matches the contribution, the students are given the covering number cards, if not, the next group gets a chance to select two numbers. The game continues until all matches have been made. See the list of scientists at the end of Chapter 3.

**Younger
Students:** Younger students match objects and their names. The version here shows living things and their names. When students match the picture with the name of the picture, a match is made.

Concentration—living things board game

		Rose	Mouse	
Palm tree	Fish	Ostrich		Elephant
Pine tree			Owl	Beetle
		Penguin		Dolphin
	Spider			Snail
Oak tree		Butterfly		

ACTIVITY 2.10 ■ Trivial Pursuit

Grade Level: Intermediate to upper elementary

Type of Activity: Motivational (large group)

Materials: Bank of quiz questions and category cards

Teacher Preparation: Prepare a list of low-level questions for the game. Questions should be related to information that has been previously taught.

Trivial pursuit question bank

Question	*Answer*
Category: Animals	
1. Name for a group of animals with 6 legs.	Insects
2. Name of a soft-bodied animal that carries its "house" on its back.	Snail
3. Name for the world's largest animal.	Whale
4. An insect that lives in a hive, lives in colonies.	Honeybees
5. Animal that lays eggs in nests, warm blooded.	Bird
Category: Plants	
1. Name of trees that are green all year long, keep their leaves.	Evergreen
2. The part of the plant that takes in water.	Root
3. The part of the plant that makes almost all of the food.	Leaf
4. The container that holds a baby plant and its food.	Seed
5. The part of the carrot plant we normally eat.	Root
Category: Magnetism	
1. The name of the ends of a magnet.	Poles
2. The opposite end from the north pole.	South
3. In magnets, like poles _____.	Repel
4. In magnets, unlike poles _____.	Attract
5. Type of material picked up by a magnet.	Iron (steel)
Category: Human Body	
1. The organ that pumps blood.	Heart
2. The organ responsible for thinking	Brain
3. Structures that hold up or support the body.	Bones
4. Largest organ in the body.	Skin
5. The main organ of vision.	Eye

Conducting the Activity: Divide the students into groups and have each group select a captain. Give each group a question in rotation. Each time a group correctly answers the question it receives a point. The group with the most points at the end of the game wins.

ACTIVITY 2.11   ■   **Dinosaur Extinction**

Grade Level: Intermediate to upper elementary

Type of Activity: Instructional (large or small group)

Materials: Bank of vocabulary words for current unit of study, take-apart dinosaur, and masking tape

Teacher Preparation: Prepare the take-apart dinosaur model by coloring and cutting out the figure. Place a tape roll on the back of each piece of the dinosaur and tape the dinosaur on the board.

Conducting the Activity: Say to the students: "Dinosaur Extinction is played like the old game of Hangman. I'll put blanks on the board, each blank representing one letter in a vocabulary word that we are using. For each incorrect guess, I'll remove one piece of the dinosaur from the board. The objective is to guess the word before the dinosaur becomes extinct (all pieces are removed from the board)."

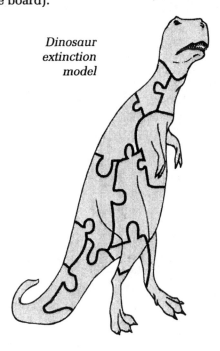

Dinosaur extinction model

CHAPTER SUMMARY

One of the primary objectives of elementary science education is to interest and involve students in learning science and in considering participation in science-related careers in adult life. Motivational factors are rooted in behavioristic, humanistic, and cognitive psychology traditions. Research indicates that the use of six motivational factors—level of concern, feeling tone, success, interest, status, and knowledge of results—increases the likelihood that children will be encouraged to learn science. The use of motivating factors also increases the likelihood that classrooms will become culturally affirming environments, places where culturally diverse students will be encouraged to continue their study of science and perhaps to engage in science careers in adult life.

 TOPICS TO REVIEW

- Psychology viewpoints on motivation (behavioral, humanistic, and cognitive)
- Six factors that increase motivation
- Nine characteristics of rich educational tasks
- Six steps to break the cycle of failure
- Discrepant event
- Three types of feedback

 REFLECTIVE PRACTICE

1. How are humanistic, cognitive, and behavioristic views on motivation similar? How do they differ?

2. What is meant by "making classrooms culturally affirming environments"? What specific ways can you identify that could be used to produce such environments?

3. Identify six strategies for motivating culturally diverse students. How could each of these be used to make your classroom more appealing to culturally diverse students?

4. How can you modify assignments so that they are motivating for culturally diverse students?

5. In your opinion, why are all motivational factors not equally effective for all students?

CHAPTER 3

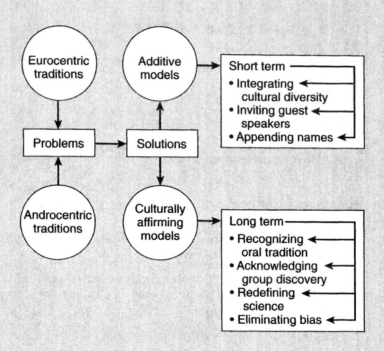

The History of Science:
A Culturally Affirming
Perspective

POINTS TO PONDER

- How many women scientists can you name?
- How many culturally diverse scientists can you name?
- What are the roots of modern science and medicine?
- Do all cultures view "discovery" in the same manner?
- What can be done to make the history of science more culturally affirming for all students?

My mother-in-law was a curandera, a healer. Her yard was a beautiful, aromatic pharmacy, filled with plant species garnered from remote corners of the desert, where she spent her entire life. As a young bride, she moved from the city of El Paso, Texas, to the isolated, rural railroad section where my father-in-law worked, at Swanee, New Mexico. Four or five decades ago, Swanee was home to a dozen Chicano families, in the middle of nowhere, 50 miles from the nearest town and the nearest doctor.

The women and men who lived in this remote area developed a special kinship with the land; they came to regard the desert as a source of food, housing, and medicine. From the desert came clay with which to make adobes and to build homes capable of withstanding the heat of summer and the cold of winter. In properly irrigated and cultivated desert soil, they could grow food for their families. Finally, desert plants served as medicine, for a trip to the doctor was undertaken only for life-threatening illnesses. During her years in Swanee, my mother-in-law learned the skills of midwifery through hands-on practice. She also learned the uses of the plants that grew around her home—aloe, yucca, peppermint, ironweed, and stinkweed. Soap to disinfect wounds, salves to soothe cuts, teas to reduce fevers, and liniments to ease the pain of muscle strains can be derived from desert flora.

Modern medicine has its roots in traditional folk medicine. The current rush of pharmaceutical companies to the vanishing rainforests of the world testifies to the curative value of plant species (although one can't assume that all folk medicine is good medicine). As we teachers speak to children of science careers, we often forget to tell them of their heritage, of their families' and communities' historical place in science and medicine. We forget to validate their scientific traditions and to remind them that science is for all Americans.

OUR POINT OF VIEW

Traditionally, science has been taught in U.S. schools from a Eurocentric or androcentric viewpoint. The science curricula in schools have emphasized "the scientific method" and famous scientists (primarily of European extraction) as the originators of our knowledge base regarding science. This view of the history of science excludes the contributions of many culturally diverse individuals and groups and deprives children of vitally needed role models. One goal of science education, as expressed in *The Liberal Art of Science,* is "to increase the numbers of women, blacks, and Hispanic/Latino students who major in natural sciences and pursue science and science-related careers" (American Association for the Advancement of Science [AAAS], 1990, p. 64). Reaching this goal will require that culturally diverse children be involved in learning and doing science. In setting forth U.S. standards for science education, the National Research Council has stated that "all students, regardless of age, sex, cultural or ethnic background, disabilities, aspirations, or interest and motivation in science, should have the opportunity to attain high levels of scientific literacy" (1996, p. 20). Making science accessible to all students means finding ways to convey the messages that "you too can do science" and "you too come from a long tradition of contributing to scientific knowledge."

This chapter seeks to examine the historical, axiological, and epistemological roots of science as it is presented in "traditional" science textbooks and curricula in U.S. public schools and to propose a culturally transforming model of science for incorporation into science education classes and instructional materials. A colleague who teaches social studies at a large Western university begins his course each semester by asking "Who discovered America?" He gets the usual answers about Columbus and Leif Erikson and other

Science is for all Americans.

early European discoverers from his students. Then he asks a second question: "Was America ever lost?" From a Native American perspective, the United States of America couldn't have been found, because it was never lost. Many of us tend to view U.S. history from a European viewpoint, while ignoring our Native American heritage; it is as if life began when European explorers and settlers arrived on these shores.

The history of science has also been shaped and presented to U.S. school children in our current science education programs from a European, white male–dominated viewpoint. U.S. children find few examples of culturally diverse role models in their textbooks or classrooms. A classic study of textbooks (which has been repeated several times in recent years with similar results) revealed that the most widely used elementary texts in science, math, reading, spelling, and social studies contained females and culturally diverse individuals in fewer than one-third of the illustrations (Sadker & Sadker, 1979). Excluding culturally diverse individuals and females from textbooks deprives children of a source of culturally diverse role models. Before children can capitalize on their interest in science, they must be made aware that people like them can participate in scientific endeavors.

The Eurocentric Tradition in the History of Science

The European tradition in the history of science is embodied in the "scientific method" and in the contributions of European scientists (and scientists of European heritage) to that body of knowledge (Al-Daffa & Stroyls, 1984). From this tradition scientists derive the questions that they ask, the ways that they explore the world around them, their sources of data, and the ways that they view truth and knowledge. Because writers of textbooks and curricular materials for children are normally trained or educated in this Eurocentric scientific tradition, their writings—the textbooks and instructional materials provided to U.S. children—reflect their training. As described in many older science textbooks (American Chemical Society, 1988; Bierer, Lien, & Silberstein, 1987; Merrill Publishing, 1987; Oram, 1986; Slesnick, Balzer, McCormack, Newton, & Rasmussen, 1985), the "scientific method" is a five-step method for investigating the natural world that includes (1) stating the problem, (2) collecting information, (3) forming a hypothesis, (4) testing the hypothesis, and (5) drawing a conclusion. Within this tradition, Jean Lamarck is credited with discovering a theory of evolution, James Watson and Francis Crick with discovering the structure of the DNA molecule, and Robert Boyle with discovering the gas laws. Frequently, science is presented to children as a single way of investigating the world rather than as a multifaceted construct.

If a scientist or a group of people does not follow this formula, is the "discovery" science? Probably not, at least according to U.S. science textbooks and curricular materials. For thousands of years, the Native Americans of the southwestern United States and Central America have cultivated corn. Each year the biggest and the best ears of maize were saved by the harvesters and used as seed the following year. The tradition of sowing only genetically superior seeds improved maize from a stubby little weed into the well-formed ears of corn that we know today. The Native Americans certainly followed the scientific method: They identified the problem, collected information about which were the best ears of maize, formed their hypothesis that planting the biggest seeds would result in an improved plant, conducted experiments in plant growth for thousands of years, and passed their findings orally to their children. However, we do not view Native Americans as the founders of genetics research.

Native Americans did not keep written records of their research, nor did they present their findings for peer review in the scientific community. Credit for the discovery of genetics research has gone to Gregor Mendel. Did Gregor Mendel alone discover genetics research, or did others walk that path before he did? Who discovered genetics research? The Eurocentric view of science, which includes the notion that the scientific method must be used (that is, keeping copious notes, writing reports of findings, and reporting findings to scientific societies), excludes the research of generations of Native Americans.

Eurocentric science is dominated not only by the "scientific method" but by discoveries attributed to white males. In 1721 Onesimus, an African American slave, explained to his master, Cotton Mather, how he had been in-

Native Americans conducted genetics experiments on corn.

oculated against smallpox when he was a child (Sammons, 1990). Everyone in Onesimus's tribe knew that it was common sense to transmit a less virulent form of smallpox to children to prevent them from getting a deadly form of the disease. African parents taught their children this simple inoculation procedure through a tradition of oral history and learning. Cotton Mather wrote to Dr. Boylston explaining the smallpox inoculation procedure that his slave Onesimus had shown him. Boylston tried the procedure on his son and two slaves and reported his findings in a letter to a colleague. For his discovery, Boylston was called to London and was honored in the scientific community by being made a fellow of the Royal Society. Onesimus, the slave who bridged the knowledge gap between the oral medical practices of his homeland and the European world, received no credit. Who then discovered the smallpox vaccination?

*Annie Jump Cannon
(1863–1941) Astronomer,
Harvard University*

It can indeed be argued that the genetics research of the Native Americans and the discovery of a smallpox vaccination by the Banyoro tribe in Africa were pre–scientific revolution discoveries and thus fall in a category of quasi-scientific discovery. However, even when culturally diverse and female scientists did make scientific "discoveries" using the scientific method, those discoveries were frequently claimed by white male colleagues. The discoveries of the functions of the honeybee's antennae, the expulsion of drones from the beehive, and the fertilization flight of the queen bee made by Maria Aimee Lullin (1750–1831) were published under the name of her husband, François Huber (Alic, 1986). As sometimes was the practice during this time period, discoveries made by women were viewed as less credible than those made by men, which led women to publish their findings under a male name. The lack of female and minority role models in current science textbooks is in part a function of our Eurocentric view of the world and in part a reflection of the roles that women and culturally diverse individuals held in our society in the past.

The Andocentric Tradition in the History of Science

The androcentric model of the history of science gives credit for scientific "discoveries" to individuals. Within this tradition, Dimitri Mendeleyev is credited with discovering the periodic table of elements, Joseph Priestley with discovering that plants produce oxygen gas, and Henri Becquerel with discovering X rays. Group discoveries of knowledge are rarely acknowledged within the androcentric tradition of science.

Charles Finch has recorded a story of obstetrical procedures from the history of science in East Africa (Van Sertima, 1986). In 1879, a missionary doctor named Felkin observed a Banyoro surgeon in Uganda performing a cesarean section. A young woman was lying in a hut preparing to deliver her first child. The delivery had been particularly difficult, and the tribal surgeon had given the young mother-to-be some banana wine to ease the pain of childbirth. Banana wine was commonly used by the Banyoro as a pain-killing drug. When it became apparent that both the mother and child were in difficulty and that both might die, the surgeon poured banana wine on the mother's abdomen and on his surgical knife. The wine acted as an antiseptic. Next the surgeon made an incision in the mother's abdomen and lifted the baby out. The abdominal cut was sealed with hot irons, a procedure that we call cauterization today. Finally, the wound was closed with sharp cactus spikes (in place of stitches) and bound with a hand-woven grass mat soaked in the same banana wine. Did Joseph Lister alone invent the antiseptic? Who invented pain killers? The cesarean section? Cauterization? Staples to close a surgical wound? Were they "invented" at all, or are they part of a long heritage of healing passed from one generation to the next? By insisting on identifying a particular individual as a "discoverer" of knowledge, we ignore the many cultures who do not value individualism and "discovery" but rather see the group good as the important consideration.

Moving toward a
Multicultural Perspective

There is little readily available in current science textbooks, filmstrips, videos, the World Wide Web, and supplementary science education materials that describes the contributions to science made by culturally diverse men and women and by white woman. In fact, sometimes women and those from culturally diverse backgrounds are relegated to footnote status in science writings. Though these omissions may not be intentional, the hidden message is that women and culturally diverse individuals cannot be important scientists. This message victimizes all of us. Men and women of color and white females lack successful science role models, and white males develop a feeling of unfounded superiority. All human beings are short-changed by this lack of knowledge and perspective (worldview orientation).

Additive Models

One strategy for handling the lack of culturally diverse role models in science education materials is through the use of an additive model (Gilbert & Gay, 1985). The additive model of history holds that providing underrepresented minority students with successful culturally diverse scientists as role models addresses the need of students to have significant others in their lives. When using the additive method of restructuring the history of science in textbooks or classes, one could mention that an ancient Chinese scholar (Shen Kua) had invented the compass in about 1070 A.D. (Daintith, Mitchell, & Tootill, 1981). One could mention that Percy Julian, an African American male, had synthesized cortisone from soybeans and that cortisone is routinely used in the treatment of many illnesses, including arthritis. Additionally, we could include women in the history of science by adding the names of Chien-Shiung Wu, Anna Comstock, Annie Jump Cannon, Elizabeth Blackwell, Rosalyn Yalow, and Barbara McClintock to a list of famous scientists contained in science textbooks or on special "Scientist of the Day" bulletin boards.

By appending culturally diverse role models and women to the list of white male European scientists already mentioned in textbooks, web pages, filmstrips, and instructional materials, the additive model makes a beginning at restructuring the androcentric nature of science. Yet although the addition

Scientists such as Luther Burbank may be highlighted on bulletin boards and in class displays.

of information about the contributions of women and culturally diverse individuals may improve the quality of instruction for children, this action alone does not address the Eurocentric nature of science. Only when the contributions of women and culturally diverse individuals are woven into the fabric of our instruction will the basic axiological and epistemological foundations of science become inclusive rather than exclusive.

A Culturally Diverse Viewpoint

If the history of science taught in our schools is to be truly inclusive in nature rather than exclusive, certain fundamental changes need to be made in the ways that we view science and scientific discovery. Suzuki (1984) suggests that we use a culturally transforming model for education. In science, a culturally transforming model would require the addition of culturally diverse individuals and groups to our current curriculum materials and a review of the structure and values upon which the discipline is based. First, science instruction needs to include in the history of science that we present to children the oral tradition of recording information. Second, we should tell children that scientific discoveries are not always made by individuals. Some cultures value group discovery, not individual initiative. Third, our instruction should adopt a broadened definition of the scientific method that includes valid "discoveries" that research has shown to be effective and that may not have been derived through traditional Eurocentric channels. Finally, the bias in reporting the discoveries of culturally diverse individuals and women (i.e., attributing "discoveries" to the wrong author or ignoring the contributions of certain individuals or groups) needs to be eliminated from our curricular materials.

Recognizing the Oral Tradition of Science

The oral tradition is often not recognized as a valid method for transmitting information in the scientific community. Thus, some scientists and historians of science have labeled traditional scientific practices from culturally diverse groups as folk medicine. Some discount contributions made without the controls and written documentation that accompany scientific "discoveries." Certainly, some folk medicine practices are scientifically unfounded and unjustified in the scientific realm, but these should not taint all folk practices as "bad science."

Many Hispanic parents know that the flowers of the daisy fleabane plant can be boiled into a tea that is an effective medicine for children's illnesses. For hundreds and probably thousands of years, Hispanic and Native American parents have been passing on oral traditions about the medicinal use of herbs to their children. *Manzanilla* (made from the flowers of daisy fleabane) is a mild analgesic that contains acetylsalicylic acid. In herbal tea form, manzanilla is a traditional cure of healers or curanderos for fevers, aches, and pains in children. In 1853 the German chemist Charles Gerhardt discovered acetylsalicylic acid ($C_9H_8O_4$) as a natural byproduct of coal tar; he called his discovery *aspirin*. If the history of science is to be made meaningful for Hispanic children, the inclusion of the discovery of aspirin by curanderos needs to be validated. The oral tradition as a means of communicating information from one generation to another needs to be included in classroom discussions of the nature of science that teachers hold with children.

Acknowledging Group Discoveries in the History of Science

For centuries the Quechua-speaking Incas of the Andes had used *quina-quina* or the "bark of barks" to cure cramps, chills, heart-rhythm disorders, and a variety of illnesses. When Europeans arrived in the Americas, they brought with them malaria, a disease carried by the anopheles mosquito. Malaria, characterized by chills and fever, was a dreaded disease during medieval and colonial times. It is estimated that about 20% of the colonists of Virginia were infected with malaria and died within a year of contracting the disease (Weatherford, 1988). Historians estimate that approximately two million people a year died from malaria during the period of European colonization.

When malaria arrived in Peru, the Quechua-speaking Incas used their traditional "Peruvian bark" to combat it. Peruvian bark—quinine—became a standard cure for the disease. Quinine was exported from Peru to Europe, North America, and throughout the world. In 1902 Sir Ronald Ross was awarded the Nobel Prize in medicine for discovering that the anopheles mosquito carried malaria from one person to another. The discovery of the cure for malaria made by the Native Americans three hundred years before was never honored. Surely, Sir Ronald Ross was deserving of the Nobel Prize for the discovery of the method of transmission of malaria, but the Quechua-speaking Incas are also worthy of recognition for their cure of a disease that killed two million people a year. The inclusion of group "discoveries" in the mainstream fabric of science instruction will enhance the quality of science education for all students.

Broadening the Definition of Scientific Method

There is a snobbery within the scientific community about which scientific discoveries are worthy of note. Many scientists and historians of science give weight only to scientific discoveries that use the European language and standards of science and deny the merit of discoveries derived from other investigative methods. Historically, in China when women gave birth, a dish of boiled pig's feet was prepared for the mother to eat. The dish is made by combining the pig's feet with a strong concentrated black vinegar. During the preparation, the vinegar dissolves the bone tissue in the pork and produces a thick broth rich in calcium ions. When the new mother eats the pork, the calcium replenishes the minerals lost during childbirth and stimulates lactation. In Asian communities throughout the United States this tradition of nourishing new mothers with a sweet-and-sour pork dish is still practiced.

If a licensed physician were to prescribe a calcium supplement for a new mother, we would tend to call this medicine. Homemade calcium supplements such as that provided by the dish of pig's feet are commonly viewed as quackery and folklore. Both the prescription bottle of calcium pills and the homemade pork dish redress the calcium deficiency in the new mother's body. Validated "discoveries" derived from investigative means other than a five-step "scientific method" need to be included in discussions with children of the history of science.

Eliminating Bias in Reporting Discoveries

The fourth barrier to the inclusion of culturally diverse individuals and women scientists in mainstream science is much more complicated because it focuses upon the oppressive nature of U.S. society. Many women and culturally diverse researchers have been plagued by a lack of financial resources, a lack of collegiality, and a lack of opportunity to participate in mainstream science activities. For example, George Washington Carver taught only in black colleges, his laboratory furnished with discards collected from the city dump, while the laboratories of his white peers were equipped by endowments from their universities. Carver was forced to work in an industrial arts setting rather than in a mainstream science laboratory. The lack of a properly equipped working environment crippled Carver's ability to conduct the in-depth studies he wished to.

Culturally diverse scientists and women scientists have frequently been isolated from the rest of the scientific community. Scientists such as George Washington Carver taught primarily in black institutions, isolated from their colleagues. Black research scientists such as Charles Turner, Percy Julian, Luther Burbank, and Ernest Just were excluded from full participation in the U.S. scientific community, as were white females such as Annie Jump Cannon, Carolyn Herschel, Elizabeth Blackwell, and Katharine Burr Blodgett. All were denied the professional interactions, laboratories, and access to public libraries accorded their white male counterparts and denied the opportunity to mentor the next generation of scientists.

*George Washington
Carver, Biochemist*

Addressing the Needs of
Culturally Diverse Learners

Just as students are learning that to say Columbus "discovered America" is in-accurate, they need to know that people from all cultures have contributed to our knowledge of science. Some scientific practices have been handed down through oral tradition for hundreds of years, practices often shaped by many individuals from specific communities. Because the United States has strong Eurocentric roots, discoveries are often credited to white male members of our society. Unfortunately, as Pearson and Bechtel (1989) point out, cultur-ally diverse scientists and women have traditionally worked in isolation, have lacked the advanced training afforded other scholars, have had their scholarly works usurped by others, have had their works relegated to foot-notes, and have been excluded from full participation in the scientific com-munity. Our science curricula will become more accurate and alive when teachers and their students have better access to information about the con-tributions of culturally diverse individuals and women (see Table 3.1).

TABLE 3.1 ■ Culturally Diverse Scientists

Name	Dates	Field	Country	Contribution
Al Khwarizmi, Muhammad ibn Musa	(800–847)	Mathematics	Khiva, SSR	Invented algebra—1st and 2nd degree equations
Albategnius	(858–929)	Astronomy	Turkey	Sine tables for astronomical calculations
Albuzijani	(940–998)	Mathematics	Persia	Trigonometry—tangents and cotangents
Alhazen	(965–1038)	Physics	Iraq	Spherical and parabolic mirrors
Alvarez, Luis	(1911–	Physics	United States	Liquid hydrogen bubble chamber
Anderson, Elizabeth	(1836–1917)	Medicine	England	First woman physician in England
Arnald of Villanova	(1235–1313)	Chemistry	Spain	Alchemist—tinctures, carbon monoxide
Arzachel	(circa 1080)	Astronomy	Spain	Planetary orbits are ellipses
Ashby, Winifred	(1879–1975)	Medicine	United States	Hematology techniques with red blood cells
Averroës	(1126–1198)	Medicine	Spain	Commentaries on Aristotle
Avicenna	(980–1037)	Medicine	Iran	Encyclopedia on medicine, function of human eye
Ayala, Francisco	(1934–	Biology	Spain	Molecular evolution—genetic variation
Bailey, Liberty H.	(1858–1954)	Biology	United States	Founded the discipline of horticulture
Banneker, Benjamin	(1731–1806)	Physics	United States	Honeybee research, wooden striking clock
Bascom, Florence	(1862–1945)	Geology	United States	Optical crystallography
Bhabha, Homi	(1909–	Physics	India	Cascade theory—cosmic rays
Blackwell, Elizabeth	(1821–1910)	Medicine	England	First female physician in United States
Blodgett, Katharine	(1898–1979)	Physics	United States	Nonreflecting glass
Bluford, Guion	(1942–	Astronomy	United States	First black American in space
Bose, Jagadis	(1858–1937)	Physics	India	Short radio waves, plant tropisms
Bose, Satyendra	(1894–1974)	Physics	India	Electromagnetic properties of ionosphere
Brahmagupta	(598–665)	Astronomy	India	Cyclic quadrilateral equation
Burbank, Luther	(1849–1926)	Botany	United States	Plant genetics
Callinicus	(circa 670)	Chemistry	Egypt	Nature of combustion, "Greek fire"
Cannon, Annie	(1863–1941)	Astronomy	United States	Spectroscopic analysis of stars
Cano, Juan	(1460–1526)	Astronomy	Spain	First to circumnavigate the globe (not Magellan)
Carson, Rachel	(1907–1964)	Ecology	United States	Interdependence of plants and animals
Carver, George	(1864–1943)	Biochemistry	United States	Uses for peanuts, sweet potatoes; soil sciences
Chandrasekhar, Subrahmanyan	(1910–	Astronomy	Pakistan	Stellar evolution, structure, and energy transfer
Chang, Min	(1908–	Biology	China	In vitro fertilization, oral contraception

(continued)

TABLE 3.1 ■ Continued

Name	Dates	Field	Country	Contribution
Chang Heng	(78–142)	Astronomy	China	Value of pi, armilliary sphere, 1st seismograph
Chen, Shiing-shen	(1911–	Mathematics	China	Differential geometry
Chou Kung	(c. 1200 B.C.)	Mathematics	China	Proofs for Pythagorean theorem, square root
Chu Shih-Chieh	(c. 1300)	Mathematics	China	Algebraic signs—negative numbers
Clarke, Edith	(1883–1959)	Mathematics	United States	Theory of symmetrical components
Comstock, Anna	(1854–1930)	Zoology	United States	Entomological drawings and illustrations
Cori, Gerty	(1896–1957)	Medicine	Czechoslovakia	Heredity of glycogen-storage diseases
Curie, Marie	(1867–1934)	Physics	Poland	Discovered radium and polonium
D'Elhuyar, Don Fausto	(1755–1833)	Geology	Spain	Discovered tungsten and wolframite
Del Rio, Andres	(1764–1849)	Geology	Spain	Discovered vanadium
Drew, Charles	(1904–1950)	Medicine	United States	Established blood banks
Ebashi, Setsuro	(1922–	Biochemistry	Japan	Relaxing factor (contraction) in muscle tissue
Egas Moniz, Antonio	(1874–1955)	Medicine	Portugal	Angiography, prefrontal leukotomy
Esaki, Leo	(1925–	Physics	Japan	Semiconductors—electron tunneling
Esau, Katherine	(1898–1990)	Botany	United States	Ontology of phloem in plants
Fell, Dame Honor	(1900–1989)	Biology	England	In vitro cultivation of cells
Fernandez-Moran, Humberto	(1924–	Biophysics	Venezuela	Brain research
Finlay, Carlos	(1833–1915)	Medicine	Cuba	Yellow fever virus research
Fleming, Williamina	(1857–1911)	Astronomy	Scotland	Spectral classification of stars
Foot, Katherine	(1852–1920)	Biology	United States	Cytology studies—photomicrographs
Franklin, Rosalind	(1920–1958)	Chemistry	England	Graphitizing and nongraphitizing carbons
Furukawa, Junji	(1912–	Chemistry	Japan	Chemistry of oligomerization—polymers
Gagarin, Yury	(1934–1969)	Astronomy	Former USSR	First human in space
Garcia, Manuel	(1805–1905)	Medicine	Spain	Inventor of the laryngoscope
Geber	(circa 1300)	Chemistry	Spain	Spread Arabian chemistry to Europe
Gilbreth, Lillian	(1878–1972)	Engineering	United States	Founded the discipline of industrial psychology
Gleason, Kate	(1865–1933)	Engineering	United States	Designed worm gear, low-cost housing
Hagihara, Yusuke	(1897–1989)	Astrophysics	Japan	Stability of satellite systems
Hall, Julia	(1859–1925)	Chemistry	United States	Electrolytic reduction of alumina to aluminum
Hamilton, Alice	(1869–1979)	Medicine	United States	Founded industrial medicine, identified occupational disease
Harvey, Ethel	(1885–1969)	Biology	United States	Embryology studies with hydra
Herschel, Caroline	(1750–1848)	Astronomy	England	Discovered eight comets

Name	Dates	Field	Country	Contribution
Hironaka, Heisuke	(1931–	Mathematics	Japan	Mathematics—singularity of algebraic varieties
Hodgkin, Dorothy	(1910–	Biochemistry	United States	X-ray diffraction of penicillin, vit. B-12, insulin
Honda, Kotaro	(1870–1954)	Chemistry	Japan	Magnetic alloys
Hopper, Grace	(1906–1993)	Computer Science	United States	One of developers of first computers
Houssay, Bernardo	(1887–1971)	Medicine	Argentina	Internal secretions of adrenal and thyroid glands
Hyde, Ida	(1854–1945)	Medicine	United States	Inventor of the microelectrode
Hyman, Libbie	(1888–1969)	Biology	United States	Invertebrate studies, embryology, morphology
Hypatia	(370–415)	Mathematics	Greece	Neoplatonic school in Alexandria
I-Hsing	(681–727)	Astronomy	China	Length of meridional line
Ishimure, Michiko	(1927–	Medicine	Japan	Heavy metal poisoning
Isidore of Seville	(560–636)	Biology	Spain	Encyclopedia of natural world
Jabir ibn Hayyan	(721–815)	Chemistry	Iran	Father of Arabic chemistry
Joliot-Curie, Irène	(1897–1956)	Physics	France	Formation of electrons and positrons, alpha rays
Julian, Percy	(1899–1975)	Chemistry	United States	Synthesis of physostigmine, chemistry of indole
Karle, Isabella	(1921–	Chemistry	United States	Structural analysis by X-ray diffraction
Kaufman, Joyce	(1929–	Physics	United States	Three-dimensional quantum chemistry calculations
Khan, Fazlur	(1929–	Engineering	Bangladesh	Structural architectural tube buildings
Khorana, Har	(1922–	Chemistry	India	Synthesis of nucleotide triplets, 1st artificial gene
Kihara, Hitoshi	(1893–1988)	Biology	Japan	Cell studies of wheat
Kimura, Motao	(1924–	Biology	Japan	Random drift—mutant genes
Kitasato, Shibasaburo	(1852–1931)	Biology	Japan	Antitoxins of diphtheria and tetanus
Ko Hung	(283–343)	Chemistry	China	Alchemist—elixir of gold cinnabar, tin sulfide
Kovalevskaya, Sofya	(1850–1891)	Mathematics	Russia	Partial differential equations
Kuno, Hisashi	(1910–	Geology	Japan	Crystallization of pyroxenes from magmas
LaFlesche, Susan	(1854–1903)	Medicine	United States	Culturally syntonic or harmonious medicine
Lamme, Bertha	(1869–1954)	Engineering	United States	Theory and design of motors and generators
Latimer, Lewis	(1848–1928)	Physics	United States	Carbon filament for electric light bulb
Leavitt, Henrietta	(1868–1921)	Astronomy	United States	Variable stars
Lee, Tsung-Dao	(1926–	Physics	China	"Weak" interactions of particles—nuclear physics
Leloir, Luis	(1906–	Biochemistry	Argentina	Glycogen synthesis
Li, Choh	(1913–	Biochemistry	China	Pituitary hormones—ACTH, somatotropin
Lim, Robert	(1897–1969)	Physiology	Singapore	Nerve receptors are chemosensitive
Lin, Chia-Chiao	(1916–	Mathematics	China	Hydrodynamics and turbulent flow
Lonsdale, Kathleen	(1903–1971)	Physics	Ireland	Crystal structure analyses, hexamethylbenzene
Maloney, Arnold	(1888–1955)	Medicine	Trinidad	Action of picrotoxin on barbiturate poisoning
Manton, Sidnie	(1902–	Biology	England	Embryology and morphology of crustacea
Matuyama, Motonori	(1884–1958)	Geology	Japan	Magnetic field reversals of Earth

(continued)

TABLE 3.1 ■ Continued

Name	Dates	Field	Country	Contribution
Maury, Antonia	(1866–1952)	Physics	United States	Spectral analysis of northern stars
Mayer, Maria	(1906–1972)	Chemistry	United States	Nuclear shell structure—atomic structure
McClintock, Barbara	(1902–	Biology	United States	Behavior of chromosomes—jumping genes
Meitner, Lise	(1878–1968)	Chemistry	Germany	Discovered thorium C and protactinium
Mela, Pomponius	(circa 44)	Geology	Spain	Climatic regions, first geographical work
Milstein, Cesar	(1927–	Biology	Argentina	Structure of immunoglobulins, phosphoenzymes
Minoka-Hill, Lillie	(1876–1952)	Medicine	United States	Nutrition research
Noether, Emmy	(1882–1935)	Physics	Germany	Noether's theorem—law in particle physics
Noguchi, Hideyo	(1876–1928)	Biology	Japan	Cultivated syphilis and yellow fever bacterium
Nomura, Masyasu	(1927–	Biology	Japan	Ribosomes contain RNA
Ochoa, Severo	(1905–	Chemistry	Spain	Synthesized RNA (ribonucleic acid)
Omar Khayám	(1050–1123)	Astronomy	Iran	Quadratic equations and astronomical tables
Onesimus	(circa 1700)	Medicine	Africa	Inoculation for smallpox
Paulze, Marie	(1758–1836)	Chemistry	France	Chemical nature of respiration
Peebles, Florence	(1874–1954)	Zoology	United States	Tissue regeneration in hydra
Perlmann, Gertrude	(1912–1974)	Biochemistry	Czechoslovakia	Protein chemistry—phosphoproteins
Ponnamperuma, Cyril	(1923–	Chemistry	Sri Lanka	Synthesized ATP, adenine
Raman, Chandrasekhara	(1888–1970)	Physics	India	Molecular spectroscopy and acoustics
Ramanujan, Srinivasa	(1887–1920)	Mathematics	India	Real analysis and number theory
Ramón y Cajal, Santiago	(1852–1934)	Biology	Spain	Discovered the neuron—nerve cell
Reed, Dorothy	(1874–1964)	Medicine	United States	Reed-Sternberg cells in Hodgkin's disease
Reynolds, Doris	(1899–1987)	Geology	England	Granitization of rock
Rhazes	(850–923)	Chemistry	Iran	Differentiated between smallpox and measles
Ride, Sally	(1951–	Astronomy	United States	First U.S. woman in space
Sabin, Florence	(1871–1953)	Medicine	United States	Origin of lymphatic vessels
Sager, Ruth	(1918–	Medicine	United States	Non-Mendelian inheritance
Saha, Meghnad	(1894–1956)	Physics	India	Thermal ionization of stars
Salam, Abdus	(1926–	Physics	Pakistan	Weak and electromagnetic interactions
Santos-Dumont, Alberto	(1873–1932)	Engineering	Brazil	Invented tail-first pusher biplane
Scharrer, Berta	(1906–	Medicine	Germany	Invented neuroendocrinology
Servetus, Michael	(1511–1553)	Medicine	Spain	Circulation in heart and lungs
Shen Kua	(1031–1095)	Geology	China	Discovery of magnetic compass
Shirane, Gen	(1924–	Physics	United States	Phase transitions in solids
Slye, Maude	(1879–1954)	Medicine	United States	Hereditary basis of cancer

Name	Dates	Field	Country	Discovery
Stearns, Mary	(1925–	Physics	United States	Photonuclear reactions and meson spectroscopy
Stevens, Nettie	(1861–1912)	Biology	United States	Chromosome is the basis for sex determination
Su Sung	(1020–1101)	Astronomy	China	Astronomical clock (escapement)
Takamine, Jokichi	(1854–1922)	Chemistry	Japan	Superphosphates, starch-digesting enzyme
Tamiya, Hiroshi	(1903–	Biology	Japan	Physiology of mold—*Aspergillus oryzae*
Taussig, Helen	(1898–1980)	Medicine	United States	Surgical correction of congenital malformations
Ting, Samuel	(1936–	Physics	United States	Discovered J particle in the atom
Tomonaga, Sin-Itiro	(1906–1979)	Physics	Japan	Theory of relativistic quantum electrodynamics
Trotter, Mildred	(1899–	Medicine	United States	Comparative anatomy by skeletal structure
Tsai Lun	(50–118)	Chemistry	China	Inventor of paper
Uyeda, Seiya	(1929–	Geophysics	Japan	Paleomagnetism—ancient magnetic fields
Vennesland, Birgit	(1913–	Biochemistry	Norway	Radioactive carbon as a tracer
Williams, Cicely	(1893–1980)	Medicine	United States	Described kwashiorkor
Wrinch, Dorothy	(1894–1980)	Chemistry	Argentina	Specificity of genes resides in amino acids
Wu, Chien-Shiung	(1912–	Physics	China	Beta disintegration (radioactive decay)
Yalow, Rosalyn	(1921–	Physics	United States	Radioimmunoassay
Yang, Chen	(1922–	Physics	China	Yang-Mills theory
Yukawa, Hideki	(1907–	Physics	Japan	Binding force in nucleus—strong force

Note: Sources of information about culturally and linguistically diverse scientists include: Addison-Wesley, 1993; Al-Daffa & Stroyls, 1984; Alic, 1986; Allen, 1989; Archibald, 1949; Asimov, 1964; Broker, 1983; Cajori, 1980; Campbell, 1982; Crow Dog, 1990; Daintith, Mitchell & Tootill, 1981; Deloria, 1988; Erdrich, 1984; Eves, 1976; Ferrio, 1991; Green, 1992; Herzenberg, 1986; Hinding, 1979; Howard, 1951; Ireland, 1962; Kass-Simon & Farnes, 1990; Kahle, 1985; Melson, Joseph & Williams, 1993; Ogilvie, 1993; Pearson & Bechtel, 1989; Rennert, 1995; Roessel, 1981; Ronan, 1982; Rubalcava, 1991; Sarton, 1952; Struik, 1987; Taton, 1963; Van Sertima, 1986; Weatherford, 1988; Yost, 1943.

CLASSROOM PRACTICE

Changing the presentation of information in science textbooks from a Euro-centric/androcentric model of science to a culturally affirming model of science will take time. In the interim, there are steps that you as a teacher can take to make science education an inclusive experience for all children, such as:

- Deliberately and consistently including the contributions of culturally diverse scientists and groups of individuals in each unit of science instruction.
- Setting up bulletin boards featuring the "Scientist of the Day" or of the week (see Table 3.1).
- Conducting a search on the World Wide Web or Internet to find information about culturally diverse scientists (one starting point: http://www.sjsu.edu:80/depts/ Museum.aamenu.html).
- Selecting videos, filmstrips, CD-ROMs, and other audiovisual materials that focus on the contributions of culturally diverse scientists and incorporating those materials into your instruction.
- Inviting culturally diverse scientists and women scientists to the classroom to speak about their work and their educational backgrounds.
- Assigning students to research the lives and works of culturally diverse individuals and then presenting the information orally, visually, or in written form for others in the class.
- Having students make a notebook of "famous scientists," including the names of culturally diverse individuals in that list.
- Allowing students to construct electronic timelines of scientific invention and discovery using software such as Chronos or TimeLiner.
- Reading biographies of culturally diverse scientists aloud to students when working with listening skills.
- Encouraging students to set up an electronic database of "famous scientists" using computer software such as HyperStudio, HyperCard, File-Maker Pro, Microsoft Works, Claris Works, or The Digital Chisel.

CHAPTER SUMMARY

Modern-day science is often presented to children through a Eurocentric/androcentric model of reporting, that is, an instructional model that primarily focuses on the contributions of white males of European descent. The contributions to the history of science made by groups, culturally diverse individuals, and white females are rarely mentioned in science classrooms. If all children are to be actively engaged in "doing science," the ways that we present information to children need to be restructured. Restructuring science education to make it inclusive would require that science curriculum materials include oral traditions, group discoveries, a redefinition of science, and unbiased reporting of the contributions of culturally diverse individuals. In the short term, as a teacher you can include the contributions of culturally diverse individuals in your instructional program so that all children find role models in science.

TOPICS TO REVIEW

- Scientific method
- Additive models
- Culturally transforming models

REFLECTIVE PRACTICE

1. Why is the presentation of information about famous scientists important to students?

2. What images or perceptions of science do you hold? How were those images formed?

3. Is there a former teacher or person in your life who helped you make your career decision? What did this person do to influence your career choice?

4. If you were making specific recommendations to publishing companies regarding the historical content of their science textbooks, what recommendations would you make? Why?

5. If you served on a school library committee that made recommendations about purchases of resource materials for children, what criteria would you recommend be considered in the purchasing process? Why?

6. Beyond the suggestions made in this chapter, what strategies can you identify as appropriate for providing information about famous scientists to culturally diverse learners?

CHAPTER 4

Approaches to Educational Psychology

Theory	Writers	Focus	Concepts
Behaviorism	Pavlov Thorndike Skinner Gagné	Human behavior	Reinforcement Punishment Behavior modification
Humanism	Rogers Combs Maslow	Human attributes	Self-esteem Self-worth Self- actualization
Cognitive Theory	Piaget Ausubel Vygotsky Norman	Knowing and learning	Structure of knowledge Organization Learning

Ways of Knowing Science

 **POINTS TO PONDER**

- How do children learn?
- What assumptions do you hold about teaching and learning?
- Do all children learn in the same way?

About a decade ago, I worked with some colleagues to develop a series of math/science problem-solving activities for use in the middle school science and mathematics classrooms. After a year of work, we were ready to field test the materials with "real kids." We finished developing the materials at the beginning of summer, and the only children we could round up for our field test were those enrolled in summer school. I have observed that children typically attend summer school for two reasons—either they are bright-eyed and bushy tailed, eager to get ahead in the academic world, or they are reluctant learners who need extra time to master the content of the course. We selected the reluctant learners for our study, thinking that if the materials would work with them they ought to work with any students.

One lesson in particular delighted us, a study on the mathematics of fruit. In this activity, the children were divided into teams, and each team was assigned the task of describing the physical attributes of their piece of fruit—the length, width, mass, volume, seed-to-mass ratio, and so forth. The apple, grape, tangerine, pear, avocado, lemon, and orange teams had little difficulty with the tasks. Throughout the morning, they weighed and measured their pieces of fruit and prepared presentations to share with the rest of the class. The watermelon team was a different story.

Our watermelon team was comprised of two boys and two girls, delightful youngsters who were intent on solving the problems that we presented to them. The first difficulty they encountered was the question, "What is the mass of your piece of fruit?" The other groups had been able to weigh their fruits using the pan balances that we had provided. The watermelon was so large that it "maxed out" the balance; the group had to use a bathroom balance, which presented a new difficulty—the watermelon kept rolling off the balance. The group tried many ways of standing and placing the watermelon on the balance, to no avail.

Finally, Kizzy, one of the Native American girls in the group, thought of a solution. An expression of delight spread across her face. She held the watermelon in her arms and looked down at the bathroom balance, started to place her foot on the balance, and then stopped. Kizzy examined the other members of her group for a moment and finally grabbed the smallest of the boys by the arms and stood him on the balance. She noted his weight and wrote it down. Next she dropped the watermelon into his arms and wrote down the weight of Matt plus watermelon. She subtracted Matt's weight from the weight of Matt plus watermelon and smiled as she recorded the mass of the melon.

Another dilemma experienced by the watermelon group was the question, "What is the volume of your piece of fruit?" By now, the watermelon group was behind the other groups in data collection, so they watched the other groups, hoping to find some shortcuts to lighten their workload. They had observed the orange group solve the volume problem by using the formula for the volume of a sphere ($3/4 \prod r^3$) found in the appendix of their mathematics textbook. The watermelon group had also observed the solution worked out by the pear group, who had solved the volume problem by water displacement. They had filled a large beaker full of water, submersed their pear, and measured the volume of water displaced by the pear. The water-displacement solution seemed to be a viable solution; after all, the watermelon group couldn't find the formula for the volume of their fruit in the math book.

It was obvious to everyone in the watermelon group that their piece of fruit would not fit into any beaker they could find. Jason emptied the papers from a large trash can into another can and signaled for his group to follow him outside, where he directed the group to fill the trash can with buckets of water. Finally, he dropped the watermelon into the trash can and watched in horror as the water gushed out in all directions, thoroughly soaking everyone's sneakers.

Kizzy again came to her group's rescue. She located a large kitchen knife in the lab area and with quick thrusts cut the ends from the watermelon. She placed the two ends together and said, "If we put the ends together, we have a sphere. The rest of the melon is a cylinder." The group quickly located the formulas for spheres and cylinders in their math books and proceeded to calculate the volume of a watermelon.

At the end of the day's lesson, I asked Kizzy about her problem-solving abilities. She was a wonderful teacher. She taught me that there are many ways

I had never thought of to think and to solve problems. When I asked how she had figured out how to weigh the watermelon, Kizzy explained that she had seen her grandmother weigh newborn lambs in this manner. Her grandmother weighed each lamb in order to identify those that were sickly, those that would need extra care. I asked Kizzy how had she figured out that a watermelon could be divided into a sphere and a cylinder. Kizzy smiled and said, "Oh, that's easy, it's just like pottery." She told me how she had learned to make pottery from her mother, who had shown her how to break complicated designs into simpler ones. By her own evaluation, Kizzy was a terrible math and science student. She couldn't understand math and science as they were presented in class (thus her enrollment in summer school). In reality, she was a wonderfully talented problem solver. The ways that we view teaching and learning determine the ways that we present information to children. This chapter deals with views of teaching and learning and with ideas on teaching children.

TEACHING AND LEARNING

Teaching and learning are independent but highly related processes. Frequently, teaching leads to learning, but not always. **Teaching** may be operationally defined as a system of actions by the teacher that are intended to encourage learning on the part of the student. **Learning** may be defined as a process by which knowledge, behavior, values, attitudes, and beliefs are formulated, modified, or changed. The ways that we view teaching and learning depend on our sociological, historical, and psychological assumptions.

THINKING AND LEARNING

From a neurobiological viewpoint, learning science or any subject involves the processes by which sensory input is transformed, reduced, elaborated, stored, recovered, and used (Reed, 1988, p. 3). Learning begins with **sensory stimuli** from the physical environment (see Figure 4.1). The human body is constantly receiving information about the physical world from the eyes, ears, skin, tongue, and nose. Most of the information received by human senses is lost or not attended to. As we actively listen to someone speak, we focus on receiving information through aural means. However, at the same time, our bodies continue to receive visual, tactile, olfactory, and gustatory input, information permanently lost or not attended to.

Many of us have had the experience of getting up from bed in the middle of the night and walking across a darkened room. In the process, we have stumped our big toe on a piece of furniture. In that moment, our entire body seems to focus on tactile input. Pain sensors in the toe take precedence over

FIGURE 4.1 ■
Diagram of
Human Memory

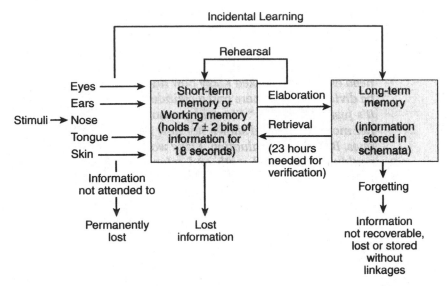

all other sensory receptors in our body, and we block out incoming information from our nose, eyes, ears, and tongue. We focus on the big toe. **Selective perception,** attending to one stimulus rather than all stimuli, is the first step in learning. By attending to sensory input from one set of receptors rather than all receptors, we filter information.

After selective perception has occurred, information moves into **short-term memory.** A series of mental processes have already altered incoming information from the moment of perception. Changes in perception may be small or large. Short-term memory may be thought of as a temporary receptacle for information. Information may be retained in short-term memory for approximately 18 seconds. Short-term memory has a very limited holding capacity; only seven plus or minus two bits of information may be retained at a time. After 18 seconds, information may be retained in short-term memory only if it has been **rehearsed.** Information that is not rehearsed is permanently lost or forgotten. Thus, when we want to remember a telephone number, we need to repeat it over and over to ourselves, rehearsing it until we use the information to dial the phone, to write it down, or to transfer it to long-term memory.

When information passes from short-term memory into **long-term memory** it again has been transformed by mental processes. These mental processes include **chunking** of similar information, extracting meanings from words, and identifying patterns or relationships in the information. Long-term memory may be viewed as a **semantic network,** as a web of interconnected words or concepts. Information in long-term memory is organized into schemata or data structures. Schemata (plural of schema) may be defined as cognitive structures created through the abstraction of experiences or acquired through instruction.

A schema provides an organizational structure into which new information may be fitted. Typically, new information is linked to existing information in long-term memory. Norman states that **schemata** are organized packets of knowledge gathered together to represent single units of self-contained knowledge (1982, p. 54). Information that moves from short-term memory into long-term memory has been transformed by mental processes involved with **elaboration**—adding meaning by connecting one bit of new information with other associations or with existing knowledge (Woolfolk & McCune-Nicolich, 1984, p. 208). Short-term memory has a limited capacity but can absorb information rapidly. By contrast, the input capacity of long-term memory is relatively slow, but long-term memory has a nearly limitless capacity. Access to information in long-term memory is dependent upon the way that information is stored. Short-term memory or working memory can retain information for only a short time, whereas long-term memory has the capacity to retain information for the life of the organism.

Learning involves moving information from short-term memory into long-term memory. Remembering or **retrieval** involves the movement of information from long-term memory into working memory or short-term memory. To remember is to have managed three things successfully: the acquisition, retention, and retrieval of information. Failure to remember means failure at managing one of those three things. Forgetting something may mean that we never learned the information in the first place. It may also mean that information was not organized in a way that makes access easy. Finally, forgetting may mean that information was learned in a very limited context and cannot be retrieved without that context.

Learning and Culturally Diverse Children

Research indicates that culture may influence the stimuli that we attend to, our focus in the learning process. For a long time, there was a popular belief that all children learn in the same way; the opening vignette regarding Kizzy and the watermelon may help to dispel this myth. Although it is true that the same neurobiological processes occur in all human beings, each of us has been socialized to learn within a cultural context. Consideration of the cultural context of learning also requires that teachers avoid stereotypical assumptions about children and their learning styles. Although many unassimilated Hispanic/Latino children prefer a photonovela format for printed materials (a highly visualized comic book–like textbook featuring embedded linguistic scaffolding techniques), not all Latino children share this preference. Level of assimilation into mainstream culture, country of origin, and family beliefs, values, and attitudes all influence the degree to which children are culturally and linguistically socialized to home culture and school culture.

Erickson (1984, p. 528) reports that Polynesian children are taught to navigate ships through an apprenticeship model. In this situation, children are taught to model themselves after an experienced navigator. They are taught to watch the characteristics of the waves, color of the water, movement of the water, and positions of the stars for navigating across hundreds of miles. While these neophyte navigators are incapable of passing traditional Western pencil-and-paper tests of mental abilities associated with navigational expertise, they are completely capable of sailing a boat from one place to another. Polynesian children in this situation have been socialized to attend in the learning process to visual phenomena associated with water movement and stellar positioning.

Hvitfeldt (1986) found that Hmong students have been socialized to learn in a different manner than Western or European learners. In her study with unassimilated adult learners, Hvitfeldt found that Hmong students have been socialized to work in cooperative groups and that students automatically engage in peer tutoring in order to improve the performance of all members of the community. Hmong learners typically rely more heavily on oral learning than do their Western counterparts. Additionally, unassimilated Hmong learners tended to rely heavily on external motivational factors in classroom learning rather than on internal motivation. Hmong learners have been socialized to view the world holistically and thus tend to have difficulty wrestling with ideas and concepts unless they are presented in context.

Researchers working with unassimilated Native American children have found them to rely on oral communication as their primary means of learning. Many Native American children have been socialized to observe

Many Native American children are socialized to learn in group settings.

adult performance as a means of learning. Olion and Gillis-Olion (1984) point out that Native American children are taught to listen and to wait until their years of experience have prepared them to learn enough and to be influential enough to attract listeners. Additionally, Native American children have been socialized to depend on memory rather than written notes in the learning process. Social mores such as cooperation, anonymity, submissiveness, humility, and sharing valued in the Native American community sometimes conflict with school ways of doing and knowing.

The interrelationship between culture and learning is frequently overlooked in the classroom. Teachers need to develop a sensitivity to the fact that not all children have been socialized to learn in the same fashion. Although some children have been taught by their parents and community to value reading books, other children have been taught to value listening to elders. An understanding of the connection between home culture and school culture is vital in understanding the learning process. Learning occurs within a sociocultural context. The **sociocultural aspect** of learning includes the culture of the classroom, as well as the culture that the child brings to the classroom from home. A consideration of the psychological assumptions that underpin learning theories needs to consider the child as well as the culture of the child.

Behavioral Psychology

Behavioral psychology is grounded on theories of stimulus-response learning. Behavioral psychologists and teachers socialized to teach children from this viewpoint place a heavy emphasis on external rewards and reinforcement, on controlling the educational environment to maximize the learning of children. From a behavioral perspective, the job of the teacher is to construct a learning environment that will have a high probability of reinforcing students' correct responses and behaviors while extinguishing undesirable behaviors. Educational goals within this context focus on organizing, sequencing, and presenting information to children so that learning is achieved. Writers ascribing to behavioral psychology traditions include Ivan Pavlov, E. L. Thorndike, B. F. Skinner, E. R. Guthrie, and Robert Gagné.

Pavlov

Ivan Pavlov, a Russian psychologist, conducted most of his studies of learning in the context of animal research. Experimentation with dogs (e.g., Pavlov's puppies) form some of the empirical evidence for behaviorist learning models. Pavlov identified food as a stimulus and salivation as a response in his experiments, in which he presented dogs with bowls of food at the same time that he rang a bell. After a period of time, he discovered that the dogs responded to the sound of the bell by salivating as well as to the sight and smell of the food. The dogs became conditioned to associate the ringing of the bell with the presence of food and salivated whether food was presented or not.

FIGURE 4.2 ■ Pavlov's Stimulus-Response Theory

In Pavlov's experiments, the food was an unconditioned stimulus, one that dogs responded to without previous training. Salivation was an unconditioned response, that is, an automatic response as opposed to a trained response. After a period of time, the dogs responded to the sound of the bell and associated it with food; thus the ringing of the bell became a conditioned stimulus (see Figure 4.2). Pavlov referred to this type of stimulus-response learning as conditioning. Conditioning is still used as an acceptable education model, especially in military training.

Thorndike

E. L. Thorndike was noted for his theory of connectionism. Thorndike was a behaviorist who believed that connections between stimuli and responses became ingrained or stamped on human memory. While Pavlov's work focused on the learning of dogs, Thorndike's work involved the learning of cats. His first principle of learning, the law of effect, states that when a situation results in a satisfying state of affairs, a connection is formed. Rewards or extrinsic motivational devices increase the strength of these connections. His law of effect was based on Thorndike's observations of a cat in a cage pulling a string to obtain a food reward.

Thorndike's second principle of learning, the law of exercise, states that the more a stimulus-response connection is practiced the stronger it becomes. Likewise, if a stimulus-response connection is not practiced, the bond becomes weaker. In educational terms, Thorndike's principles lead to drill-and-practice activities, including computer-assisted instruction, and to tangible rewards such as stars on students' papers to reinforce "good" work.

Skinner

Among all behavioral psychologists, B. F. Skinner (1904–1990) is perhaps the best known. Skinner's animal research involved the behavior of rats in mazes. In terms of human learning, Skinner's writings focused on operant conditioning. Skinner believed that most human behavior takes the form of operant responses, which include behaviors such as driving a car, reading a book, writing a letter, and talking with others. At the beginning, an individual's responses tend to be random in a particular situation.

When some responses are reinforced as appropriate, a child will perform these with greater frequency; thus operant conditioning is taking place. For example, a young child tends to explore the world in a rather random fashion. The young child may touch the toilet brush, put toy blocks in her or his mouth, open a storybook, and bite the family dog. Although the parent may smile and offer to pick up the child when the child opens the storybook, the parent typically will say "No" and will remove the seductive object when the child plays with the toilet brush or bites the family dog. After a time, certain responses become more dominant than others–operant conditioning.

Gagné

Robert Gagné's writings (1987, 1988) build a bridge between traditional behavioral psychologists and cognitive psychologists. Much of his work has been used as the basis of industrial and military training models. Gagné believes that the purpose of instruction is to provide support to the internal processes of learning. Additionally, Gagné believes that learning occurs in five domains: **attitudes, motor skills, verbal information, intellectual skills,** and **cognitive strategies.** By arranging the events of instruction (see Figure 4.3), the teacher can control or influence the learning of the student.

According to Gagné, learning begins with stimulation of neural receptors (eyes, ears, nose, skin, and tongue) by external stimuli. This stimulation produces patterns of neural activity that are briefly registered by the sensory registers. Information from the physical environment is transformed into a

FIGURE 4.3 ■ Gagné's Events of Instruction

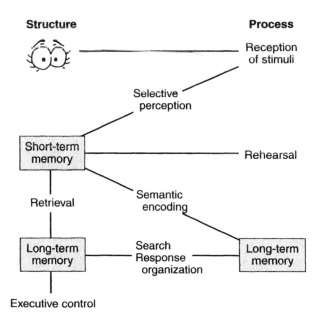

form that is usable in short-term memory. Since information may be lost from short-term memory due to decay, rehearsal strategies are necessary to maintain information in memory until it can be transformed by semantic encoding into long-term memory. Gagné summarizes the events of instruction as:

- *Attention,* which determines the extent and nature of reception of incoming stimuli;
- *Pattern recognition or selective perception,* which transforms stimuli into information that may be stored in short-term memory;
- *Rehearsal,* which maintains items stored in short-term memory;
- *Semantic encoding,* which prepares information for long-term memory;
- *Retrieval or search,* which moves information to working memory;
- *Response organization,* which selects and organizes performance;
- *Feedback,* which provides the learner with information about performances; and
- *Executive control,* which selects and activates cognitive strategies.

The products of learning, according to Gagné, include intellectual skills, cognitive strategies, verbal information, motor skills, and changes in attitudes (Table 4.1). Gagné has defined intellectual skills as those entities that enable individuals to interact with their environments in terms of symbols or conceptualizations (Gagné, Briggs, & Wager, 1988, p. 43). Gagné points out that intellectual skills are the most basic and pervasive structures of formal education. Cognitive strategies are a second product of schooling. Intellectual skills, according to Gagné, may be arranged in a hierarchy that includes (1) signal learning, (2) stimulus-response learning, (3) chaining, (4) verbal learning, (5) discrimination learning, (6) concept learning, (7) rule learning, and (8) problem solving. Cognitive strategies are the capabilities that govern an individual's own learning, remembering, and thinking behaviors. The third outcome of learning is the development of verbal information in the learner. Gagné states that verbal information is the kind of knowledge that can be stated; it is declarative knowledge. The fourth outcome of learning, according to Gagné, is the development of motor skills in the learner. Motor skills may include making a microscope slide, determining the mass of an object using a pan balance, and assembling water displacement apparatuses. The final outcome of learning is a change in the learner's attitudes toward objects, persons, or situations—change in the affective domain. Robert Gagné's writings thus bridge the information-processing theories of cognitive psychology and "traditional" behavioral psychology.

Behavioral Psychology in the Science Classroom

Behavioral psychologists typically advocate using social reinforcers (smiles, hugs, and social acceptance), tokens (points, grades, prizes, and play money), and activities (music-listening time, free play, computer time) as motivational devices in the classroom. Theories of behavior modification, where "good" or

TABLE 4.1 ■ Gagné's Products of Learning

Outcomes or Capabilities	Examples of Performance
Intellectual skill	Identifying the diagonal of a rectangle. Demonstrating that water freezes at 0° Celsius. Predicting plant growth based on water, soil, sunlight, etc.
Cognitive strategy	Constructing a chart to organize data. Working backwards to solve a problem. Breaking a problem into its component parts.
Verbal information	Naming the parts of a plant cell and their functions. Identifying common insect vectors. Stating Newton's laws of thermodynamics.
Motor Skill	Constructing a microscope slide, wet mount. Assembling a distillation apparatus. Determining the mass of an object using a pan balance.
Attitude	Electing to sign out a book on dinosaurs from the library. Voluntarily visiting a space museum on a Saturday. Choosing to make an insect collection.

desirable behaviors are reinforced while "bad" or negative behaviors are ignored, are also vestiges of behavioral psychology theories in the classroom. Programmed instruction, drill-and-practice activities, computer-assisted instruction, and mastery learning have their origins in theories of behavioral psychology.

Operant conditioning typically involves five specific steps: (1) specifying the desired behavioral objectives or educational outcomes, (2) dividing the lesson or task into small, incremental steps, (3) sequencing instruction with a consideration of prerequisite learnings, (4) providing instruction with accompanying feedback, and (5) reinforcing correct responses (answers, study habits, and classroom behaviors). Practitioners of operant conditioning consider schedules of instruction and schedules of feedback vital components of instruction.

Critics of behavioral learning models point out, first, that these models rely heavily on drill-and-practice activities and low levels of information processing. Second, not all teachers are skilled in identifying prerequisite skills and in breaking down complex tasks into simple components. Third, the use of behavioral or mastery learning models encourages students to develop poor study habits by learning only the information necessary to pass a test. Fourth, the use of mastery learning models or drill-and-practice models may lead students to assume that they have mastered the content in a particular academic area, when indeed they have only a superficial understanding of the concepts. Finally, some critics of behavioral learning models point out that the heavy reliance on extrinsic reward structures and on behavioral modification techniques raises ethical concerns about the misuse of these instructional models.

Humanistic Psychology

Most humanistic psychologists believe that concern for the individual's feelings, perceptions, beliefs, and purposes is the foundation of the teaching and learning process. Humanists believe that in order to understand another person, it is necessary to see the world from that person's viewpoint. Thus, in order for a teacher to understand the behavior of a student, the teacher must first determine how the child perceives its own actions in a particular situation. The teacher sees the wearing of "colors" by an African American or Hispanic/Latino child (that is, wearing a Raider's jacket, "bagging" trousers, and

The wearing of colors is often an attempt to achieve peer acceptance, not antisocial behavior.

wearing a handkerchief as a hat) as gang-related activity. The child views this behavior as a way to gain approval from one's peers or sometimes as simple survival behavior on harsh inner-city streets. (Increasing numbers of inner-city public schools are requiring students to wear uniforms to decrease the impact of gang-related wearing apparel.)

Humanistic psychologists believe that the way a person feels is as important as how the person thinks or behaves. Humanistic psychology is sometimes referred to as existential psychology, phenomenological psychology, or perceptual psychology. It is an attempt to understand human behavior from the viewpoint of the learner, rather than from the viewpoint of the teacher. The major proponents of humanistic psychology include Carl R. Rogers, Arthur Combs, Abraham H. Maslow, George Brown, and William Glasser.

Rogers

Carl Rogers (1902–1987) is a psychologist who advocated making learning and teaching more humanistic, more personal, and more meaningful. Rogers's notions of teaching and learning include learning principles that speak of (1) the desire to learn, (2) learning and change, (3) the learning environment, (4) self-directed learning, and (5) the significance of learning. Rogers's approach to educational psychology may be characterized as person-centered or child-centered learning.

In writing of the desire to learn, Rogers pointed out that all human beings are endowed with a natural curiosity or desire to learn, evidenced in the eagerness of young children to explore their natural surroundings. Classrooms based on humanistic psychological principles provide opportunities for children to satisfy their curiosity, to explore for themselves, and to pursue their own academic endeavors.

Rogers's second principle of learning involves learning and change: Children need to be taught to accept change as a natural part of learning. What children learn in school is soon outdated; therefore, children need to be encouraged to be lifelong learners to fill gaps in their knowledge base as new technologies produce new products. Rogers would argue that schools ought to produce individuals who are capable of learning in a changing environment.

The third principle of learning advocated by Rogers involves the learning environment: Learning is best acquired and retained in an environment free from threat. From a humanistic perspective, learning occurs best when children are free to fail without penalty. Effective learning environments are those where children can test their skills, talents, and abilities without fear of criticism or ridicule.

Self-directed or self-initiated learning is the subject of Rogers's fourth principle of successful schooling. Learning how to learn is a major goal of humanistic educational advocates. Rogers would say that being able to choose the direction of one's learning is highly motivating for children. Additionally, he would point out that self-directed learning focuses the child's attention on the process of learning as well as the product of learning. In terms of outcomes, Rogers stated that self-directed learning teaches children to be self-reliant and independent.

Rogers's final principle of learning concerns the significance of learning and focuses on the child's perceptions of the value of learning. Humanistic psychologists would point out that learning is meaningful when children perceive it as relevant to their own needs and to their own world. According to Rogers, children learn best and most rapidly when learning is significant or of personal value to them. For Rogers, the teacher is a facilitator of learning in the classroom, not a dispenser of knowledge.

Maslow

Abraham Maslow (1908–1970) has long been recognized as a proponent of humanistic psychology. The majority of Maslow's work dealt with the gratification of needs as a motivational force in the educational process. Maslow's hierarchy of needs (Maslow, 1962a) is an attempt to prioritize human needs in educational terms (Figure 4.4). Within the hierarchy of human needs, physiological needs for food, shelter, water, and sleep are primary. Once these needs have been attended to, other needs may be satisfied. At the second level of the hierarchy are safety needs, which could include the desire for security from danger and the aspiration for good health. Maslow's third level of identified needs includes the desire to belong to a group and the desire for

FIGURE 4.4 ■ Maslow's Hierarchy Revisited

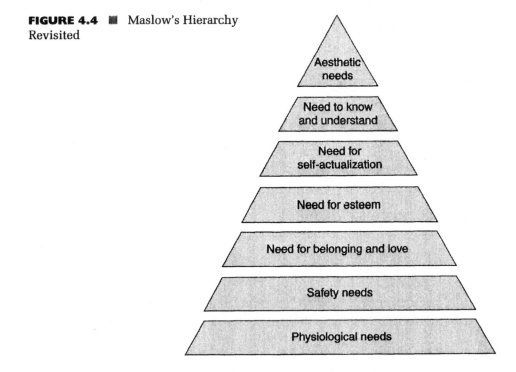

Aesthetic needs

Need to know and understand

Need for self-actualization

Need for esteem

Need for belonging and love

Safety needs

Physiological needs

affection or love. All children desire to be accepted in their family and peer group. All desire the respect, admiration, and confidence of their social group. The need for esteem, highly related to the need for belonging, constitutes the fourth level of the hierarchy. Self-actualization or self-fulfillment is the fifth level; here children focus on their need to develop to their full potential, to become "all they can be." At the self-actualization level, children pursue hobbies, develop their athletic prowess as far as possible, and develop expertise in the performance of some skill, job, or talent. The need to know and to understand falls at the sixth level of Maslow's continuum. This level embraces the concepts of curiosity, acquiring understanding, and pursuing knowledge. The final and highest level of Maslow's hierarchy is concerned with aesthetic values and appreciations. Here children seek to fulfill aesthetic needs for such conditions as closure, order, and symmetry. Maslow has defined the first four levels (physiological, safety, belonging, and esteem needs) as deficiency needs, while the higher levels of the hierarchy (self-actualization, knowing, and aesthetic needs) are growth needs or being needs.

Maslow's work in humanistic psychology emphasizes the intrinsic nature of motivation. Additionally, his work provides explanations of why students' attempts to fulfill their personal deficiency needs may at times conflict with a teacher's educational goals. Students who come to school tired, hungry, or feeling rejected at home may have difficulty learning until the basic physiological, safety, or belonging needs in their lives have been met. Teachers who ascribe to Maslow's theory would seek to move students from lower-order needs to higher-order needs or needs associated with self-fulfillment and aesthetic appreciation.

Humanistic Psychology in the Science Classroom

In general, humanistic psychologists value educational goals that help students learn more about themselves, relate to others, and make independent decisions. This psychological perspective is concerned with the feelings and perceptions of the individual learner. Translating the writings of humanistic psychologists into classroom practice has produced the confluent educational movement, open education environments, values clarification activities, and an emphasis on social skills training. Confluent education, developed at the Center for Humanistic Education at the University of California, Santa Barbara, is a process of integrating affective experiences with cognitive learning. This approach to learning involves students in understanding the content while personalizing the information in terms of their individual experiences.

Open education is a humanistic approach to education that differs from traditional education in terms of instruction, diagnosis, evaluation, provisions, and humanness. Proponents of open education encourage children to freely move around the classroom, to use manipulative materials to learn about the physical world. Most open education proponents encourage children to work on their own, to pursue their own interests. Typically, open classrooms are highly individualized learning environments where tests are few and teacher-directed learning infrequent. Open education provides students the freedom to select their own activities and encourages teachers to serve as facilitators of learning rather than as dispensers of information.

Values clarification activities (mentioned in Chapter 13) are derived from humanistic psychology foundations. In terms of science education, values clarification is incorporated into science/technology/society instruction. This vestige of humanistic psychology is a vital part of producing scientifically literate citizens capable of decision making in a democratic society. Values clarification helps students examine their personal value system so that they may arrive at informed decisions.

Social skills development, the ability to work with others, is closely akin to values clarification. Modeling, role playing, peer tutoring, and cooperative learning activities are examples of social skills training from the humanistic psychology tradition that have been infused into modern elementary science education.

Criticism of Humanistic Approaches

Over the years, humanistic psychology approaches to education have been criticized in terms of (1) self-directed learning, (2) goals, (3) program planning, (4) evaluation, and (5) affective components. Many critics point out that students are not always capable of directing their own learning, that students may lack the "big picture" as to what is relevant and necessary for lifelong learning. In terms of goals, critics of humanistic psychology traditions point out that a lack of direction or purpose is frequently evident in many humanistic classrooms. In the same context, humanistic educational programs are criticized as lacking conceptual frameworks for students' learning. Evaluation of learning in humanistic classrooms is difficult due to the lack of appropriate assessment tools or tests. It is difficult for humanistic educators to show that their programs have made a difference in terms of children's concept acquisition and in their attitudes, values, and beliefs. Finally, the reliance on affective components makes the outcomes of humanistic education difficult to quantify. It is a challenge to show that children have truly learned in a humanistic classroom when the emphasis is on internal control of learning.

Cognitive Psychology

In writing of teaching and learning, Anderson points out that a "complete theory of education should eventually include a synthesis of neurobiological and cognitive scientific principles in addition to philosophical and cultural contexts" (1992, p. 1039). Modern cognitive psychology views of teaching and learning combine a knowledge of information processing derived from medical literature with a knowledge of human cognitive development derived from the traditions of Piaget and Bruner. Modern cognitive psychologists also take into consideration the sociocultural context of learning, the culture of the child, and the culture of the classroom. Finally, cognitive psychology is based on theories of schema formation, such as those advocated by Donald Norman. The important writings in cognitive psychology include works by Jean David Ausubel, Lev Vygotsky, Robert Gagné, and David Norman. Piaget's works have added to our knowledge of the influence of a child's physical and mental development on the child's learning. Ausubel's writings, on the other hand, deal with the area of verbal reception learning. Vygotsky's writings are concerned with the influence of the child's culture on learning. Gagné's writings build a bridge between traditional behavioral psychology and modern cognitive psychology. Norman's works are typical of cognitive psychology writings that focus on information-processing approaches to teaching and learning. The writings of cognitive psychologists focus on how children acquire new knowledge, how they organize that knowledge, and how they feel about what they have learned.

Piaget

In terms of cognitive psychology, Jean Piaget (1896–1980) was a pioneer in describing how children think and how they make sense of their world. By studying vast numbers of children and their behavior, Piaget developed the **stage theory of learning.** He believed that all children move through a series of four cognitive or developmental stages (see Table 4.2). Piaget is frequently

TABLE 4.2 ■ Piaget's Cognitive Stages

Stage	Age in Years	Characteristics
Sensorimotor	0–2	Child begins to use imitation, memory, and thought. Objects cease to exist when they are hidden from view. Child moves from reflex actions to goal-directed learning.
Preoperational	2–7	Child experiences language development and gradual ability to think in symbolic form. Unidirectional thinking is possible. Difficulty using multiple perspectives.
Concrete	7–11	Child is able to solve concrete or hands-on problems in a logical fashion. Child understands the laws of conservation and reversibility. Child is able to classify and seriate.
Formal	11–15	Child is able to solve abstract problems in a logical fashion. Thinking becomes more scientific. Child develops concern for societal problems and issues.

referred to as a developmental psychologist, one who focused on children's stages of intellectual development.

According to Piaget, the earliest stage of learning is the **sensorimotor stage.** This stage is so named because development focuses on sensory input and on resultant body movements. Object permanence, that is, the belief that objects exist only when they are within the visual range of the child, is the dominant mental indicator of this stage. Learning occurs at this stage of mental development through imitating of the behaviors of others.

Piaget's second developmental stage, the **preoperational stage,** is characterized by the development of language and the ability to think in symbolic

FIGURE 4.5 ■ Piagetian One-Way Logic Task

Teacher's Map of the Neighborhood

Child's Map of the Neighborhood

form. Symbolic manipulation, that is, using pictures or symbols to represent real world objects, is first developed during this stage. Piaget theorized that children at the preoperational stage are very egocentric or self-oriented in their thinking. Additionally, he believed that as the child moves from the sensorimotor to the preoperational stage, the ability to engage in one-way logic develops but not the ability to understand the concept of conservation of matter.

One-way logic may be operationally defined as the ability to sequence objects or events. For example, if a child is presented with a "road" and a set of objects, the child should be able to arrange the objects in sequence. In this Piagetian task, the teacher presents the child with a map of the neighborhood (see Figure 4.5) and a set of manipulative materials. Children functioning at the preoperational stage typically are capable of completing this task.

When teachers work with students at the preoperational stage, lessons need to include concrete props and visual aids whenever possible. Children at this stage have difficulty following instructions, so directions need to be relatively short. Most kindergarten programs feature the use of manipulative materials that encourage children to move from a preoperational to a concrete stage of functioning. Additionally, programs for early elementary children include opportunities for children to develop experiences in exploring and operating in the physical world.

Most children in the early grades of elementary school function at the preoperational stage and have not yet mastered the idea of conservation of matter. For example, if a child sees a teacher pour a glass of water into a different-shaped container, the child is unable to understand that the volume doesn't change although the shape of the liquid has changed. In this Piagetian task, the teacher fills one container with liquid and then pours it into a different-shaped container in the presence of a child. Children at the preoperational stage will say that one container holds more liquid than the other (see Figure 4.6), even though both containers actually hold the same amount of liquid.

The ability to understand the concepts of conservation of liquids and length is an indicator that a child is functioning at the **concrete operational stage.** Other indicators of this stage of mental reasoning include the development of the ability to solve problems in a logical fashion using concrete,

FIGURE 4.6 ◾
Piagetian Conservation of Volume Task

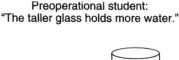
Preoperational student: "The taller glass holds more water."

Concrete operational student: "Both glasses hold the same amount of water."

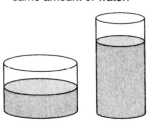

hands-on materials. Just as children are able to understand the idea of conservation of quantity at this stage, they are also able to understand reversibility (recounting events backwards). In teaching students at this stage of mental development, teachers need to continue to supply manipulative materials to students. Additionally, students learn best when lectures and readings are well organized and short. The use of concrete examples from the physical world benefits all students operating at this cognitive stage, especially students who have not yet acquired English language proficiency.

Formal reasoning is the last level of Piaget's stage theory. At the formal level of reasoning students are able to solve abstract problems in a logical and sequential manner. Students' thinking at this stage also becomes more scientific. Children typically show concern with societal issues when they reach this level of mental ability. When teaching students who are operating at this stage of mental reasoning, teachers should encourage them to engage in problem-solving activities and should ask them to explain their solution paths. Where possible, teachers should encourage students to "get the big picture," to wrestle with broad concepts.

In addition to his observations of children's developmental stages, Piaget pointed out that certain environmental factors may influence a child's mental development. Piaget believed that physical maturation, physical experience, social interaction, and equilibrium (the self-control or regulation of learning) were salient variables in children's intellectual development. Many of Piaget's beliefs and theories about children's learning continue to be widely applied in classrooms, as is apparent in the discussion on scaling in Chapter 8.

Ausubel

In contrast to the many cognitive psychologists who favor inquiry-based learning, including discovery learning, David Ausubel favors expository teaching techniques and reception learning. Ausubel emphasizes the idea that expository teaching is useful in helping teachers present large amounts of information to students while focusing on relationships within the content to be learned. Ausubel's theory explains how lecture and textual material, when properly organized, can lead to as much retention and understanding as discovery or inquiry learning. He explains that in the process of meaningful learning, the student relates new information to existing knowledge structures. Meaningful learning occurs when students "understand" (as opposed to memorizing by rote) that which is to be learned, and when they connect new information to existing knowledge structures.

Ausubel's theory of teaching is based on a **three-phase model:** (1) advance organizer, (2) presentation of the information or task, and (3) strengthening the cognitive organization. During the first phase of learning, information can be communicated to learners either by some form of reception learning that presents the information in its final format or by some type of discovery learning that obligates learners to discover all or part of the information independently of the teacher. In the first phase of learning, the teacher clarifies the aim of the lesson and presents an advance organizer. The **advance organizer** serves to identify the attributes of the concept, to provide examples of the concept, and to use the concept in context. The use of advance organizers does not automatically increase students' learning. Rather, advance organizers seem to benefit students most when the information to be learned is poorly organized or when students lack prerequisite skills, abilities, or conceptual knowledge.

During the second phase of teaching, the teacher presents the material or task to be learned to the students. At this time, the teacher makes the organization of the material explicit for the students. Additionally, the teacher uses the process of progressive differentiation to help students assimilate and retain new information. **Progressive differentiation** is a strategy by which teachers present the most general applications of the concept first, followed by less inclusive applications of the concept. For example, to teach the concept of insect, the teacher would begin with the broad definition: An insect is an arthropod (an animal with jointed legs) with three body segments, six legs, two eyes, two antennae, and usually one or two pairs of wings. The teacher could mention that bees, butterflies, and grasshoppers are insects. Next the teacher would mention that ants (which in most cases have no wings) are also insects. Finally, the teacher would mention less-known examples of insects such as bedbugs, lice, and springtails. By the time the teacher reaches the less-known examples of the concept, students have a cognitive structure in place to accommodate the new information.

The final phase of Ausubel's teaching and learning model involves strengthening cognitive organization. Ausubel refers to this stage as **integrative reconciliation** in which the learner integrates new information with existing information. This phase of learning promotes active reception learning, clarifies information for the learner, and prepares the student for new learning. In the case of the concept "insect," the teacher would encourage students to compare insects with centipedes, millipedes, and spiders, asking "Are these organisms insects? Why or why not?"

According to Ausubel, reception learning is meaningful learning. Information is logically organized when it is presented to the learner in its final form. Students are encouraged to relate new information to existing cognitive structures. It should be noted that Ausubel is not opposed to discovery learning. In fact, he is a strong advocate of the occasional use of discovery learning, particularly for elementary school children. Ausubel points out that young children still functioning at a concrete level need tactile, kinesthetic learning experiences. Much of Ausubel's writing has been incorporated into Madeline Hunter's mastery teaching model (Hunter, 1982).

Vygotsky

Much of Lev Vygotsky's writing deals with the sociocultural context of learning, that is, the culture that the child brings to school and the culture of the classroom. Vygotsky, a Russian cognitive psychologist, was concerned with the influence of culture on children's learning. Vygotsky's work focused on combining what was known of the neurological and physiological functioning of the brain with knowledge acquisition. His writings focus on the importance of culture, the role of language in learning, and the development of higher mental functioning.

Vygotsky pointed out that children under guidance, in groups, and in collaboration with one another can perform tasks they have not mastered independently (1978, p. 87). He points out that learning has both external and internal aspects. When children learn, they negotiate meaning. They assign meaning to objects and events as they speak with each other and with adults. Children solve practical tasks with the help of their speech, as well as with their hands, eyes, and other senses. Learning is dependent upon the external environment, but also on the child's internal processing of information. Vygotsky pointed out that culture makes social processes possible. Social processes bring about the learning of language. Ultimately language makes thought possible.

Children's play, according to Vygotsky, is the primary means of their cultural development. In their play, children project themselves into adult activities of their culture and rehearse their future roles and values. Play is a means by which children begin to acquire the motivation, skills, and attitudes necessary for social participation. By the time children enter school, they have developed a way of learning based on their culture of origin. In terms of culturally diverse children in U.S. schools, this means that children have frequently been socialized to learn at home in a way that may be different from school ways of knowing and learning. From a Vygotskian perspective, a child's level of assimilation with mainstream U.S. culture may have a tremendous impact on the child's learning at school.

Language, according to Vygotsky, not only makes thought possible, it also regulates behavior. Vygotsky describes three stages in the development of language: social, egocentric, and inner. Social language or external speech is the first stage of language development. During this stage children typically utter statements such as "juice," "milk," or "cookie." Egocentric language or speech is the second stage of language development and typically occurs between ages three and seven. During this developmental language stage children talk to themselves in an effort to guide their own behavior. They may say things like "I'm going to the bathroom," "I'm going outside," and "I'm a good girl." Inner speech, the last stage of language development, is silent self-talk; this inner speech makes all higher mental functioning possible.

Norman

Donald Norman states that learning involves purposeful remembering and skillful performance. According to his theory of cognitive psychology, which takes an information-processing approach to teaching and learning, learning involves at least three distinct modes: accreting, structuring, and tuning. **Ac-**

cretion is the addition of new knowledge to existing knowledge structures, a gradual process of accumulating new knowledge and of appending that knowledge to existing conceptual frameworks. **Structuring,** according to Norman, involves the formation of new knowledge structures. Structuring occurs when existing schemata will no longer suffice, when new knowledge cannot be appended to existing knowledge and new conceptualizations occur. Finally, **tuning** is the fine adjustment of knowledge to a task.

Norman points out that learning, memory, and performance are interrelated. Learning, according to Norman, tends to emphasize the acquisition of information. Memory tends to emphasize how information is retained and then retrieved when needed. Performance emphasizes how information is used. As children learn, they gain expertise in certain areas of their lives. Expertise is characterized by smoothness, automaticity, decreased mental effort, performance under stress, and point of view.

Smoothness, by Norman's definition, is the apparent ease with which a professional or an accomplished learner performs. Automaticity refers to the lack of conscious awareness that characterizes expert performance. As students become expert in performing a particular task, or as they master a skill, they show decreased mental effort. Norman points out that once something is learned, it is performed even under stressful conditions without a deterioration in the quality of the performance. Finally, Norman asserts that one's point of view changes as one gains expertise.

Special Needs Students

In every elementary school in this nation, there are children who in one or more ways depart from the norm. These children may be more creative, more intelligent, or superior artistically, or they may have exceptionally well developed motor skills. Other children may seem less creative, less intelligent, lacking in motor skills, or physically impaired. In total, these children may be described as exceptional in some way or another. With the passage of Public Law 94-142 in 1975, schools were required to provide the least restrictive environment possible for all children.

The passage of Public Law 94-142 meant that children who had been isolated from the rest of the academic community were now to be included in the educational mainstream to the greatest extent possible. First, this law protects a child's right to due process in educational placement, thus eliminating arbitrary placement in "special educational programs." Second, the law attempts to protect exceptional children from undue bias and discriminatory practices in testing and educational placement. Finally, the law mandates that every exceptional child is entitled to an individual educational plan to meet that child's unique educational needs. The result of this legislative act is that more children are included in mainstream science education activities than ever before. Accommodating the needs of exceptional children requires that teachers understand the educational needs of children and attend to those needs.

In affirming the right of all students to have access to science education experiences, the framers of the *National Science Education Standards* (National Research Council, 1996) state:

> Science is for all students. This principle is one of equity and excellence. Science in our schools must be for all students: All students, regardless of age, sex, cultural or ethnic background, disabilities, aspirations, or interest and motivation in science, should have the opportunity to attain high levels of scientific literacy. The *Standards* assume the inclusion of all students in challenging science learning opportunities and define levels of understanding and abilities that all should develop. They emphatically reject any situation in science education where some people—for example, members of certain populations—are discouraged from pursuing science and excluded from opportunities to learn science. (p. 20)

Physical Exceptionality

From a neurobiological perspective, children with physical exceptionalities have less sensory receptors with which to receive information than do other children. Many times, children who are physically challenged, those with sensory deficits, and those with cerebral palsy are perfectly capable of functioning in a regular elementary science classroom. At other times, students may need the support and assistance of resource teachers, classroom aids, or peer tutors. Many of the activities described in this book provide for multiple means of knowledge representation and are therefore appropriate for children with a wide range of abilities or capabilities. For example, auditorially challenged children, even with hearing aids, may not be able to hear what is being said in the classroom. These same children are capable of exploring their natural environment through the use of written words, pictures, icons, and realia. In providing the least restrictive environment for all children, teachers should provide multiple means of representing information.

To accommodate the needs of all children, many educational materials and resources are readily available. For example, most elementary science reading materials are available in braille editions for those who are visually challenged. Hardware such as the Arkenstone reader, large-font editions of science textbooks, and text-to-speech computer software allow students who are visually challenged to access text-based information sources.

Hearing aids and signers (those trained in the use of sign language) are available to assist auditorally challenged children. Sticky Fingers and Sticky Keys are computer software packages that allow students with palsied conditions to express themselves in written form. Voice recognition systems, head mice, and tongue mice are computer-based adaptations that allow paraplegic students to actively participate in science classes. Finally, minor modifications of hands-on learning activities make learning environments accessible

The National Science Education Standards *hold that science is for all students.*

to physically challenged children. Elementary science experiences enrich the lives of all children and should be a vital part of every child's educational experiences.

Social-Emotional Exceptionality

Children with social-emotional exceptionalities may range from those with negative behaviors (autism, conduct disorders, hyperkinesis, and schizophrenia) to those with positive behaviors (leadership skills and invulnerability). In most cases, children with social-emotional exceptionalities are capable of functioning well in elementary science classrooms. Environments that feature cooperative learning groups provide positive and affirming peer role models for children uncertain as to appropriate social behaviors. At the same time, group work environments provide situations where children who exhibit excellent leadership skills may thrive and prosper.

Intellectual Exceptionality

Just as there is a continuum of physical and social-emotional abilities among children, there also exists a continuum of intellectual abilities. At one end of the continuum are children with exceptional academic giftedness—superior intellect, high creativity, and high motivation. At the other end are students with mild, moderate, or profound retardation and children with information-processing disorders (learning disabilities). Research has shown that learning environments that provide open-ended tasks—problems that may be solved by many solution paths—profit students at both ends of the continuum. With proper supporting services, all children may be accommodated in learning science. By allowing children multiple modes of knowledge representation in learning environments, and multiple means of performance to demonstrate learnings, teachers provide for the needs of a wide range of learners.

CLASSROOM PRACTICE

In practice, most classroom teachers are highly eclectic in their beliefs about human development and human learning. Classroom teachers typically borrow ideas from behavioral psychology, humanistic psychology, and cognitive psychology. In practice most teachers use a variety of teaching strategies during the course of a day, month, or academic year. Some may be derived from one school of educational psychology, others from other schools of educational psychology. Good teaching involves finding an appropriate instructional strategy to match the instructional goal for a particular lesson or activity. A knowledge of children and of the material to be learned frequently determines which instructional strategies are appropriate.

CHAPTER SUMMARY

Theories of behavioral psychology focus on the behavior of the learner. Pavlov, Thorndike, Skinner, and Gagné are well-known behavioral psychologists. Typically, behavioral psychologists believe that teachers can increase students' learning by changing the variables in the educational environment. Educational concepts derived from behaviorist traditions include reinforcement, behavior modification, and punishment.

Humanistic psychology centers on the individual learner. Rogers, Combs, and Maslow are among humanistic psychology theorists. Theories of self-actualization, self-esteem, and self-worth have their origins in humanistic literature.

Finally, cognitive psychology focuses on the ways that people learn and the ways they know about the world around them. Cognitive psychology is concerned with theories of information processing, organizing information, and learning strategies. Piaget, Ausubel, Vygotsky, and Norman are writers who reflect cognitive psychology theories and traditions.

TOPICS TO REVIEW

- Teaching
- Learning
- Sensory stimuli
- Selective perception
- Short-term memory
- Long-term memory
- Semantic network
- Schemata
- Five domains of learning
- Eight events of instruction
- Eight intellectual skills
- Operant condition
- Hierarchy of needs
- Stage theory
- Modes of learning

REFLECTIVE PRACTICE

1. What are the basic tenets or assumptions of behavioral psychology? Which of these assumptions do you hold?

2. What are the basic tenets or assumptions of humanistic psychology? Which of these assumptions do you hold?

3. What are the basic tenets or assumptions of cognitive psychology? Which of these assumptions do you hold?

4. What current educational practices used in elementary schools reflect behavioral psychology traditions? Explain your answer.

5. What current educational practices used in elementary schools reflect humanistic psychology traditions? Explain your answer.

6. What current educational practices used in elementary schools reflect cognitive psychology traditions? Explain your answer.

7. The author has written that most teachers are pragmatic in their educational practices and thus combine behavioral, humanistic, and cognitive psychology traditions in their classrooms. Would you agree or disagree with this statement? Justify your answer.

CHAPTER 5

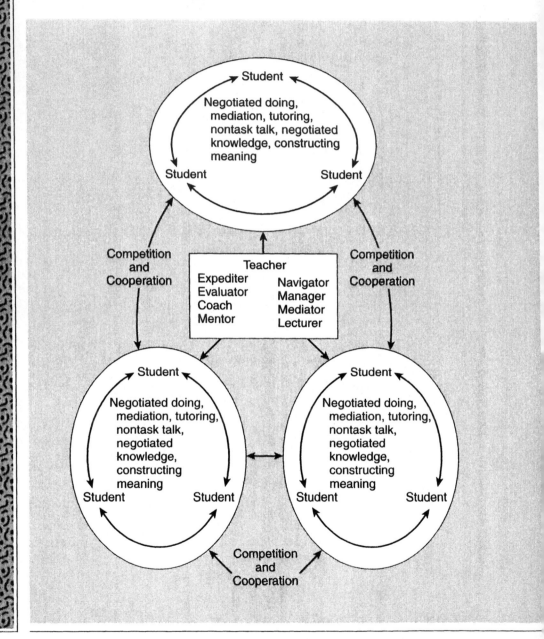

Groups in the Science Classroom

![] POINTS TO PONDER

POINTS TO PONDER

- In what situations is group learning appropriate?
- In what situations is individualized learning appropriate?
- Do you prefer individual or group learning activities? Why do you feel that way?

Connie Rausch is a wonderful and dynamic kindergarten teacher who makes learning fun for her students and for all who enter her classroom. Each August, during the first week of school, Connie conducts the Baggie Lift Activity (Activity 5.7) with her students. She begins the Baggie Lift by challenging the students in her class to lift her off the floor. One after another, the kindergartners come forward, place their arms around Connie's waist, and attempt to move her 145-pound frame off the floor. No one is successful.

With the class watching, Connie places a gigantic plastic bag on the floor of the classroom. She tapes the bag to the floor with duct tape and covers the center of it with a sheet of cardboard. Connie sits on the cardboard and passes out straws to her students. She instructs the students to insert the straws into the top layer of the plastic and to blow on the straws. Within two to three minutes, she calls to the students to stop and to observe what has happened. Alone, none of the students were able to lift her; working together, they are able to lift her about 30 to 40 centimeters off the floor. The Baggie Lift Activity is a wonder-

ful way to illustrate the power of cooperative learning (the subject of this chapter); it is also a wonderful illustration of good science teaching in its illustration of the effects of air pressure.

LEARNING AS A SOCIAL PROCESS

In writing guidelines for school redesign and reform, the American Psychological Association (1992) has stated that learning is facilitated by social interactions and by communication with others in a variety of flexible, diverse, and adaptive instructional settings. In stressing the importance of social interactions in the science classroom, the framers of the *National Science Education Standards* have written that teachers should encourage the development of communities of science learners that reflect the intellectual rigor of scientific inquiry and the attitudes and social values conducive to science learning (National Research Council, 1996, p. 49). This same sentiment was expressed by Johnson and Johnson (1994) when they wrote that the classroom climate consists of ways in which people within a classroom interact with each other. **Learning** is a social process, based on the interactions of teachers and students.

Constructivist View of Groups

Most culturally diverse learners find that cooperative learning activities attend to their academic needs far better than do individual learning activities. Fields (1988) asserts that cooperative learning activities foster social skills, positive peer relationships, and higher levels of self-esteem in students. From a sociological perspective, many culturally diverse children are socialized to prefer group or extended family settings as primary learning environments. Constructivists (those who believe that students individually construct a knowledge of science within a sociocultural context) such as Lorsbach and Tobin (1992) point out that cooperative learning strategies allow individuals to test the fit of their experiential world with a community of others. Social psychologists assert that no aspect of human experience is more important than cooperative interaction with others.

The sociocultural aspects of learning involve constructing a knowledge of a given subject area in a group setting. Students need the opportunity to make sense of what they are learning, to compare the knowledge that they have constructed with the knowledge that others have constructed. Discussion, active listening, discovering differences between one's knowledge and the knowledge of others, justifying one's position, and arriving at a group consensus are all parts of the social process of constructing meaning, part of

cooperative learning. Knowledge is constructed and modified by individuals within a group context. Learning is not simply the act of an individual learner, but rather a product of social interactions between groups of learners.

Research on Group Learning

Why are so many teachers and science educators excited about group learning? Why is a transition occurring in U.S. schools from individual goal structures to group goal structures? Unlike many science education trends of the past, cooperative learning activities conducted in group settings are a research-based approach to science teaching and learning. Much is now known of the impact of group activities on children's science learning.

Problem Solving

Researchers commenting on the effectiveness of cooperative learning situations indicate that the use of cooperative learning groups improves students' problem-solving abilities (Stasson, Kameda, Parks, Zimmerman, & David, 1991; Tobin, 1990). As a university student, I remember learning computer programming for the first time. Our second class assignment was to write a BASIC program to generate the Fibonacci sequence (1, 1, 2, 3, 5, 8, 13, 21 and so forth). I understood that the sequence was developed by adding the previous two numbers together to generate the next number in the series. I spent an entire weekend working on that project; no matter how hard I tried, I couldn't get my program to work. Finally, on Monday morning, a classmate showed me an error in my program. I had forgotten to initialize my variables. Had it not been for peer tutoring and sharing, I would not have been able to get a working program. Cooperation and sharing increase our problem-solving abilities.

Retention of Knowledge

Cooperative learning activities also promote mastery and retention of declarative or conceptual knowledge among many groups of learners (Humphreys, Johnson, & Johnson, 1982). Walking is a wonderful illustration of this idea. I go out for a walk nearly every day. If you were to ask me what I saw and learned on yesterday's walk, I probably won't remember much about it. However, several years ago, I went on a walk with some visiting friends who belong to the Audubon Society. As we walked through the woods, they named the birds that we saw, they whistled imitations of the birds' songs so that I might remember their calls, and they told beautiful and wonderful stories about the habits and habitats of the birds that we encountered. That walk differed from others in that my knowledge base grew; it grew because others shared their knowledge and expertise with me. Group interaction helps us to increase our knowledge base, to remember what we have learned.

Academic Achievement

The use of cooperative groups benefits culturally diverse students in terms of academic achievement (Okebukola & Ogunniyi, 1984; Sharan, 1985; Watson, 1991). Some culturally diverse learners lack knowledge of the English language. Cooperative groups provide children with the opportunity to engage in peer tutoring in their native language or home language, and at the same time to broaden their understandings of English vocabulary and usage through social interactions. Group work also affords the opportunity for active learning, a means for learning that appeals to children used to learning through tactile and kinesthetic experiences.

Attitudes toward Learning

Cooperative learning activities have been shown to improve students' attitudes toward learning (Humphreys, Johnson, & Johnson, 1982). As long as I can remember, I have had a fear of high open places. For that reason, I have always tried to avoid walking on roofs, climbing trees, and ascending ladders. In other words, I had a terrible attitude toward high places. My oldest son, Ray, developed an interest in rock climbing during his freshman year of college. He was determined to share his joy of rappelling with his mother. When I trudged up the side of Glorieta Baldy near Glorieta, New Mexico, with my son and his friends, they were thrilled and I was filled with apprehension and fear. With a lot of coaxing, coaching, and outright lying, my son and his friends convinced me that rappelling was just like climbing out of bed in the morning. It wasn't, but I did learn that rock climbing was not as horrible as I thought. My attitude changed due to a group effort. Cooperating with others can help us change our attitudes toward learning new tasks.

Self-Concept

Cooperative learning improves culturally diverse students' self-concepts (Johnson, Johnson, Scott, & Ramolae, 1985; Sharan, 1985). Many culturally diverse children have been socialized to work in groups. Feedback from peers and members of our social group are far more important than letter grades or other types of rewards for many of us. Recently, I watched a group of children build Puffmobiles (Activity 5.2) as part of a unit of study on alternative energy sources. Fernando, a shy Chicano boy, assumed social status in his group during the construction process. The other students in the group were having great difficulty attaching the wheels (beads) to the axles (straws) of their Puffmobile. To the delight of his group, Fernando picked up the straws and pins and proceeded to attach the wheels so that they stayed on. While Fernando's English-speaking ability was weak, his hands-on problem-solving ability was strong. Fernando was suddenly a very valued member of the group. Peer praise and acceptance are important variables in improving one's self-esteem and self-concept.

Race Relations

Studies with culturally diverse learners indicate that participating in cooperative groups improves students' abilities to work with others and improves race relations in classrooms (Johnson, Johnson, Scott, & Ramolae, 1985; Okebukola & Ogunniyi, 1984; Sharan, 1985). When we work with others, our viewpoint frequently changes. Recently, I observed a group of children newly arrived from Somalia during their first year in Southern California schools. On the first day of school, the Somalian children sat by themselves on one side of the classroom, while their American peers sat on the other side of the room. Each group of children thought that the other group looked strange, spoke with a dialect, and wore funny clothing. When I returned to the classroom several months later, I found the American and Somalian children fully integrated and working together. Strangeness and distrust had given way to respect and friendship. Daily contact had changed the children's perceptions of each other and their level of racial tolerance.

Student Preferences

Okebukola (1986) suggests that most culturally diverse students prefer cooperative learning situations to competitive learning environments. Okebukola's work in cooperative or group learning was conducted among tribal groups in Africa. His findings are probably generalizable to children in this country. Most children prefer to work with others; however, they like to be graded not on the work of others but on their own initiative. When group work is used as an instructional strategy, teachers should allow children to individually produce a record of the learning activity. For example, Connie, the kindergarten teacher with the Baggie Lift Activity, should allow students

Cooperative groups improve race relations.

to individually report on their learnings even though everyone in the class participated in the activity itself. Cooperative learning activities improve students' learning in terms of cognitive knowledge, social skills, motor skills, and attitudes.

Competitive Learning Situations

While most teachers today advocate a cooperative or group approach to learning, many of them still rely heavily on individualized or competitive goal structures in their classrooms. Learning alone, working by oneself, is firmly ingrained in the U.S. educational system. Before continuing the discussion of cooperative learning structures as viable instructional strategies for use in the multicultural classroom, it would be best to examine the arguments for the use of competitive learning strategies. Many of us, whether we will admit it publicly or not, continue to view learning as an individual act. Therefore, it is a good idea to examine our attitudes toward competition and toward individualized learning before turning our attention to cooperative learning strategies.

Teachers frequently believe individual learning situations are best.

The view of learning as an individual endeavor is firmly rooted in the sociological, psychological, and historical foundations of education. Johnson and Johnson (1994) report that there are five traditional arguments for individual learning activities in schools: (1) the competitive nature of U.S. society, (2) development of leadership skills in students, (3) real world applications of the process of schooling, (4) student preferences for instructional strategies, and (5) building self-confidence and self-esteem in children.

Competitive Nature of Society

Johnson and Johnson (1994) point out that advocates of competition insist that schools must reflect the dog-eat-dog theory of survival in the occupational world. Teachers who use competition in their classrooms frequently do so because they believe that the job market is highly competitive and that they are preparing students for competition in adult society. Based on these assumptions, teachers set up games, competitions, and individual learning activities to prepare students for this perceived real world application of schooling. While this argument for competition superficially makes sense, in reality, modern corporations depend upon cooperation and teamwork rather than competition to survive in the world marketplace.

Developing Leadership Skills

Another reason teachers frequently give for the use of individual competitive activities in the classroom deals with building leadership skills in students. Montagu (1965) pointed out that competition in schools is based on the notions of social Darwinism, and on concepts such as survival of the most "fit," the struggle for existence, and competition as the lifeblood of the nation. Advocates of classroom competition perceive that achievement, success, outstanding performance, and superhuman effort give rise to leaders with drive, ambition, and motivation—to individuals who enjoy competing with others. Those who advocate the use of individual learning activities perceive that these activities will produce rugged individuals capable of competing in an impressive array of human endeavors. Fernando, the Chicano boy who excelled in the Puffmobile activity, developed leadership skills during a group activity, not through competition. Most successful athletes will pause at the moment of their greatest victories and acknowledge their parents and coaches for their contributions. Contrary to popular opinion, leadership in the athletic or academic arena comes only with a well-developed support network—a system of caring, loving others who help us meet our goals in life.

Real World Applications

Johnson and Johnson (1994) point out that supporters of individual goal structures believe that competition is character building and that it toughens the young for life in the real world. Enjoying the thrill of victory and learning to endure the agony of defeat are sometimes thought to be character-building activities. In our society, some businesses thrive and prosper, while others become bankrupt. Teachers who observe this economic phenomenon believe that they can prepare students for adult living by teaching individual competition to children at an early age, and that competition is preparation for life in the real world. In response to this position, one could point out that all of us experience temporary failure in our lives, and that we learn from our mistakes only when others support us in our temporary failure and show us where we went wrong and the lessons to be learned from our mistakes.

Children's Preferences

Individual competition in the classroom also receives support from teachers who hold the homegrown or naive belief that children *prefer* to compete with each other in the classroom. Greenberg (1932), in a classic study of children's goal structures, found that children seem to enjoy competitive reward structures as long as they are winning. Frequently, teachers use classroom competitions such as spelling bees, chess tournaments, bulletin boards of exemplary work, and honor-student competitions believing that these activities will encourage students to strive for academic excellence and that all students profit academically from such activities. During my elementary school years, I dreaded spelling bees. It wasn't that I was a bad speller, it's just that I was terribly shy and hated standing in front of my peers. I frequently became nervous when it was my turn to spell a word and forgot what I was doing. I'm sure that my teachers meant well, but I can't say I liked the competition of the classroom spelling bees.

Building Self-Esteem

Greenberg's classic study (1932) further pointed out that while children enjoy winning, they do not enjoy losing. Since Greenberg's time, we have learned the devastating effects of losing on children's emotional development. Children who perceive themselves to be "losers" frequently spend years trying to develop positive feelings of self-worth. In commenting on individual learning activities conducted in competitive environments, Johnson and Johnson (1994) point out that under appropriate circumstances competition can be exciting and enjoyable. On the other hand, they state, the inappropriate use or overuse of competition (due in part to a series of myths passed down from one generation of teachers to the next) may have destructive outcomes that interfere with successful instruction. Additionally, these authors point out that prejudice and discrimination against minority groups increase and are perpetuated under competitive conditions.

Growing up, I had an uncle who ate Wheaties every morning. When I asked him about this, he used to reply that he liked Wheaties. No matter how much we enjoy an activity or a food, a steady diet of the same thing becomes boring for most of us. Group work every minute of every school day is just as dull and boring as constant competition. Good teachers balance the class-room diet by providing a mixture of small group and large group activities for students.

Sociocultural Aspects of Learning

Schooling is a social process, in the sense that students are placed in groups called classes and an adult or teacher is given the responsibility for managing the instruction of those students. Within the typical classroom, a series of social interactions occurs on a daily basis, including (1) student-to-student, (2) teacher-to-student, and (3) group-to-group interactions.

Student-to-Student Interactions

Few studies in education have dealt with social interactions in small group settings. One of the first such studies was conducted by Wallace (1986) in British schools. By watching children interact with each other in dyads and triads (cooperative groups of two or three students) over a protracted period of time, she developed a system for classifying children's interactions with each other. Wallace contends that children engage in six types of student-to-student communications, including (1) negotiated doing, (2) social mediation, (3) tutoring, (4) nontask talk, (5) negotiated knowledge, and (6) constructing meaning.

Negotiated Doing.   Wallace (1986) has described negotiated doing to include arranging apparatus and turn taking in conducting "experiments." Cheng (1992) points out that approximately 65 percent of language is conveyed through nonverbal channels. Negotiated doing, where students hand materials to each other, exchange supplies and equipment, and take turns using manipulatives, is a primary means of nonverbal communication among children. Subtle negotiations about who touches the materials, who hands materials to whom, and so forth are frequently worked out among students without overt verbal negotiations.

Social Mediation.   Removing tension is a second type of student-to-student communication commonly found in small groups. Any time social interactions occur, disappointments and disputes will arise between the participants. Removing tension, agreeing to who performs what job in the group, is a vital part of the learning experience and of social mediation. Even when teachers assign jobs to specific individuals within the group (e.g., facilitator, equipment manager, clean-up person, recorder, and so forth), students still need to define their job function and parameters within the small group setting. Does the clean-up person clean up after everyone in the group, or just check to make certain that the work area has been cleaned? Does the recorder take one set of notes for the entire group or make certain that everyone has performed this task? How are minor disputes to be handled in the group? What happens when someone goes out of turn? Removing tension is a form of social mediation that allows learning to take place in a group environment.

Tutoring.   A third type of student-to-student communication, tutoring may be defined in terms of giving and receiving help. For limited English proficient students, linguistic tutoring is perhaps the most useful function of small group work. Peer tutoring allows students to append new knowledge to existing knowledge structures. Limited English proficient students find that a small group environment allows them the opportunity to develop new vocabulary and to try their oral communication skills in a friendly or nonthreatening setting. Peer tutoring allows students the opportunity to teach what they have just learned to each other and to restate information to each other in terms of culturally familiar examples and analogies.

Nontask Talk.   Nontask talk is the fourth type of student-to-student communication identified by Wallace as occurring in cooperative settings. Wallace (1986) has operationally defined nontask talk to include greetings and "strokings" as students settle into their small groups. Adults would probably refer to nontask talk as small talk (i.e., talk about the weather, Saturday's football game results, a television show, or the school lunch menu). Although nontask talk is necessary for social interactions, it is not known to have particular educational value, other than to allow children the opportunity to begin social discourse with each other.

Negotiated Meaning.   A fifth type of student-to-student communication, negotiated meaning (also discussed in Chapter 7), involves a give and take between children as they struggle to make sense of the world, as they attempt to compare the knowledge that they have constructed with the knowledge that their peers have constructed. For limited English proficient students, negotiated meaning may also entail defining terms in English or the student's home language, and appending English name tags to concepts that they have formed in their home language.

Constructed Meaning.   Constructed meaning is the final type of student-to-student communication mentioned by Wallace (1986) in her study of group interactions. Solomon (1989) points out that while teacher interaction through brainstorming or question-and-answer periods has long been advocated to help pupils understand new learnings, this style of teaching brings another message to students, namely, the importance of "getting it right" or winning the teacher's approval. Edwards and Mercer (1987) point out that teacher-led classroom discussions might appear to be relatively open and pupil oriented, but in reality most teachers in these situations manage to maintain close control over the selection, expression, and direction of ideas and activities.

Constructing meaning in a small group setting involves students in corroboration and active participation with others. Group environments are places where students examine their personal renditions of knowledge and restructure that knowledge based on the notions, perceptions, and feedback provided to them by others in the group. A consensus effect (Solomon, 1989) is tangible evidence that the group process is working and that students are restructuring their conceptions of the natural world based on their interactions with their peers.

Teacher-to-Student Interactions

When cooperative group activities are introduced in classrooms, the role of the teacher changes from that of dispenser of knowledge to facilitator of learning. In classrooms, Fields (1988) points out, the use of cooperative learning groups (1) allows teachers to use hands-on learning activities with a minimum of materials, (2) provides teachers more opportunity to interact with groups and individuals, (3) fosters social skill development in students, (4) encourages peer tutoring, and (5) produces higher levels of self-esteem in students. In their daily interactions with students, teachers serve in many different capacities and function in many different roles. Typically, when cooperative learning groups are used in the classroom, teachers function as expediters, evaluators, coaches, mentors, navigators, managers, mediators, and lecturers.

Teacher as Expediter. As expediter, the teacher brings together children and objects from the physical world in a way that will facilitate the learning of each child. The teacher not only establishes the physical environment in which learning can occur but defines the task that will facilitate the learning of the child. As Wheatley (1991) states, the teacher's role is to provide stimulating and motivational experiences. According to Wheatley, appropriate tasks for cooperative learning experiences are those that (1) are accessible to all students at the start, (2) invite students to make decisions, (3) encourage students to ask "what if" questions, (4) prompt students to use their prior knowledge, (5) promote discussion and communication, (6) lead students somewhere, (7) contain an element of surprise, (8) are enjoyable, and (9) are extendable to other learning situations. Finally, as expediter, the teacher provides the materials, physical space, and work time that allow children to complete the task at hand.

Teacher as Evaluator. As evaluators, teachers function as judges, as those who evaluate children's learning. By watching what children do and say, the teacher gains insights into the ways that they have constructed knowledge. Teachers are able to make inferences about children's thinking, development, and the knowledge that they have constructed. At times teachers evaluate children in formal testing situations and at other times teachers assess children informally to determine what children are capable of understanding. Information gained from assessing or evaluating children's understandings of science influences (1) the choice of concepts that are taught, (2) the choice of learning experiences made available to children, and (3) the presentation of the purposes of the proposed activities (Driver, Guesne, & Tiberghien, 1985).

Teacher as Coach.   High school football coaches demonstrate, encourage, and provide feedback to football players. Elementary science teachers use these same strategies to coach children to acquire knowledge of the physical world. Sometimes teachers model a performance that they want children to emulate and watch while children perform the skill or task. At other times teachers encourage children to try again or to attempt a different solution path when they have met with temporary "failure." Finally, teachers coach by providing corrective or reinforcing feedback.

Recently I observed Gwen, a third-grade teacher, teaching a lesson on dinosaurs. Gwen had designed a lesson that combined science and art in which children were to make three-dimensional clay models of dinosaurs from black-and-white line drawings. As Gwen approached Sarah's desk, she noticed that Sarah had constructed a Stegosaurus-shaped pancake rather than a three-dimensional dinosaur model. No matter what she said to Sarah, Gwen couldn't convey the idea that dinosaurs were round, not flat. Finally, Gwen picked up a ball of clay and made a round body. Suddenly, Sarah got the idea; she modeled a Stegosaurus body after Gwen's dinosaur model and began to attach the legs and plates to her model. Gwen had encouraged, modeled, and provided feedback to Sarah until she mastered the skill; she had coached her to perform spatial visualization skills.

Teacher as Mentor.   In the role of mentor, the teacher functions as a master learner, while students function as apprentices. This teaching role is based on theories of motivation and modeling. In the framework of the apprenticeship setting, a teacher models learning, problem solving, social interactions, investigation of the natural world, and so forth in the elementary multicultural science classroom. The following conversation from a fourth-grade classroom illustrates this concept:

Ms. Kitano:	Suppose that I went on a camping trip to the mountains and forgot to take along matches or a lighter, what would I do? I have a package of frozen hotdogs in my cooler ready to eat for lunch, and suddenly I don't have any way to start a fire. Can anyone give me some ideas about what to do?
Jenny:	Maybe you could start a fire with sticks or rocks.
Ms. Kitano:	That's one way I could solve the problem. That's a real good idea, Jenny. Does anyone know how to start a fire with sticks?
Jenny:	Not really, I heard it on TV, but I think we could get it to work.

Ms. Kitano: Maybe we could work with sticks and rocks to figure out how to start a fire. Before we try that, does anyone else have another possible solution to my problem?

Mark: You could eat the hotdogs raw. I think hotdogs are already cooked before they're sold.

Ms. Kitano: Now that's an idea I hadn't thought of, Mark. That's a second way that I could use to solve my problem. I think Mark is correct, I could safely eat frozen hotdogs if I needed to do so. But, suppose I don't care for frozen hotdogs, is there another idea about how to cook them or warm them up if I don't have matches to start a fire?

Ricardo: You could make a solar cooker. We did that in scouts last year. We took a sheet of aluminum foil and some cardboard and string and made a big curved mirror type of hotdog cooker. Then we tried to find the place where the sun's rays focused and we placed a hotdog on a stick at that point. It worked pretty well. It took a while to get it working, but we could cook our food without making a fire.

Ms. Kitano: Good Ricardo, you've given us a way to heat the food without building a fire. Solar cooking is a third way to solve my problem.

In this vignette, the teacher is modeling brainstorming or identifying multiple solution paths for the students. She is mentoring students in problem-solving skills by acting as a master learner, as one who identifies possible solution paths and evaluates them before solving the problem.

Teacher as Navigator. The teacher in the cooperative learning classroom also plays the role of navigator. Teachers are accustomed to thinking of themselves in this capacity, in that they are used to determining goals or charting the course for students. In a cooperative group setting, however, the navigator is also analogous to a ship's navigator. On a cruise ship, a navigator is also a passenger in the sense that he or she is traveling on the ship along with others. The ship's navigator and the passengers experience the journey together. Just as the splendor of sunrises and sunsets may be enjoyed by all aboard the ship, so too everyone aboard experiences the rough waves and stormy conditions. In a cooperatively grouped classroom, the teacher charts the course but together with the students experiences the adventure of exploring the natural world.

Teacher as Manager. Teachers also function as managers in the classroom, structuring the environment to maximize the learning of all students. Managerial tasks in the cooperative classroom include (1) arranging the physical layout of the classroom, (2) maintaining records of student performance and task completion, (3) establishing and coordinating cooperative learning groups, (4) assigning roles to individuals in groups, (5) requisitioning supplies and materials, (6) establishing minimal performance and behavior standards, and (7) coordinating activities of the classroom with outside agencies (e.g., the total school community and the students' homes).

When teachers function as managers, they may inform students when the work atmosphere becomes too boisterous or when students are off task. Additionally, within their managerial role, teachers may assign tasks to specific individuals in a group. The Inquiry Role Approach developed by Seymour, Padberg, Bingman, and Koutrieck (1974) stresses the importance of assigning such roles as coordinator, technical advisor, data recorder, and process evaluator. In this model, part of a teacher's managerial role is to transfer responsibility for learning to specific individuals in each group.

Teacher as Mediator.   When teachers function as mediators, they are serving in a counseling or advising capacity in the classroom. In this role, a teacher mediates disputes between students and addresses longstanding social inequities that may separate students. Teacher as mediator is a concept familiar to most educators. Most teachers feel comfortable with this traditional mediation role in the classroom. However, a second facet to mediation involves a social concern for the educational and social needs of low-income or "minority" students.

Cohen, Lotan, and Catanzarite (1990) point out that a student's status characteristics may be altered by the actions of the classroom teacher. **Status characteristics,** according to these authors, are socially evaluated attributes based on qualities associated with a student's ethnicity and social class. A child from a less affluent socioeconomic background may be held in low esteem by students from more affluent ones. Teachers may confer status on such students by providing feedback to the child's peers regarding the student's contributions to the group's activities. If a teacher is standing by a group and hears a "low status" student make a suggestion to the group, the teacher could make a statement such as, "That's a really good idea, Mary. You've provided the group with another way to solve the problem." The teacher is valuing Mary's contribution to the group and in the process attending to a sociological problem, namely, differential status between students.

Teacher as Lecturer.   The teacher as lecturer is the final role of the teacher in the cooperative classroom, as identified by Wheatley (1991). Direction giving is necessary in all educational settings. Even in the most child-centered learning situations, there needs to be an adult in charge, someone responsible for the health and safety of the children. In the role of lecturer, the teacher provides instructions that insure the well-being of the children in the classroom. If an activity involves the use of a flame or a heat source, the teacher might give instructions such as, "Be sure to wear your safety goggles," "Be careful not to touch hot glassware," and so forth. Matters of health and safety cannot be left to discovery learning but need to be addressed by the teacher in a straightforward expository manner.

Group-to-Group Interactions

Just as there are social interactions within groups, there are interactions between groups. Social interactions between groups may be of a cooperative, neutral, or competitive nature. Neutral interactions exist when no formal or informal interactions occur between groups in the classroom. In this situation, students work within their own groups, and their group activities are independent of those of other groups in the classroom. Traditional reading groups are an illustration of this type of group noninteraction. When using reading groups, a teacher normally meets with one reading group while other groups of students in the classroom work on some other task, either independently or under the direction of a classroom aide.

Research Team Approach. Cooperative interactions between groups imply the sharing of responsibility for the parts of a learning task. One model of this type of intergroup sharing is illustrated by the Research Team Approach developed by DelGiorno (1969). When using this approach, the teacher and students distribute the responsibility for the learning task across many groups in the classroom. Each group develops expertise in some part of the learning task and reports its findings to the other groups in the class. For example, in a class studying the behavior of mealworms, one group might investigate the preference of mealworms for wet or dry conditions. Another group might investigate the behavior of mealworms in light and dark environments. A third group might attempt to determine whether mealworms prefer oat or wheat bran flakes as a food source. Each group would develop expertise in a specific area and would then share this knowledge with the other groups.

DelGiorno (1969) has identified four phases as vital to the Research Team Approach: (1) lecture, (2) independent study, (3) experimentation, and (4) discussion. In the mealworm example just discussed, the teacher would introduce the concept of habitat through a large group lecture. The teacher would also establish the task (e.g., to determine the habitat of the mealworm) for the class. Groups of students would assume responsibility for developing expertise in a portion of the learning. During the second phase, independent study, each group would search out resource people, books, and so forth for information about their assigned topic. Students would also plan a way to investigate the environment to find answers to their group's question. During experimentation, the third phase of DelGiorno's model, the group would manipulate materials to learn about mealworms. During the fourth phase of learning, each group would report its findings to the other groups in the class. The last phase of the Research Team Approach may also serve as a time of evaluation, where the teacher, other groups of students, or both might evaluate the findings of each group and critique its performance. The Jigsaw Approach (Lucker, Rosenfield, Sikes, & Aronson, 1976; Slavin, 1982) to cooperative group work contains many of the elements of shared responsibility for learning and disseminating of findings found in the Research Team Approach.

Team Competition.   In addition to intergroup cooperation, intergroup rivalry has been found to be a highly effective approach to instruction in the classroom (Slavin, 1982). Group or team competition seems to be preferred to individual instruction by many culturally diverse students (Hadfield, Martin, & Wooden, 1992; Okebukola, 1985). In group competition settings, students enjoy intragroup cooperation while competing with other groups in the classroom. A team environment is created when students collaborate in solving a problem and then compete against other groups in the classroom. The Puffmobile (Activity 5.2) in this chapter is an example of a team competition activity. In this activity, students collaborate to build a wind-propelled vehicle that will travel faster or farther than similar vehicles made by other groups in the classroom. By working together, students tackle the problems of friction, wind propulsion, navigation, and so forth. The contest is fair in the sense that every group is supplied with the same raw materials. Win or lose, competition in a Puffmobile derby is a nonthreatening experience for students. Competing together in a group is a culturally familiar learning experience for many culturally diverse students in the multicultural science classroom.

CLASSROOM PRACTICE

The decision as to whether students should work individually or in groups is a pedagogical decision best left to each classroom teacher. Decisions about which pedagogical strategies to use in the classroom depend on the characteristics of the students, the information to be learned, and the goals or purposes that a teacher has in mind. Indeed, there is no one right way to learn anything. In this section, a series of activities are presented that are designed to be used in competitive and cooperative learning environments.

ACTIVITY 5.1   ■   Egg Drop Contest

Purpose: To develop spatial visualization skills

Type of Activity: Competitive (individual)

Materials: 25 plastic straws, 100 straight pins, and 1 raw egg for each person, and 1 meter stick to measure heights

Teacher Preparation: Allow students to construct their containers at home prior to the egg drop contest. (Note: the use of straws and pins addresses equity issues, as nearly all students have access to these simple materials.)

Student
Directions: Using the straws and pins, construct a container that will protect the egg during free-fall and landings. The container that successfully protects the egg from the greatest height is the winner.

Egg drop container

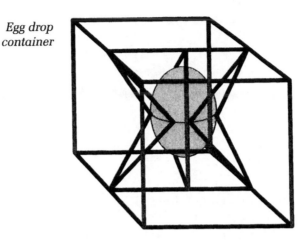

Conducting
the Activity: On the day of the egg drop, cover an area of schoolyard with a plastic tarp or large plastic bags. Bring garbage bags to contain the losers and a bucket of warm, soapy water to rinse the target area. Access to a ladder is also advisable. Drop the containers in a uniform manner starting with a height of about 2 meters.

ACTIVITY 5.2 ■ Puffmobiles

Purpose: To develop a wind-driven vehicle—exploring alternative energy-sources

Type of
Activity: Cooperative (team competition)

Materials
(per group): 10 soda straws, 25 straight pins, sheet of 8½" × 11" paper, and four macramé beads (with holes large enough to fit over the straws)

Group
Directions: Construct a wind-powered vehicle capable of traveling the fastest over the racecourse.

Conducting
the Activity: 1. Allow students to construct and field test their Puffmobiles in small cooperative groups.
2. Remind students to reserve one straw for the propulsion system.

Puffmobile

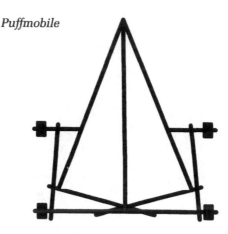

3. All materials must be attached to the car. No "leftovers" are allowed.

4. Set up a racecourse on a smooth surface (concrete pad, gymnasium floor, tiled hallway). Use masking tape to denote a start and a finish line about 10 meters or 25 to 30 feet apart.

5. Have students place all "wheels" of the puffmobile behind the starting line. The first car to get all of its tires across the finish line wins. Students are allowed to follow their car down the racecourse blowing through their straws to supply wind power.

ACTIVITY 5.3   ■   Boxosaurus

Purpose: To develop a dinosaur model from recycled materials

Type of Activity: Cooperative (groups)

Materials: Assorted cardboard boxes, glue, scissors, paints, egg cartons, yarn, paper cups, milk cartons, dinosaur sketches, colored photographs of modern-day reptiles

Group Directions: Using cardboard, build a boxosaurus. A boxosaurus is a model of a dinosaur built using recycled materials.

Conducting the Activity: 1. Allow each group to "adopt" a dinosaur from the sketches or drawings.

Boxosaurus

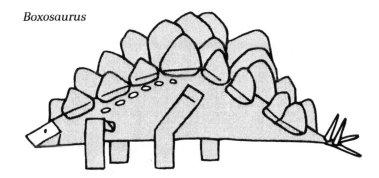

2. Encourage students to research their dinosaur and to learn about its physical characteristics.
3. In group settings, allow students cooperatively to build models of dinosaurs from the scrap materials.
4. Before students paint the dinosaurs, show them photographs of present-day reptiles or modern descendants of dinosaurs (coral snakes, Gila monsters, pine lizards, and so forth). Have the students note the patterns on the skin of the modern-day reptiles and allow them to make inferences about dinosaur skin colors and patterns based on their knowledge of living reptiles.

ACTIVITY 5.4 ■ Clay Boats

Purpose: To develop a clay boat—illustrates surface area

Type of Activity: Competitive (teams)

Materials: Clay, bucket of water (or small swimming pool), metric stacking masses (or washers or metric weight set)

Group Directions: Build a boat out of clay that holds the largest possible mass.

Conducting the Activity:
1. It may be useful to show students pictures or drawings of boats before beginning the activity (rowboats, canoes, sailboats, barges, etc.).
2. Instruct the students to form their clay ball into a boat. Allow students to test their boats to determine the amount of mass the boat will hold without sinking.

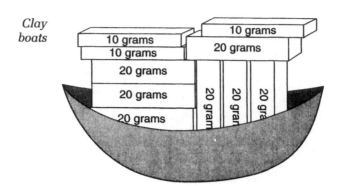

Clay boats

3. Conduct a contest in which students add stacking masses slowly to their boats until they sink. The group whose boat holds the greatest mass before sinking wins.

ACTIVITY 5.5 ■ Magnet Scavenger Hunt

Purpose: To explore properties of a magnet

Type of Activity: Competitive (individual or teams)

Materials: 1 magnet per person or per group

Student Directions: Attract as many objects as possible to your magnet during the time allowed.

Conducting the Activity: For older students, give each student a magnet and have them generate a list of objects that are attracted to it. A time period of 15 to 30 minutes is sufficient for the activity. Modify the activity for early elementary students by having them draw each of the objects attracted to the magnet.

ACTIVITY 5.6 ■ Meltathon

Purpose: To investigate the properties of insulating materials

Type of Activity: Competitive (teams)

Materials: Ice cubes, metric balance, paper towels, newspapers, wax paper, aluminum foil, plastic wrap, etc.

Group Directions: Insulate the ice cube so that it melts as little as possible during a given time period. The objective of the contest is to prevent meltdown.

Conducting the Activity: Give each group of students an ice cube whose weight you have noted. Instruct the students to wrap the ice in materials so that it is insulated as much as possible. After about one hour, ask the students to weigh their ice cubes. The group with the least amount of "lost ice" wins.

ACTIVITY 5.7 ■ Baggie Lift

Purpose: To investigate air pressure

Type of Activity: Cooperative (groups)

Materials (per group): One heavy-duty garbage bag, soda straws (one for each child in the group), duct tape

Group Directions: Lift a classmate off the floor without touching her or him.

Baggie lift

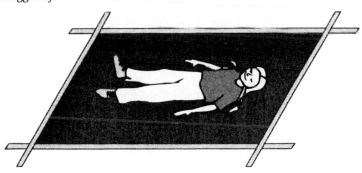

Conducting the Activity: Place the children in groups of six to eight. Tape the plastic garbage bags flat to the floor using the duct tape. In each group, have one student sit or lie down on the garbage bag. Ask the other students to insert their straws into the garbage bag, to blow air into the bag, and to observe the student sitting on top of the bag.

ACTIVITY 5.8 ■ Paper Airplanes

Purpose: To investigate properties of an airfoil

Type of Activity: Competitive (individual)

Materials: One sheet of notebook paper and one paper clip per student; 1 metric measuring tape

Student Directions: Make a paper airplane that will fly the farthest distance.

Conducting the Activity: Have students fold the patterns of the paper airplanes as shown and adjust the position of the paper clip, flaps, and edges of the plane until they develop a model that will fly the farthest distance possible. Conduct a paper airplane contest. Allow students to throw their airplanes and measure the distance that each plane flew.

Paper airplane pattern

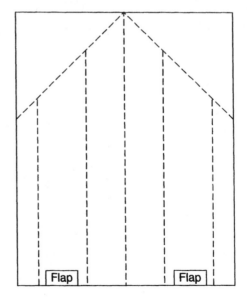

Flap · · Flap

CHAPTER SUMMARY

Learning is a social process involving interactions between students and teachers. Student-to-student interactions in group situations include negotiated doing, mediation, tutoring, nontask talk, negotiated knowledge, and constructing meaning. When group activities are used in the elementary science classroom, teachers function as expediters, evaluators, coaches, mentors, navigators, managers, mediators, and lecturers. In cooperatively grouped classrooms, interactions between groups may be competitive, cooperative, or neutral in nature. The use of group activities has been found to benefit many culturally diverse learners in terms of students' academic achievement, problem-solving skills, attitudes toward science, self-concepts, and social growth and development.

 ## TOPICS TO REVIEW

- Six research-based reasons for cooperative learning
- Five arguments for competitive learning
- Six types of student-to-student interactions
- Types of group interactions
- Research Team Approach

 ## REFLECTIVE PRACTICE

1. Compare and contrast individual learning activities and cooperative group activities in terms of students' learning and social interactions.

2. What are the traditional arguments for competitive learning environments? Do you agree or disagree with these arguments? Why or why not?

3. In your opinion, when are competitive learning environments useful in the classroom? When are cooperative learning environments useful? Justify your answers.

4. It has been said that "cooperative learning environments proportionally benefit culturally diverse students." Do you agree or disagree with this statement? Justify your answer.

5. What is the role of the teacher in the competitive classroom? The cooperative classroom? Compare and contrast the role of the teacher in competitive and cooperative classrooms.

6. A classic argument against the extended use of cooperative learning environments is that "bright students are objectified" (that is, they carry a disproportionate burden or responsibility for the learning of slower students). How do you react to this statement? Do you agree or disagree? Justify your answer.

CHAPTER 6

Affective Domain

Unobtrusive	*Obtrusive*
Library	Drawings
Mini-museum	Likert
	Semantic
	differential
	Essays
Social	Surveys
interactions	Checklists

Cognitive Domain

Traditional	*Authentic*
Norm-	Portfolio
referenced	Concept
Criterion-	mapping
referenced	Task tests
Self-	Journal
referenced	writing
	Group
	discussion

Psychomotor Domain

Laboratory Activities

Checklists
Rubrics

Assessing Knowledge in the Science Classroom

POINTS TO PONDER

- What is the purpose of testing or evaluation?
- How can we assess what children have learned?
- How can assessment be made more culture-free and culture-fair?

Jack was a wonderful, kind, elderly gentleman. During my childhood, he used to hunt for squirrels, rabbits, opossum, and pheasants on our family farm. Toward sunset one beautiful autumn day, Jack came to the door of our farmhouse and handed me a fistful of freshly picked pheasants. Being a rather rude teenager at the time, I informed him that I didn't care for pheasants, that I'd rather eat a McDonald's hamburger any day, but that I'd take the pheasants to my parents. Knowing that Jack had only a grade school education, I deliberately used 25¢ words rather than my normal 5¢ words. My father was standing behind the kitchen door listening to my remarks. As I went into the house, my father bolted over to Jack and apologized for my rude behavior and lack of manners.

When my father entered the house, he scolded me for my conduct and informed me that he would personally oversee my education the following day. When I protested that I couldn't possibly stay home from school, my father told me that he would personally talk to the high school principal about my absence. At 4 o'clock the next morning, my father woke me and ordered me to get dressed. It was a moonless sky that greeted us as we walked into the woods together in those predawn hours. I was cold and angry. Why had my father kept me home from school? Why were we walking about in the woods at this ridiculous hour? A dozen similar thoughts flashed through my mind. Finally, we reached the banks of White Clay Creek, which ran behind the edge of our property. My father sat on a rock, lit his pipe, and said, "Okay, get me some breakfast."

I protested that there wasn't any food, that we didn't have any pots and pans, and that I couldn't possibly fix a meal under such primitive conditions. My father informed me that when he and Jack went hunting they always paused here for breakfast, and Jack could whip up a tasty, fresh-cooked meal in about an hour using the same basic ingredients that I now had at hand. I stormed around, stamped my feet, and generally made a fool of myself. When I was done, my father told me to get started on gathering food for his breakfast. This was one of the worst mornings of my life, I thought. I gathered some old berries and a handful of mushrooms and defiantly marched back to my father. My father looked up and smiled, "Dear, those pokeberries are poisonous and so are those mushrooms."

By now, I was reduced to tears. My father sat me down, patted me on the head, and began to teach me some of life's lessons that I hadn't gotten in school. He informed me that Jack didn't have much "school learning" but that he held a wealth of knowledge about the natural world. He said you can't judge someone's education or knowledge level by their degrees or a test score. He told me how Jack hunted and fished to support his family, and how he always gave the best of what he killed to the farmer whose land he used. The night before, I had turned up my nose at Jack's gift, pheasants that I wished I had at this minute. Jack always took care of others before himself. He acted out of love; he gave because he wanted to, not because he had to. Finally, my father gave me some words to live by that remain with me still. "The more education you have, the more people you ought to be able to communicate with, not fewer."

My father took me to school later that day, having served as my teacher that morning. Many months later, I had the opportunity to go hunting with Jack. He taught me about blackberries, raspberries, and pokeberries, which were edible and which were not. I learned to eat the greens of the fields, roots of the cattail, acorns, persimmons, and fish from the creek. Once in a while, I still fix his recipe for pheasant with wild rice and chestnut stuffing. My memory of Jack wonderfully illustrates the value of assessment in the educational process. Sometimes we really do not measure what people know and what they have learned. Traditionally, schools have measured only a small part of the knowledge that children have acquired.

ASSESSMENT AND EVALUATION

The *National Science Education Standards* operationally define *assessment* as the process for effectively communicating the expectations of the science education system to all concerned with science education (National Research Council, 1996, p. 76). In the past, many teachers tended to regard evaluation and assessment as processes for gathering information to make judgments and decisions about individuals in their classrooms. In actuality, evaluation and assessment involve a consideration of the child, the curriculum, the community, and the teacher. Certainly teachers want to evaluate students in order to determine their academic progress, grade placement, and promotion from one grade to another; but as part of the evaluative process teachers also need to use assessment tools to reflect on their own teaching and on the curriculum they are using. The authors of the standards posit the notion that teachers, students, educational administrators, parents, the public, policymakers, institutions of higher education, business and industry, and government are all consumers of information about student performance in the science classroom (1996, p. 76).

EVALUATING CHILDREN'S UNDERSTANDINGS

Grading papers and reporting academic growth or achievement to parents and the community are only a small part of the total assessment process. Evaluation of children's understanding of the world around them involves an assessment of the **affective** (attitudes, values, and beliefs), **cognitive** (facts, concepts, rules and principles, and problem solving), and **psychomotor** (motor skills, including science processes) domains. For culturally diverse students nontraditional assessment tools such as oral interviews, portfolios, concept maps, and authentic assessment tools (e.g., drawing tests, oral tests, visual tests) are vitally needed in most elementary schools in order to assess changes in their knowledge structures in all three domains.

Affective Domain

Throughout our lives we are thrilled with the beauty of sunrises and sunsets, starry nights replete with shooting "stars," wildflowers blooming in the spring, and autumnal foliage in deciduous hardwood forests. Science is the study of the natural world, a physical world that impacts the lives of all who share this planet. Every child has affective responses to natural phenomena, yet such responses—values, attitudes, and beliefs—are infrequently assessed in the typical elementary school science curriculum. Measurements of the affective domain were rarely undertaken in the past because attitude constructs are difficult to define and to measure.

Bloom (1971) divided the affective domain into five categories: (1) receiving, (2) responding, (3) valuing, (4) organizing, and (5) internalizing a value system. **Receiving,** the first level of the affective domain, involves sensitivity to or awareness of stimuli and events. If students watch a public television show on the plight of whales, they are receiving information. At the second level or **responding** level of Bloom's affective domain, students do something about or respond to the stimulus. If, after viewing a show on whales, a student goes to the library and signs out a book on whales to learn more about them, that student is functioning at a responding level. At the third level of Bloom's taxonomy (**valuing**), the student develops a criterion or standard for determining the worth of behaviors, things, and events. According to Bloom, students functioning at the fourth level (**organizing**) of his affective taxonomy begin to formulate a value system. The final step or stage of the affective domain involves the **internalization** of a value system. It is only when students act on their interests, appreciations, attitudes, and values that teachers are able to assess those attributes.

Feelings and values are also incorporated into McCormack and Yager's (1989) taxonomy of science education. These authors divide knowledge into five domains: (1) knowing and understanding, (2) exploring and discovering, (3) imagining and creating, (4) feeling and valuing, and (5) using and applying. In this classification system, knowing and understanding includes the learning of facts, concepts, laws, and theories of science. These authors define exploring and discovering as being the processes of science. Imagining and creating are defined in this taxonomy as including the abilities (1) to produce a mental image, (2) to visualize, (3) to produce alternate or unusual uses for objects, (4) to solve problems and puzzles, (5) to fantasize, and (6) to dream. McCormack and Yager have defined feeling and valuing in much the same manner as Bloom defines valuing, that is, assessing values, attitudes, and beliefs. The final domain in this taxonomic system for science education includes using and applying knowledge.

In recent years, advances in **psychometric** or test design procedures have resulted in new instruments with which to assess the affective domain. These instruments allow classroom teachers to readily measure students' values, attitudes, and beliefs and to determine whether those attitudes and beliefs change as a result of instruction. Whether one uses a three- or five-domain taxonomic system for classifying knowledge, assessment of children's attitudes before, during, and following instruction is vital to understanding those attitudes and how they change over time and as a result of instruction.

Unobtrusive Measures

Unobtrusive or indirect measurements have long been used to assess students' attitudes or preferences. School cafeteria workers in most elementary schools are proficient at measuring students' attitudes toward particular foods. As children walk through the cafeteria line and select entrees, the workers inventory their food preferences. Cafeteria managers prepare greater quantities of foods that students like and avoid wastage by cooking smaller quantities of foods that children avoid. This same principle of unobtrusive assessment may be used in a classroom setting.

Library Selections.   If children visit the school library and are allowed to select books for their own reading pleasure, teachers may get a crude indicator of their interests. Suppose Mr. Hun, a fourth-grade teacher, wants to determine if his unit on dinosaurs is making a difference in children's attitudes toward the study of ancient life. At the end of the weekly library period, he could unobtrusively observe and tally the topics and numbers of the books that his students had voluntarily checked out. After several weeks of teaching a dinosaur unit, Mr. Hun could again use a simple tally count of library books to determine if his students' reading habits had changed. If his first survey revealed that only 2 children in his class of 30 students had checked out books

Children's reading patterns are an unobtrusive measure of their interests.

on dinosaurs, he would conclude that only a few children were interested in the topic. Mr. Hun could tentatively conclude that his instruction had made a difference in his students' attitudes toward dinosaurs if half the students in the same class signed out books on dinosaurs after his unit of instruction. This same procedure may be used to evaluate student interest in the selection of science fair topics, multimedia courseware, and field trip activities. Unobtrusive observation of voluntary performance is one way to assess students' affective domains.

Mini Museums.   A second unobtrusive measure sometimes used to assess students' attitudes toward a particular topic is the mini-museum. Sometimes a teacher establishes a museum corner in the classroom and allows students to make voluntary contributions to the museum. Each morning as students bring in objects, each item is labeled with its name and the name of the student contributor. After each unit of study, the teacher allows students to take the realia home. To assess student interest, a teacher could keep an informal tally of the percentage of students who voluntarily contribute materials to a particular unit of study.

Using mini-museum contributions to assess attitude is an imprecise measure because real world objects are more readily available for some units of study than others (e.g., plant materials are far easier for children to obtain than realia associated with chemistry). Other unobtrusive measures of children's attitudes could include materials self-selected for reading during silent reading periods, computer software self-selected for study during a class activity time, students' choices of book report topics, and children's self-selected activities carried out in a learning center environment. Unobtrusive measures of voluntary performance are powerful devices for determining children's attitudes toward school and the subjects taught in the classroom.

Obtrusive Measures

Purposeful measurement of children's attitudes toward science and related topics has become easier in recent years with the development of new assessment tools. Newer psychometric tools described in this chapter offer teachers ease of test administration and scoring. Drawing tests, pictorial tests, iconic response categories, and oral tests allow teachers to assess children's attitudes even though the children may not be highly proficient in the use of the English language. Additionally, many of these tests eliminate much of the cultural bias associated with traditional pencil-and-paper assessment tools. While no test is completely culture free or culture fair, recently developed attitude instruments do seem to minimize the testing bias that has flawed many of their predecessors.

Drawing Tests. The Draw-A-Scientist Test (Mason, Kahle, & Gardner, 1991) is one of the easiest attitude instruments to administer to elementary-aged children. In this test, the child is given a blank sheet of paper and is directed to draw a scientist. Children are allowed 15 to 30 minutes to draw their perceptions of a scientist. Since this is a drawing instrument, it is appropriate for younger children and for children with limited proficiency in the English language. An upper elementary child's perception of a scientist is shown in Figure 6.1.

This test is scored by counting the number of standard stereotypical indicators in the drawing. A child may score from 0 to 11 points on the standard indicator scale. A list of standard indicators is presented in Figure 6.2. A high score indicates the child holds a strong negative (more stereotypical) stereotype of a scientist, while a lower score indicates that the child holds a more realistic or less stereotypical image of a scientist. Teachers may administer this test as a pretest and a posttest either over the school year or during a particular unit of study.

FIGURE 6.1 ■ An Elementary Student's Perception of a Scientist

FIGURE 6.2   ■   Indicators for the Scientist Stereotype

1. Laboratory coat
2. Eyeglasses
3. Facial hair
4. Symbols of research
   a. Flasks
   b. Test tubes
   c. Microscope
   d. Bunsen burner
   e. Other laboratory equipment
5. Symbols of knowledge
   a. Books
   b. Filing cabinets
   c. Chalkboard
   d. Other educational supplies
6. Symbols of technology (the products of science)
   a. Solutions in glassware
   b. Machines
   c. Robots
   d. Computers
   e. Other inventions
7. Captions (e.g., "Eureka, I've got it!!!" "He's a nerd.")
8. Male
9. Signs and labeling (e.g., Fire Exit, Poison)
10. Pencils and pens in chest pocket
11. Unkempt appearance (e.g., uncombed hair, dirty lab coat, "high water" trousers)

Likert Instruments.   Among all attitude instruments, the most reliable and valid are Likert instruments. Likert instruments normally feature five response categories ranging from "strongly agree" to "strongly disagree." Such instruments are developed in a highly constrained environment and are subjected to numerous reliability and validity checks prior to their publication, thus they are sensitive to even slight changes in students' attitudes. Among Likert instruments used in science education, perhaps the most widely known is the Science Attitude Scale (Shrigley, 1974; Thompson & Shrigley, 1986). Numerous versions of this scale have been produced over the years (see Figure 6.3).

The science attitude scale has been translated into approximately 20 languages and has been administered throughout the world. It has been used

FIGURE 6.3 ▧ Science Attitude Scale

1. I feel uncomfortable in the science classroom.

1	2	3	4	5
Strongly agree	Agree	Undecided	Disagree	Strongly disagree

2. Learning science is important to me.

1	2	3	4	5
Strongly agree	Agree	Undecided	Disagree	Strongly disagree

3. I fear that I will be unable to learn science adequately.

1	2	3	4	5
Strongly agree	Agree	Undecided	Disagree	Strongly disagree

4. Learning science takes too much time.

1	2	3	4	5
Strongly agree	Agree	Undecided	Disagree	Strongly disagree

5. I enjoy the lab period in science classes.

1	2	3	4	5
Strongly agree	Agree	Undecided	Disagree	Strongly disagree

6. I have a difficult time understanding science.

1	2	3	4	5
Strongly agree	Agree	Undecided	Disagree	Strongly disagree

7. I feel comfortable with the subjects in my science class.

1	2	3	4	5
Strongly agree	Agree	Undecided	Disagree	Strongly disagree

8. I would be interested in working in a science lab.

1	2	3	4	5
Strongly agree	Agree	Undecided	Disagree	Strongly disagree

9. I look forward to coming to science class.

1	2	3	4	5
Strongly agree	Agree	Undecided	Disagree	Strongly disagree

FIGURE 6.4 ■
Likert Iconic
Response Categories

Strongly agree   Agree   Undecided   Disagree   Strongly disagree

in its traditional pencil-and-paper form with older elementary children and orally with younger children. Additionally, iconic response categories featuring "smiley" and "frowny" faces have been developed over the years for early elementary children and for limited English proficient students (Figure 6.4).

Checklists.   For older elementary children, attitude checklists are highly effective devices for measuring attitudes toward science. One easily administered instrument is Zuckerman's Affect Adjective Checklist (Docking, 1978). This checklist may be used to measure anxiety toward the study of science. Zuckerman's Affect Adjective Checklist consists of 21 key words embedded in a total of 60 adjectives. Students are instructed to circle whatever words describe how they feel about science. The 11 words designated (+) are scored as 1 if they are circled and 0 if they are not circled. The 10 words designated as (–) are scored 0 if they are circled and 1 if they are not circled. Each child's total anxiety is obtained by summing the scores for the 21 key words. The re-

FIGURE 6.5 ■ Zuckerman's Affect Adjective Checklist

Directions: The words below could describe how you feel about school science. Read through the list of words and underline those which describe how you generally feel about multicultural education. You may underline as many or as few words as you wish.

absorbed	afraid	aimless	ambitious	annoyed
aware	bored	calm	careless	cautious
challenged	cheerful	cheated	comfortable	confused
contented	creative	curious	dedicated	desperate
disappointed	efficient	entertained	excited	fearful
fortunate	frightened	happy	hopeless	impatient
incapable	inspired	interested	joyful	lazy
loving	miserable	misplaced	nervous	organized
overloaded	panicky	pleasant	pleased	productive
pushed	refreshed	regretful	rewarded	satisfied
secure	serious	shaky	steady	tense
terrified	thoughtful	upset	weary	worried

maining 39 adjectives are ignored in the scoring process. The instrument exhibits good validity and reliability characteristics. Children's scores on the Zuckerman instrument may range from 0 (no anxiety) to 21 (extreme anxiety). This instrument may be used as a pretest and posttest to measure the effectiveness of science instruction in the affective domain.

Semantic Differential Scales. Semantic differential scales have been used for several decades to assess student attitudes toward a variety of topics. Semantic scales typically consist of a list of bipolar adjectives (e.g., beautiful/ugly, wonderful/awful) that may be applied to a particular topic. A five- or seven-point continuum is placed between the two adjectives. Students indicate the strength of their feelings about the subject by circling the appropriate response category. Information about a student's attitudes can be determined at the beginning of a course or unit of study and again at the end. From these measures a determination may be made about changes in students' attitudes. A sample of a semantic differential instrument is shown in Figure 6.6.

Essays and Surveys. Open-ended essay questions or interviews may also be useful in assessing students' attitudes toward science. Writing starters such as "Shorelines ought to be preserved for everyone to use, not just a few individuals," "Explain why you agree or disagree with this statement," and "Do you think endangered animals such as the whale ought to be preserved? Why or why not?" are effective devices for assessing students' attitudes. Oral interviews about the unit under study are useful for students who have difficulty communicating in written English. Interview questions such as "Have you gone to a science museum lately? If so, what did you enjoy most? Least?" "Have you visited a state or national park? If so, which one?" and "What science movies have you seen during the past month on television? Did you enjoy them? Why or why not?" provide insights into students' attitudes and interests.

FIGURE 6.6 ■ Semantic Differential Scale

SCIENCE IS . . .

Exciting	1	2	3	4	5	Boring
Good	1	2	3	4	5	Bad
Fun	1	2	3	4	5	Dull
Useful	1	2	3	4	5	Useless
Important	1	2	3	4	5	Unimportant
Easy	1	2	3	4	5	Hard

Social Interactions

Social interactions are vital to each child's success in the multicultural science classroom, in the total school community, and in the community at large. Historically, most teachers have used a simple rating of "satisfactory" or "unsatisfactory" under a vague category of "citizenship skills." However, social skills are a complex construct and may be operationally defined as consisting of cluster skills, task skills, and camaraderie skills. (See Table 6.1.)

Cluster skills include the ability to move into small groups, sharing materials in a small group setting, turn taking, contributing ideas, and active listening (Ostlund, 1992). **Task skills** in a social context might include asking questions, receiving and giving peer tutoring, asking clarifying questions, elaborating on the ideas of others, justifying answers, and assisting the group in reaching consensus. Finally, **camaraderie skills** would include encouraging the learning of others, avoiding giving negative feedback to peers, pro-

TABLE 6.1 ■ Social Skills Checklist

Skill			
How are my cluster skills? Do I . . .	*Always*	*Sometimes*	*Never*
Move into a group rapidly?			
Share materials with others?			
Take turns with others?			
Contribute ideas to the group?			
Listen to others?			
How are my task skills? Do I . . .	*Always*	*Sometimes*	*Never*
Ask questions of others?			
Give and accept help from others?			
Ask questions when I don't understand?			
Explain my answers?			
Help others reach agreement?			
How are my camaraderie skills? Do I . . .	*Always*	*Sometimes*	*Never*
Encourage others?			
Avoid giving negative feedback to my peers?			
Praise others for good ideas?			
Share my feelings with others?			

viding verbal support to others, and sharing feelings with others when appropriate. Each of these clusters of social skills may be evaluated with checklists as teachers circulate from one group to another, or by the students themselves.

Cognitive Domain

Assessing declarative knowledge, knowledge that can be stated, is the most common form of evaluation used in elementary schools. Tremendous attention has been paid to cognitive assessment instruments during the past several decades. The "back to basics" movement of the 1980s focused national attention on children's mastery of declarative knowledge. Historically, most cognitive assessment has taken the form of end of the unit or **summative evaluation. Formative evaluation** (in-process evaluation), knowledge of how children are progressing, is also necessary in informing students and parents of children's progress in mastering new knowledge.

Bloom (1971) classified knowledge in the cognitive domain into a hierarchy consisting of (1) knowledge, (2) comprehension, (3) application, (4) analysis, (5) synthesis, and (6) evaluation. Within Bloom's taxonomic system, information at the **knowledge** stage consists of recall of facts and principles. Bloom defined **comprehension**-level knowledge as the understanding of facts and ideas. Applying facts and ideas to new situations comprises the **applica-**

Questioning skills are vital in the multicultural classroom.

tion or third level of Bloom's taxonomy. **Analysis,** the ability to break concepts down into parts and to see their relationships, is the fourth level of Bloom's taxonomy. According to Bloom, **synthesis,** the fifth level of knowledge, is the ability to put facts and ideas together to make a new whole. Finally, Bloom classifies **evaluation,** that is, the ability to judge the value of facts and ideas, as the highest level of thinking skill.

Other authors have defined the cognitive domain as including intellectual strategies and information. McCormack and Yager (1989) define the cognitive domain as including knowledge and understanding. Gagné, Briggs, and Wager (1988) analyze the cognitive domain into levels of complexity of intellectual skills: (1) discriminations, (2) concrete concepts, (3) rules and defined concepts, (4) higher-order rules, and (5) problem solving. Within their taxonomic system, **discriminations** involve making different responses to stimuli that differ from each other along one or more physical dimensions (p. 57). **Concrete concepts,** according to Gagné, Briggs, and Wager, are object properties or attributes (color, shape, etc.). By **defined concepts and rules,** these authors mean the ability to attribute particular characteristics to objects, events, or relations. When a learner is able to respond with a class of relationships among classes of objects or events, these authors would say that the child is functioning at the **higher-order rules** level. Finally, when a student is able to generalize previously learned knowledge to a new situation, Gagné, Briggs, and Wager would say that the learner is functioning at the **problem-solving** level. Regardless of how we classify knowledge in the cognitive domain, the assessment of that domain has long been central to assessment in elementary classrooms.

Traditional Assessment Tools

Pencil-and-paper tests have long been a staple in elementary schools in the United States. Weekly spelling tests, end of unit tests, and annual achievement tests are familiar to all students and former students of U.S. public schools. The reported purpose of these instruments is to determine student progress in mastering the curriculum and to compare students to others of the same age and grade level. Many traditional pencil-and-paper assessment instruments come from a tradition of **objectivism.** There is an underlying assumption in these tests that there is a basic body of knowledge that students are to master and that the purpose of testing is to determine how successful students have been at this endeavor.

Norm-Referenced Tests.   Norm-referenced tests are used to rank and compare students in such areas as scholastic aptitude, language proficiency, and academic attainment. The Scholastic Aptitude Test, the Iowa Test of Basic Skills, and the California Achievement Test are examples of norm-referenced tests. The purpose of these instruments is to compare individual students to other students of the same age and grade level. Data from these instruments have been used as a source of information for comparing individuals, schools, and school districts with others in the same locality and throughout the nation. Additionally, these instruments are commonly used to identify gifted and talented students and students who qualify for special education programs.

From a multicultural perspective a great deal of attention has focused on the primacy of these instruments in assessing the achievement and aptitude of culturally diverse students. In spite of years of test analysis and construction, many norm-referenced tests remain biased against poor children and those from ethnic minority groups. Underlying norm-referenced instruments is an assumption that all children have been exposed to certain educational experiences in their lifetimes.

One popular neuropsychological measure uses black-and-white line drawings to assess children's knowledge of real world objects. One black-and-white line drawing depicts an igloo. When presented with this line drawing, the child is expected to respond with its name. Many unassimilated Hispanic/Latino and Native American students from the Southwest identify this icon as a *horno*, an outside bake oven familiar to those who live in the rural Southwest. Because this test consists of sixty such items, incorrectly labeling only a few may mean that a child scores significantly below her or his actual intellectual level. Not all children have had the same mainstream educational experiences, and cultural bias in testing may systematically alter the achievement levels of certain groups of culturally diverse children.

Criterion-Referenced Tests. Criterion-referenced tests measure how well a student is progressing or achieving the objectives of the course of study. Criterion measures are normally constructed by textbook-publishing companies or by individual teachers. For example, suppose Mrs. Deal, a sixth-grade teacher, wants students to label the parts of a plant cell as an objective for a unit of study on cells. The objective might be that "given a line drawing of a plant cell, the student will be able to label the nucleus, cell wall, cell membrane, chloroplasts, and cytoplasm with 80 percent accuracy." Mrs. Deal would pretest the students before beginning instruction to determine if they know the parts of the cell. She would then present a series of activities designed to teach students the cell parts. Finally, she would administer a criterion-referenced posttest that included a question about labeling the parts of the plant cell. The test would inform Mrs. Deal as to her students' progress in mastering the objective. Students in Mrs. Deal's class who do not meet the objective would be provided with remedial instruction and additional opportunities to master the objective. An example of a criterion-referenced test is shown in Figure 6.7.

Criterion-referenced tests became popular with the development of individualized instruction during the 1960s. They experienced a resurgence in the educational community during the early part of the 1980s, during the "mastery learning" decade. Criterion-referenced assessment instruments are

FIGURE 6.7 ■ Criterion-Referenced Test

Cell Test

Part A. Cell Drawings

Directions: Draw a typical animal cell and label the nucleus, cell membrane, and cytoplasm.

Part B. Multiple Choice

Directions: Select the letter for the correct answer and place it on the line at the left.

___ 1. Which of these is not a basic need of all living cells?
    a. energy   b. space   c. oxygen   d. blood

___ 2. Plant cells make food in the process of _____.
    a. reproduction   b. photosynthesis   c. metabolism   d. competition

___ 3. Cell reproduction takes place in the cell _____.
    a. membrane   b. wall   c. cytoplasm   d. nucleus

___ 4. Plant cells obtain energy from the _____.
    a. soil   b. sun   c. chlorophyll   d. fertilizer

___ 5. The protective layer of the cell is called the _____.
    a. cell membrane   b. cytoplasm   c. vacuole   d. meiosis

___ 6. Which of these is not a basic cell process?
    a. movement   b. reproduction   c. metabolism   d. growth

Part C. Compare and Contrast

Directions: Write a paragraph or two telling how plant and animal cells are alike and how they are different.

---

grounded in a tradition of training models. They are based on philosophies and theories of education that hold that children may be trained to respond to certain educational stimuli, and that children will learn under certain conditions. This behaviorist worldview holds that children learn best under stimulus/response instructional strategies. Aside from its use in mastery learning programs in elementary schools, criterion-referenced assessment is also widely used in military training modules and in corporate training programs.

Historically, criterion-referenced tests have tended to focus on low levels of cognitive knowledge, since questions at these levels are easier to construct than are those dealing with higher-level knowledge. Programmed instructional units are today the most familiar context of criterion-referenced tests. Many textbook companies produce criterion-referenced assessments to accompany their textbooks. From a multicultural perspective, criterion-referenced tests have frequently been criticized as an impediment to student learning, especially when students must perform at a particular level before moving to new instruction. For limited English proficient students, and for students who find mastery learning dull, repetitious, and boring, the criterion-referenced test has frequently become a barrier to advancement to higher-level mathematics and science courses.

Multiple choice, true and false, short answer, and short essay questions are the primary means by which teachers assess student knowledge in the cognitive domain. These kinds of test items are commonly used because most teachers view them as being easy to administer, easy to score, and flexible—an easy way to assess a wide range of content area knowledge. Pencil-and-paper assessments using these formats are deemed by many to be highly effective for assessing students' prior knowledge.

Self-Referenced Assessments.   Self-referenced assessments are most frequently found associated with Individual Educational Plans (IEPs) in special education programs. Self-referenced assessments are used primarily to measure learnings individual students must attain before moving to another level of instruction. When self-referenced assessment is used, the student is typically administered a pretest, instruction, and a posttest. A student's achievement in meeting a particular goal is carefully assessed.

Suppose one goal for a particular fifth-grade student is to construct a bar graph from a table of data. The student would be assessed regarding the ability to construct a bar graph prior to instruction. Next the student would be given a series of activities designed to develop competency in graph construction. Finally, the student's skill in constructing a bar graph would be assessed. If the student is now capable of constructing a bar graph, a new goal in graphing skills would be generated for the student. If the student were unable to perform the bar-graphing task, then remedial activities would be undertaken to assist the student in performing the particular skill. Self-referenced assessment is most useful when teaching skills to a single student.

Authentic Assessment Tools

From a constructivist viewpoint, the purpose of assessment is to identify the ways that students have constructed knowledge. In science study, the focus of assessment ought to be to accurately assess students' ability to do science. Former secretary of education William Bennett has stated:

> The problem of assessment also constrains the spread of "hands-on" science. It is relatively easy to test children's knowledge when they have been asked to memorize lists of data for a test. It is much harder to design tests that measure learning derived from experience. (1986, p. 3)

Certainly diagnostic testing is necessary to determine students' entry-level knowledge and experience. It is also necessary to monitor instructional processes to determine whether children are receiving information as the teacher envisioned. However, most traditional assessment and evaluation procedures have little to do with what children are learning in the science classroom.

The purpose of "authentic assessment" is to match assessment procedures with what children are learning, and to provide students with feedback about their progress in mastering new knowledge. If children have been learning to classify living insects to order using a dichotomous key, then a pencil-and-paper question that asks students to select a dictionary definition for the term *dichotomous key* from a list of definitions in a multiple-choice format is a difficult task. Classifying insects to order using a dichotomous insect key is a multifaceted construct that involves observing, understanding insect anatomy, gathering data, and evaluating the quality of one's answer. Asking students to identify a formal definition of the term *dichotomous key* has little to do with the actual instruction. In this instance, we would say that there is little **congruency** or **consistency** between instruction and assessment. The methods of authentic assessment mentioned in this chapter are performance-based approaches to assessment that seek to provide the teachers and students with insights into the ways that children have constructed a knowledge of science.

Portfolios. Using a **portfolio** to assess children's understanding of science is a practice gaining popularity among elementary science teachers. The use of problem-solving, thematic approaches to learning dictates that teachers find appropriate means to assess what children are learning. Hamm and Adams define *portfolio* as "a container of evidence of a person's skills" (1991, p.18). Most adults are familiar with an artist's or a photographer's portfolio. In the classroom, a portfolio is a collection of a child's work. It is evidence of what the child can do in science and of the child's growth as a learner. A portfolio should reflect a child's growth in acquiring scientific knowledge, skills or processes, and attitudes as well as a child's mastery of knowledge.

When portfolios are used as assessment tools, four questions need to be addressed by the teacher: (1) What is being measured? (2) What constitutes evidence? (3) Who determines what goes in the portfolio? and (4) How will portfolios be assessed? Typically, portfolios are used to show growth in acquiring a knowledge of science and science processes. The first question, what specific science content areas and processes are being measured, needs to be determined by the teacher, the students, or both before a portfolio project is undertaken. The second question involves the matter of evidence or proof of learning and is best addressed by discussion and negotiation between students and their teacher. Typically, portfolios may include students' written work, journal entries, laboratory notebooks, records of students' investigations and laboratory activities, data entries and logs, rough drafts and finished products, and samples of students' individual and group assignments. The third question, regarding who determines the content of the portfolio, is usually a shared responsibility. Some entries in the portfolio may be mandated by the teacher, with other entries left to the discretion of the students. Finally, there is the matter of portfolio evaluation. Scoring rubrics have been shown to be one useful device for assessing the content of a student's portfolio.

Portfolios encourage students to collect, organize, and reflect on their own learning and to identify their strengths and weaknesses. For limited English proficient students, portfolios offer the opportunity to perform in nontraditional and non-language–dependent media. Videotapes, audiotapes, drawings, and projects may be used to show evidence of learning in science. Additionally, electronic portfolios, such as the Grady Portfolio and the Scholastic Portfolio, are multimedia tools for storing students' documents in an electronic format. Portfolios may allow students to show competency in mastering science concepts through multiple means of knowledge representation.

Concept Mapping.   Concept mapping or word webbing is an authentic assessment tool in which students try to convey to teachers the ways that they have constructed knowledge of a particular concept or idea. Novak (1991) states that a "concept map can be used to organize and represent knowledge." The visual organizer at the beginning of each chapter of this book may be thought of as a concept map. If the purpose of assessment is to determine what knowledge of science students have constructed and how that information is organized, then a concept map is a valuable tool for assisting teachers to understand students' perceptions of the world. A third-grade student's concept map of plants is shown in Figure 6.8.

From this concept map, the teacher could infer that the student has some prior knowledge of plants, of edible plants, and of the parts of a plant. If a goal of the unit were to have students develop an understanding of the interdependence of plants and animals, then the teacher would examine stu-

FIGURE 6.8 ■ Student's
Concept Map of Plants

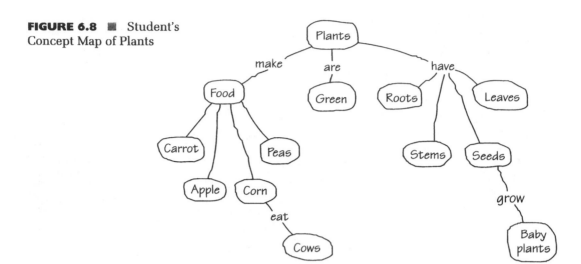

dents' concept maps at the end of the unit to determine if students had incorporated this new information into their existing schemata. Students who indicated in their concept maps that plants produce food and oxygen for animals to use and that animals produce carbon dioxide and fertilizer necessary for plant growth would show evidence of the learning that the teacher had sought to elicit. Concept maps and word webs provide teachers with insights into the ways that students have constructed knowledge and have integrated new knowledge into their existing schemata.

Task Tests.   Task tests are a third tool for assessing the state of students' reasoning abilities. Typically, task tests elicit a performance of a science process from students and require them to justify or explain their answers. The purpose of this authentic assessment tool is to gain insights into the ways that students engage in problem-solving skills. A typical Piagetian task uses the illustration shown in Figure 6.9.

The purpose of this task is to determine students' abilities to engage in proportional reasoning. In this problem the student is given a small paper clip and is asked to measure the height of Mr. Short in paper clip lengths. Next, the student is given a large paper clip and is asked to predict the height of Mr. Short in paper clip lengths without actually measuring the figure. Students who can function at a formal operational level are able to establish a ratio between the size of the paper clips and to determine the height of Mr. Short by comparing the large paper clip to the small one. If a student is functioning at a concrete operational level, then the student will be unable to write an algebraic statement or ratio comparing the lengths with the two paper clips. Other task tests may be used to determine students' abilities to

FIGURE 6.9 ▓ Mr. Short, a Task Test Figure

engage in conservation of matter, seriation, classification, combinatorial reasoning, identification and control of variables, and hypothetical-deductive reasoning. Task tests are normally used to determine a child's level of cognitive development at different Piagetian stages.

Clarkson (1991) points out that task tests are highly appropriate for use with culturally diverse students in that Piagetian measures are highly correlated with mathematical achievement, particularly problem-solving skills. Task tests allow bilingual students to demonstrate computation, measurement, and mathematical language abilities far better than do other assessment instruments. Additionally, these instruments are well correlated with a student's language ability (whether home language or English). For culturally diverse learners, task tests may provide an alternative form of assessment that provides the teacher with an understanding of the ways that students have constructed a knowledge of science.

Journal Writing. Journal writing, another authentic assessment tool, encourages reflective learning. The process of writing about learning encourages students to (1) assess their prior knowledge, (2) think about the process of schooling, (3) formally state what they have learned in the classroom, and (4) integrate language arts and science skills in the classroom. Journal writing is highly beneficial in the science classroom because persuasive writing requires the analysis and presentation of data in an organized manner. Additionally, descriptive writing requires students to make detailed observations, organize information in a logical pattern, and develop precision in their writing styles.

Journal entries provide teachers with insights into the ways that students have constructed knowledge and into their levels of conceptual understandings. Liftig, Liftig, & Eaker (1992) point out that students need practice in journal-writing skills, specifically students who (1) are unaccustomed to responding in a written fashion, (2) have been coached in schools to respond to low-level questions, (3) need practice in elaborating answers, and (4) have difficulty communicating with the intended audience. As teachers change from traditional pencil-and-paper measures to authentic assessment tools, they need to mentor children in the use of these assessment devices.

Group Discussion and Projects.   Group discussions and projects, the final authentic assessment tools mentioned in this chapter, have been infrequently used in the past for assessing students' understandings of science. Projects such as posters, videos, drama productions, interactive bulletin boards, songs, poems, debates, and so forth may be used to assess children's understandings of science. For many culturally diverse students, group performance is a more comfortable means of displaying knowledge than individual testing situations. Care must be taken with group work to provide individuals the opportunity to be accountable for their portion of the project.

Students who do not contribute to a group project and yet reap the benefits of the work of others present a problem in this type of grading situation. Projects provide a viable alternative for assessing students' growth, but grading of these projects needs to reflect concern for the contributions of each student. Allowing students to participate in the grading process is one technique that may help counteract this difficulty. Students may be asked to rate each other and their personal participation in the project. Teachers frequently use a multitiered scoring system to evaluate group work, deriving part of the grade from the total project and part of the grade from each individual's contributions to the work.

Recently, an upper elementary teacher wanted to assess her students' understandings of water. She assigned groups of students in the class to draw science fiction cartoons about water. Students were to incorporate their knowledge of the properties of water into their cartoons. Cartoons were scored on scientific content, creativity, and grammatical skills. Additionally, each student received a second grade from the teacher, based on the teacher's observations of the student's working ability in the group. One of the products of this activity is shown in Figure 6.10. The cartoon is an illustration of the use of authentic or alternative assessment procedures in a group setting. Authentic assessment instruments provide teachers with additional tools for assessing students' cognitive knowledge of science.

FIGURE 6.10 ▨ Group Assessment Project

The Story of Wally Water

Once upon a time, there was a drop of water named Wally.
Wally lived in a beaker of water in Dr. Lightfoot's laboratory with
his brothers and sisters.

Wally was a favorite among the other
drops of water because he was slow to anger.
He had a high boiling point (about 100 degrees Celsius).

Wally enjoyed hanging around with the other drops of water in
his family. They were a very cohesive group.

(continued)

FIGURE 6.10 ■ **Continued**

One day Dr. Lightfoot was working with some soil samples in
his laboratory. Dirt, a mean and vicious little monster, got all over the sleeve
of Dr. Lightfoot's lab coat. The dirt monster was ugly, sticky,
and caused Dr. Lightfoot a lot of discomfort.

At first Dr. Lightfoot called upon his old friend Al Cohol
to help get rid of Dirt. Al tried, no matter what he did Dirt wouldn't move.

Then a great idea struck Dr. Lightfoot, "Wally Water will help me."

Dr. Lightfoot poured Wally out of the beaker. Wally went right to work.
He had been weight lifting and working out his bipolar muscles.
Wally hit Dirt with his positive end, and then his negative end.
Time after time, Walley Water threw punches at Dirt.

The fight was long and hard, but Wally overcame Dirt. His electrons spun
with joy, as he claimed the victory. Dr. Lightfoot's lab coat gleamed
like new and Wally was still the Champion of Polar Solvents.

The End

Psychomotor Domain

Assessment of the psychomotor domain involves an evaluation of children's motor skills or manipulation of materials. Simpson (1972) devised a taxonomy of the psychomotor domain, shown in Figure 6.11.

From this domain, certain hands-on science activities correspond to the levels of motor development. For example, at the **perception level** students would be able to recognize that insects are different sizes. Students functioning at the **set level** would know which insect is bigger than another. At the **adaptation level,** students would be able to correctly identify an insect that they had not previously encountered.

Laboratory Activities

Laboratory practical examinations are commonly used to assess students' psychomotor skills in the science content area. Normally these instruments assess children's competency in using science processes. During laboratory skills tests, students are asked to manipulate equipment and materials, observe, reason, record data, and interpret results. Hands-on testing allows the teacher to assess students' abilities to (1) work with basic science equipment (e.g., thermometers, balances), (2) manipulate objects (e.g., simple laboratory equipment), (3) collect data, (4) record data, (5) observe and classify, (6) perform laboratory procedures, and (7) communicate.

FIGURE 6.11 ■ Taxonomy of the Psychomotor Domain

---

1. *Perception.* Using sense organs to obtain cues needed to guide motor activity.
   1.1. Sensory stimulation
   1.2. Cue selection
   1.3. Translation
2. *Set.* Being ready to perform a particular action.
   2.1. Mental set
   2.2. Physical set
   2.3. Emotional set
3. *Guided response.* Performing under guidance of a model.
   3.1. Imitation
   3.2. Trial and error
4. *Mechanism.* Being able to perform a task habitually with some degree of confidence and proficiency.
5. *Complex or overt response.* Performing a task with a high degree of proficiency and skill.
6. *Adaptation.* Using previously learned skills to perform new but related tasks.
7. *Origination.* Creating new performances after having developed skills.

Assume that Ms. Czienski, a fifth-grade teacher, had completed a unit of instruction on the metric system. During this unit, her students had learned to measure linear distances using a metric ruler and a meter stick, to measure volume with a graduated cylinder, and to determine the mass of an object using a spring balance and a pan balance. In order to assess her students' knowledge of measuring, Ms. Czienski could set up a rotating laboratory test while the students were at recess. The test would consist of 35 lab stations, and the students would move from station to station once each minute. Each station would assess each student's abilities to use metric measuring tools. A portion of this rotating lab test on the metric system is shown in Table 6.2.

In this testing situation, students move from station to station performing specific measuring skills. Laboratory examinations may measure performance, including the processes of observing, manipulating, and measuring. They may measure investigative processes, including planning and designing investigations or experiments. Finally, laboratory practical examinations may be used to assess students' reasoning abilities, including interpreting data, formulating generalizations, and developing models.

Assessment in the psychomotor domain is frequently overlooked in the elementary science classroom. Laboratory practical examinations (1) require more planning time than do pencil-and-paper examinations, (2) necessitate access to manipulative materials, (3) need more space than do other instructional activities, (4) require clean-up time, and (5) obligate the teacher to a

TABLE 6.2 ■ Part of a Rotating Lab Test on Metrics

Station Number	Question Card	Materials
1	What is the height of the chair at this station?	Meter stick
2	What is the length of this line segment?	Metric ruler Paper with line segment
3	How much water does this container hold?	Bucket of water Container Graduated cylinder
4	What is the mass of this object?	Spring balance Object to weigh
5	What is the mass of this object?	Pan balance Object to weigh

lengthy set-up process. However, in spite of the difficulties of test preparation, laboratory practical examinations do accurately assess student learning. From the viewpoint of limited English proficient students, hands-on manipulative testing tends to present the teacher with a more accurate picture of the child's learning than "traditional" pencil-and-paper instruments.

Checklists and Scoring Rubrics

At times, teachers seek to evaluate just one skill or science process at a time. In these instances, checklists and scoring rubrics are highly effective evaluative tools. In most instances, evaluation is seen as a summative activity, to be conducted at the end of a period of instruction. If assessment is to be effective in providing students with feedback, to be corrective in nature, then it must also be formative in nature. Assessment ought to be part of the learning process, not an end result. Checklists assist teachers in providing feedback to students; they are a tool for reflective learning, for helping students to get a handle on what they know and what they need to learn. Observation checklists are among the easiest and most flexible ways to implement different assessment methods (Nott, Reeve, & Reeve, 1992).

Suppose a teacher wishes to assess students' abilities to use a Bunsen burner. The teacher could develop a checklist of specific behavioral objectives and assess students on those skills, moving from group to group. Such a checklist might look like the one in Figure 6.12.

From this checklist, the teacher could evaluate the student's knowledge of safety rules, ability to light a burner and adjust the flame, and skill in handling hot materials. This checklist establishes a standard for performance and judges the student's skills against that standard. For example, does the student wear safety goggles? If so, how often? Always? Sometimes? Never? From

FIGURE 6.12 ■ Checklist for Assessing Use of a Burner

Behavioral Objective	Always	Sometimes	Never
Wears safety goggles			
Lights burner properly			
Adjusts flame correctly			
Heats objects carefully			
Handles hot materials carefully			
Cleans work area			

this data, the teacher and the student can begin a dialogue about the student's progress in mastering science processes.

In addition to checklists, teachers may wish to use scoring rubrics to assess student progress in the psychomotor domain. Scoring rubrics typically contain a limited number of well-defined categories for describing a student's performance. To evaluate a student's ability to observe and record data on a table during a laboratory investigation, the teacher could use a scoring rubric such as that shown in Table 6.3.

Using this rubric, the teacher can translate observations of a student's behavior into a numerical grade. Additionally, this rubric allows the teacher to distinguish between students performing the process poorly and those performing with expertise. When properly used, rubrics and performance checklists have great potential for providing productive feedback to students and their teachers about the appropriateness of student performance.

EVALUATING TEACHING AND CURRICULUM

As teachers evaluate and assess students, they also need to reflect on their own teaching practices and the instructional materials that they are using. Sometimes children fail to learn because of their own lack of effort and motivation. At other times, students fail to learn because the teaching materials are inappropriate for them. Finally, students fail to learn because the teacher has used inappropriate teaching strategies or has failed to provide an appropriate classroom environment for learning to occur. A child's failure in the science classroom is a two-edged sword. Failure of a student indicates that the child has failed to learn at this particular time, but it also indicates that the teacher has failed to reach the child. Just as teachers evaluate and assess students, they also need to evaluate themselves and the curriculum materials that they use with children.

TABLE 6.3 ■ Scoring Rubric to Assess Observing and Recording Abilities

Points	Characteristics
0	Fails to observe or record data
1	Seems to observe correctly; doesn't record data accurately
2	Observes and records data accurately
3	Observes and records data with great expertise

Reflective Teaching

Reflecting is part of every teacher's professional growth and development. Four basic questions should guide the teaching process and teacher's reflections on that process: (1) What do my students know? (2) What do I want my students to learn? (3) How will I help them learn? and (4) What have they learned? The first question, What do my students know? refers to the knowledge that students bring to the classroom. Assessment of prior knowledge may involve formal pretesting, concept mapping, or simple conversations. Exploring what students know also involves an assessment of children's language abilities and their experiences in the real world. Frequently, teachers may find that students need to broaden their background before they are ready to learn new material or information. For example, many kindergarten science programs introduce students to a study of common farm animals, or use farm animals as a basis for building a knowledge of living things. Because inner-city students may not have been exposed to life in the rural United States, these students may need to visit a farm and gain experience in seeing, touching, and hearing animals before they are ready to tackle learning that presupposes a knowledge of these animals.

The second question, What do I want my students to learn? involves an examination of the goals and objectives of the teacher, the school, the school district, and sometimes state curriculum frameworks and requirements. Frequently, teachers interpret local and state recommendations as themselves being the course, or a mandate for teaching, rather than as guideposts or suggestions. In schools where teachers rely heavily on textbooks as central to the curriculum, teachers need to remember that publishing companies frequently include far more materials than can be mastered in a year or in a course of study. What do I want my students to learn? is a question that involves professional decision making based on a knowledge of the students and of the curriculum.

The third question, How will I help them to learn? is a pedagogical question based on a knowledge of the students, their prior knowledge, and the science concepts to be learned. For students in the multicultural classroom, a consideration of how to help them learn involves a knowledge of the ways that children have been socialized to learn. Not all children learn in the same manner. Although a highly verbal presentation of information may be appropriate for teaching a certain topic in one setting, the same teaching strategy may not work in another setting. Many culturally diverse children are socialized to work in groups. Additionally, if a teacher is working with large numbers of limited English proficient students, the teacher may choose teaching strategies that use peer tutoring, multiple modes of knowledge representation, and multiple modes of performance.

What have they learned? is a reflective teaching question that involves assessment. Assessment involves a knowledge of children's cognitive, affec-

TABLE 6.4 ■ Changing Emphases in the *National Science Education Standards*

Less Emphasis On	More Emphasis On
Assessing what is most easily measured or assessed.	Assessing what is most highly valued or regarded.
Assessing discrete or individual packets of knowledge.	Assessing the depth of students' knowledge and understandings.
Assessing scientific knowledge.	Assessing students' reasoning and scientific understandings.
Assessing what students do not know.	Assessing what students have learned and understand.
Assessing only achievement.	Assessing students' achievement and providing opportunities to learn.
End of term assessment by teachers.	Continuous assessment of their work and that of their peers by students.
Development of external assessments by measurement experts working alone.	Involvement of teachers in the development of external assessments.

tive, and psychomotor domains. Historically, schools have focused on assessing children's cognitive growth without adequately assessing changes in attitudes, values, beliefs, and science processes. *National Science Education Standards* speaks to changes in the way that we view teaching and learning, specifically urging teachers and administrators to change their emphases in assessment (see Table 6.4).

CLASSROOM PRACTICE

As a teacher, assessment provides you the opportunity to make students part of the teaching and learning process. Assessment allows you and your students to examine goals and to determine the progress that collectively you are making in achieving those goals. Evaluation of the cognitive, affective, and psychomotor domains provides an opportunity for you and your students to reflect on what is being learned. Finally, assessment encourages students to become reflective learners and to assess what they are learning, why they are learning it, and how to express what they have learned.

This section provides specific examples of assessment devices that may be used in the multicultural classroom. Each is a model of the types of assessment activities that may be used to measure specific content knowledge, processes, or attitudes of students.

ACTIVITY 6.1 ■ Phases of Matter Quiz

Type of Activity: Task test (individual)

Materials: Small container of oobleck for each child

Teacher Preparation: Oobleck is a mixture of corn starch and water. Pour corn starch into a container and add sufficient water so that the corn starch is completely moistened (thick, not runny).

Conducting the Activity:
1. Provide each student with a paper cup or plastic container of oobleck and tell them, "I have a new substance for you today. It is called oobleck. I want you to play with the oobleck for a few minutes and then answer some questions about it."
2. Write the following on the board and also read it aloud to your students: "What phase of matter (solid, liquid, or gas) is oobleck? Explain your answer."
3. Encourage students to write their observations of oobleck and to classify oobleck as a solid, liquid, or gas based on their prior knowledge of the phases of matter. Oobleck or the mixture of corn starch and water is really a non-Newtonian fluid. Most students will classify it as a liquid.

Scoring: In evaluating students' responses, focus on the students' knowledge of the characteristics of the phases of matter.

ACTIVITY 6.2 ■ Weather Quiz

Purpose: To assess literary expression

Type of Activity: Assessment (group)

Materials: Tape players and record players

Conducting the Activity: Assign students to work in groups and to write a song (including rap songs) or poem that expresses some of their ideas about weather. Encourage students to incorporate as much knowledge of weather as possible into their product. When students have completed their song or poem, allow them to perform their rendition for the class. If students have written a poem, encourage them to perform a choral reading of the poem for the class.

ACTIVITIES

Scoring: Use the following scoring rubric to assess students' knowledge of weather.

Scoring rubric for weather activity

Points	Characteristics
0	Students did not perform any knowledge of weather.
1	Students performed an imitation of an existing song or poem.
2	Students performed an original piece, but knowledge of weather was lacking.
3	Students adequately performed a song or poem about weather that showed a conceptual understanding of the causes and/or types of weather.
4	Students expertly perfomed a song or poem about weather that demonstrated outstanding conceptual understanding of the causes and/or types of weather.

ACTIVITY 6.3 ■ Energy Quiz

Purpose: To assess energy knowledge

Type of Activity: Assessment (individual or group)

Materials: Poster board or newsprint for each student or group of students, magazines, felt tipped markers, scissors, glue, crayons, etc.

Student Directions: Create a bulletin board that displays your knowledge of energy. Be certain that the display includes a definition of energy and an array of the types of energy.

Scoring: Use the following scoring rubric to assess students' knowledge of energy.

Scoring rubric for energy activity

Points	Characteristics
0	Display shows no evidence of a knowledge of energy.
1	Students are able to operationally define energy.
2	Students are able to operationally define energy and show a knowledge of at least 3 types of energy.
3	Students are able to define energy and give examples with expertise.

ACTIVITY 6.4 ■ Insect Test

Type of Pictorial test
Activity:

Student (read orally to students)
Directions: Examine each picture. Place an X on each drawing that is *not* an insect
and explain your answer on the line below the drawing. On a separate
sheet of paper, explain your answers.

Pictorial testing

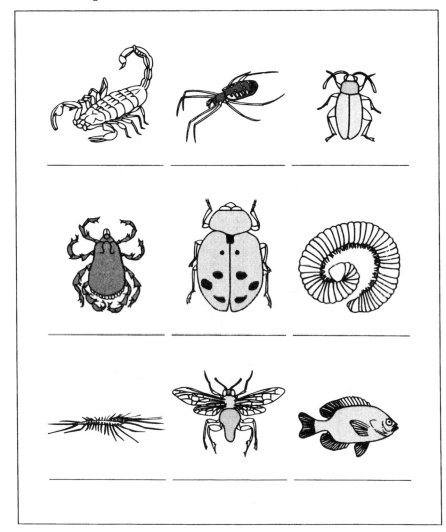

ACTIVITY 6.5   ■   Magnet Task

Type of Activity: Task test

Student Directions: (read orally to students)

Mario wanted to find out which of three magnets was the strongest. He had a bar magnet, a truck-shaped refrigerator magnet, and a U magnet. He found a jar of nails in the kitchen that his mother used to make repairs around the house. How could he use these materials to find out which magnet is the strongest?

Magnet task problem

 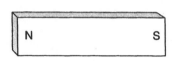 

CHAPTER SUMMARY

Classroom evaluation and assessment involve a consideration of what children know, what they will learn, how they will be exposed to new information, and what they have learned. Assessment of children's learning ought to be both formative and summative in nature, with children and teachers considering what children are learning as well as the final product of their learning. Additionally, assessment ought to consider affective and psychomotor outcomes as well as cognitive outcomes. Traditional pencil-and-paper assessment has focused on the cognitive domain, on conceptual learning. Learning may be expressed through multiple modes of knowledge representation. Authentic assessment, which involves multiple means of presenting learning, ought to be incorporated into all elementary science classrooms.

▨ TOPICS TO REVIEW

- ▬ Assessment
- ▬ Affective domain
- ▬ Cognitive domain
- ▬ Norm-referenced tests

- Criterion-referenced tests
- Self-referenced tests
- Authentic assessment tools
- Portfolio
- Concept map
- Task tests
- Journal writing

REFLECTIVE PRACTICE

1. Standardized tests have long been popular in public schools as tools for insuring accountability from the educational system. What are the benefits of using standardized tests? What problems are associated with the use of standardized tests? (Focus your response on the needs of culturally diverse children.)

2. In what ways is authentic assessment more relevant to the needs of culturally diverse children than traditional assessment tools?

3. If you were to use authentic assessment tools in your classroom, what types of public relations work might you need to do with parents before implementing them? Elaborate on your answer.

4. Assume you have been given the responsibility for developing a new report card for your school that would report to parents on the progress of their children. Based on what you have learned in this chapter, what might that report card look like? Explain your rationale.

5. Assume that you have just completed a unit of instruction on rocks and minerals. Design an assessment tool that will assess children's (1) attitudes toward the study of rocks and minerals, (2) ability to identify the characteristics of common minerals, and (3) knowledge of rocks and minerals.

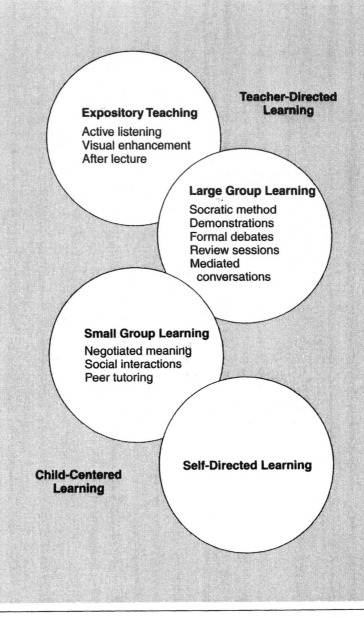

CHAPTER 7

Expository Teaching

Active listening
Visual enhancement
After lecture

Teacher-Directed Learning

Large Group Learning

Socratic method
Demonstrations
Formal debates
Review sessions
Mediated
    conversations

Small Group Learning

Negotiated meaning
Social interactions
Peer tutoring

Self-Directed Learning

Child-Centered Learning

Instructional Strategies for Culturally Diverse Learners

POINTS TO PONDER

- What are teaching strategies?
- What is meant by the expression "There's no one right way to teach anything"?
- Why do many teachers use a variety of instructional strategies throughout the day and the school year?

When my youngest son, Aáron, completed driver's education training and had received his first driver's license, his experience in learning to drive an automobile caused me to reflect on the many ways we learn in life. My son began driver's training by reading a book and memorizing the rules of the road. When he passed a written examination on driving, he began simulator training (sitting in a car seat chair in the classroom and watching a movie about driving). Next he advanced to the school's driving range where he practiced starting, stopping, braking, parallel parking, and a multitude of other non-traffic-related skills. Finally, he was issued a learner's permit and was permitted to drive on highways when accompanied by a licensed adult. In other words, he first acquired a strong declarative knowledge (i.e., knowledge that can be stated, or "head knowledge") of the rules of the road and then he began to acquire a procedural knowledge (a "how to" knowledge) of driving. Needless to say, it was many months before his parents allowed him to make his first solo flight.

I, on the other hand, can't remember a day when I didn't drive. As a toddler, I sat on my mother's or father's lap as they drove tractors from one field to another. I learned steering, shifting, and braking by emulating my parents. By age 5, I was given the responsibility of driving a tractor and wagon from the corn field to the house. I still remember my first solo trip. My father told me to drive the John Deere (a green tractor with yellow wheel rims) up to the house, disengage the hand clutch, step on the brake, and wait for my mother to come and get me. My mother came from the house quickly when she saw me. I still remember the discussion she had with my father about 5 year olds and tractor driving. As a teenager, I learned the rules of the road and acquired a driver's license. After driving a tractor, truck, and combine, I didn't consider driving a car much of a challenge. Unlike my son, I acquired a procedural knowledge of driving first; later I acquired a declarative knowledge of the rules of the road.

Some of us learn to drive by first reading about driving. Some of us learn to drive by first steering a moving vehicle. I am not valuing one method over the other, only pointing out that there are many ways to learn to drive or to learn to do anything in life. Sometimes one way is better than another, sometimes two ways are equally good, and sometimes one is worse. Teachers make decisions every day of their professional careers about teaching methods, about which method or strategy is best to teach children. This chapter is designed to introduce you to a variety of teaching strategies appropriate for use with culturally diverse learners in the elementary science classroom.

CHILDREN'S UNDERSTANDINGS

Children's understanding of the physical world grows naturally as a result of their ordinary interactions with adults and with other children. A knowledge of the world is constructed by each individual child within a social context, through social interactions with others. Learning in the multicultural classroom, indeed in all classrooms, should "begin and end with students. This means that the teacher's understanding of students should form the basis of all instruction" (Marshall, 1989, p. 60). Children are like natural scientists bent on making sense of the world (Elementary Grades Task Force, 1992, p. 12). Instructional activities should be selected by teachers to assist students to make sense of the world. While hands-on, experience-oriented activities conducted in heterogeneous, cooperative groups have been shown to be particularly effective with students of varied language backgrounds and achievement levels (Mechling & Oliver, 1983; National Research Council, 1996; Science Curriculum Framework and Criteria Committee, 1990), other instructional activities or strategies are highly effective and appropriate for the elementary science classroom. Most teachers use a variety of instructional strategies during each class period and throughout the school day.

Variety in Teaching Strategies

If a teacher desires to have students investigate the causal agents in a volcanic eruption, an inquiry approach to learning would probably not be appropriate. It is difficult to imagine finding a volcano where students could control the variables that lead to an eruption. Even if a teacher could find such a volcano, no one would care to have children randomly adjusting the pressure on the magma chamber or causing a volcano to erupt. In this instance, the teacher would need to provide a means for students to acquire a knowledge of volcanoes that does not involve hands-on manipulation of the real world object. Filmstrips, movies, textual passages, and multimedia computer programs could be used as data sources for children as they attempted to construct a knowledge of phenomena associated with volcanic eruptions. Volcanic eruptions and the atmospheric conditions on other planets in our solar system are topics more appropriately taught with expository than inquiry-based instructional strategies.

INSTRUCTIONAL STRATEGIES

Four clusters of instructional strategies are commonly used in elementary science classrooms: (1) self-directed activities, (2) small group negotiations, interactions, and peer tutoring, (3) large group verbal interactions, and (4) expository sessions. Expository instructional techniques are the most teacher-centered or teacher-directed pedagogical methods, and self-directed activities the most child centered. A continuum of instructional strategies is shown in Figure 7.1.

Self-directed Learning

Self-directed learning or individualized learning is most effective when it is child initiated rather than teacher initiated. A child working alone in the classroom completing a teacher-made ditto page is not an example of self-directed learning. Self-directed learning is self-motivated, the self-initiated act of a child who wants to explore a portion of the world alone. Teachers and parents can support and nurture this type of learning, but it should be controlled by the child, not mandated by an adult.

FIGURE 7.1 ■ Continuum of Instructional Strategies

Teacher centered			Child centered
Exposition	Large groups Mediated conversations	Small groups Peer tutoring, negotiation, and interactions	Self-directed learning

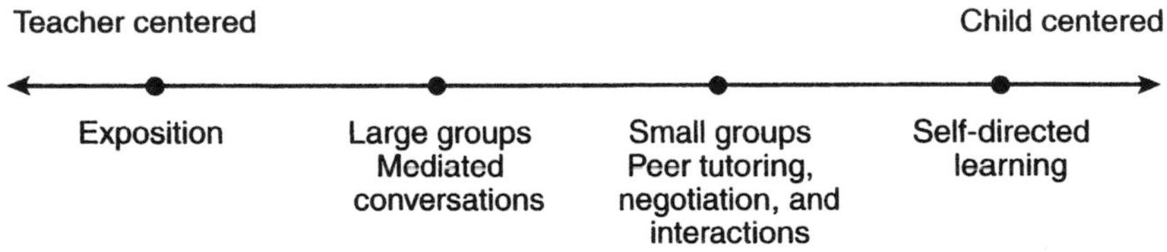

Elementary classrooms should contain the elements of interactive learning commonly found in good museums or libraries. Science classrooms for children should burst at the seams with things to do and things to learn. Niches, nooks, crannies, and corners of classrooms should literally bulge with "stuff" (e.g., library books, interactive bulletin boards, multimedia workstations, listening stations, mini museums filled with realia, and activity corners). Sometimes, elementary classrooms resemble adult workplaces, with rows of neat orderly workstations, professionally designed visual displays, and rigorously controlled supplies and materials. For self-directed learning to occur with children, there must be (1) time for self-initiated activities, (2) resource materials for individual learning, and (3) encouragement to pursue one's interests.

Time for self-initiated activities can be formally or informally provided by the teacher. Studies have shown that when "dead time" or transitional time (time between instructional activities or time between classes and recess, etc.) is eliminated from classrooms, student learning is increased. Physical resources in the form of library books, mini museums, interactive bulletin boards, computer software, and learning centers need to be provided in each classroom in order for students to engage in self-directed learning. Finally, teachers need to encourage students to continue learning after the formal instructional period has ended.

It is difficult to imagine that a third grader wouldn't want to learn more about dinosaurs, or that a first grader could avoid exploring the world with a magnet if given the opportunity. If students are to actively share with others what they have learned, they need the opportunity to develop individual expertise, to acquire new knowledge and insights they can share with others. Self-directed learning provides the opportunity for students to pursue their interests and to continue learning after the planned instructional activities have ended. Creativity, a sense of freedom to learn, a knowledge of science processes, and a feeling of success are the products of self-directed learning (Wolfinger, 1984).

Small Group Learning

Small groups or cooperative groups (discussed in more detail in Chapter 5) are environments in which negotiations, interactions, and peer tutoring provide support for the learning of each child. Groups may be viewed as an extension of the home environment of the child into the school environment. For many culturally diverse children, working in a group in the classroom closely resembles working with family members or with extended family groups that they have encountered in settings outside school. Group learning provides a culturally syntonic or culturally harmonious supporting environment for the child. In speaking of the primacy of group learning, Lev Vygotsky wrote, "Children can perform under guidance, in groups, and in collaboration with one another learning which they have not mastered independently" (1978, p. 87).

Students perform in groups work they can't do by themselves.

In a small group, children have the opportunity to try out their ideas within a supportive, nurturing environment. A group is a place of sharing, a place where individuals can externalize and share with other group members their understandings of their shared experience (Vygotsky, 1978, p. 132). Learning is a social process; children's knowledge of the world is derived from their social interactions with others. Children solve practical tasks with the help of their speech, as well as their eyes and hands (Vygotsky, 1978, p. 26). The use of speech in problem solving or in task completion implies group work, a sharing of possible solution paths with others. Speech is a social process, not an individual endeavor. Groups provide places where children can (1) negotiate meaning, (2) engage in social interactions, and (3) give and receive peer tutoring.

Negotiated Meaning

In a small group, children interact with peers in an attempt to make sense of the world. Group work fosters reflective learning and articulation. Within the social context of the small group, children should reflect on what they have learned and on the applications of that learning. Meaning for ideas and objects is achieved by the speaker and listeners through a process of collaboration and negotiation (Greeno, 1989, p. 51). The process of **semantic negotiation,** of using speech to make sense of the world, occurs as a collaborative act that is accomplished only when the speaker and listeners agree that something meaningful has been added to the collection of information that they share as common ground (Greeno, 1989, p. 51). An example of semantic negotiation or group collaboration to achieve meaning is shown in this scenario in which a group of second graders are attempting to apply what they know of the concept *fruit:*

> Tom: We're supposed to look at each picture and to decide if each one is a fruit. This first picture's a carrot. [Tom points to the picture while the rest of the group looks on.]
>
> Li: I think a carrot's a vegetable because my mother buys 'em in the vegetable section of the store.
>
> Wilma: Yeah, and when you cook 'em and eat 'em, they don't have any seeds inside.
>
> Felipe: The teacher said fruits are supposed to have seeds in 'em.
>
> Li: Yeah. That's right. Carrots are roots, they grow in dirt, they don't have any seeds.
>
> Tom: Carrots grow from seeds, but the stuff we eat doesn't got any seeds.
>
> Li: Fruits grow on trees.
>
> Felipe: Not all the time, tomatoes have seeds in 'em and they don't grow on a tree. My parents have a garden . . . I know that tomatoes don't grow on any old trees.
>
> Wilma: Well, some fruits grow on trees. Oranges and apples grow on trees. The teacher said they're fruits.
>
> Tom: The teacher said a fruit is supposed to be a package of seeds. I don't think the part of the carrot we eat's a fruit.
>
> Felipe: Yeah, that's right. This picture [Felipe points to the picture of the carrot] shows a root of the plant, not a fruit. Root, not a fruit. Hey, that rhymes.

During this conversation, the children added what they knew from personal experience, from their personal rendition of the concept *fruit.* They each contributed their interpretations of the information that the teacher provided them, and their own real world experiences with vegetables and fruits. Together they are forming a definition of the concept *fruit* through reflecting on their own learning and through articulating that knowledge.

Social Interactions

A second function of the small group environment is to provide social interactions for children. Within the small group, the child has the opportunity to (1) develop social interaction skills (e.g., active listening and responding), (2) build self-esteem, (3) develop efficacy in the use of the English language, and (4) learn leadership skills. The socialization of children is a primary, often unmentioned, goal of schooling. Small group instructional environments provide places for children to develop social skills.

In speaking of the social value of small group learning, Cohen (1984) states that learning curriculum content in a peer group is positively related to the frequency of interaction within the group, and that frequency of interaction is correlated with social status in the classroom. Cohen also points out that teachers sometimes need to intervene on behalf of some students to encourage their participation in group activities and to assist students by conferring status on them. She points out that when students are put in the position of using each other as resources for learning, status characteristics become salient and relevant to the social interaction (Cohen, 1984, p. 18). In the small group, the student has the opportunity to build self-confidence and self-esteem. Each child should be viewed by teacher and peers as a valuable part of the whole. Each child brings unique skills, talents, and abilities to a group, attributes that can enrich the learning of others and can enhance the performance of the total group.

Peer Tutoring

A third function of small group instructional settings is to provide an opportunity for peer tutoring. Educational literature has revealed that peer tutoring (1) improves students' academic performance, (2) improves students' attitudes toward the content area, (3) facilitates students' acquisition of English language proficiency, and (4) enhances students' acquisition of science processes. Both the tutor and tutee benefit from peer tutoring in the science classroom. Every child can function as a tutor or a tutee in a group, depending upon what is being taught and what is being learned.

Learning as an Apprenticeship

When small group work is used, the function of the teacher in the classroom changes. Teachers who rely on small groups as the primary environments for teaching and learning find that their responsibilities include modeling, coaching, scaffolding, articulation, and reflection (Garcia & Pearson, 1990). The teacher models behaviors and attitudes for students, such as the procedure for making a microscope slide or fostering a positive attitude toward recycling natural resources. As teachers move from one group to another in the classroom they engage in coaching, providing students with corrective feedback as well as encouragement to continue learning. Small group work requires that the teacher provide a framework or a scaffolding for students' learning. As students become adept at guiding their own learning and in reflecting on that learning, the responsibility for learning is transferred from the teacher to the students. Teachers need to articulate what is being said or read or verbalized to the class and to explain new ideas and concepts to students. The teacher should expound on students' responses and encourage students to apply what they are learning to new situations. Finally, teachers need to reflect on what students are learning and encourage students to engage in their own reflective learning activities. When teachers engage in modeling, coaching, scaffolding, articulation, and reflection they are using an apprenticeship model of teaching and learning (Garcia & Pearson, 1990). In this scenario, the teacher becomes the master learner and students become apprentices.

Learning as an apprenticeship

Large Group Interactions

Large group verbal interactions between teachers and students have long been recognized as appropriate pedagogical techniques in science instruction. Too frequently, what may be called large group discussions are actually lectures interspersed with review questions. In a true discussion, the students talk as much and preferably more than the teacher (Wolfinger, 1984, p. 211). Five types of large group verbal interactions are commonly used in elementary schools: (1) Socratic teaching, (2) demonstrations, (3) formal debates, (4) review sessions, and (5) mediated conversations. Socratic teaching and demonstrations are the most teacher-directed large group verbal interactions; mediated conversations are the most child-directed. Formal debates and review sessions allow for constrained interactions between teachers and students.

Socratic Method

In the Socratic teaching method, the teacher attempts to assist students to develop a simple concept through oral questioning. The teacher begins by asking a broad general question. The next question should begin to narrow the range of responses from the students and to focus the learners on the topic. Periodically, review statements are mixed with the questions in order to keep the salient points in the forefront of the discussion. The final question in the sequence should bring the students to the desired concept. A sample of a sequence of Socratic questions used in a fifth-grade classroom appears in Table 7.1.

While Socratic teaching is a large group discussion activity, it rarely produces a mediated learning environment. As the teacher begins the instruction, the desired end point is known and students are verbally "forced" to-

TABLE 7.1 ■ Script of Socratic Teaching

Teacher Question	Probable Student Answer
1. Has anyone ever seen a chicken or a picture of a chicken before?	1. (All hands are raised.)
2. What do chickens eat?	2. Worms, seeds, insects, corn, chicken feed
3. Yes, chickens eat a lot of different things, but what do they eat most of the time?	3. Mostly they eat grain or seeds from plants.
4. This is a gastrolith. It is a fossil. It came from a Stegosaurus, a plant-eating dinosaur. This fossil was found inside the rib cage of the Stegosaurus.	4. (Students examine gastrolith.)
5. What can you tell me about the gastrolith?	5. They're round. They're like stone balls. They are different colors. They are very smooth.
6. [Teacher summarizes what students have observed through manipulating the gastrolith.]	
7. Why do you suppose the Stegosaurus had gastroliths inside its rib cage?	7. Maybe they had something to do with eating?
8. How would round stones have something to do with eating?	8. Maybe it's like a chicken.
9. How do chickens eat differently from other animals?	9. Chickens have a gizzard.
10. What's a gizzard?	10. It's part of the digestive system used for grinding food.
11. Can you explain that a little more?	11. My grandmother raises chickens on her farm and she explained how baby chickens pick up pieces of gravel and they store them in their bodies.
12. Why would chickens store gravel in their bodies?	12. To grind up corn and other seeds.
13. How is this gastrolith from a Stegosaurus like the gravel in the chicken's gizzard?	13. The stegosaurus was a plant eater. Maybe it ground up food in a gizzard or a similar organ like the chicken grinds up corn and grain.
14. What is a gastrolith?	14. It's probably some stones in the Stegosaurus's stomach or gizzard that grind up food.
15. How did the stones get inside the Stegosaurus?	15. Maybe the Stegosaurus picked up the stones with its food.
16. Why are the stones round?	16. The grinding made them smooth, like a rock tumbler or something.
17. Would someone summarize what we have learned about gastroliths?	17. [Teacher calls on a student to summarize the discussion.]

ward that end point. Socratic teaching, while interactive, is a highly teacher-centered instructional technique. Reciprocal teaching, where teachers and students share learning with each other, typifies mediated conversations and is lacking in this instructional strategy.

Demonstrations

A demonstration is a large group activity in which some person (normally the teacher) stands before the class and shows or demonstrates something. Typically, a demonstration is followed by a period of student questions. Demonstrations are appropriately used in the science classroom when (1) there is a danger to students due to the use of chemicals or flammables, (2) a piece of science equipment is to be used for the first time, (3) a model is used as a visual enhancement device, and (4) a discrepant event is used as an advance organizer. In order for a demonstration to be effective, it must be visible to the entire class simultaneously and it must "work."

Safety is also vitally important in demonstrations. If the teacher is demonstrating an activity because it presents a hazard to students, proper precautions need to be taken to protect the audience during the demonstration. For example, some demonstrations need to be viewed outdoors to prevent students from inhaling smoke or fumes. At other times, especially with chemistry demonstrations, a safety shield should separate the viewers from the demonstration. Finally, the audience needs to be far enough away from the demonstration to prevent any risk of injury to the audience in case something goes wrong during the demonstration.

It has been jokingly said that "the only one who learns from a demonstration is the teacher." To preclude this result, the teacher needs to use the demonstration as a motivational device to interest and involve students in the scientific process. The teacher should gather the required materials and try out the demonstration ahead of time to be certain that the desired event does indeed happen. For a demonstration in the classroom, everything needs to be enlarged in order for students in the back of the room to see what is occurring. If a demonstration calls for a beaker of liquid, for example, the teacher should plan to use a large battery jar instead. Lengthy demonstrations in elementary science classrooms will produce only inattentiveness and restlessness rather than learning. Finally, demonstrations need to be accompanied by a question and answer period. Children should be engaged in the demonstration by being allowed to ask questions at its conclusion. Demonstrations can be highly effective large group instructional devices, but, as with salt, they are best used sparingly.

Formal Debates

The formal debate is a highly effective verbal teaching strategy rarely used in elementary classrooms. The best debates present controversial information. "Should oil drilling be allowed off the Delaware coast?" "Should genetic engineering be used to produce new animal species?" "Should government agencies set off mild earthquakes in fault zones to prevent the likelihood of large earthquakes?" "Should people be allowed to keep threatened animal species as household pets?" "Should nuclear waste from around the nation be stored in New Mexico?" Such questions lend themselves to formal debating in classrooms. The debate itself is the public presentation of what has been previously learned. The library research, organization of information, and preparation of opening statements are normally conducted in small groups prior to the formal presentation in a large group setting.

The following modifications of formal debating procedure seem to best meet the needs of elementary-aged children:

- Brief speech from the affirmative side;
- Brief speech from the negative side;
- Second speech from the affirmative side that rebuts the statements of the negative side;
- Second speech from the negative side that rebuts the statements of the affirmative side;
- Short period of questions for both sides from the audience;
- Summary by the affirmative side captain; and
- Summary by the negative side captain.

Formal debating is appropriate for use with culturally diverse learners only when all students are encouraged to participate in the process. Every child can contribute to the data gathering and organizing efforts of the team. Many students who have difficulty expressing themselves in written language find the oral medium of debating comfortable. Debating also provides an opportunity for students to develop oral communication skills within the science content area.

Review Sessions

Reviewing prior knowledge or new learning is a highly effective use of the large group instructional environment. In a review situation, the teacher asks a series of questions that provides students with the opportunity to verbalize what they have learned. Review questions may be convergent or divergent in nature. In **convergent questioning,** the teacher attempts to focus the child on a single answer, to encourage the child to reproduce what has been previously stated in class. When **divergent questioning** is used, the student is encouraged to combine background knowledge with new information to generate a creative or novel way of looking at things.

Traditionally, large group question-and-answer periods have been plagued by three categories of problems: (1) rapid-fire questioning rates, (2) selective disengagement of some students, and (3) a preponderance of low-knowledge-level questions. Each of these difficulties can be addressed by careful planning on the part of the teacher. First, teachers need to be sure that they allow students time to process information, perhaps engaging in wait time before accepting answers from the class. Second, teachers need to include all students in the activity and to eliminate "target" students whenever possible. Finally, teachers need to distribute questions across a range of knowledge levels.

Wait Time.   Research has shown that teachers using large group discussion techniques typically ask as many as 150 questions during the average class period (Melnik, 1968). When question-and-answer periods are used as an instructional technique, teachers tend to ask low-level-knowledge questions in rapid-fire order (Rowe, 1974a, 1974b). For many children, the science classroom resembles a television game show in which the objective is to score points with the teacher by playing a live version of Trivial Pursuit. Children who may be embarrassed by their lack of English proficiency and children who are unused to performing in front of a large group find this a very uncomfortable environment. When low-order-knowledge questions become the focus of instruction, students are encouraged to memorize facts, to engage in shallow information processing. This type of question asking and student responding precludes effective use of discussion sessions that emphasize reflective thinking and inquiry (Collette & Chiappetta, 1989, p. 209).

When question-and-answer periods are used as instructional devices, teachers should strive to ask open-ended questions, questions that encourage divergent thinking on the part of students. Rowe (1974a, 1974b) proposed that teachers should pause and wait 3 to 5 seconds after asking an open-ended question. This pause after a question is asked is referred to as **wait time.** The use of wait time by the teacher gives students an opportunity to think, to reflect, and to formulate an answer. Research has shown that the use of wait time by the teacher (1) increases the length of student responses, (2) decreases the failure of students to respond, (3) increases the number of unsolicited but appropriate responses, (4) changes the number and type of questions asked by the teacher, (5) improves the performance of "slow" students, (6) increases students' confidence in their answers, (7) increases the variety and type of students' verbal responses, (8) increases the students' incidence of comparing their findings with others, (9) increases the number of questions that students ask, (10) produces a higher incidence of speculative responses, and (11) results in a higher incidence of evidence-inference statements by students (Atwood & Wilen, 1991; Riley, 1986; Rowe, 1974a, 1974b, 1983; Tobin & Capie, 1981). Tobin (1984) states that wait time improves the quality of the learning environment and increases achievement in subjects such as mathematics and science, where higher cognitive-level outcomes are often a concern.

The active use of wait time during question-and-answer periods benefits all students. When wait time is used in the classroom, students listen to one another, rather than listening for the next question; this reinforces the self-worth of each child and tends to build self esteem. By allowing children time to formulate answers to questions, teachers who use wait time are encouraging children to activate their existing mental structures and are providing the opportunity for children to mentally translate information stored in their home language into school language. The use of wait time allows children time to evaluate the quality of their answers, to build confidence in their ability to respond to questions. Wait time is a vital tool in encouraging the participation of culturally diverse learners in large group verbal interactions.

Target Students. The interaction of the teacher and the student with the curriculum is the heart of the educational process. Research has shown students do not interact equally with their teachers in the classroom (Barba & Cardinale, 1991; Parakh, 1967; Tobin & Gallagher, 1987). Tobin and Gallagher (1987) reported that in nearly every classroom there are three to seven "salient" students who tend to monopolize or control student interactions. Parakh (1967) reported that high-ability or highly verbal students tended to interact with their teachers more often than did low-verbal students. According to Tobin and Gallagher (1987) and Barba and Cardinale (1991) target students—those who engage in frequent verbal interactions with their teachers—generally tend to be assertive white European males, rather than white females or culturally diverse learners. The following trends have emerged, according to the research on teachers' targeting behaviors (Connery, 1990; Gallagher & Tobin, 1987; Gooding, Kephart, Swift, Swift, & Schell, 1990; Okebukola & Ogunniyi, 1986; Tobin & Gallagher, 1987):

- Most teachers tend to direct questions at random to the whole class, behavior that favors those who raise their hands and those who call out responses;
- Teachers feel that students who raise their hands probably know the answer and deserve to be recognized;
- Teachers occasionally attempt to call on students who do not raise their hands, but not in a concerted manner;
- Teachers generally ask low-level questions and random but direct high-level questions to those whom they perceive to be more capable;
- Teachers generally "target" students because they feel that these students will facilitate learning and content coverage;
- Target students generally receive better feedback from their teachers; and
- Some target students are teacher selected, while others self-select to become target students.

In assessing the effect of teachers' targeting behaviors, Barba and Cardinale (1991) point out that nontarget students have fewer interactions with their teachers and thus receive less attention in the classroom. Over time, nontargeted students may feel that the teacher avoids them because they are less capable than other students. Systematic disengagement of students during classroom verbal interactions results in a situation in which some students feel that they do not have meaningful information to contribute to the class. For white females and culturally diverse students, the lack of interaction with their teacher during science instruction may lead them to feel that they have low ability in sciences, and they may remove themselves mentally from the study of science and from science careers. When using large group verbal interaction teaching techniques, teachers need to equitably distribute questions across the class in order to avoid such targeting behaviors.

Levels of Questioning.   Educational journals and trade magazines frequently run articles that exalt the use of "higher-order" thinking skills, while degrading the use of "low-level" thinking skills. One criticism of large group verbal interactions is that this environment fosters "low-level" learning. The terms *low level* and *high level* generally refer to Bloom's (1956) taxonomy of the cognitive domain. Research has shown that during verbal interactions, teachers tend to rely heavily on questions at the knowledge and comprehension levels of Bloom's taxonomy while avoiding questions at the application, analysis, synthesis, and evaluation levels (Barba & Cardinale, 1991; Melnik, 1968; Parakh, 1967; Riley, 1986; Rowe, 1983; Tobin, 1984).

In his taxonomy of the cognitive domain, Bloom (1956) asserted that cognitive knowledge could be classified as being at the knowledge, comprehension, application, analysis, synthesis, or evaluation level. The knowledge level includes factual information that the student recognizes or recalls. At the comprehension level the student understands the information. Application refers to the students' ability to use scientific knowledge in a new situation. Using cognitive knowledge at the analysis level involves the ability to break information into component parts. When students function at the synthesis level, they are, according to Bloom, able to put information together to form a new whole. Finally, at the evaluation level, students are able to develop criteria and to judge the relative worth or merit of ideas, solutions, and methods. A summary of each level of Bloom's taxonomy appears in Table 7.2.

Mediated Conversations

Among all large group instructional techniques, the mediated conversation is the most productive in terms of students' learning. In a mediated conversation, teachers and students teach each other and learn from each other. The teacher should serve as a mediator whose job it is to assist students in examining their mental constructions and to guide them as they engage in cognitive restructuring. Through questioning, the teacher redirects, guides, channels, and in general assists the students in accommodating new information so that their internal mental structures are more consistent with empirical data about the external world. A constructivist learning model modified from the works of Saunders (1992, p. 139) is presented in Figure 7.2.

FIGURE 7.2 ■ A Model for Constructing Knowledge

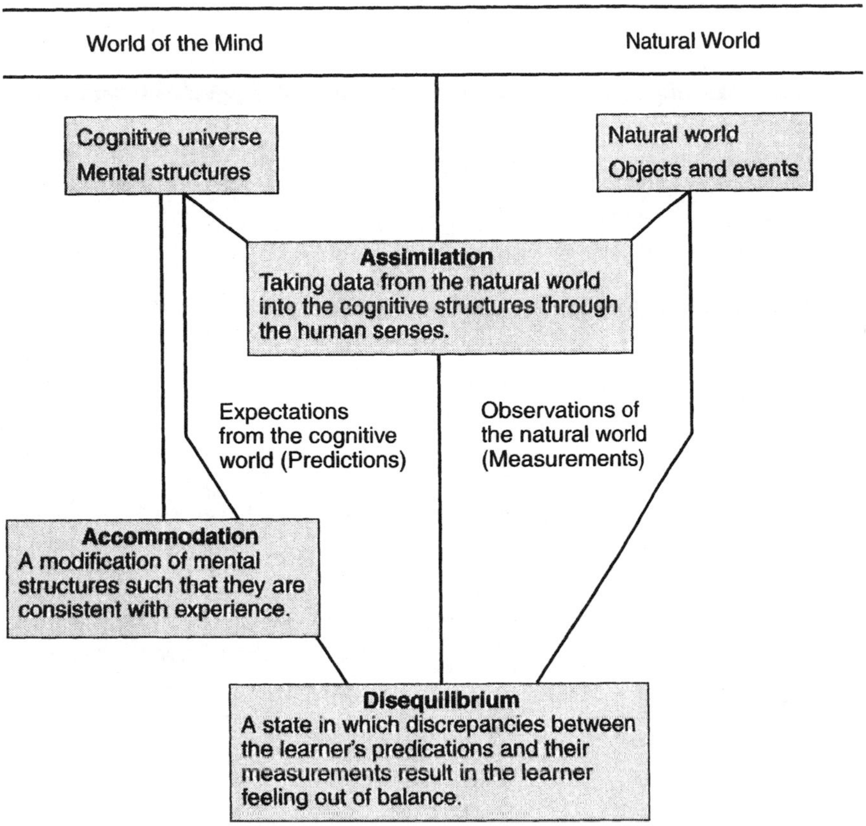

World of the Mind	Natural World

Cognitive universe
Mental structures

Natural world
Objects and events

Assimilation
Taking data from the natural world into the cognitive structures through the human senses.

Expectations from the cognitive world (Predictions)

Observations of the natural world (Measurements)

Accommodation
A modification of mental structures such that they are consistent with experience.

Disequilibrium
A state in which discrepancies between the learner's predications and their measurements result in the learner feeling out of balance.

In this constructivist model of learning, assimilation occurs when students take data through their sensory organs into the existing cognitive structures. If these data do not "fit" with the existing mental structures, a state of cognitive dissonance or disequilibrium develops within the learner. In science education we sometimes refer to the event that causes cognitive dissonance as a **discrepant event.** For example, all of us are familiar with the properties of rocks and minerals. If we were to see someone pick up a rock and struggle to heave it into a pond or lake, we would expect the rock to sink. If that rock floated, we might be hard-pressed to explain why. Unless we had a prior knowledge of pumice, a rock normally lighter than water, we would not be able to accommodate this new information. We would be in a state of disequilibrium. After a period of playing with pumice, of manipulating it and determining that indeed it is a very lightweight rock, we would be able to accommodate this new knowledge. We would restructure our existing schemata to accommodate the fact that this one rock floats, that it is less dense than water.

TABLE 7.2 ■ Bloom's Taxonomy with Levels of Questions

Descriptors	Appropriate Questioning Verbs		Sample Activities or Questions

Knowledge *Definition:* to recall or to know

- Lowest level of learning
- Remember terms, facts, concepts, or methods
- Recall information
- Bring to mind stored knowledge
- Remember previously learned material
- Recite learned information
- List previously learned information
- Remember stored knowledge

Arrange
Ask
Check
Choose
Cite
Define
Describe
Label
List
Match
Name
Outline
Pick
Point out

Quote
Recall
Recite
Repeat
Say
Select
Show
Spell
State
Tell
Touch
Underline
Write

- Label the parts of an insect.
- Write the definitions for the words.
- Locate the parts of the animal cell.
- Write the symbols for the elements.
- List the names of the birds.
- Group the minerals by color.
- Locate biomes on the map.
- Name the parts of the microscope.
- Label the parts of the flower.

Comprehension *Definition:* to understand or explain

- Interpret charts and graphs
- Grasp the meaning of new material
- Predict consequences
- Interpret material
- Estimate future trends
- See relationships among things
- Understand facts and principles
- Project effects of ideas
- Summarize material
- Communicate in a new way
- Explain ideas

Alter
Annotate
Calculate
Change
Construe
Convert
Define
  operationally
Demonstrate
Expand
Explain
Moderate
Offer
Project

Propose
Qualify
Spell out
Submit
Transform
Translate
Vary

- Summarize the reading.
- Give reasons for the dinosaurs becoming extinct.
- Explain why we have lab safety rules.
- What factors contributed to the scientific revolution?
- Restate the reasons for climatic changes on the earth.
- Interpret the line graph showing the heating of the liquid.
- Outline the steps in preparing a "wet" mount.

Application *Definition:* to use ideas

- Requires higher levels of understanding than comprehension
- Make use of knowledge
- Apply concepts to new situations
- Apply scientific principles in a real world situation.
- Demonstrate correct use of a procedure or method
- Construct graphs and charts
- Solve mathematical problems

Adopt
Apply
Avail
Classify
Collect
Construct
Employ
Exercise
Manip-
  ulate
Operate

Organize
Profit by
Put in
  action
Put to use
Relate
Solve
Try
Use
Wield

- How do you use simple machines at home?
- Put this information in a bar graph.
- Organize the survival gear from most needed to least needed.
- Plan posters, skits, and activities that will promote a recycling ethic in your peers.
- Sketch a mural that relates your feelings about the environment.

Descriptors	Appropriate Questioning Verbs		Sample Activities or Questions

Analysis   *Definition:* to break down into component parts

- Break into components
- Understand the organizational structure
- Analyze the elements
- Analyze relationships between parts
- Understand content and form
- Recognize principles involved

Audit
Break-
 down
Deduce
Diagram
Differen-
 tiate
Dissect
Divide
Examine
Include
Inspect
Look into

Reason
Screen
Search
Section
Separate
Sift
Simplify
Study
Subdivide
Survey
Take apart
Test for
Uncover

- Compare and contrast plants and animals.
- Identify the problems associated with nuclear waste materials.
- Uncover the unique characteristics of horseshoe crabs.
- Examine a toy and identify the simple machines you find in it.
- Compare and contrast lava and magma.
- Examine a cartoon and identify the scientific errors you find.

Synthesis   *Definition:* to form a new whole

- Take something apart and pattern it in a new way
- Put parts together in a new whole
- Create new and original things
- Work with abstract relationships
- Communicate an idea in a new way
- Tell a personal experience effectively

Build
Cause
Combine
Compile
Compose
Conceive
Construct
Create
Design
Develop
Effect
Evolve

Formulate
Generate
Make
Mature
Modify
Originate
Plan
Produce
Rearrange
Reorganize
Revise
Structure

- Formulate a scheme for classifying wildflowers from your neighborhood.
- Develop a plan for schoolwide recycling.
- Using straight pins and soda straws construct a bridge that will hold at least 500 grams of mass.
- Create a rap song to tell others about the elements of the periodic table.
- Write a theme describing how you would invent a new robot to help with your schoolwork.

Evaluation   *Definition:* to judge or critique

- Highest level of learning
- Ability to judge the value of material
- Ability to indicate logical fallacies in arguments
- Use of a definite criteria for evaluations
- Value judgments based on a defined criterion

Appraise
Arbitrate
Assay
Classify
Conclude
Criticize
Decide
Determine
Discri-
 minate
Evaluate

Grade
Judge
Justify
Prioritize
Rank
Rate
Referee
Rule on
Umpire
Weigh

- Summarize what you have learned this year.
- Rank the list of scientific discoveries in order of importance to you.
- Decide which solution to the problem is best and why.
- Determine the criteria for a "good" paper airplane and justify your selection criteria.
- Read two different accounts of the "discovery" of DNA, decide which is most accurate, and tell why.
- Judge your peers' science fair displays, decide which is best, and give rational for your decision.

One job of the teacher is to help students restructure their schemata so that their interpretations of the natural world are more in accord with those of the community of scientists and not homegrown conceptions or misconceptions about the world. Verbal interactions between students and teachers are a medium for this restructuring process.

Just as the teacher guides and directs the students, students guide and direct their teacher. Through the questions that they ask and through the statements that they make, students communicate to the teacher their level of understanding of scientific knowledge. Unfortunately, teachers are not always good listeners; they do not always attend to what students say about their levels of understanding. The following conversation illustrates this point:

Ms. Chan: We have just finished looking at some insects. We've written a list of insect characteristics on the board. Would someone review for us the characteristics of insects? . . . [The teacher uses wait time.] . . . Carlos?

Carlos: Insects have six legs, three body parts, and some of them got wings.

Ms. Chan: Good, Carlos, that's a very good beginning. Did anyone else find some characteristics that all of the insects seemed to have in common? [The teacher again uses wait time.] . . . Yes, Lisa, what did you want to add?

Lisa: Our group collected a spider. It was real yucky. When we were outside, our group noticed that insects are animals. They move from one place to another. Some of them walked and some ran.

Ms. Chan: That's right. Lisa has just told us that insects are animals, that they move from place to place. What else do we know about insects? . . . [The teacher pauses.] . . . Tim?

Ms. Chan missed a "teachable moment," the opportunity to assist Lisa and others in the class in restructuring their knowledge of insects. In this conversation, Lisa mentioned that a spider was an insect, Ms. Chan complimented Lisa on knowing that insects were animals, but she neglected to notice that Lisa had included spiders in the same group as insects. Many students in the class probably shared the same mental image of insects that Lisa did, that is, that insects are "small animals." Ms. Chan should have allowed Lisa and her classmates the opportunity to count the number of legs on several insects and then to count the number of legs on a spider. Had she done this, Lisa and her classmates would have been faced with a dilemma: Insects have six legs, and spiders have eight legs. Being placed in a state of cognitive dissonance or disequilibrium would have allowed Lisa and her peers the opportunity to accommodate new knowledge. One role of the teacher is to assist students to alter their schemata to bring their predictions or expectations more in line with their observations of the natural world.

A mediated conversation is a class meeting. In this large group setting, the principles of modeling, coaching, scaffolding, articulating, and reflecting are practiced by students and their teacher. Large group instructional environments should be places where students and teachers (1) develop plans to explore the natural world, (2) share their findings regarding phenomena, objects, and events in that world, (3) wrestle with explanations and interpretations of data, and (4) attempt to make sense of the world around them.

Exposition

Exposition or expository instructional strategies may be operationally defined as those in which some authority (e.g., teachers, textbooks, computer programs, CD-ROM disks, laser disks, filmstrips, or videotapes) presents oral and/or written information to students without active verbal interactions occurring between the students and the authority figure. Although extensive use of exposition is not recommended with elementary-aged children, expository instructional techniques certainly have a place in the multicultural science classroom. However, Hunter reminds us that often "telling is not teaching" (1982, p. 33).

Long, monotonous lectures devoid of visual enhancement are not an appropriate pedagogical strategy for use with young children. But sometimes telling *is* teaching. Speaking frankly and succinctly to the subject is a highly effective instructional technique in certain instances. If you wish to train young children in behaviors appropriate for use in emergency situations, then expository teaching is best. In an earthquake, for instance, students should be taught to "duck, cover, and hold." When crossing the street children should remember that they are to "stop, look, and listen." On a field trip to a state or national forest, students should be encouraged to "hug a tree" and wait there until help arrives if they get separated from the rest of their group. Direction giving is one very appropriate use for exposition.

In the past when expository instructional techniques have been used in the classroom, the teacher has been viewed as the controller of knowledge, the person who transmits knowledge to students who are blank slates and must therefore be attentive and quiet. This view of teaching and learning is based on objectivist epistemological precepts that view knowledge as a truth to which humans have access. From this viewpoint, the function of the teacher in the classroom is to "teach" this truth or knowledge to children. The teacher from this perspective dispenses knowledge and structures the learning environment to maximize the learning of the children. In writing about expository instructional strategies, Vygotsky (1978) stated that the mere exposure of students to new materials through oral lectures allows for neither adult guidance nor collaboration with peers.

Extended use of expository instructional techniques is usually viewed as inappropriate with elementary-aged children in the science classroom because (1) verbal presentations are difficult for children to understand, (2) children have a limited attention span and thus tend to become restless,

(3) children tend to be passive learners when expository techniques are used, and (4) what is said is not always what is heard or what is interpreted (Wolfinger, 1984). Additionally, children are typically not coached in schools to assimilate and accommodate information presented orally and/or in writing.

For culturally diverse learners, expository teaching techniques pose a set of problems related to the way that such children have been taught to interact or work in small cooperative groups or in extended family settings. For these children, sitting silently in a large group, facing front, and not interacting with peers while attending to the words of one adult is a highly unpleasant and culturally unfamiliar experience. Frequently, teachers build an invisible wall between themselves and their students when they lecture. They sometimes pace the perimeter of the classroom or stand at a lectern, physically removing themselves from the children in the classroom. Sometimes children perceive these teacher actions as hostile and conclude that the teacher doesn't like them or care about them. Learning is difficult when children view the classroom as a hostile environment. Making expository instructional periods user friendly for culturally diverse students can be accomplished by (1) increasing the level of student interactivity through notetaking and active-listening activities, (2) using multiple modes of knowledge representation or visual enhancement, (3) conducting short, concise lecture periods, and (4) using small groups after lectures to summarize points.

Active Listening and Interacting.   Lectures, filmstrips, laser disks, textbooks, videos, and computer software are all appropriate for use in the classroom, especially for providing background information on a particular topic (e.g., the volcano example used earlier in this chapter). Expository instructional techniques are excellent for providing students with access to science content knowledge they cannot easily derive through inquiry-based instruction. However, expository techniques need to include elements of active participation for students to receive their full benefit. In coaching elementary-aged children to attend to what is being said, the teacher may wish to design the focusing questions ahead of time, as guideposts to facilitate students' listening and processing skills. Studies have shown that students benefit from expository presentations only when they actively listen, process what they have heard, and write down words or phrases that will activate their mental structures at a later time (Anderson & Armbruster, 1986; Lazarus, 1991; Peper & Mayer, 1986).

Visual Enhancement.   When expository teaching techniques are used with elementary-aged children, especially with those culturally diverse children who may have difficulty acquiring meaning from spoken or written words, visual enhancement is especially appropriate. When students represent their knowledge during problem-solving situations, they use real world objects (or realia), spoken words, written words, pictures, and icons (Lesh, Landau, &

FIGURE 7.3 ■ Modes of Knowledge Representation

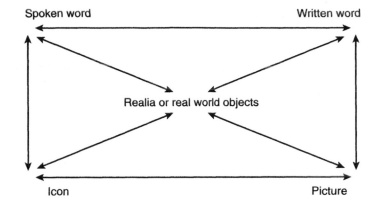

Hamilton, 1983). These modes of knowledge representation may be used effectively to present information to children (see Figure 7.3).

Since icons, realia, and pictures are not language dependent, their use in the multicultural classroom profits limited English proficient students who have not yet mastered the English language. Icons, real world objects, and pictures serve to activate a student's prior knowledge, knowledge that sometimes was constructed in the students "home language" or native tongue. Research has shown that multiple means of knowledge representation proportionally profit students who have difficulty obtaining meaning from printed words; that is, students who are not "high-verbal" learners in English (Allen, 1975; Conway, 1968; Dwyer, 1978; Levie & Levie, 1975; Severin, 1967; Sless, 1983). Teachers who use slides, transparencies, photographs, drawings, and diagrams to enhance their verbal presentations are attending to the linguistic needs of multicultural students.

Concise Lecture Periods. Periods of expository teaching need to be short and sweet. Elementary teachers should remember that children at this age level are able to attend to verbal presentations for only 10 to 15 minutes.

Students should know in advance what they are expected to learn from the presentation. A highly appropriate way to begin a lecture is to use an advance organizer (Ausubel, 1963), a verbal device that provides relevant introductory information. Advance organizers help students explain, integrate, and interrelate prior learning with new knowledge. Short stories, analogies, and questions may be used as advance organizers. Advance organizers may be comparative or expository in nature. A teacher beginning a unit of study on wildflowers, for example, may say, "Do you remember when we learned to group or classify insects? Today we are going to begin to learn about grouping wildflowers." A comparative organizer relates new learning to previous knowledge, to familiar experiences. Expository organizers inform learners of what is to be learned, knowledge with which they are unfamiliar. When introducing a unit of study on monerans, the teacher could say, "Today we are going to begin to study monerans. The name *moneran* refers to bacteria, tiny single-celled living things." With this statement the teacher is informing the students of what is to be learned and is assisting students to identify the salient information that will be presented during the lecture.

Following the introduction of the subject, the teacher should move to the body of the lecture. Here information should be presented in a clear, concise fashion. The attention span of children is far shorter than that of adults, so lengthy expository presentations are inappropriate for young children. Children tend to remember best what they hear at the beginning and at the end of the expository presentations, least what is said in the middle. We refer to this as *primacy* and *recency*.

When providing information on a new concept, the teacher should (1) identify the critical attributes, (2) select examples from the students' own lives whenever possible, (3) provide examples that may be less than ideal but still present the appropriate characteristics, and (4) provide unusual examples (Hunter, 1982; Wolfinger, 1984). A teacher who wanted to teach the concept *mammal* to students in an expository manner should begin by stating the critical attributes: "A mammal is a warm-blooded animal whose body is covered more or less with fur. Mammals have milk glands to nourish their young, a diaphragm used in respiration, and a four-chambered heart." Next the teacher would provide examples of mammals from the lives of students: "Cats, dogs, and people are examples of mammals that you are familiar with." In reinforcing the concept, the teacher would provide additional examples of mammals more removed from the students' direct experiences: "Cows, monkeys, horses, deer, and pigs are also mammals." Finally, the teacher would provide little-known examples of mammals: "The bat is a mammal. Even though it flies, it is a mammal and not a bird. The bat has hair rather than fur on its body. It provides milk to its young. The whale is also a mammal. The whale lives in water and looks like a fish, but it is really a mammal. The whale's body does not have scales like a fish. It feeds its young milk from its own body." Visual enhancement through photographs, slides, and transparencies is vital in expository teaching. Each example of a mammal mentioned by the teacher should be accompanied by a pictorial, iconic, written, or real world representation of the organism. During the conclusion of the lecture, the teacher should reiterate the main points and ask students to reflect on what they have just learned.

Instructional Strategies and the Standards

The framers of the *National Science Education Standards* (National Research Council, 1996) have written about the changing instructional paradigm in terms of what science education used to look like in the classroom and what instructional practice should be (see Table 7.3).

TABLE 7.3 ■ National Science Education Standards Recommendations

Less Emphasis On	More Emphasis On
■ Expository teaching methods	■ Inquiry-based teaching models
■ Lecture and reading about science	■ Investigation and inquiry
■ Separation of scientific and pedagogical knowledge	■ Integration of scientific and pedagogical knowledge
■ Individual learning	■ Group learning and collaboration
■ Separation of theory and practice	■ Integration of theory and practice in school settings
■ Teacher as technician	■ Teacher as reflective practitioner
■ Teacher as consumer of knowledge about teaching and learning	■ Teacher as generator of knowledge about teaching and learning

CLASSROOM PRACTICE

As a teacher, part of your job is to determine the best instructional strategies for meeting the needs of your students. There are times when you will find expository teaching to be the most appropriate method. Sometimes, you may find that students will learn best in a small group setting. At other times, you will want to engage your students in a mediated conversation. Finally, there will be times when you will want to help students engage in self-directed learning, extending what they have previously learned. The decision as to which instructional strategy is appropriate is one that you will make many times a day, depending upon (1) the content knowledge to be mastered by the students, (2) the characteristics of your students, and (3) your purpose in teaching a particular concept or body of knowledge.

Fostering self-directed learning in students is perhaps the most difficult task that teachers face. This section focuses on the development of an activity corner designed to provide resources that invite students to engage in self-directed learning. Many times it is difficult to determine what will excite students, what will turn them on to learning.

Nearly all parents share the experience of carefully selecting a holiday or birthday gift for their child, only to find the child unappreciative of it. The parents have spent endless hours shopping for an age-appropriate toy that will actively engage the young child in meaningful play only to find that the child prefers to play with the wrapping paper or the box. The same phenomenon occurs in classrooms; what teachers find engaging and interesting, students sometimes find dull and boring.

"Pogo sticking" with a purpose or exploring one thing after another on your own is the heart of self-directed learning. One vehicle for self-directed learning is an activity corner, which ought to be a place where students can continue learning begun in a larger class setting, a place where alone, or together with one or two others, students can pursue their interests. Activity corners should be stocked with materials that elicit curiosity in children, such as computer workstations, microscopes, library books on the current topic of study, filmstrip-viewing stations, a mini museum (displays of child-collected realia), and individual learning kits or shoeboxes.

Individual learning kits or shoebox science activities are normally teacher-made learning activities that children can do on their own. Several shoebox science activities are provided here as examples of the types of materials that can be used with students.

ACTIVITY 7.1   ■   Floaters and Sinkers

Grade Level:	Primary
Purpose:	To observe, classify, collect data, interpret data
Type of Activity:	Motivational (small group)
Science Concept:	Some objects float and others sink.
Materials:	(list taped to the lid of the shoebox) Cotton ball, penny, soda straw, small piece of paper, button, popsicle stick, Ping-Pong ball, plastic cup
Teacher Preparation:	Assemble the materials and place them in the shoebox.
Student Directions:	(included in the shoebox) 1. Make sure that all the materials are in the shoebox. 2. Fill your cup 2/3 full of water. 3. Pick up one object and place it in the water. 4. Does it float or sink? 5. Draw the object on the correct column of the data sheet. 6. Repeat for each object.

Float or sink?   Sink   Float

Data sheet for "Float or Sink?"

Directions: Draw each object in the correct column.

Floater   *Sinker*

ACTIVITY 7.2 ■ **Fishing with Magnets**

Grade Level: Primary or intermediate

Purpose: To observe, classify, infer, predict, collect, and interpret data

Type of Activity: Self-directed

Science Concept: Some materials (e.g., those made of iron or steel) are attracted to a magnet.

Materials: (list taped to the lid of the shoebox)
Twenty to thirty pieces of "junk" (e.g., marble, staples, paper clip, erasers), ruler, string, magnet, plastic tray

Teacher Preparation: Assemble the materials and place them in the shoebox.

Student Directions: (included in the shoebox)
1. Assemble a fishing pole by tying the magnet to the string and attaching it to the end of the ruler.
2. Make a fishing hole by placing the assorted items in the plastic tray.
3. Catch the objects from the fishing hole. Write the name of each object that is attracted to the magnet on one side of the data sheet and the names of the objects left behind on the other.

Magnet data sheet

Attracted to the Lure (Magnet)	*Not Attracted to the Lure (Magnet)*

ACTIVITY 7.3 ■ **Heartbeats**

Grade Level:	Upper elementary
Purpose:	To observe, use numbers, and record, interpret, and graph data
Type of Activity:	Motivational (small group)
Science Concept:	Variables such as the type of exercise affect heart rate.
Materials:	(list taped to the lid of the shoebox) stopwatch, graph paper
Teacher Preparation:	Assemble the materials and place them in the shoebox.
Student Directions:	(to be included in the shoebox)

1. Rest for one minute. To find your pulse, place two fingers on your neck under your chin. Move your fingers carefully, pressing gently on your neck until you feel your pulse. Count the number of beats of your heart for one minute. Record your heart rate on the data sheet.

Heart rate data sheet

Activity	Heart Rate (Beats/Minute)
Resting	
Jumping rope	
Jogging	
Lying down	

2. Jump rope for two minutes. Now determine your heart rate. Record your results on the data sheet.
3. Jog in place for two minutes. Determine your heart rate. Record your results on the data sheet.
4. Lie down for two minutes. Record your heart rate.
5. Make a bar graph of your results.
6. What happens to your heart rate as you exercise?

CHAPTER SUMMARY

In this chapter, four clusters of instructional strategies were discussed: (1) self-directed learning, (2) small group interactions, (3) large group instruction, and (4) expository teaching. Expository teaching techniques are the most teacher centered; self-directed teaching strategies are the most child centered. In all four clusters of teaching strategies mentioned in this chapter, the role of the teacher is to assist children in exploring the natural world. Teachers assist children by modeling, coaching, scaffolding, articulating, and reflecting on learning and how to learn. The choice of an appropriate instructional strategy is situational: It depends on what is to be learned, the characteristics of the learners, and the teachers' understanding of their students and the ways that they learn.

 TOPICS TO REVIEW

- Self-directed learning
- Small group learning
- Large group learning
- Expository teaching

 REFLECTIVE PRACTICE

1. Explain what is meant by the concept "appropriate use" of instructional strategies. In other words, when might a particular teaching strategy be appropriate? Inappropriate?

2. Many authors state that knowledge is "constructed within a sociocultural context." Having read this chapter, what does this expression mean to you?

3. Identify some reasons why social skills are important in science learning. Explain your reasons.

4. Reflecting on your own skills and competencies, which teaching "jobs" or functions are you most comfortable with? Least comfortable with? In which teaching roles do you have the most expertise? In which teaching roles do you need to develop expertise?

CHAPTER 8

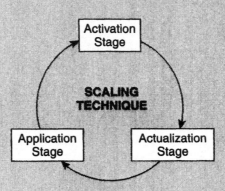

Constructing a Knowledge of Science and Language

 POINTS TO PONDER

- How do language and hands-on experiences help children build a knowledge of science concepts?
- How should science instruction be modified to accommodate the needs of limited English proficient children?
- In what ways is science like children's play?

In San Diego, California, Ms. Gonzales's 31 third graders enter their classroom after recess to find two sizes of soda straws (one with a larger diameter than the other) and a slice of raw potato on their tables. Ms. Gonzales begins class: "While you were at recess, I placed straws and potato slices on your tables. Today we are going to make potato pistols. To make the pistol, place your thumb over the end of the large straw and press it into the raw potato." Ms. Gonzales waits while the students repeat the action. "Now pull the straw out of the potato and turn it upside down. Then put your thumb over the other end of the straw and insert it into the potato. You should have a plug of potato in each end of your straw. Now we take the thinner straw and push it into one of the potato plugs in the big straw. What happens?" Ms. Gonzales waits for the students to perform the action.

As the students practice "shooting" their potato pistols (see Figure 8.1), Ms. Gonzales walks around the room from group to group using encouraging

FIGURE 8.1   ■   Potato Pistol

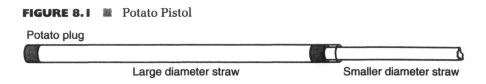

Potato plug

Large diameter straw   Smaller diameter straw

comments to keep the students on task. At each group, Ms. Gonzales pauses and checks with the children to be certain that they have understood her instructions. When she encounters a Chicano boy who seems to be having difficulty with the task, she quickly and quietly translates her previous instructions into Spanish and encourages the child to begin manipulating the materials. As she passes a group with two Vietnamese children, Ms. Gonzales says, "Tran, I remember that you speak Vietnamese; would you be sure that My San understands what we are doing? Help her by translating my instructions into Vietnamese. Be sure that she knows the English names for straw and potato."

After a walk through the room and a quick visit to each group, Ms. Gonzales has determined that everyone has been successful in getting their potato pistol to "fire." Ms. Gonzales calls the class to order and begins to lead a discussion in English. "What happens when you push the plunger or the small straw into the potato inside the larger straw?" Ms. Gonzales waits for student answers. "What would happen if we used a longer straw? A shorter straw? What happens when we push the plunger slowly? Very rapidly? What would happen if we put two or three potato plugs in the larger straw? How could we find out?" Ms. Gonzales pauses after each question and allows the children to formulate "guesses" about what they think would happen. She encourages the children to justify their answers, to develop a rationale for their decision making.

Ms. Gonzales encourages the students to design their own activities in their small groups. She provides the class with metric measuring tapes so they can measure the distance that the potato plugs travel. She also encourages students to record their observations and the results of their activities in a journal or a science notebook, to keep a record of their investigations. As the students work in their small groups, she encourages them to think about the activities they have just done and to formulate additional questions that they can answer by manipulating the straws and the potato plugs.

We call these child-generated questions operational questions (so named by Dorothy Alfke while she was on the faculty of the Pennsylvania State University). An **operational question** *is one that either directly or by implication states what must be done with science materials to obtain an answer to a student-generated question. Ms. Gonzales allows the students to formulate a series of activities that will help them develop the experiential background necessary for understanding the phenomena they are observing. As the students work in their small groups, Ms. Gonzales encourages them to help each other; she encourages students with stronger English language skills to help others in their* *group in naming objects and events. Additionally, Ms. Gonzales encourages every student to become actively involved in manipulating the potato pistols, in exploring the scientific phenomena.*

Finally, after about 30 minutes, Ms. Gonzales asks the class to put away the materials, to pick up potato plugs that may be on the floor, and then she leads them in a large group discussion of the activity. As students speak of their experiences, Ms. Gonzales introduces the term air pressure to the class. Together, Ms. Gonzales and her students operationally define the term. **Operational definitions** *are working definitions, as opposed to formal science definitions. They are definitions based on the children's understanding of the phenomena that they have observed, and they are refined by each child as he or she grows older and has more experiences in the physical world. In this case, the students may define air pressure as a "squeezing of the air inside the large straw that causes the potato plug to shoot across the room." Ms. Gonzales asks the students to put down the manipulative materials and says, "We have been working with materials that illustrate the concept of air pressure. Can you think of another example of air pressure? What experiences or events in your past or at home could also be considered an illustration of air pressure? I want you to look for examples of air pressure around you. Tomorrow, we will have another activity or two in which we will apply our new understanding of air pressure. Right now, I would like you to share with me what you have learned about air pressure today. Some of you may choose to write a journal entry describing what you have learned today, some of you may choose to draw a word web sharing your new learning and some of you may choose to make a drawing sharing your ideas. Take about 15 minutes now and find a way to tell me what you have learned about air pressure." Ms. Gonzales again moves around the classroom speaking to individual students and encouraging them to develop a plan for reporting their new learning.*

The story of Ms. Gonzales and her third-grade students is an example of a modified learning cycle lesson, of a scaled activity. Scaling is an instructional strategy that enables students to investigate the natural world in much the same manner of professional scientists investigating the world.

INTERACTIVE SCIENCE INSTRUCTION

Science is more than a collection of facts about the natural world; it is a way of thinking, of approaching problems objectively by theorizing about what might be from careful observation of what is, and then testing the hypothesis. Science instruction in U.S. public schools should help all children to think as scientists, to become familiar with the laws and principles of the natural world, to develop proficiency in the use of the English language, and to become scientifically literate citizens in a democracy. Showalter has stated that a **scientifically literate** individual is one who:

1. Understands the nature of scientific knowledge;
2. Accurately applies appropriate science concepts, principles, laws, and theories in interacting with his universe;
3. Uses process of science in solving problems, making decisions, and furthering his own understanding of the universe;
4. Interacts with the various aspects of his universe in a way that is consistent with the values that underlie science; and
5. Has developed a richer, more satisfying, and more exciting view of the universe as a result of his science education and continues to extend this education throughout his life." (1974, p.2)

The authors of the *National Science Education Standards* define scientific literacy as "knowledge and understanding of scientific concepts and processes required for personal decision making, participation in civic and cultural affairs, and economic productivity (National Research Council, 1996, p. 22). The ability to understand and apply science concepts, processes, and vocabulary to everyday life is vital for all children. That each child develops scientific literacy, regardless of which definition one selects, is the primary goal for all science teaching and learning.

Historical Foundations of Scaling

Translating the work of scientists into a pedagogical approach for children has resulted in a "learning cycle" (Karplus, 1974) or inquiry approach to science teaching. Expanding and modifying the learning cycle to include language acquisition skills and to accommodate the needs of culturally diverse learners has resulted in a scaling technique for teaching and learning. **SCALE** is an acronym for Science Content and Language Expansion. Scaling knowledge involves the acquisition of science concepts, science processes, and scientific vocabulary as a unified whole. As used in this chapter, scaling knowledge involves the use of a three-stage, inquiry-based teaching strategy that allows the child the opportunity to construct a knowledge of scientific phenomena and its associated vocabulary. Scaling allows children to build new science concepts, practice science processes, and develop vocabulary knowledge through scientific investigation and questions. It allows children in the elementary classroom to function as scientists investigating their natural world.

The Learning Cycle Approach

Scaling is a highly modified form of the learning cycle approach to science teaching. The learning cycle was designed by Karplus and Atkin in 1962 as a three-phase inductive teaching approach (Lawson & Renner, 1975, p. 339).

Originally, the learning cycle was developed to accompany an elementary science curriculum project called the Science Curriculum Improvement Study (SCIS) project. Since development, the learning cycle has proven an appropriate teaching strategy in middle schools (Barman, 1989; Lawson, Abraham, & Renner, 1989), high schools (Abraham & Renner, 1986; Lawson, 1975; Lawson, Abraham, & Renner, 1989; Lawson & Renner, 1975; Purser & Renner, 1983), and universities (Lawson, Abraham, & Renner, 1989; Marek & Methven, 1991; Schlenker, 1983). Today, modified forms of the learning cycle are used as the pedagogical foundation in the Biological Sciences Curriculum Study elementary science program (Science for Life and Living; Integrating Science, Technology, and Health) and in the Lawrence Hall of Science Full Option Science System (FOSS) program.

The learning cycle as it was originally conceived consists of three phases: exploration, concept introduction, and concept application.

Exploration Phase

During the first phase of the learning cycle, students are very active. The emphasis of the exploration phase is on students learning through their own actions and reactions in a new situation. During this phase students interact with materials in the physical world and with each other. The teacher functions primarily as an observer who assists individual students and small groups. The exploration phase provides children with concrete experiences to help them build mental images of new ideas or terms.

Exploration, according to Lawson and Renner (1975) involves students in concrete, real world experiences. As a result of the exploration phase, learners encounter new information for which they have no mental structure

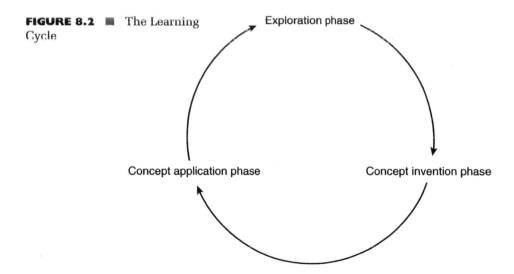

FIGURE 8.2 ■ The Learning Cycle

by which to assimilate it. When students do not have existing mental structures to accommodate new information, they enter into a state of disequilibrium, that may give rise to cognitive restructuring.

Concept Invention Phase

During the concept invention phase of the learning cycle, the teacher assists students in naming objects and concepts. Concept invention serves "to introduce a new concept or principle that leads the students to apply new patterns of reasoning to their experiences. This step, which aids in self-regulation, should always follow exploration and relate to the exploration activities" (Karplus et al., 1977, pp. 5–9). During this phase the teacher assumes a more "traditional" teaching role, gathering information from students about their experiences in the exploration phase.

Concept Application Phase

During the final phase of the learning cycle, concept application (sometimes called the expansion phase), students apply what they have learned in the first two phases of learning cycle to new situations or problems. In this last phase, the students apply the new concept or reasoning pattern to additional examples. The application phase provides children with the opportunity to use new ideas or terms in different situations. This phase permits students to generalize their learning, thus reinforcing the newly acquired knowledge.

Research Findings

In reviewing the literature regarding the learning cycle, Lawson, Abraham, and Renner (1989) state, "the learning cycle approach appears to have considerable promise in areas of encouraging positive attitudes toward science and science instruction, developing better content achievement by students, and improving general thinking skills. It has shown superiority over other approaches, especially those that involve reading and demonstration-lecture activities." While science laboratory–based experiences have proved to be more effective than lecture techniques (Hykle, 1992), the learning cycle has proven especially useful in the science classroom. Specifically, research has shown that learning cycle activities (1) increase a student's opportunity for social interaction (Marek & Methven, 1991), (2) provide opportunities for hands-on learning activities in the classroom (Barman, 1989; Marek & Methven, 1991), (3) assist students in developing scientific vocabulary (Barman, 1989), (4) facilitate students' development of problem-solving skills (Barman, 1989; Lawson, Abraham, & Renner, 1989), (5) aid in students' cognitive growth (Pollard, 1992; Rubin & Norman, 1989; Silberman & Zipp, 1986), (6) improve students' attitudes toward science (Granger, 1986), and (7) help students build mental images of new ideas (Barman, 1989; Koran, Koran, & Baker, 1980) .

Accommodating the Needs of Culturally Diverse Learners

The learning cycle dealt with science concept and process acquisition. The scaling approach used in this book has modified the learning cycle to accommodate the needs of culturally diverse learners. Incorporating English language acquisition opportunities and multiple modes of performance into the structure of the learning cycle calls for a new teaching strategy. This strategy, called scaling, incorporates the strengths of a hands-on/minds-on, inquiry-based approach to learning with a language acquisition model suitable for bilingual/bicultural and regular science classrooms. Scaling, like the learning cycle, is a three-step inquiry-based strategy for science teaching (see Figure 8.3).

Rationale for Scaling

SCALE accommodates the needs of culturally diverse learners by providing (1) multiple modes of declarative knowledge representation, (2) an opportunity for science process acquisition, (3) a vehicle for English language acquisition, (4) peer tutoring in the student's home language, (5) a cooperative learning environment, (6) a means for socialization between students, (7) an avenue for students to bring home learning into the school environment, and

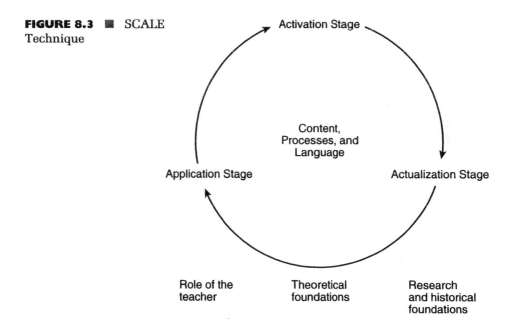

FIGURE 8.3 ■ SCALE Technique

(8) an environment in which children demonstrate their learning orally, in writing, and visually.

The use of the three-tiered SCALE technique described in this chapter allows teachers to present declarative information to children by multiple modes of representation, that is, with real world objects, icons, spoken words, written words, and pictures. Scaling uses an inquiry-based approach to learning that allows children to develop science process skills (e.g., observing, comparing, ordering, categorizing, relating, inferring, and applying). Limited English proficient children in this instructional environment are paired with peers who have developed more competency in the English language; thus there is the opportunity for each child to acquire language skills and science concepts simultaneously. The activity-based approach fostered by scaling presents new information to children in a manner that encourages the activation of mental structures in the child's home language, while appending English nametags to objects and concepts. This approach helps children attach two sets of nametags to the same objects or events, one set in the child's native language and one in English. Scaling decreases the chances that a child will develop two different mental structures for the same concept (one in English and one in the child's home language).

Stages of Scaling

Scaling meets children's needs for social interactions by encouraging children to work in cooperative groups, where together with others they can negotiate meaning regarding the natural world. When scaling is used as an instructional technique, each child is urged by the teacher to bring examples, analogies, metaphors, and other elaborations from their own experience into the science classroom, to connect their home learning to school learning. Finally, scaling allows students to present their new learning to their teacher and to their peers, to engage in reciprocal teaching, in a manner that is culturally familiar and in keeping with their English language proficiency.

Activation Stage

During the activation stage of the scaling technique, students activate their prior knowledge of the events, materials, and concepts that are being introduced in the class. Ms. Gonzales began the activation stage by allowing her students to explore the potato pistol. Students investigated the potato pistol using their prior notions and knowledge. All of the students had experience in using straws and in eating potatoes. However, few of the students would have prior experience with "potato pistols." Most students would not possess mental structures with which to accommodate this new experience. There would probably be a lot of "oohing" and "aahing" in Ms. Gonzales's class as

Activation engages students in manipulating realia.

students manipulated the straws and potato plugs for the first time. The unexpected happened in class: pieces of potato shot across the classroom. Ms. Gonzales was providing a real world experience that helped students to develop a mental structure to accommodate the concept of air pressure. Additionally, Ms. Gonzales was providing the opportunity for students to see, touch, hear, and in general manipulate a real world object (the potato pistol). During this stage children recall what they already know about the realia that they are manipulating. For bilingual students and for students not yet entirely comfortable with speaking English, this is an opportunity to expand and develop their English vocabulary by learning the English names for physical objects and concepts.

Actualization Stage

During the actualization stage, the teacher assists students to build their vocabularies and use the formal language of science. Students assume "ownership" of new knowledge and construct a personal rendition of the science concept. In Ms. Gonzales's class, the students encountered the concept of air pressure and developed an operational definition for air pressure based on their experiences with the potato pistol. Sometimes textbooks, audiovisual materials, and other sources of information are called on to help students develop the concept.

During the actualization stage of the learning process, students first construct and name a new concept. In this stage students accommodate new learning. The teacher guides students' thinking toward constructing appropriate labels for the relationships they have just discovered. The actualization stage lends itself to reciprocal teaching (Johnson & Johnson, 1987). As children share what they have learned with the teacher, the teacher shares the formal terminology of science (sometimes in more than one language) with the students. Teachers and students teach each other and learn from each other during this stage of scaling.

Application Stage

The concept of air pressure developed in Ms. Gonzales's class could be expanded through related activities such as making a homemade barometer or investigating the workings of a squirt bottle. The application stage of scaling is necessary to extend the concept to new settings and new environments. Unless students are presented with numerous examples of the newly learned concept, their application of the concept will be constrained to the single setting in which the concept was first learned. Additionally, this stage allows children to use the new concept to explain phenomena in their own lives in a different manner. A student may connect the concept of air pressure as seen in the potato pistol to the functioning of a staple gun that their father or mother uses at home, to a toy squirt gun, or to a condiment dispenser stored in the refrigerator. The application stage of the scaling technique is a time for students to formally report to the teacher and to their peers what they have learned through the activity and through their interactions with their peers.

Theoretical Foundation of Scaling

Learning in the science classroom involves acquiring knowledge by means of a constructive process in which the learner interacts with the external world, mentally considers data, and renders it meaningful in terms of prior knowledge. Learning is always an interpretive activity, characterized by individual constructions (Tobin, 1989). Learning is the act of the individual learner. To "know" something requires that the learner receive, interpret, and relate incoming information to already existing knowledge. "Principles of constructivist epistemology are clearly evident in guided discovery science instructional models, particularly in the learning cycle" (Staver, 1991, p. 123) and in scaling techniques.

In the real world, "doing science" involves higher-order thinking skills and problem solving, and it involves interacting and sharing with one's colleagues. The use of the scaling technique in the classroom allows children to function as scientists—to formulate hypotheses, to design experiments, to gather data, to interpret data, and to make sense of their natural world.

SCALing builds science concept knowledge, science processes, and language skills.

Role of the Teacher

When using scaling techniques, the role of the teacher is (1) to facilitate students' knowledge construction by designing learning experiences or tasks, (2) to provide the physical resources necessary to complete the tasks, (3) to establish a classroom climate in which students are free to discuss and exchange ideas, (4) to form cooperative groups for peer interactions, and (5) to foster sharing about the learning experience to mediate conversations about the new concepts. The teacher moves from being an authoritative source of information to being a facilitator of learning. The "teacher in the science classroom is someone who understands that their role is to engage children in working with natural phenomena, someone who assists children in making sense of the world. A teacher is someone who cares about some part of the world and how it works and who wants to make it accessible to children" (Duckworth, 1987).

During the activation stage of the scaling technique, the teacher functions as an expediter and an observer who supplies the manipulative or instructional materials and who watches and encourages children as they interact with those materials. The role of the teacher changes to that of a conductor or a guide during the actualization stage of the scaling process. Here the teacher channels or focuses the students on the concept and vocabulary that they have just learned. Finally, during the application stage, the teacher serves as a controller, a mediator, or a reference librarian, directing students to new sources of learning or to new places where the concept may be applied. The use of a scaling technique transforms the role of the teacher from a "sage on stage" to a facilitator of learning. Scaling allows the teacher to assist children in building linguistic and cultural bridges between their home environments and the school environment.

CLASSROOM PRACTICE

This section presents a series of lessons appropriate for all learners, especially culturally diverse children in multicultural classrooms. These lessons provide specific examples of the scaling technique. They are written in far more detail than usual to offer a model of the types of questioning, coaching, mentoring, and so forth that should be used with students. While these lessons have been widely used with children in classrooms, they have been modified here to show their usefulness with culturally diverse learners. I encourage you to modify each lesson so that it is appropriate for your students. Remember that many science lessons may be used with students of different ages and ability levels. For example, we may grow seeds in paper cups in kindergarten classrooms, but we also grow seeds hydroponically (in water) in graduate-level science classes. While the activity may be the same, the level of sophistication of the activity varies with the age and intellectual development of the learner. Older elementary students or students in gifted and talented classes are typically capable of controlling more than one independent variable at a time. Frequently students in upper elementary classrooms are capable of determining the "average" or mean during a number of trials and are able to use more sophisticated graphing techniques than younger children. Determining the instructional level of students is a decision best left to the professional discretion of the individual teacher.

Each of the scaling lessons presented in this section provides an opportunity for you and your students to construct investigations of natural phenomena together. Keep in mind that the extra detail provided in these lessons is shown here only to give you a flavor of the modifications necessary for lessons to meet the needs of culturally diverse students. Work with your own students to develop plans for exploring the natural world through the use of operational questioning. During the activation stage, encourage students to explore phenomena briefly on their own or in small groups. For culturally diverse learners, especially those who are bilingual or limited English proficient, place special emphasis on social interactions and on allowing students opportunities to develop their English language proficiency as they work with others. The activation stage, as used in the scaling lessons presented here, becomes a vehicle for activating the child's prior knowledge and for preparing students to integrate new learning with their existing mental structures. When working with bilingual or second language students, strive to (1) simplify the input (e.g., use a slower but natural speech rate with clear enunciation and avoid scientific jargon); (2) focus on the manipulative materials; (3) draw on the students' prior background and experiences; (4) expand, restate, and reinforce important ideas; (5) identify the key concepts and whenever possible translate (or have a peer or classroom aide translate) the naming words for manipulative materials and concept names into the student's home language; (6) encourage all students to actively engage in using manipulative materials; and (7) encourage all students to verbally interact with each other (California State Board of Education, 1990, pp. 170–171).

Scaled activities provide the opportunity for all students to become actively involved in the learning process. When using manipulative materials, be especially sure to encourage female students to become actively involved. Research has shown that female students tend to be passive observers in laboratory or hands-on settings, to watch their male peers manipulate the materials. In making your classroom a culturally affirming environment for all students, be certain to engage all students in hands-on learning.

During the actualization stage, encourage students to design investigations that answer "what if" and "what happens when" questions. In other words, encourage students to formulate operational questions that can be answered with the manipulative materials. In the past, many teachers using the traditional learning cycle approach focused on operational questioning during the exploration phase of learning cycle. When working with limited English proficient students or low-verbal learners struggling with vocabulary development, operational questioning is best done in groups, where students receive assistance in acquiring and negotiating meaning for new vocabulary words.

Finally, during the application stage of the scaling process, encourage students to connect their new learning to their prior experiences. For example, if you are teaching the concept "fruit" (operationally defined as a package of seeds produced by the parent plant), encourage students to mention fruits with which they are familiar. What fruits has the student eaten or grown or seen? For children in the multicultural classroom, the application stage might be better viewed as an expansion stage where the student brings home learning to class and combines it with school learning. Students should be encouraged to apply new learning both to new situations and to explain experiences they have had in life.

From a linguistics viewpoint, the activation stage should be viewed as a time when students manipulate real world materials and activate their prior knowledge about those materials. The actualization stage should be used to invent the new science concept, while building English language proficiency. The application stage should be a time when students apply the newly learned concept to new situations and use the new concept to explain events or phenomena in their prior experience.

ACTIVITY 8.1 ■ Bottle Rocket

Purpose: To explore the concepts of air pressure or the laws of motion through communicating, observing, ordering, relating, inferring, and applying.

Type of Activity: Scaling (group)

Content

    Theme: Energy

    Basic Field of Study: Physical science

Science Concepts: Force (A force is a push or pull.)

    Related Concepts and Terms: Work, energy

Activation Stage

Teacher Preparation: Collect a sufficient supply of empty detergent bottles so that there is one for each group in the class. Using a pair of pliers, remove the cap from the bottle and the plastic "stem" from inside the center of the top of the bottle. Wash out the bottles with clean water to remove the excess soap and detergent. Allow the bottles to dry before using them in class.

Materials (for each group): Empty detergent bottle (see teacher preparation, ball of clay, thin plastic soda straw, three thicker plastic soda straws (thicker than the straw used on the "rocket launcher")

Procedure
1. Have the students assemble the bottle rocket launcher. In assembling the launcher, place the thin straw at the top of the detergent bottle and mold the clay around the straw so that the top of the bottle is sealed off. Have the students check to be certain that air can escape only through the straw.
2. Have students assemble a rocket by placing a small amount of clay on one end of a soda straw (a straw with a larger diameter than the straw used on the rocket launcher.
3. Instruct the students to test-fire their bottle rockets. Place the rocket on top of the launcher and squeeze the center of the detergent bottle. What happens?
4. If you have a large number of limited English proficient students in your class, take time to name the objects that you are working with (e.g., *straw, clay, detergent bottle*). Also, explain that you are making a model of a *rocket launcher* and a *rocket* from these materials, that

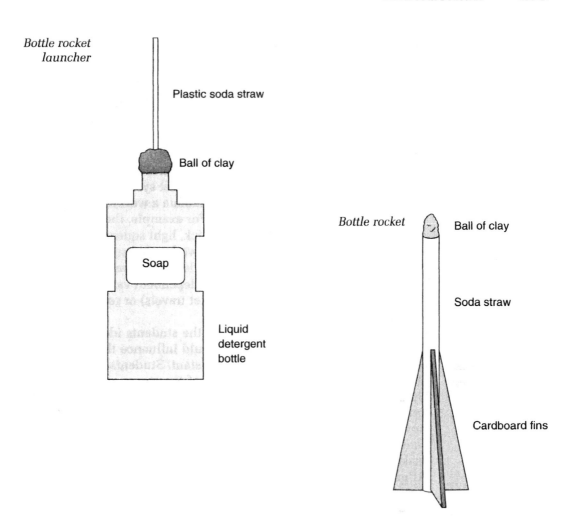

Bottle rocket launcher

Plastic soda straw

Ball of clay

Soap

Liquid detergent bottle

Bottle rocket

Ball of clay

Soda straw

Cardboard fins

ACTIVITIES

the clay serves as a *payload*, etc. Be sure to build the students' vocabulary as you work.

5. When all students have had the opportunity to test-fire their rockets, assemble the students in a large group and allow them to discuss their observations about the bottle rockets.

Actualization Stage

Materials: Empty detergent bottle (see teacher preparation work), ball of clay, thin plastic soda straw, three thicker plastic soda straws (thicker than the straw used on the "rocket launcher"), metric measuring tapes, graph paper, calculators (optional—for older students where multiple rocket firings will be carried out and where the average or mean distance that the rocket travels will be calculated)

Procedure

1. Encourage the students to generate a list of questions that they could answer with the materials that they have; for example, What would happen if the rocket were shorter? Longer? What would happen if I squeezed the squirt bottle harder? Softer? What would happen if I had a heavier payload (ball of clay) on the rocket? What would happen if I added paper "fins" to my rocket? How many fins should I add? Where should I place the fins?

2. Assume that the students have decided to investigate the "squeeze" as the important variable in the bottle rocket system. Allow the students to operationally define (i.e., formulate a working definition) a soft, a medium, and a hard squeeze. For example, the students may decide that a soft squeeze means a quick, light squeeze of the detergent bottle, while a hard squeeze is a two-handed squeeze.

3. After identifying the squeeze as the independent variable in the activity, allow the students to define the dependent variable (normally it would be the distance that the rocket travels) or responding variable.

4. Before conducting the activity, have the students identify extraneous variables (those variables that could influence the flight of the rocket) that the class will all hold constant. Students might identify the angle of the launcher, the length of the straw, and the mass of the payload as extraneous variables.

5. Establish a means for recording results. Have the students decide how each group will collect and record data and how they will present their findings to the class. You may wish to have students make a table of data or a bar graph of their results.

6. After students have had the opportunity to design and conduct an investigation using their bottle rockets, engage students in discussing their results. Finally, introduce students to the concept of force (a force is a push or pull). Encourage the students to talk about the relationship between the squeeze on the rocket launcher and the distance that the rocket travels.

Application Stage

Materials: Bottle rocket launcher (assembled previously), straws, glue, cardboard, scissors, tape, miscellaneous art supplies (string, markers, etc.)

Procedure

1. Ask students the following question: Could we build a better rocket? Provide students with a box of scrap materials and allow the students to design and test-fire rockets of other designs. When students have developed the best possible rocket, allow them to share their designs with the rest of the class. Sharing may include draw-

ings, graphs, diagrams, actual models, and so forth. Allow multiple means of reporting to accommodate the needs of limited English proficient students.

2. Tell students the rocket travels because of air pressure, because of the force with which we squeeze the bottle. Ask; What is another example of a force, something that results in a push or a pull?

3. Ask: Can you think of an example of a force that you have seen or experienced in the past?

4. Ask: How is your rocket like a real rocket? How is it different?

ACTIVITY 8.2   ■   Bubbleology

Purpose: To explore the concept of a bubble or a film by observing, communicating, comparing, applying.

Type of Activity: Scaling (group)

Content

Theme: Scale and structure

Basic Field of Study: Physical science

Science Concepts: Bubble (A bubble is a thin film of liquid forming a ball around air or gas.)

Related Concepts and Terms: Film, gas, surface tension

Activation Stage

Materials: Straw, liquid detergent, water, paper towels (for clean up)

Procedure
1. Instruct the students to pour some water on their tables or desks. Add four or fivr drops of liquid detergent to the puddle of water.
2. Tell students to insert a soda straw into the water and blow a bubble. What happens?
3. Be certain to help children with limited English proficiency name the manipulative objects.

Actualization Stage

Materials: Straw, liquid detergent (several different brands may be desirable), water, paper towels (for clean up), metric measuring tapes, calculators (optional—for older students to use in determining the average size of bubble footprints)

Procedure

1. Allow the students to generate a series of operational questions about bubbles, such as: How can you make a larger bubble? A smaller bubble? What would happen if we used a larger straw? A smaller straw? What would happen if we used a stronger concentration of detergent? A weaker concentration? What would happen if we used different brands of detergent?

2. Assume that the students wanted to investigate the concentration of detergent as an independent variable. Prepare solutions of different concentrations of soap solution (e.g., 1 drop of soap/milliliter, 2 drops/milliliter, etc.).

3. A dependent variable could be the size of the bubble footprint (operationally defined as the diameter of the bubble or the "ring" left on the table after the bubble pops).

4. Have the students identify extraneous variables that everyone will control in the same fashion, such as size of the straw, method for measuring the bubble footprint, and brand of detergent to be used.

5. Allow the students to conduct an investigation to determine how the concentration of the soap solution affects the size of bubble that they make. Depending upon the age of the students, tables and graphs are appropriate methods for recording data. You may wish to have older students record the average size of the bubble (an average of three or five or ten trials).

6. During this phase you should develop the concept of *bubble*.

7. Be certain to allow students to engage in peer tutoring, to assist others in their group with naming the objects and the concepts that they are encountering, in English and in the child's home language when appropriate.

Application Stage

Materials: Straw, liquid detergent (several different brands may be desirable), water, pieces of insulated copper wire, paper towels

Procedure

1. Allow students to continue to investigate bubbles by asking some operational questions (have students share their answers with others in the class): Can you blow a "square" bubble? What happens when two bubbles touch? Can you make a "long lasting" bubble?

2. Ask: How are bubbles useful in the real world?

3. Ask: Where do we use films of materials in the real world?

4. Provide students with many opportunities for expressing what they have learned—journal entries, drawings, and oral reporting.

ACTIVITY 8.3 ▓ Dancing Raisins

Purpose: To explore the concept of energy conversion by observing, communicating, comparing, ordering, and relating.

Type of Activity: Scaling (individual or group)

Content

    Theme: Patterns of change

    Basic Field of Study: Physical science

Science Concepts: Energy can be converted from one form to another.

    Related Concepts and Terms: Chemical change, gas, buoyancy

Activation Stage

Materials: Vinegar, baking soda, raisins, beaker, clear plastic container, or a glass (Safety note: Use plastic containers whenever possible to avoid the dangers of broken glass.)

Procedure
1. Tell students to fill a beaker one-third full of vinegar and one-third full of water. Slowly add one teaspoon of baking soda to this mixture.
2. Have students add five or six raisins to the container. Ask what happens.
3. Be certain to move around the classroom and assist students in naming the objects and phenomena that they are seeing and experiencing (*raisins, vinegar, baking soda, beaker, foam, bubbles*, etc.).

Actualization Stage

Materials: Vinegar, baking soda, raisins, beaker, clear plastic container, or a glass (Safety note: Plastic containers are preferable for elementary aged children.), stopwatch or other timer

Procedure
1. Allow the students to generate a list of operational questions (questions that can be answered using the manipulative materials), such as, What would happen if more vinegar were used? Less vinegar? What would happen if more raisins were added to the liquid? Less raisins? What would happen if more baking soda were used? Less baking soda?

2. Select one or more activities for the students to investigate. For example, they could vary the concentration of the vinegar. The concentration of the vinegar would be the independent variable and the length of time that the raisins "danced" in the container would be the dependent variable. Allow the students to identify extraneous variables that all students will control.
3. Work with the students to find ways to observe and record data. This may include producing a table and a graph showing the results of their investigation.
4. Allow time for students to share their results with others in the class.
5. Assist students in developing the concept of chemical change, or the concept that energy may be changed from one form to another (e.g., chemical energy to mechanical energy).
6. Be certain that limited English proficient students receive help or peer tutoring in expressing their ideas in English.

Application Stage

Materials: Vinegar, baking soda, empty soda bottle (Safety note: Use plastic soda bottles, not glass containers.), cork (to fit the top of the soda bottle)

Procedure
1. Tell students: Fill a soda bottle one-quarter full of vinegar. Add 2 or 3 teaspoons of baking soda to the bottle. Immediately stopper the bottle with a cork. Observe carefully. What happens? What type of energy is produced when baking soda is added to vinegar? What kind of energy is produced by this chemical reaction? What energy transfers are involved in this activity?
2. Ask: What are some sources of energy that you have seen before?
3. Ask: Can you think of instances of energy transfers that you have seen in your life? Discuss these with others in your class.
4. Provide opportunities for students to express what they have learned in a variety of ways. Allow for journal writing, drawings, demonstrations and so forth.

ACTIVITY 8.4 ■ Mysterious Minerals

Purpose: To explore the concept of *mineral* by observing, communicating, comparing, ordering, and applying.

Type of Activity: Scaling (groups)

Content

> ***Theme:*** Patterns of change
>
> ***Basic Field of Study:*** Earth sciences

Science Concept: Minerals can be grouped based on their physical characteristics.

> ***Related Concepts and Terms:*** Hardness, luster, color, cleavage

Activation Stage

> ***Materials:*** Ten to fifteen mineral specimens for each group of students
>
> ***Procedure***
> 1. Ask the students to observe the minerals and to list their characteristics.
> 2. Ask: In what ways are minerals alike?
> 3. Ask: In what ways are minerals different?
> 4. Ask: How could minerals be grouped? Have students share their system of grouping minerals with the class.
> 5. Be certain that limited English proficient students receive assistance in naming terms such as *mineral, hardness,* and so forth.

Actualization Stage

> ***Materials:*** Video or movie on minerals, ten to fifteen minerals (Try to select typical specimens so that they are the same as those shown in the filmstrip or movie.)
>
> ***Procedure***
> 1. Ask the students to identify the minerals they have been working with using the examples that they saw during the movie or video. Allow the students to share with others the reasons for their decision making.
> 2. Following the discussion, introduce the terms *mineral, luster, hardness, color,* and *cleavage* and explain that these are physical characteristics scientists use to group or classify minerals.

Application Stage

> ***Materials:*** Ten to 15 different mineral specimens (specimens not previously used by the students), mineral identification guides, field hardness testing kit (optional)
>
> ***Procedure:*** Explain to the students that they are mineral detectives and that their job is to identify each of the "unknown" minerals using the mineral identification guides. Allow students multiple means for performing what they have learned, such as charts, tables of data, oral reports, and so forth.

ACTIVITIES

ACTIVITY 8.5 ■ **What Color Is Black?**

Purpose: To explore the concept of color by observing, comparing, communicating, ordering, relating, and inferring.

Type of Activity: Scaling (groups)

Content

> ***Theme:*** Patterns of change

> ***Basic Field of Study:*** Physical science

Science Concepts: Chromatography is the process of separating the parts of a mixture.

> ***Related Concepts and Terms:*** Solutions, mixtures, capillary action, color

Activation Stage

> ***Teacher Preparation:*** Prepare one chromatography strip for each group of students. Cut strips from commercially available coffee filters and mark the strips in 1 centimeter increments. Place a large dot of black ink from a water soluble black felt-tipped pen on the "0" mark.

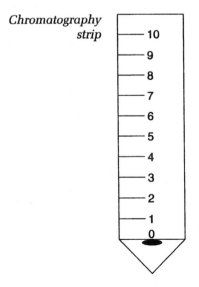

Chromatography strip

> ***Materials:*** Beakers or clear plastic cups (Safety note: Use plastic whenever possible to avoid potential injury from broken glass.), pencil and masking tape, chromatography strip

Student Directions:

1. Place 1 or 2 centimeters of tap water in the bottom of the beaker or a clear plastic cup.
2. Lightly tape the coffee filter (the chromatography strip) to a pencil and suspend the pencil on the lip of the cup so that the tip of the paper just touches the surface of the water.
3. Observe for the next 10 minutes, recording your observations? What happens?
4. After the water has reached the 10 centimeter mark of the filter paper (chromatography paper), remove the paper and allow it to dry.
5. What colors were in the black ink?
6. (Note: As students work in small groups, move around the classroom and assist limited English proficient students in naming the materials they are using.)

Actualization Stage

Materials: Video or movie on color

Procedure

1. Allow the students to discuss their observations with others. Encourage the students to formulate a series of operational questions about this phenomenon, such as: What would happen if we used a different color ink? What would happen if we left the filter paper in the water for a longer time? What would happen if we used more ink?
2. Show the students a video or movie on light and color.
3. Ask the students to explain what happened to their black dot in accordance with the new knowledge presented in the movie or video.
4. Following the discussion, introduce the terms *color, chromatography, mixture,* and *capillary action.* (Note: Allow for peer tutoring, especially for limited English proficient students.)

Application Stage

Materials: Coffee filters and pattern (shown here) for cutting the filters into chromatography strips, water-soluble markers of several different colors, masking tape, beakers or clear plastic cups (Safety note: Use plastic containers whenever possible to avoid risk of injury from broken glassware.), scissors, metric ruler

Student Directions:

1. Using the pattern, cut out four or five chromatography strips from pieces of filter paper and mark each strip in 1 centimeter increments.
2. Place a large dot of ink from the felt-tipped pens on each strip of paper. Place one color on each strip.

3. Predict what colors may appear as the water is absorbed by the filter paper.
4. Tape each strip to a pencil and suspend the pencil on the top of the beaker or cup as you did with the first chromatography strip.
5. Write down your observations.
6. When the water reaches the 10 centimeter mark, remove it from the beaker or cup. Were your predictions correct?
7. Share your findings with others. (Note: Allow for oral, verbal, and pictorial sharing of new learnings.)

ACTIVITY 8.6 ■ Magic Milk

Purpose: To explore the concept of surface tension by observing, communicating, comparing, relating, inferring, and applying.

Type of Activity: Scaling (groups)

Content

Theme: Patterns of change

Basic Field of Study: Physical science

Science Concepts: Surface tension

Related Concepts and Terms: Molecular attraction, molecules

Activation Stage

Teacher Preparation: Allow the milk to warm to room temperature for best results. Cold milk may be used in this activity but experience has shown that slightly warmed milk is best.

Materials (for each group): Milk, food coloring (three or four colors), liquid detergent, heavy duty paper plates or shallow trays, eye dropper

Procedure
1. Have students pour some milk into a paper plate so that the bottom of the plate is covered with milk.
2. Instruct the students to place two or three drops of each color of the food coloring at different locations on the surface of the milk. For example, there would be a spot of yellow food coloring at one corner of the plate, a spot of red coloring at another location, and so forth.

3. When the surface of the milk is very still, instruct the students to add one or two drops of liquid detergent to the plate and observe what happens.
4. When working with limited English proficient students, be sure to name the manipulative objects, that is, *paper plate, soap* or *liquid detergent, milk,* the colors of the food coloring and so forth.
5. Encourage the students to present their observations to others in the class.

Actualization Stage

Materials (for each group): Heavy-weight paper plates or shallow trays (metal or plastic), liquid detergent, black pepper

Procedure

1. Instruct the students to cover the bottom of their paper plates with water.
2. Tell them to cover the surface of the water lightly with black pepper.
3. When the water in the plate is very still, tell students to add one or two drops of liquid detergent. Ask: What happens?
4. Introduce the students to the term *surface tension.* Ask the students to explain how the milk activity and the pepper activity are alike. Different.
5. Allow the students to design other activities in which they investigate the phenomenon. For example, what would happen if we used skim milk instead of whole milk? What would happen if we used another brand of liquid detergent?
6. Encourage the students to record their activities and their findings in a journal or a science notebook, to share their findings with others.

Application Stage

Materials (for each group): Sewing needle, beaker or a clear plastic cup (Safety note: Remember to use plastic containers whenever possible to minimize the risk of injury from broken glass.), water

Procedure

1. Ask: Can you get the sewing needle to float on the surface of the water? What concept does this illustrate?
2. Lead the class in a discussion of surface tension using such quetions as: What is surface tension? (Have the students operationally define the concept.) How is surface tension useful? Can you think of instances of surface tension that you might have seen before? Have the students relate the new learning to their home learning.
3. Have students report what they have learned about surface tension through a word web, a journal entry or a drawing.

ACTIVITIES

ACTIVITY 8.7 ■ Planting a Mold Garden

Purpose: To explore the concept of mold growth by observing, communicating, comparing, ordering, categorizing, relating, inferring, and applying.

Type of Activity: Scaling (groups)

Content

> **Theme:**   Systems and interactions
>
> **Basic Field of Study:**   Life science

Science Concepts: Mold is a living thing.

> **Related Concepts and Terms:**   Fungi, characteristics of living things, spores, hypha, reproduction

Activation Stage

Teacher Preparation (to be done 2 to 4 days before the activity): Begin bread mold cultures for each group. Place small cubes of bread in individual plastic baggies. Add two or three drops of water to each bread cube and seal the plastic container. Place the baggies in a warm, dark place to facilitate mold growth.

Materials (for each group):   Bread mold, hand lens or tripod magnifier or dissecting microscope

Procedure
1. Present the students with a bread mold colony. Allow the students to discuss what they see and to report their observations to others in their group.
2. Have the students draw their bread mold.
3. For limited English proficient students, name the terms *bread mold, baggie,* and so forth.)
4. Lead the class in a discussion of bread mold: What is bread mold? Where does it come from? On what kinds of materials does mold grow?

Actualization Stage

(This activity will take several days to complete. Allow time for mold growth to occur.)

Materials: Plastic bags, eye droppers, magnifiers, bread cubes

Procedure
1. Tell students: Select some materials on which you think mold will grow. Also select some materials that you think will not encourage the growth of mold. Place these materials in a baggie and put several drops of water on each one. Place the sealed baggies in a dark area and allow mold to grow for several days.
2. Ask students: What conditions are most favorable for mold growth? Have students design activities in which they investigate mold growth. For example, does mold grow better in light or in darkness? In hot, warm, or cold places? How much water does mold need to grow? A little? A lot? Have students identify independent variables (variables they will control) and change those variables.
3. After several days, have students examine the mold gardens. Ask: Where did mold grow best? On what types of materials? Under which conditions?
4. Have students develop plans for reporting their findings to others.
5. Develop the concept that mold is a living thing and that mold grows better under certain conditions than under others.
6. You might want to show a filmstrip or movie at this stage of the scaling process. Since mold is difficult to observe, even with hand lenses, a filmstrip or movie might help students focus on the critical attributes of the mold organism.

Application Stage

Materials: Basic art supplies (crayons, markers, colored pencils, and drawing paper)

Procedure
1. Have the students discuss mold. Ask: Have you seen mold before? Where?
2. Ask: Is mold useful? How? Is it harmful? How? Have students write a journal entry or make a word web or concept map describing their knowledge of mold.
3. Ask: What are the characteristics of living things? How are all living things alike? How are they different? Have students make a chart showing the characteristics of living things.
4. Ask: How is mold like other living things? How is it different?
5. Assist students in connecting their prior knowledge of mold to their newly gained school knowledge of mold.

ACTIVITY 8.8 ■ Bobs and Strings

Purpose: To explore the law of the pendulum by observing, communicating, comparing, relating, inferring, and applying.

Type of Activity: Scaling (groups)

Content

Theme: Systems and interactions

Basic Field of Study: Physical science

Science Concepts: Energy can be transformed from one kind to another.

Related Concepts and Terms: Pendulum, bob, kinetic energy, potential energy, work, period of a pendulum

Activation Stage

Materials (for each group): Bobs (any objects may be used for the pendulum bobs—washers, stoppers, large paper clips, and so forth), string

Procedure
1. Construct a hand-held pendulum by attaching a weight to a string and releasing the pendulum.
2. Lead the students in a discussion of ways to make the pendulum go faster and slower.
3. If you have a large number of limited English proficient students in your class, take time to name the objects that you are working with (e.g., *bobs, washers, string*). Also, explain that you are making a pendulum and that pendulums are sometimes used in clocks. Be sure to assist students in developing their vocabulary as they work.

Actualization Stage

Materials: Bobs, string, timer or wrist watch

Procedure
1. Lead the students in reporting their findings on factors that influence the movement of the pendulum. Have the students formulate a series of operational questions that may be answered using the pendulum, such as: Does the mass affect the movement of the pendulum? Does the length of the string affect the movement of the pendulum? Does the color of string effect the movement of the pendulum?

2. Have the students develop investigations to determine which factors affect the movement of the pendulum. Students could vary the length of the strings on their pendulums; one group could have a string 50 cm. long, another 100 cm. (1 meter) long, 150 cm., and so forth. In this instance the length of the string is the independent variable and the number of swings per minute is the dependent variable. Have the students construct a table of data to record their results.

Pendulum data sheet #1

Length of the String (in centimeters)	**Period of the Pendulum (swings/minute)**
50	
100	
150	
200	

3. Allow the students to discuss their results with their peers.
4. You may wish to have students investigate other variables associated with the pendulum, such as the mass attached to the pendulum. In this instance, the number of washers attached to the pendulum could be used as the independent variable, and the number of swings of the pendulum per minute would be the dependent variable. Have the students make a second table of data to record their results.

Pendulum data sheet #2

Number of Washers	**Period of the Pendulum (swings/minute)**
1	
2	
3	
4	
5	

5. When working with the pendulum, have the students identify and control extraneous variables, that is, other factors that might influence the period of the pendulum.

6. Work with the students to develop and operationally define the concepts of potential and kinetic energy. Potential energy is stored energy, operationally defined as the energy that the pendulum has at its maximum release point. Kinetic energy is energy of motion, the energy that the pendulum has while it is moving. In a pendulum system, potential energy can be changed into kinetic energy.

7. Encourage the students to record their activities and their findings. For older children, use multiple trials and record the average result.

8. When working with limited English proficient children, encourage peer tutoring. Encourage children to apply English name tags to the science objects and concepts that they are encountering in class.

Application Stage

Materials: Bobs, string, timer or wristwatch

Procedure

1. Ask the students to make the best possible pendulum, the one that will make the most swings in a minute. Next, ask the students to construct another pendulum that will make the fewest possible swings in a minute.

2. Have the students report their findings to others. Allow for multiple means of reporting (writing, drawings, oral reporting, and so forth).

ACTIVITY 8.9   ■   Fair and Unfair Games

Purpose: To explore fair and unfair games by observing, communicating, comparing, ordering, categorizing, relating, inferring, and applying.

Type of Activity: Scaling (individual)

Content

Theme: Patterns of change

Basic Field of Study: Life science (genetics)

Science Concepts: Possibilities and probabilities are different entities.

Related Concepts and Terms: Probability, fair games, unfair games, random selection

Activation Stage

Materials (per person):   penny (Any coin will do.)

Student Directions:

1. Flip a penny 100 times and record each flip on a chart using tick marks. What do you expect to happen? What actually happened?

Coin outcome data sheet

Number of Heads	*Number of Tails*

2. What are the two possible outcomes? Do "heads" and "tails" appear with equal frequency?
3. Is flipping a coin a "fair" game (one in which each outcome occurs about the same number of times)?
4. If working with young children, a discussion of coins and their value is a natural extension of this activity at this time.

Actualization Stage

Materials (per person):   Thumb tacks (Safety note: Thumb tacks are selected due to the way that they are constructed and their center of balance. Students should be cautioned about handling thumb tacks.)

Procedure

1. Have students flip a thumb tack 100 times in the same fashion that they flipped the coin. Ask: What are the possible outcomes? (Answer: point up and point down.) Will the thumb tack land point up as often as it lands point down? Have students record findings on a table of data using tick marks:

Thumb tack outcome sheet

Point Up	*Point Down*

ACTIVITIES

2. Ask: Does each possibility (point up or point down) occur with equal frequency? Is flipping a thumb tack a "fair" game? Why or why not?

3. Lead students in a discussion of the concept. A *possibility* is an expected outcome. A *probability* is the chance of obtaining that outcome.

Application Stage

> ***Materials:***   No additional materials required
>
> ***Procedure:***   From your own experiences, what are some "fair games"? Some "unfair games"?

CHAPTER SUMMARY

Through the use of the scaling technique, students and teachers together can build a knowledge of science concepts, processes, and vocabulary. Scaling is a three-stage, inquiry-based approach to science instruction in which students function as scientists in investigating their physical world. During the first stage, activation, students' prior knowledge is activated through the use of hands-on manipulative activities. This stage also assists students in appending English name tags to existing home language, when necessary. In the actualization stage, teachers and students work together to construct an understanding of natural phenomena. Through the process of asking operational questions, formulating hypotheses, controlling variables, and collecting, recording, and interpreting data, students construct mental images of science concepts. By engaging in reciprocal teaching, in which students share their data and findings with their teacher and their peers, and teachers share the formal language of science, teachers and students together construct individual understandings of the world around them. Actualization involves each learner in constructing a personal rendition of scientific knowledge and its accompanying vocabulary. Finally, during the application stage, students apply newly learned knowledge to new situations and use this same knowledge to explain events and phenomena that they have observed in the real world. The application stage of scaling actively involves students in applying their newly formed knowledge of science and in preparing them for additional learning. This final stage of the scaling process helps students build linguistic and cultural bridges between school learning and home learning.

TOPICS TO REVIEW

- SCALE
- Scientifically literate
- Activation stage
- Actualization stage
- Application stage

REFLECTIVE PRACTICE

1. Based on your previous experiences and your prior knowledge of science teaching and learning, how is scaling similar to "traditional" laboratory activities? How is scaling different from "traditional" laboratory activities?

2. Based on your own experience, how is scaling similar to the ways scientists explore the world? How is it different?

3. In your opinion, why is there an emphasis on integrating vocabulary development into scaling activities instead of teaching the vocabulary before the activity (the most commonly used model for teaching language)?

4. Many researchers have said that learning cycle (scaling is a modified form of the learning cycle) activities are examples of thematic or integrated teaching. Do you agree or disagree with this statement? Justify your answer.

CHAPTER 9

Experimenting

Defining operationally | Investigating

Formulating hypotheses | Controlling variables

——— **Basic Processes** ↓ ↑ **Integrated Processes** ———

Using space/ time relations	Using numbers	Identifying variables
Predicting	Inferring	Communicating
Observing	Classifying	Measuring

Constructing a Knowledge of Science Processes

■ POINTS TO PONDER

- What are science processes?
- Why are science processes vital in science education?
- What types of activities assist students in forming a knowledge of science?

My love of hickory-horned devils began during the summer between seventh and eighth grades. Two old majestic walnut trees grew outside the front door of our farmhouse. Those trees provided us with shade in the heat of the summer and food during the cold months of winter. Those same trees also provided specimens for my insect collection. One warm spring day, I found a cluster of insect eggs on the underside of the leaves of one of the lower branches of one tree. Gingerly, I carried the leaf inside and placed it in a gallon-sized pickle jar with a piece of wire gauze on top. Within a week, my eggs hatched, and I was the proud owner of twenty small green larvae.

During the coming weeks, I fed my larvae walnut leaves more and more frequently, once a day at first and later four to five times a day. Gradually, the larvae became recognizable as hickory-horned devils. At maturity, they were eight to ten inches long. Their green bodies were covered with vibrant white-and-black markings, and large orange "horns" curved back over their heads. When an unsuspecting stranger approached their jar, they would rear back on their hind legs in a defensive posture. Among all larvae in the insect world, the hickory-horned devil is certainly the fiercest looking.

Toward the middle of summer, my little devils reached their maximum size and one after another began to pupate in the bottom of the jar. Within a few weeks, the pupae began to hatch. From each pupa, a newborn moth emerged. Slowly, the newly hatched moths climbed onto the sticks in the jar. Each one firmly attached itself to a branch while it pumped "blood" into its wings. In the heat of the summer sun, the wings hardened. By nightfall, each newly hatched royal walnut moth was ready for its maiden flight. As I released the royal walnut moths back into the natural environment, I reflected on my weeks of observation. It had been a joy to know these creatures for a short time. From egg, to larva, to pupa, to adult, the life cycle of Citheronia regalis *had provided me wonder and delight.*

Observing creatures in their natural environment is still a source of delectation in my life. I will always be grateful to Bea Derickson, my fifth-grade teacher, who encouraged us to observe the world around us. Each day after lunch, she bundled us up in coats and jackets and walked us through the woodlot on the school grounds. We observed that woodlot with her in the sunlight of autumnal splendor; in the cold, frozen snows of winter; and in the warming days of spring. She taught us to walk softly and quietly, to listen carefully, to look up as well as down. Mostly, she taught us to enjoy looking and seeing. Observing is the most basic of the science processes, a skill that is learned over time. It is the foundation upon which all other science processes are built.

SCIENCE SHOULD BE TAUGHT . . .

That science should be "taught as science is practiced" is an underlying theme of science education reform documents such as the American Association for the Advancement of Science's *The Liberal Art of Science* (AAAS, 1990, p. xi). In summarizing the status of science education, the AAAS has stated that "conventional science teaching suppresses students' natural curiosity and leaves them with the impression that they are incapable of understanding science" (AAAS, 1990, p. 28).

Too often in the past, teachers have viewed science as a body of facts to be learned or committed to memory. Renner and Lawson state that traditional science-teaching methods embrace the notions that (1) teaching is telling, (2) memorization is learning, and (3) being able to repeat something on an examination is evidence of understanding (1973). The overreliance in elementary schools on expository teaching techniques has resulted in generations of children who tend to view science as a list of vocabulary words to be committed to memory, rather than a way of investigating the world. In addition to a heavy reliance on expository teaching techniques, elementary schools have also depended excessively on textbooks as the major source of information and knowledge about science. In summarizing an investigation of ten recently published elementary science textbooks, Elliott (1987) stated that these textbooks neither promote nor encourage the development of scientific thinking or attitudes, nor do they engage students in applying cognitive processes that are basic to understanding the content covered.

Inquiry-based science instruction, on the other hand, engages students in actively constructing a knowledge of the natural world. The *National Science Education Standards* (National Research Council, 1996) encourage an in-depth, hands-on science education environment for students at all grade levels. As a child, I learned that I could investigate the natural world on my own, that I could generate questions and seek answers on my own. I was able to learn about the life cycle of the royal walnut moth from firsthand observation. Later, I would go to books to increase my knowledge about these magnificent creatures, but only after my curiosity had been aroused through my firsthand experiences. The skills of inquiry that I used in that experience are commonly called science processes. I was fortunate as a child to have encountered a teacher like Bea Derickson who would encourage me to use science processes daily.

RESEARCH REGARDING SCIENCE PROCESSES

The thinking processes scientists use to investigate the natural world are referred to as scientific thinking processes. These same processes are readily learned by children in classrooms that foster an inquiry- or discovery-based approach to learning. Science is the process of "finding out." It is the art of interrogating nature, a system of inquiry that requires curiosity, intellectual honesty, skepticism, tolerance for ambiguity, and openness to new ideas and the sharing of knowledge. In making sense of the natural world, students should be able to learn from direct, not vicarious, experience. "Learning science" involves careful observation; experimentation; identification of salient variables; and precise, accurate, and reliable measurements. The cornerstone of science learning is discovering or "rediscovering" the laws implicit in data, constructing and testing hypotheses, and challenging the predictive power of theories and models.

In describing the importance of science processes, the California State Board of Education (1990) stated that a knowledge of science processes is vital for all students, including those for whom considerations of gender, ethnic and cultural backgrounds, and physical disabilities are of primary importance. Science processes are dynamic, higher-level thinking skills which help students build an understanding of the natural world and its connection to our technologically advanced society. Mechling and Oliver (1983) summarized research into science processes by saying that competence in using process skills provides children with the ability to apply knowledge not only to science, but outside the classroom in everyday life. These authors pointed out that science processes learned in childhood are useful in adult life as we attempt to separate inferences from evidence in a systematic fashion.

Learning for all children begins as physical experience with objects. This experience provides students with mental models or records of what they have done and seen. From such mental models, the student is able to develop a conceptual understanding of science. In writing of the role of science processes in the classroom, Lawson and Renner (1975) stated that experience in manipulating objects, in learning science through a hands-on instructional model, helps students to build operational structures that can ultimately lead them to think abstractly about the world around them. Inquiry-based laboratory investigations conducted in small cooperative groups proportionally benefit culturally diverse students and white females (Cohen, Lotan, & Catanzarite, 1990). Additionally, research has shown that inquiry or discovery-learning activities that emphasize science processes enhance the intellectual development of students (Herron, 1952; Lawson, 1975; Lawson & Renner, 1975; Renner & Lawson, 1973).

BASIC SCIENCE PROCESSES

Science processes may be divided into two types: basic processes and integrated processes. Basic processes may be viewed as empirical and/or analytic procedures that have been derived from scientific practice and that may be used as part of every student's daily life. Science processes are thinking processes that foster lifelong learning. The simplest science processes are referred to as basic processes; those that incorporate more than one process are referred to as integrated processes. Basic science processes include (1) observing, (2) classifying, (3) measuring, (4) communicating, (5) inferring, (6) predicting, (7) using space/time relationships, (8) using numbers, and (9) identifying variables.

Observing

Observing involves using one's senses, that is, seeing, hearing, tasting, smelling, feeling, and in general experiencing the natural world. The process of observing involves children in identifying and naming the properties of objects and events in the world around them. In operationally defining observation, Wolfinger said, "Observation is a piece of information learned directly though the senses" (1984, p.89).

As adults we frequently assume that children have prior knowledge of objects and events in the world, when indeed they do not. For all children, a strong foundation of observational knowledge derived from watching, from

Observing is a basic science process.

looking, from experiencing the world is vital to later success in science. Observing is the most basic of the science processes. All other science processes are built directly or indirectly on this scientific thinking process. Historically in this nation, children came to school with a knowledge of plants and animals built from their experience in playing, working, and living in the natural world. This experiential learning base was often derived from a rural farm experience and included a knowledge of farm animals, crops, ponds and streams, and the interrelationships between people and the natural world.

Today, many children live in high-rise apartment buildings, in inner cities paved with asphalt and concrete. Teachers may no longer assume that children come to school with a wealth of knowledge of the natural world. For many children, experiences with plants may be limited to potted house plants or decorative trees and shrubs. Children's prior knowledge of animals may be limited to invertebrate household pests and common household pets. Children's experiences with energy sources may be limited to electrical appliances and battery-powered toys. Observation of the natural world, the ability to observe accurately without at first making judgments from those observations, is a vital science process that must be developed and nurtured in all children.

While students at all grade levels need practice with observational processes, those in early grades need the most practice in making and stating observations, for young children frequently lack the experiential base necessary for observing well. Observation is the basis for almost all of the other science processes; practice in observational skills is desirable for students of all ages. Activities 9.1 through 9.3 offer such practice.

ACTIVITY 9.1   ■   "Growing" a Butterfly

Grade Level: Primary, intermediate, or upper

Science Process: Observing

Materials: Butterfly eggs (approximately three to five per child), plastic vial with cap, food for butterfly larva (depends on species, for example, spice-bush swallowtails feed on spicebush, monarch butterflies feed on milkweed), ruler

Cabbage butterfly

Conducting the Activity:

1. Supply each child or cooperative group with butterfly eggs. Have the children observe the eggs and record their observations in a journal. Encourage young children or children with limited English proficiency to make drawings to record their observation. Once the eggs hatch, instruct the children to feed the larvae daily, to "water them" by sprinkling the food with water, to clean their habitats, and to make daily observations on the larvae.

Insect larva in its habitat

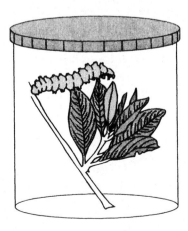

2. Instruct the children to keep a journal of their observations of their butterflies. Some species will complete a life cycle in four to six weeks in warm weather.

ACTIVITY 9.2 ■ It Smells Like . . .

Grade Level: Primary

Science Process: Observing

Materials: Ten film canisters or small opaque containers, ten food substances

Conducting the Activity: Before students arrive in the classroom, puncture holes in the lids of ten film canisters or similar containers. Place a different food (onion, apple, watermelon slice, cinnamon, orange peel, chocolate, oregano, banana, strawberry, celery) in the bottom of each container. Have the students sniff each container and make a guess as to its contents (without opening the container). After students have made a guess as to the contents of the container, allow them to open the containers and check the accuracy of their observations.

"It smells like . . ." observations

Container Number	Guess as to Contents	Actual Contents
1		
2		
3		
4		
5		
6		

ACTIVITY 9.3 ■ What's a Beetle?

Grade Level: Primary or intermediate

Science Process: Observing

Materials: Beetle or drawing of a beetle

Spotted cucumber beetle

Conducting the Activity: Present the students with a beetle or a drawing of a beetle. Pass the beetle from person to person asking the students to identify a characteristic of the beetle as it is passed. Make a list of observations on the board.

Classification

Classification is a science process that requires students to place objects into groups on the basis of the characteristics of the objects. Classification may range from a simple task such as grouping objects based on their colors to highly complex classification systems that identify the genus and species of a living organism. Classifying may be operationally defined as arranging or distributing objects, events, or information representing objects or events in classes according to some method or system (Carin, 1993). Activities that develop classification expertise involve sorting shapes, living things, and so forth by some common property.

Classification involves categorizing objects according to a predetermined property or set of properties. When working with culturally diverse learners, especially those with limited English proficiency, teachers should allow extra time to identify common attributes and to build English vocabulary associated with those attributes. Names for colors, sizes, relative masses, and so forth should be mentioned as children work with real world objects. Whenever possible, real world objects should be used in classification activities. Older students should be encouraged to develop multistage classification systems on their own. A multistage classification system for insects is shown in Figures 9.1 and 9.2. From the pictures of insects in Figure 9.1, we could develop a system for classifying insects such as that in Figure 9.2. Some activities to develop classification skills are in Activities 9.4 and 9.5.

FIGURE 9.1 ■ Common Insects

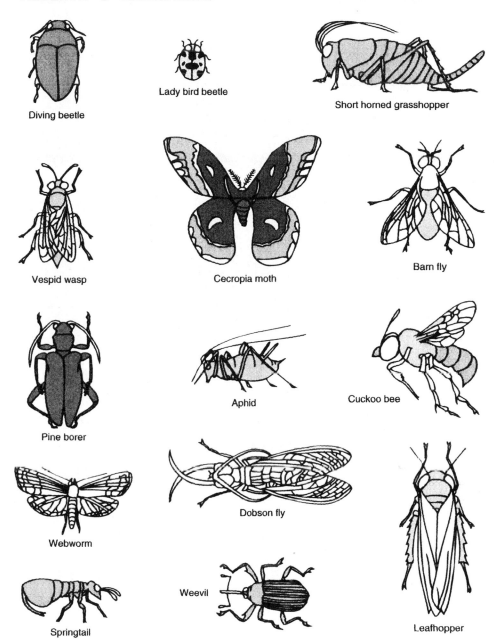

Diving beetle

Lady bird beetle

Short horned grasshopper

Vespid wasp

Cecropia moth

Barn fly

Pine borer

Aphid

Cuckoo bee

Webworm

Dobson fly

Springtail

Weevil

Leafhopper

FIGURE 9.2 ■ An Insect Classification System

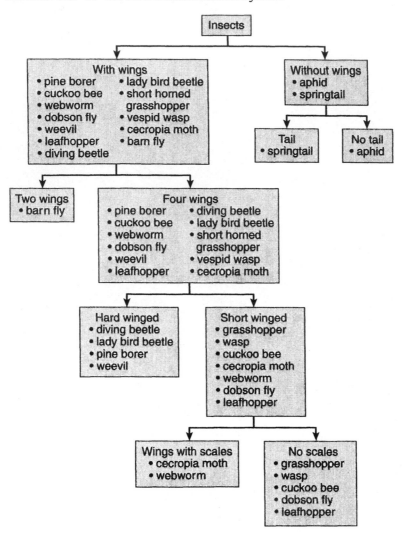

ACTIVITY 9.4 ■ Attribute Blocks

Grade Level: Primary science

Science Process: Classifying

Materials: Attribute sheet or attribute blocks

Attribute sheet

Conducting the Activity: Duplicate the attribute sheets for the students. Ask the students to cut out the shapes. Ask the students to group the shapes by common characteristics or attributes. Follow-up questions:

What are some of the ways we can group the objects?
What are some of the properties of the objects?
What shapes are the objects?
What sizes are the objects?
What patterns are there?
How many circles are there?
How many squares do you have?
How many triangles do you have?
How many of the objects are striped?
How many of the objects are spotted?
How many of the objects have a solid color?
How many of the objects are small?
How many of the objects are medium sized?
How many of the objects are large?

ACTIVITY 9.5 ■ Leaves

Grade Level: Intermediate or upper grades

Science Process: Classifying

Materials: Leaves or leaf print sheet

Conducting the Activity: Using the leaf print sheet, ask the students to group the leaves. Follow-up questions: How are the leaves alike? Different? How could you group the leaves?

Leaf print sheet

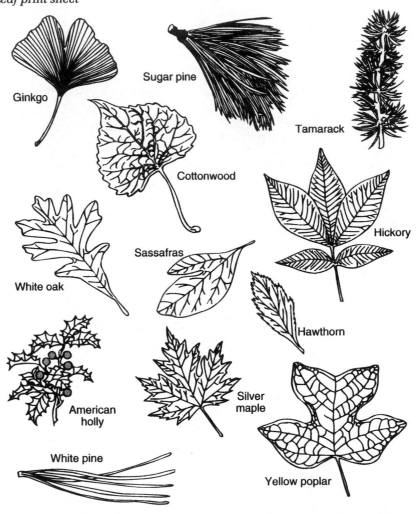

Measuring

Measuring may be defined as developing appropriate units of measurement for length, area, volume, time, and mass. Measuring at its simplest level involves comparing, that is, comparing an object of known dimensions with one of unknown dimensions (California State Board of Education, 1990). In measuring a line segment, a student compares the line segment (the object with unknown dimensions) with a ruler (an object with known or defined dimensions). According to Piaget, children need to have first attained the mental structures for conservation before they are able to understand measurement concepts (Wadsworth, 1978).

Conservation problems are some of the best known illustrations of children's levels of developmental reasoning. Assume that a young child is given two rows of pieces of candy. The child is allowed to count the pieces of candy and to determine that each row holds exactly the same number of pieces of candy. The adult aligns the candies so that there is a visible one-to-one correspondence between the pieces of candy in the top row and the bottom row (see Figure 9.3).

If the adult then rearranges the candy in one row so that it is more spread out than the other row, children who lack conservation will identify the spread-out row of candy as containing more candies than the other row (Figure 9.4). Such children lack conservation of length. Indeed, most children learn to conserve length at about 8 years of age.

In identifying the "age appropriateness" of various measuring activities, Wadsworth (1978) points out there is a strong relationship between a child's age and the child's ability to conserve different quantities. Table 9.1 lists various measurement tasks and a child's typical age for mastery of conservation.

In assisting children to develop measurement proficiency, teachers should be certain that the activity is appropriate for the age of the child. Young children who have not yet mastered conservation of liquid will have great difficulty understanding the properties of liquids (e.g., a liquid has a definite volume but will assume the shape of its container). For most children, informal measurement activities are appropriate in kindergarten through the third grade. Formal measurement using standard units of length, volume, and mass are appropriate for most children above the third-grade level.

FIGURE 9.3 ▦ Piagetian Conservation of Length Task

FIGURE 9.4 ▦ Conservation Task

TABLE 9.1 ■ Measurement Tasks and Typical Age of Conservation Mastery

Measurement Unit	Age of Attainment
Length	6 to 7 years
Number	6 to 7 years
Area	7 to 8 years
Mass	7 to 8 years
Liquid	7 to 8 years
Weight	9 to 10 years
Volume	11 to 12 years

When working with large numbers of children who have recently arrived in this country, teachers should remember that most children in the world have been taught to use metric measurement units. For example, children who have recently arrived from Mexico are used to buying milk and gasoline by the liter rather than by the gallon. These same children are accustomed to buying cloth by the meter rather than by the yard. Finally, they are used to buying flour and sugar by the "kilo" rather than by the pound. Since metric units of measurement are used in subsequent science instruction, teachers should encourage such children to continue using metric measuring units with which they are already familiar. Activities 9.6 through 9.9 assist children in mastering measurement competency.

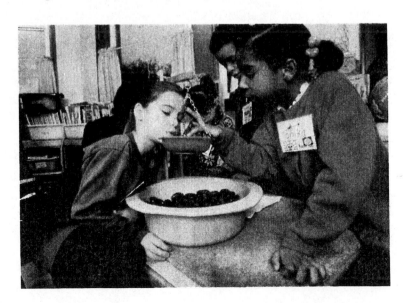

Measurement is a basic science process.

ACTIVITY 9.6 ■ Paper Clip Math

Grade Level: Primary

Science Process: Measuring

Materials: Ten small common household objects or a measuring sheet, as shown

Conducting the Activity: Ask the student to measure the length of each object using a paper clip. Instruct students to measure to the nearest whole paper clip.

Paper clip measurement sheet

Mexico

ACTIVITIES

ACTIVITY 9.7 ■ Measuring Mass

Grade Level: Primary to intermediate

Science Process: Measuring

Materials: Washers, baking cups, thread, ruler or stick, ten household objects

Student Directions:

1. Construct a baking cup balance using the baking cups, thread, and stick.

Baking cup balance

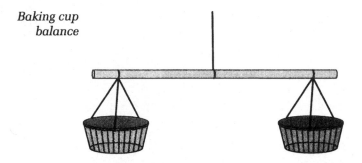

2. Place the objects in one pan (cup) of the balance. Add washers to the other cup until the two cups balance. How heavy is each object? Record the weight of each object on the table.

Baking cup balance data sheet

Object Name	Weight in Washers

Communicating

Communicating, another basic science processes, frequently involves compiling information in graphic or pictorial form. It also involves describing objects and events in detail. Communicating is the scientific thinking process that conveys ideas through social interchanges or social discourse. The process of communicating is actually the integration of language activities and mathematics in the science content area. Reporting findings is central to the work of all scientists.

Communication may be viewed as passing information from one individual or group of individuals to another (Wolfinger, 1984). Communication in the elementary science classroom ought to involve multiple means for children to express what they have learned in science. Pictographs, histograms, charts, tables of data, pictures, songs, videos, audiotaped recordings, and models are alternative means for children to express what they are learning. While written and oral communication are vital in the life of every child, not all children feel comfortable expressing their knowledge in written or oral form. Teachers working with large numbers of culturally diverse learners ought to consider alternative means of communicating or for sharing new learnings among students. When children are presented with alternative means to express their new knowledge, all children in the classroom benefit from the sharing.

ACTIVITY 9.8 ■ Candy Math

Grade Level: Primary to intermediate

Science Process: Communicating

Materials: 1 bag of M & M–like candies for each group

Conducting the Activity:

1. Allow the students to open the bag of candy. Instruct the students to divide the candy by colors (put all red candies in one pile, all yellow in another pile, and so forth). Have them complete the table of data for the candy.

Candy color distribution table

Color of Candy	Number of Pieces

2. From the table of data, ask students to make a histogram or frequency distribution showing the distribution of colors of candy in the bag.

Candy histogram

7
6
5
4
3
2
1

red green yellow blue orange brown

ACTIVITY 9.9   ■   Animal Legs

Grade Level: Intermediate

Science Process: Communicating

Materials: An animal data sheet and a piece of graph paper per student

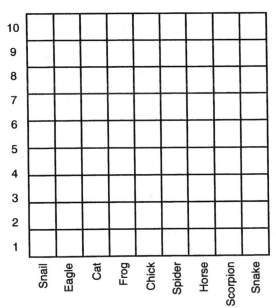

Bar graph for comparing animal legs

10
9
8
7
6
5
4
3
2
1

Snail Eagle Cat Frog Chick Spider Horse Scorpion Snake

Animal legs data sheet

Snail	Eagle	Cat
Frog	Chicken	Spider
Horse	Scorpion	Snake

Conducting the Activity:

1. Have the students examine each animal's picture and decide how many legs each animal has.
2. Instruct students to make a bar graph comparing the number of legs each animal has.

Inferring

Inferring is a basic science process that deals with ideas that are remote in time and space. Inferring involves drawing a conclusion based on reasoning to explain a set of observations. Stating that the snow melts because of the heat of the sun is an example of an inference. Inferences are guesses. They are explanations based on observations. Questions such as What can you infer from these data? What can you suggest is the reason? and Can you give evidence to support your statement? encourage students to make inferences. When students have access to a large amount of data, we tend to refer to the inference as a conclusion. A conclusion is a special type of inference based on a wealth of data rather than on a few specific cases.

Making an inference involves students in conjecturing, concluding, or suggesting new relationships based on careful observations. The process of inferring involves drawing a conclusion from what we have observed. "Mystery Boxes," Activity 9.10, encourage children to make inferences. In this activity, children guess the contents of the box based on their observations of the sound that the object makes as it moves inside the box, the relative mass of the box, and so forth. This activity encourages children to draw conclusions from their observations.

ACTIVITY 9.10 ■ Mystery Boxes

Grade Level:	Primary to upper elementary
Science Process:	Inferring
Materials:	Ten mystery boxes; each box should contain an object commonly found in the classroom and should be sealed with tape so that children cannot peek at the object.
Conducting the Activity:	Pass the mystery boxes from child to child. Instruct the children to twist, turn, and in general manipulate the box. Encourage children to write down (or draw, for younger children) a guess as to the contents of the box on a recording sheet. Before opening the boxes, encourage children to share with others their guesses about the contents of the boxes and their reasons for making their guesses.

Mystery box recording sheet

Box Number	Guess	Actual Contents
1		
2		
3		
4		
5		

FIGURE 9.5 ■ Making a Prediction

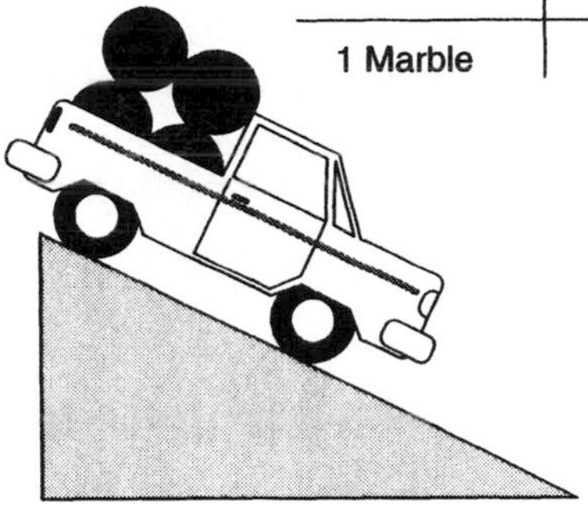

10 centimeters	20 centimeters	30 centimeters	?
1 Marble	2 Marbles	3 Marbles	4 Marbles

Predicting

Predicting involves children in forecasting a future event based on solid evidence. Abruscato states that predictions are based on observations, measurements, and inferences about relationships between observed variables (1988, p. 32). Unlike a guess, a prediction is based on careful observation. Whereas inferring involves children in drawing a conclusion based on data, predicting involves children in making informed guesses (i.e., guesses based on data) about future occurrences. Inferences are interpretations of past events; predictions anticipate future events.

Suppose a child observed a toy truck traveling down an inclined plane (Figure 9.5). When the truck was carrying one marble, it traveled a distance of 10 centimeters. When the truck carried two marbles it traveled 20 centimeters from the ramp. Three marbles loaded in the truck resulted in a trip of 30 centimeters. Based on these data, what distance would the child predict the truck would travel if it were carrying four marbles? The child's prediction would be based on observations; it would be an extrapolation or an extension beyond the existing data, and it would be a prediction of a future event based on prior observation.

ACTIVITY 9.11 ■ Marble Mania

Grade Level: Primary to upper elementary

Science Process: Predicting

Materials: Marble, ruler, piece of cardboard (approximately 20 cm. long), and piece of graph paper per student

Student Directions:

1. Elevate the piece of cardboard so that it forms an inclined plane. Raise the cardboard 2 cm. from the table. Place the marble on the cardboard and let it go. How far does the marble travel? Repeat with 4, 6, . . . cm.

Set-up for Marble Mania

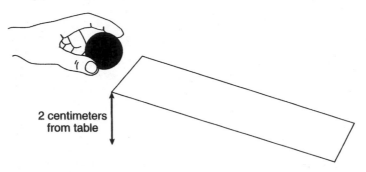

2 centimeters from table

Marble Mania recording sheet

Height of Ramp	*Distance Traveled*
2 centimeters	
4 centimeters	
6 centimeters	
8 centimeters	
10 centimeters	
12 centimeters	

2. Make a line graph showing the relationship between the height of the ramp and the distance the marble traveled.

Using Space/Time Relationships

Space/time relationships are science processes that use plane and solid geometric shapes as well as length, area, mass, and volume as part of an observation. An understanding of space/time relationships includes the ability to recognize and name two-dimensional shapes (e.g., squares, rectangles, and circles) and three-dimensional shapes (e.g., prisms, pyramids, cubes, and ellipsoids). At their simplest level, space/time relationships may include references to ordinal numbers (first, second, third). Abruscato (1988) states that this process can be broken down into a variety of categories, including shapes, direction and spatial arrangement, motion and speed, symmetry, and rate of change. For culturally diverse learners and white females, space/time relations are particularly important science processes, because many researchers have identified skill in these processes as prerequisite to success in science careers. Students who lack spatial skills are frequently unable to handle the complexity of advanced science courses. Spatial visualization skills at the lowest level include flips, flops, and rotations (see Figure 9.6).

As you visualize a notebook, think of a flip as the position of a letter after you have turned a page. A flop may be viewed as the position of a letter or numeral after you have turned up the page on a legal tablet. For a rotation, you must mentally turn an object in a 360-degree plane. Mastery of spatial visualization processes includes the ability to mentally manipulate objects, to twist, turn, and permute them. At the high school and university level, students who lack space/time relationships have extreme difficulty assembling laboratory apparatus from line drawings and mentally flipping the structures of organic molecules. A knowledge of space/time relationships is vital for success in advanced study of science and mathematics. Activity 9.12 offers practice in spatial visualization.

FIGURE 9.6 ■ Aspects of Spatial Visualization

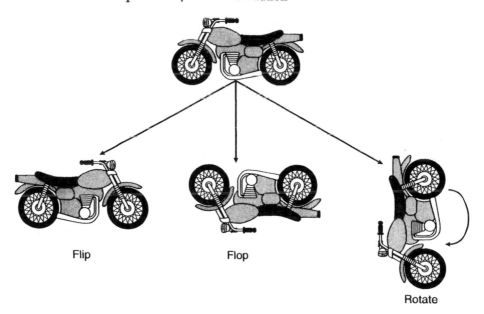

Flip   Flop

Rotate

ACTIVITY 9.12 ■ Symmetry

Grade Level: Upper elementary

Science Process: Space/time relationships

Materials: Mirror and symmetry sheet per student

Lines of symmetry

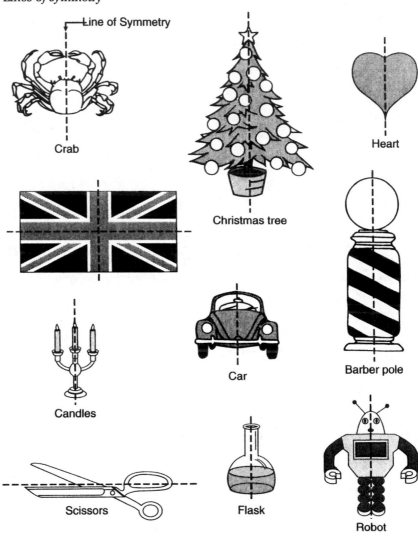

Line of Symmetry

Crab

Christmas tree

Heart

Candles

Car

Barber pole

Scissors

Flask

Robot

Symmetry data sheet

Name of Object	Symmetrical? (Yes or No)
Crab	
Christmas tree	
Heart	
Flag	
Candles	
Car	
Barber pole	
Scissors	
Flask	
Robot	

Student Directions: Examine each drawing and decide if the figure is symmetrical. Check your answer by placing a mirror on the dotted line on the figure. The dotted line is called the line of symmetry. If the figure is a mirror image of itself, if one side is the same as the other when the figure is folded in half, then the object is symmetrical.

Using Numbers

Using numbers is a basic process in which numbers other than those associated with the dimensions of an object are used to describe or quantify an activity or an experiment. Processes that require using numbers include those that apply mathematical rules or formulae in order to calculate quantities or to determine the relationships between numbers derived from simple measurements. The computation of an arithmetic average is an example of using numbers. Using numbers comprises a progression of mathematical skills that may include identifying sets and their elements, ordering numbers, serial ordering, establishing one-to-one correspondence, ordering and/or sequencing objects or events, counting, adding, subtracting, multiplying, dividing, finding averages, using decimals, manipulating fractions, and using scientific notation.

Calculators facilitate students' computation efforts and focus the attention of learners on What does the answer mean? and Is the answer reasonable? rather than on the computation itself. When using numbers in the elementary science classroom, teachers should encourage students to use mental mathematics skills, to estimate answers, and to use technology to facilitate routine computation work. Activities 9.13 and 9.14 involve children in using numbers.

ACTIVITY 9.13   ■   How Big Is a Block?

Grade Level: Upper elementary

Science Process: Using numbers

Materials: Calculator, five blocks of wood (different sizes), ruler

Conducting the Activity: 1. Have the students determine the dimensions of the wooden blocks using a metric ruler (length, width, and depth).

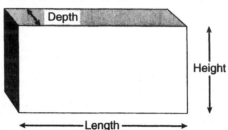

Dimensions of a rectangular solid

Volume = length × height × width

2. Have students calculate the volumes of the blocks by using the formula for the volume of a rectangular solid, using calculators, and record the results on a data sheet.

Volume of a solid data sheet

Block Number	Length	Width	Depth	Volume*
1				
2				
3				
4				
5				

*Volume = length × width × depth

ACTIVITY 9.14   ■   How Heavy Is It?

Grade Level: Upper elementary

Science Process: Using numbers

Materials: Calculator, ruler, five rectangular solids (different densities), balance

Conducting the Activity:

1. Have the students measure the dimensions of the rectangular solids (length, width, and volume). Volume = length × width × depth.
2. Have students determine the mass of each solid by weighing it on a pan balance. They should calculate the volume of the object first. Next have the students calculate the density by dividing the mass by the volume. Density = mass/volume.

Density data sheet

Number of Solid	Length	Width	Depth	Volume*	Mass	Density**
1						
2						
3						
4						
5						

*Volume = length × width × depth
**Density = mass/volume

Identifying Variables

Identifying variables is a basic science process in which the student recognizes the characteristics of objects or factors in events that are constant or that change under different conditions. Naming variables involves stating all the factors that affect an event. Variables are all of the factors within an experiment that may be changed by the experimenter.

Independent Variables

Typically, variables may be classified as being independent, dependent, and extraneous. An independent variable may be operationally defined as the variable that is changed in an experiment. Independent variables are also referred to as manipulated variables. Manipulated or independent variables may be deliberately and systematically changed by the investigator.

Dependent Variables

Dependent variables may be regarded as "responding" variables. Dependent variables respond or change according to changes in the independent variables. For elementary-aged children, dependent variables need to be those forces, actions, or quantities easily measured by children at this age.

Extraneous Variables

Finally, other factors that may influence the outcome of the experiment are referred to as extraneous variables. Extraneous variables are frequently referred to as controlled variables. They are factors or influences that may affect

FIGURE 9.7 ■ Identifying
Independent and Dependent
Variables

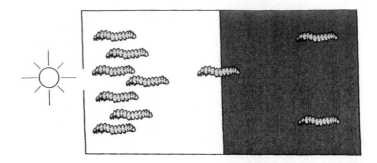

the outcome of the activity that are kept constant or unchanged during an investigation.

Suppose a researcher wanted to find out whether mealworms prefer a light or dark environment. The researcher would place the mealworms in a container with a light source at one end and darkness at the other end (see Figure 9.7). The presence or absence of light is the independent variable; it is the variable that the researcher changes. The movement of the mealworms to the light or dark end of the box is the responding or dependent variable. If most of the mealworms moved to the light end of the box, we would infer that they preferred light to darkness.

However, we need to control for extraneous variables, other factors that might influence the outcome of the experiment. Is the paper in the bottom of the box moist in some places and not others? Perhaps mealworms respond to moisture as well as light. Is the paper in the bottom of the box rough in some places and not in others? Perhaps smoothness of the paper affects the movement of mealworms. Is the temperature in the box uniform? Mealworms might respond to changes in temperature. Controlling extraneous variables or factors that may influence the outcome of the experiment is vital in all scientific investigations.

Identifying variables is a science process prerequisite for all science experimentation. Unless children are able to identify variables, they are unable to control those variables in experimental conditions. Activity 9.15 is typical of investigations that encourage children to construct a knowledge of variables.

ACTIVITY 9.15   ■   Soda-Can Catapult

Grade Level: Intermediate to upper elementary

**Science
Process:**   Identifying variables

Materials: Empty soda can (with the ring on the top), three marbles of different masses, metric measuring tape

Teacher Preparation: Before students arrive in class, pull back firmly on the tab at the top of the soda can so that the tab is at a 45-degree angle to the top of the can. This forms the top of the can into a simple catapult.

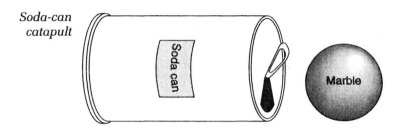

Soda-can catapult

Conducting the Activity:

1. Instruct the students to place the soda can on the floor and to place a small marble firmly against the tab. When the spring (the inverted tab) is as far back as possible, release the marble. How far does it go? Repeat with a medium and a large marble. Record the distances that the marbles travel on a data sheet.

Soda-can catapult

Size of the Marble	Distance It Travels
Small	
Medium	
Large	

2. After the students have had the opportunity to investigate the soda-can catapult, ask them to reflect on the activity and to complete the following form based on their observations. Define the terms *independent, dependent,* and *extraneous variables* for the students.

Identifying Variables

Type of Variable	Example
Independent (changes)	
Dependent (responding)	
Extraneous (other)	

INTEGRATED PROCESSES

Integrated science processes may be thought of as complex or multifaceted. They each combine two or more basic science processes. Integrated scientific thinking processes include (1) formulating hypotheses, (2) controlling variables, (3) investigating, (4) defining operationally, and (5) experimenting. Integrated processes may be thought of as "causal" processes, that is, processes that help students establish cause-and-effect relationships.

Formulating Hypotheses

A hypothesis may be defined as an educated guess. Abruscato (1988) has defined a hypothesis as a generalization that includes all objects or events of the same class. Esler and Esler (1993) have defined hypothesis formulation as making a statement that is believed to be true about a whole class of events. In constructing a hypothesis, the student is making a statement that is tentative and testable. Hypothesis formulation is an integrated process in that it combines observing, predicting, naming variables, communicating, and using numbers.

In formulating a hypothesis, students are attempting to explain a class of events in a reasonable fashion, and in a way that may be verified through their own experimentation. When adults formulate a hypothesis, they frequently express the hypothesis in the form of a Boolean statement, that is, an "if . . . then" statement. For children, hypothesis formulation is best done within the context of operational questioning. An operational question is a child-generated question that may be answered by children through their manipulation of simple, readily available materials. Examples of operational questions for children include: If I added salt to water, could I make an egg float? What would happen if I added a paper clip to the nose of a paper airplane? and How could I shape a clay boat to make it hold more mass? For children, formulating a hypothesis is an attempt to explain a phenomenon in their world, as Activity 9.16 illustrates.

ACTIVITY 9.16   ■   Paper Parachute

Grade Level: Primary to upper elementary

Science Process: Formulating hypotheses

Materials: Piece of cloth approximately 30 cm. square or a paper towel or napkin, thread, washers, meter stick or metric measuring tape

**Student
Directions:**
1. Assemble a toy parachute. Drop the parachute from a height of 1.5 meters. What happens?

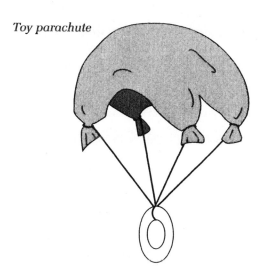

Toy parachute

2. Read each operational question, formulate a hypothesis, and record it on the following data sheet. Then conduct an investigation using the parachute to answer the question. (Hint: Use one parachute as a control before beginning to manipulate variables.)

Parachute data sheet

Operational Question	*Hypothesis*
What would happen if the parachute were dropped from a greater height?	
What would happen if more washers were added to the parachute?	
What would happen if a larger parachute were used?	
What would happen if a smaller parachute were used?	

Controlling Variables

Identifying variables is a basic science process that involves students in identifying which factors affect the outcome of an investigation. Controlling variables involves students in manipulating variables, that is, in changing some objects and/or conditions while keeping others constant. Abruscato (1988) states that controlling variables means managing the conditions of an investigation. As stated earlier, a variable is an object or quantity that may be changed and that may affect the outcome of an investigation. Controlling variables is an integrated science process which combines many basic science processes, including observing, classifying, measuring, communicating, inferring, using space/time relationships, using numbers, and identifying variables.

A logical step after identifying variables is to control variables in a systematic fashion. For example, if students carrying out the mealworm activity earlier in this chapter believe that moisture may be a salient variable in the behavior of mealworms, then students could design an investigation to determine if mealworms prefer moist or dark environments. Likewise, if children believe that exercise might affect human heart rate or respiration rate, they could design a simple investigation to determine if the two were related. Controlling variables requires mental maturation on the part of the child. Young children are rarely able to control variables by themselves. Controlling variables only becomes possible when the child has reached the formal operational level of thinking (the final stage of development hypothesized by Piaget).

The investigation in Activity 9.17 illustrates an activity in which children may manipulate variables and determine the relationship between them.

ACTIVITY 9.17 ■ Film-Can Cannon

Grade Level: Intermediate to upper elementary

Science Process: Controlling variables

Materials: Film can (empty 35 mm plastic film canister), vinegar, water, baking soda, graduated cylinder

Student Directions:
1. Place 9 ml. of water and 1 ml. of vinegar in a camera can. Add 5 grams (or a level teaspoon or measuring spoon) of baking soda. Quickly cap the canister. (This is best done as an outdoor activity with children. Alka Seltzer tablets may be substituted for the vinegar and baking soda.)

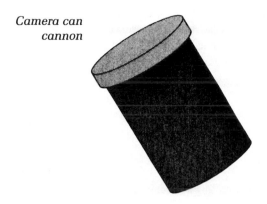

Camera can cannon

2. What happens? How far does the cap travel? Repeat for different amounts of water and vinegar while holding the amount of baking soda constant. Record the distances on the data sheet. What happens to the distance the cap travels as the concentration of vinegar increases?

Camera-cannon data sheet

Amount Water	Amount Vinegar	Distance
10 ml.	0 ml.	
8 ml.	2 ml.	
6 ml.	4 ml.	
4 ml.	6 ml.	
2 ml.	8 ml.	
0 ml.	10 ml.	

Investigating

Investigating is an integrated science process that incorporates manipulating materials and recording data. This integrated process is built on the basic processes of observing, classifying, measuring, communicating, inferring, predicting, and using space/time relationships. Typically, students investigating in the classroom use science process skills to gather data in a discovery learning situation or by following teacher directions when not employing the formal scientific process.

Investigating may be seen as replicating an activity. Investigations provide an opportunity for students to acquire expertise in handling or treating materials and equipment. As part of the manipulation of materials, students should be engaged in analyzing data, in looking for patterns and relationships between variables. Activities that provide students with the opportunity to develop investigative skills include using a microscope and noting the ways that it works and manipulating bulbs and batteries in order to make a circuit (Activities 9.18 and 9.19). Investigation typically strengthens students' motor development as well as their observational proficiency.

ACTIVITY 9.18 ■ Letter E

Grade Level: Intermediate to upper elementary

Science Process: Investigating

Materials: Newspaper, microscope, slide, cover slip, scissors

Student Directions:

1. Cut a letter *e* from a newspaper. Place it on a microscope slide and cover with a cover slip (this is called a dry mount). Place the slide on the platform of the microscope so that the letter *e* faces you. Look through the eyepiece and adjust the coarse and fine adjustment knobs so that the *e* is in focus.

Microscope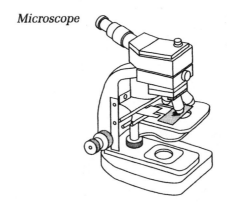

2. Draw the letter *e*. What did you expect the letter *e* to look like? How is it different under the microscope? Move the slide to the left. What happens to the letter *e*? Move the slide to the right. What happens to the letter *e*? Move the slide up. What happens to the letter *e*? Move the slide down. What happens to the letter *e*?

ACTIVITY 9.19 ■ Bulbs and Batteries

Grade Level: Intermediate to upper elementary

Science Process: Investigating

Materials: Battery, bulb, piece of insulated copper wire for each student

Bulbs and batteries

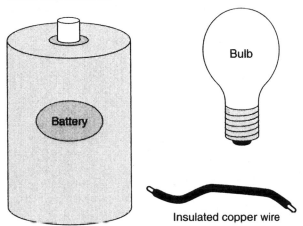

Bulb

Battery

Insulated copper wire

Student Directions:
1. Connect the bulb and battery with the wire so that the bulb lights. Draw your circuit.
2. Try another way of getting the bulb to light. Draw this circuit.
3. How many different arrangements of the bulb, battery, and wire can you make that will light the bulb?

Defining Operationally

Operational definitions may be thought of as working definitions. Because they are based on a child's experience in the natural world, they lack the sophistication of formal science definitions. Normally, operational definitions are associated with identifying and controlling variables. To formulate an operational definition, the student defines all variables as they are used in an experiment. For example, in the Soap Boat activity (Activity 9.20) the best soap boat might be defined as one that travels the farthest.

FIGURE 9.8 ■ Cocoons

An operational definition in the context of the physical sciences is based on what is done and what is observed. Operational definitions in life sciences tend to be descriptive. For example, an insect's cocoon may be defined as a container made by the insect, which holds an insect's pupa. The formal science definition of a cocoon is: "Cocoon—in general, any tough, protective covering which encloses the eggs or young, and sometimes adults of animals, as the silken envelope enclosing the larva or pupa of an insect" (Steen, 1971, p. 107).

As children have the opportunity to investigate the natural world, their knowledge and understanding of the world increases and their operational definitions begin to more closely resemble formal science definitions. An operational definition may be thought of as a working definition, one that will be refined by the child over time.

ACTIVITY 9.20   ■   Soap Boat

Grade Level: Intermediate to upper elementary

Science Process: Defining operationally

Materials: Three cardboard boats, three slivers of different brands of soap from worn-down soap bars (best done by the teacher in advance), pan of water, measuring tape

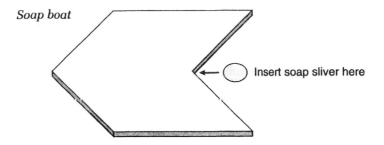

Soap boat

Insert soap sliver here

Student Directions:

1. Assemble the soap boats by inserting the soap slivers at the back of each boat. Fill a shallow pan about one-half full of tap water. Place the three boats in the center of the pan of water at the same time. Observe the boats and measure the distance that they travel before stopping. Record the results on the following data sheet.

Soap boat data sheet

Brand Soap	Distance

2. [operationally defining terms] Which boat was the best boat? Why? Which soap is best as a fuel for soap boats? Why? How do you decide the distance that the soap boat travels?

Experimenting

Experimenting is the last of the integrated science processes. It involves students in using all other processes. The best experiments are student-generated, activities students want to perform because they are interested and motivated. Experimenting typically involves extending classwork into a new domain. At its simplest level, experimenting may be defined as performing the activity. Experimenting encompasses all of the basic and integrated

ACTIVITIES

processes. Experimenting involves children in formulating operational questions that they can answer by manipulating materials. Additionally, experimenting involves children in identifying and controlling variables, designing an activity to test a hypothesis, formulating operational definitions, observing, gathering data and using numbers, making inferences, interpreting data, and drawing conclusions based on those data.

In nearly every elementary classroom there are children who do not have the opportunity to experiment on their own, to carry on an activity beyond the regular instructional period, due to a lack of resources and materials at home. Schools need to be places where children are encouraged to pursue their learning beyond the scope of the curriculum. All children ought to be encouraged to learn on their own, to pursue their interests, to develop expertise in a field of their own choosing.

ACTIVITY 9.21   ■   Balloon Rocket

Grade Level: Intermediate to upper elementary

Science Process: Experimenting

Materials: For each student, balloon, string (5 to 10 meters in length), metric tape, soda straw, scissors, tape, paper clip

Student Directions: 1. Place a thread or fine string in a short piece of soda straw. Tie the ends of the thread to chairs (spaced 5 to 10 meters apart). Blow up the balloon, twist the end and temporarily close the end with a paper clip. Place a piece of tape over the soda straw so that the balloon is attached to the straw. Place the balloon at one end of the rocket course, undo the paper clip and let go of the balloon. How far does it travel? Repeat with a balloon with a small amount of air, a medium amount of air, and a large amount of air inside. The size of the balloon may be measured by placing a string around the balloon to measure its circumference. Record your results.

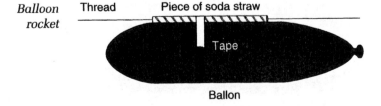

Balloon rocket   Thread   Piece of soda straw

Tape

Ballon

Balloon rocket data sheet

Size of Balloon	*Measurement*	*Distance Traveled*
Small		
Medium		
Large		

2. Experiment: Try to design the best balloon possible, the one that will go the farthest. What happens if you add fins? Add a nose cone? How many fins are best? How should the nose cone be shaped? Should mass be added to the nose cone? Keep a log of your experiments and your results.

CLASSROOM PRACTICE

Reflection is vital in the life of all teachers. As a teacher, you will reflect on your teaching on a daily basis. Reflection is guided by questions such as: What do my students know? What do I want my students to learn? How will I assist them to learn this? and What have my students learned? Activities that encourage students to use science processes are educationally rich.

Work through the electromagnet activity (Activity 9.22) first as a student. Experiment with constructing an electromagnet, investigate the properties of the electromagnet, and perform the activity as if you were a student. When you have finished the activity, reflect on your learning. What science processes have you used while doing this activity? What conceptual knowledge have you gained?

Each activity in this chapter is designed to enhance students' knowledge of science processes and to assist students in their conceptual development. Even though activities have been listed under specific science processes, in fact, all of the activities teach more than one science process. Review the activities and attempt to identify all of the processes fostered in the activities.

ACTIVITY 9.22 ■ Electromagnet

Materials: Dry cell battery, insulated copper wire, nail, metal paper clips

Student   1. Assemble the electromagnet as shown.

Directions: 2. Conduct an investigation to determine what happens to the strength of the electromagnet as more wraps of wire are added to the nail. Record your results.

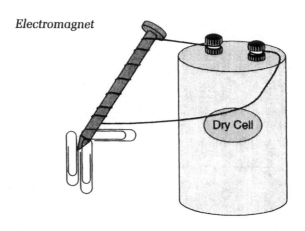

Electromagnet

Dry Cell

Electromagnet data sheet

Wraps of Wire	Number of Paper Clips Lifted
5	
10	
15	
20	
25	
30	

3. What happens to the strength of the electromagnet as more wraps of wire are added to the nail?

CHAPTER SUMMARY

One role of the elementary science teacher is to assist students to develop the thinking processes that characterize the scientific enterprise. Science as it is practiced aims to be testable, objective, and consistent. The goal of develop-

TABLE 9.2 ■ Overview of Science Processes

Science Process	Definition	Example
Basic Processes		
Observing	Identifying and naming the properties of objects and events in the physical world	Observing an insect's life cycle
Classifying	Arranging objects, events, or information according to a method or system	Grouping living things
Measuring	Comparing an object of unknown dimensions to a known dimension	Measuring line segments
Communicating	Conveying ideas through social interchanges	Journal writings of findings
Inferring	Making a conclusion based on reasoning to explain a set of observations	Mystery Boxes activity
Predicting	Forecasting some future event based on solid evidence	Weather forecasting
Using space/time relationships	Using plane and solid geometric shapes as well as length and so forth for observation	Leaf Symmetry
Using numbers	Applying mathematical rules or formulae to calculate quantities	Computing work and force
Identifying variables	Recognizing the characteristics of objects or events that are constant or changing	Soda-Can Catapult activity
Integrated Processes		
Formulating hypotheses	Making a statement believed to be true about a class of events	Paper parachute activity
Controlling variables	Changing objects and/or conditions while keeping others constant	Film-Can Cannon activity
Investigating	Gathering data in a discovery learning situation through manipulating materials	Bulbs and Batteries activity
Defining operationally	Generating working definitions in the context of an investigation	Soap Boat activity
Experimenting	The process that encompasses other processes	Balloon Rocket activity

ing scientific literacy in all students can be met only when students have mastered the scientific thinking processes. The basic science processes of observing, classifying, measuring, communicating, inferring, predicting, using space/time relationships, using numbers, and identifying variables are vital for all students. As students grow and mature, they ought to be encouraged to develop expertise in using integrated science processes: formulating hypotheses, controlling variables, investigating, defining operationally, and experimenting.

TOPICS TO REVIEW

- Observing
- Classifying
- Measuring
- Communicating
- Inferring
- Predicting
- Using space/time relationships
- Using numbers
- Identifying variables
- Formulating hypotheses
- Controlling variables
- Investigating
- Operationally defining
- Experimenting

REFLECTIVE PRACTICE

1. Think about the Soap Boat activity (Activity 9.20). What science processes will students use when working through this activity? Explain where in the activity each process is used.

2. The "Growing" a Butterfly activity (Activity 9.1) illustrates the process of observation. Actually, other processes might be taught with this activity. Name them. Explain where you see evidence of these other processes being used.

3. In your opinion, why are children discouraged from experimenting in the elementary science classroom? What could be done to change this?

4. In what ways could teaching children using process-based lessons benefit culturally diverse students? Explain your answers.

CHAPTER 10

Instructional Technology Approaches

```
┌─────────────────────────┐        ┌──────────────────────────────┐
│  Traditional Design      │        │  Information Processing       │
│                          │        │                               │
│  • Mathemagenic models   │        │  • Cognitive strategies       │
│  • IDI models for design │        │  • Visualization              │
│                          │        │  • Information processing     │
│                          │        │  • Feedback and motivation    │
└─────────────────────────┘        └──────────────────────────────┘
```

```
┌──────────────────────────────┐
│  Current Microcomputer        │
│  Applications in Science       │
│                               │
│  • Graphic packages           │
│  • Instrument interfacing     │
│  • Simulations                │
└──────────────────────────────┘
```

```
┌──────────────────────────────────────────────┐
│                FOUNDATIONS                     │
├──────────────────────────────────────────────┤
│  Historical    Pedagogical      Research       │
└──────────────────────────────────────────────┘
```

Technology in the Multicultural Classroom

▓ POINTS TO PONDER

- In what ways can technology facilitate teaching and learning in the science classroom?
- In what ways do you personally use technology to improve your science teaching?
- In your opinion, how can technology be used to address the needs of culturally and/or linguistically diverse learners?

Change is part of all of our lives. Change is good, healthy; it refreshes us; it sometimes bewilders us. The summer that my family moved from New Mexico to Pennsylvania illustrates the nature of change in my own family's lives. We traveled at the beginning of August so that we could arrive in Pennsylvania before the start of the school year. My children, who had spent their entire lives in the warmth and comfort of family surroundings, were moving thousands of miles from home. As parents, we wanted to make sure that they had time to adjust to their new home before the infamous first day of school.

In spite of our efforts, the first day in a new academic environment proved to be a disaster for our sons. Our middle son, Javier, came home from school complaining that the school cooks were attempting to poison him. He had been raised on school lunches of burritos, tacos, nachos, green chili stew, chili cheeseburgers, and tort burgers. According to Javier the cooks in Pennsylvania served rotten food. The hot dog was gray and swollen and tasted "nasty." The cooks must have left the potato salad out too long before serving it, he said, because it had become warm. Finally, they served some kind of rotten, "squishy," spoiled lettuce. According to Javier, except for the hot dog bun, the entire meal was inedible. When I called the school in the late afternoon to complain about the spoiled food, I learned that he had been served a Pennsylvania Dutch meal of knackwurst on a bun, hot German potato salad, and sauerkraut. Pennsylvania food was a culture shock to a boy from New Mexico.

My other son had an equally disappointing day. As a first-day assignment he was asked to write a composition about his summer vacation. It seemed to me that a composition about one's summer vacation on the first day of school is a fairly routine assignment. When I pressed Aáron about the nature of his complaint, I learned that the teacher had asked him to write the composition using pencil and paper. I thought this was fairly reasonable, until I saw through Aáron's eyes. From kindergarten through fifth grade, he had done all of his compositions on a computer. He was used to writing with the assistance of a prewrite package, a spelling checker, and a primitive grammar checker. His first day in a new school seemed like a visit to another planet. Having been raised as part of the computer generation, he viewed his new school as undeveloped, as technologically illiterate. Changes in technologies have resulted in changes in the ways that we teach children.

TECHNOLOGY IN SCIENCE TEACHING AND LEARNING

Movie projectors, cassette tape players, television monitors, microcomputers, interactive video workstations, and access to the World Wide Web are examples of technologies that have at one time or another entered the science classroom as tools to facilitate the teaching/learning process. Since the first school museum opened in St. Louis in 1905 (Saettler, 1968, p. 89), science educators have looked to technology for solutions to pedagogical problems. In 1913, Thomas Edison proclaimed that "books will soon be obsolete in our schools. . . . It is possible to teach every branch of human knowledge with the motion picture projector." Edison went on to predict that our school systems would be radically changed by motion picture projectors within ten years.

Magic lanterns (stereopticons and stereoscopes) became instructional tools in the science classroom during the latter half of the nineteenth century. Edison's movie projector was the visual tool of choice for science teachers during the 1910s. Following World War I, motion pictures with accompanying sound became popular instructional tools in the science classroom. Educational applications of technology multiplied during World War II. Military applications of instructional technologies included the use of overhead projectors for large group instruction, slide projectors for teaching aircraft recognition, audiotape instruction for teaching foreign languages, and multimedia flight training simulators (Olsen & Bass, 1982). Following World War II, teachers adopted these technologies for instructional purposes in the science classroom.

The 1950s and 1960s were the decades of instructional television. Educational television during this period was viewed as a means of quick, efficient, and inexpensive science instruction. The National Defense Education Act: Title VII, in effect for one decade, spent more than $40 million on 600 projects (Filep & Schramm, 1970), including instructional television. Private foundations such as the Ford Foundation, which spent $170 million during this period, supported instructional programming as a means of improving instruction nationwide. With minor exceptions, however, the disappearance of educational television has left science instruction fundamentally unchanged.

In 1951, Remington Rand introduced the first commercially available computer system, the UNIVAC I, which was constructed of vacuum tubes. By the middle of the 1950s the vacuum tubes of the UNIVAC had been replaced by transistors. The second generation of computers was faster and more complex than its predecessor. Early in the 1960s, a third generation of computers, run by integrated circuits, became commercially available. Widespread science classroom usage of microcomputer technology began in the 1970s with the invention of the fourth generation, microcomputers based on microchip technology.

The invention of CD-ROMs, modems, and digital video technologies in the late 1980s has allowed for the development of a new generation of computer-based learning environments that incorporate sound, graphics, video, and text. Multimedia courseware allows for multiple modes of knowledge representation, thus meeting the needs of learners who have difficulty functioning in a text-based learning environment. Since the introduction of computer technologies in schools, an entire generation of children has been raised using computers as readily as textbooks.

Most recently, the development of the World Wide Web has provided science teachers with additional resources to improve teaching and learning. February 1995 is cited as the date on which the amount of information stored electronically on the World Wide Web surpassed that stored in paper-based formats. Web-based learning is an emerging technology that will dramatically impact science teaching and learning, especially in terms of the amount of information available for teachers and students. An abbreviated history of the World Wide Web is shown in Table 10.1.

TABLE 10.1   ■   An Abbreviated History of the Information Superhighway

Year	Event in Internet History
1940s	Invention of first practical computers
1969	Internet founded as ARPANET at four sites
1974	Internet management transferred to the U.S. Defense Agency
1981	BITNET founded (Because It's Time Network)
1986	National Science Foundation links five supercomputers (NSFNET) as the "backbone" of the Internet
1987	National Science Foundation assigns IBM, MCI, and Michigan Education Research Information to manage the network
1991	Infomercials begin on the Internet
1994	Mosaic and other multimedia Internet services begin
1995	Two-way interactive communication, CU See Me
1996	Wireless remote modems make Internet accessible worldwide

CHANGES IN SOFTWARE

Just as a revolution in technology has allowed the microcomputer to become an affordable instructional tool in the science classroom, the software that runs that hardware has evolved. The first generation of educational software in the science classroom consisted of networked programs such as PLATO, which required the computing power of mainframe computers (Denenberg, 1988, p. 313). The first microcomputer software widely used in science classrooms was written in BASIC and required the regular science teacher to have a knowledge of BASIC commands (such as "LOAD <FILENAME>" and "RUN <FILENAME>"). By the beginning of the 1980s "Press <RETURN> to continue" became the instructional standard of the second generation of science software (Jonassen, 1988, p. 151). Software in the early 1980s became menu driven and user friendly, but the pedagogical base of that software remained rooted in a mathemagenic, drill-and-practice model. Multimedia CD-ROM products represent a fourth generation of computer software that includes multiple modes of knowledge representation and in many cases a constructivist view of teaching and learning.

The model of software design used in first-, second-, and third-generation software development was rooted in stimulus/response or behaviorist learning theory. This model holds that the software provides a stimulus and the learner responds or "learns." This is a "sage-on-stage" learning model in which the computer becomes the source of authority or information and the students are "empty vessels" waiting to be filled with knowledge. In this model, information is transmitted from the computer to children whose minds are receptive empty slates. Indeed, 85% of the software used in public schools in the United States today is drill-and-practice software (Cohen, 1983), written from this pedagogical perspective.

The behavioral principle of **connectionism,** which served as the basis of first-, second- and third-generation software, assumes that enough practice ultimately produces correct performance (Jonassen, 1988, p. 151). This **mathemagenic model** for computerized instruction has failed to achieve the desired results in the science classroom because (1) it fails to accommodate the principles of educational psychology, (2) it results in shallow or low levels of information processing, and (3) microcomputer and interactive video technologies have outgrown programmed instructional models. With fourth-generation software, computer-mediated learning is evolving from stimulus-response learning, beyond information-processing learning models to constructivist views of teaching and learning.

Fourth-generation software that encourages high levels of user interactivity and metacognitive processing is beginning to find its way into the science classroom. The term *interactivity* here refers to the user's ability to engage in direct and continual two-way communication with the computer. Fourth-generation science software establishes a transactional triangle between the learner, the microcomputer, and the natural world (see Figure 10.1).

Additionally, fourth-generation software allows children to construct meaning for themselves in an electronic environment, to negotiate meaning through interactions with the courseware. This newer software is built upon a cognitive psychology foundation that holds that children construct knowledge based on their experiences and their interactions. From this perspective, software in the future ought to allow the learner in the multicultural class-

FIGURE 10.1 ▥ Science Software's Transactional Triangle

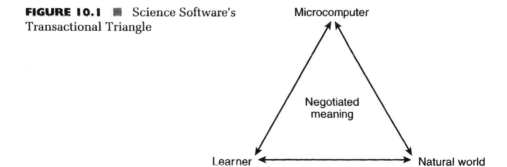

room to explore the natural world and relationships in that natural world, to "do science," rather than to watch science or to read about science. As science software is modified and refined, microcomputers will become tools for learning rather than teachers. The computer in the immediate future will become a resource to aid children in negotiating meaning regarding natural phenomena.

Embedded Cognitive Strategies

The goal of multimedia software in the science classroom ought to be to support the acquisition, retention, and retrieval of information by the individual learner. It should promote and guide active mental processing on the part of the student, to foster metacognition or an awareness of learning. To do this, multimedia courseware needs to have embedded generative cognitive strategies (Wittrock, 1978) that facilitate the transfer of information from short-term to long-term memory. Fourth-generation science software should allow the learner to actively explore the natural world as it supports the activities of the learner in that world. Placing the learner in control of the software, rather than the computer in charge of the learner, is a pedagogical decision that profits all children.

Culturally diverse learners, who frequently need multiple modes of information presentation in the learning process, particularly benefit from embedded cognitive strategies. Wittrock (1978), in addressing the status of microcomputer software, states that meaning for material presented by computer or interactive video instruction is generated by activating and altering existing knowledge structures within the learner. There is a recognition that learning is an active process, not a passive one. New learning comes as the individual consciously and intentionally relates new information to existing knowledge structures. Hence, instructional materials need to facilitate this interaction by including learning strategies.

Learning strategies generate not only learning about science, but information about how to learn science. Generative activities such as outlining, underlining, paraphrasing, summarizing, mnemonic devices, cognitive mapping, metaphors, categorizing, and note taking are mental operations or procedures that the student may use to acquire, retain, and retrieve knowledge and performance skills (Rigney, 1978). Such learning strategies may be taught explicitly, or they may be embedded in the instructional materials themselves. Embedding learning strategies directly into software can not only assist students with constructing meaning from the material at hand, but also facilitate students' development of metacognitive strategies for future learning.

We know from research (Carrier, 1983) that students who engage in active note taking perform better than students who do not overtly organize information. The active use of organizational strategies such as outlining and

FIGURE 10.2 ■ Electronic Notebook

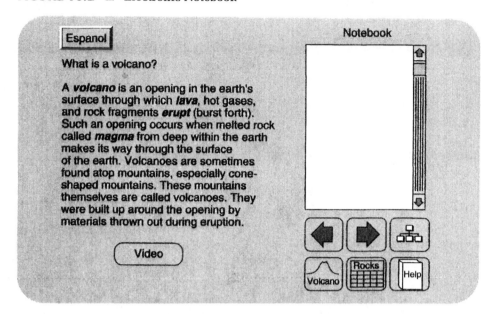

analyzing key ideas and of information-integration strategies such as paraphrasing and exemplifying increase schemata formation in learners. When students engage in active study strategies such as using electronic notebooks embedded in science software they develop deeper levels of information processing. Electronic notebooks embedded in courseware (Figure 10.2) allow students to organize, manipulate, and retrieve information; they assist the child in constructing knowledge of the physical world.

Visualization Strategies

Visualization strategies have been recognized for several decades as important to the learning process (Allen, 1960; Chu & Schramm, 1967; Day & Beach, 1950; Levie & Dickie, 1973). Visualization increases learner interest, motivation, curiosity, and concentration. Additionally, increased visualization provides instructional feedback, facilitates information acquisition, spans linguistic barriers, increases the reliability of communication, and emphasizes and reinforces printed instruction. Research has shown that enhanced visualization, including the use of the fotonovela or photonovel, is the most effective means for conveying verbal information to culturally and linguistically unassimilated learners. Students learn more declarative knowledge from textual materials printed with enhanced visualization than with traditional textbook or screen formats.

FIGURE 10.3 ■ Embedded Visualization Strategies

Hockberg's (1962) research into the visualization continuum indicates that plain line drawings and shaded line drawings are the most meaningful for all classes (low, average, and high verbal) of learners. When drawings are embedded into science software, they can focus the attention of the learner on critical attributes and provide multiple channels of information to assist the learner in acquiring information. Pictorial representations of knowledge provide additional modes for conveying meaning about the subject (see Figure 10.3).

Simple line drawings and shaded line drawings can be used for pictorial testing of students' knowledge and comprehension as well as for instruction. In reporting on the advantages of pictorial testing, Gibson (1947) pointed out that pictorial tests are as reliable and as valid as verbal instruments. Pictorial testing has been infrequently used in science classrooms because it was cumbersome and time consuming to produce visual questions. Newer computer applications make the possibility of visual testing as routine as traditional pencil-and-paper testing procedures. In the future, science software will routinely include questions in a visual format. Students will benefit from the change in questioning format because visual questions (1) are more accurate and more easily understood, (2) reduce the emphasis placed on reading skills, (3) provide motivating situations, and (4) assess information not easily evaluated through a verbal format (Lefkowith, 1955, pp. 15–21). Researchers have recognized that visualization strategies embedded in textual material facilitates the learning and assessment of that learning among low-verbal students and students for whom English is a second language (Dwyer, 1978; Koran, 1972; Shapiro, 1975).

Information-Processing Strategies

Multimedia software products allow students to access on-disk encyclopedias, dictionaries, pictorial dictionaries, and a multitude of reference sources with a single keystroke or click of the mouse (see Figure 10.4). Additionally, multimedia software packages allow children to control the linguistic environment in which they are working.

As the memory capacity of microcomputers has increased, and as CD-ROM technologies have developed, microcomputers are able to hold larger bodies of information in memory. This increase in the memory capacity of computers allows for a greater individualization of instruction to accommodate the needs of the individual child. Students who need additional infor-

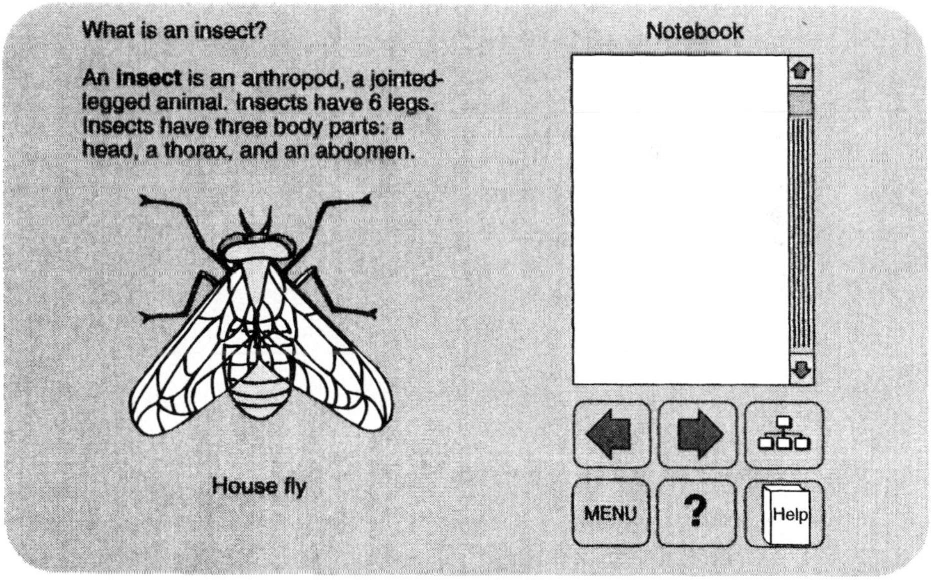

FIGURE 10.4 ■ Embedded Information-Processing Strategies

mation on a topic will be able to readily access glossaries, dictionaries, or information data bases to assist them in constructing new knowledge. Naisbitt (1982) has pointed out that we live in an information-processing age. Yet, our pedagogical methods do not reflect the times in which we live. We do not teach students to actively access multiple sources of information as they engage in learning, nor have we allowed students to control the pace of their instruction. One goal of newer software is to allow students to engage in reflective learning (that is, thinking about learning as they learn) as they work in electronic environments.

Feedback and Motivational Strategies

"Feedback or a knowledge of results facilitates meaningful learning cognitively, primarily through clarification and correction, rather than by reinforcing correct responses"; furthermore, feedback is "less important for meaningful learning than for rote learning because the internal logic of meaningfully learned material allows for more self-provided feedback than do inherently arbitrary association" (Ausubel, Novak, & Hanesian, 1978, p. 310). Computer software may contain various types of feedback, including feedback that is confirmatory, response correcting, or explanatory, depending on the nature of the learning activity. Fitting feedback to the learning activity so that the feedback is meaningful is a valuable feature in science software. Gone are the days when courseware simply flashed "Right!" or "Wrong, try again!" on the screen. Software that analyzes student answers and provides corrective feedback to the student makes learning meaningful. Feedback can assist students in making sense of new information in the electronic environment.

"Motivation is absolutely necessary for the sustained type of learning involved in mastering a given subject matter discipline, such as science" (Ausubel, Novak, & Hanesian, 1978, p. 397). Attention to motivational variables in science software design will make future courseware more effective as a learning tool in the science classroom. Gaming techniques, perceptual arousal, culturally familiar elaborations, learner control over the instructional program, and metalinguistic capacities will improve the electronic environment in which students construct knowledge. Metacognitive strategies, such as the use of instructional maps in science software, can be used to provide students with a knowledge of their progress in moving through the electronic microworld (see Figure 10.5). Instructional maps can function as motivational devices to assist learners in structuring their learning experiences.

Research into Electronic Learning

Computer-mediated instruction (CMI), the use of the microcomputer as an instructional tool, has been available to science teachers for several decades. During the past two decades, hundreds of research studies have been con-

FIGURE 10.5 ■ Embedded Metacognitive Strategies

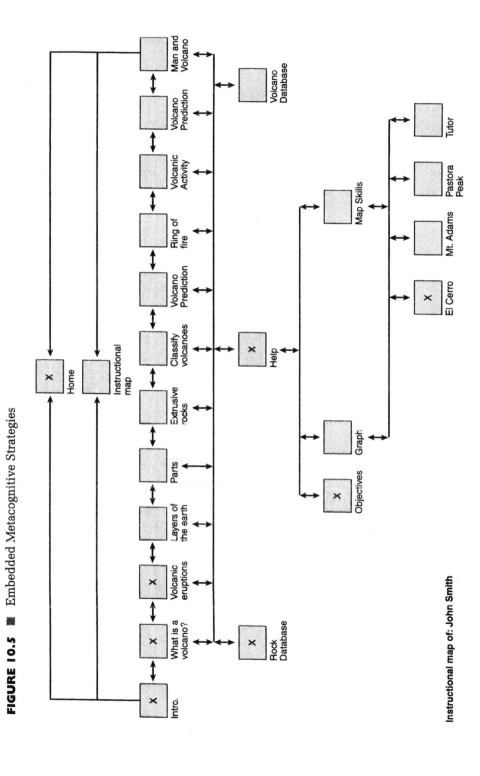

Instructional map of: John Smith

ducted into the effectiveness of electronic learning. Unfortunately, most of them have been flawed by poor research designs, improper control of variables, and inappropriate use of statistics (Kracjik, Simmons, & Lunetta, 1986). From studies that used proper controls on variables it has been learned that computer-mediated instruction, including multimedia instruction, makes significant differences in student learning in four interrelated areas: achievement, learning retention, learning time, and learner attitude.

Achievement

Perhaps the most comprehensive study of the effectiveness of computer-aided instruction was undertaken by Kulik, Bangert, and Williams (1980). These researchers used a meta-analysis technique to examine and synthesize 51 studies into computer-mediated instruction involving students in grades 6 to 12. They found that generally students who received computer-assisted instruction scored higher on objective tests than did students who received "traditional" instruction. Results from their meta-analysis indicated that the average student in the control groups scored at the 50th percentile, while the average student treated with computer-assisted instruction scored at the 63rd percentile. The gain for students treated with computerized instruction was .32 of a standard deviation.

Technology enhances students' acquisition of declarative knowledge.

Studies conducted by the Educational Testing Service indicate that students who use computerized drill-and-practice packages for knowledge- and comprehension-level information as little as ten minutes a day score significantly higher on achievement measures than do students who do not have access to microcomputers (Bracey 1982). Studies by Bowman (1996), Sprayberry (1994), and Alifrangis (1990) have found this same trend in multimedia courseware, that is, multimedia courseware is highly effective in conveying low-level information to students. Roblyer (1985), in summarizing the results of computer-assisted instruction studies, reports that computer-based instruction achieves consistently higher effects than other instructional treatments in experimental situations.

Science teachers need to integrate this body of research into their everyday instructional practice. Information at the lowest levels of Bloom's taxonomy (knowledge and comprehension) lends itself readily to electronic learning. Hence, factual information, such as the symbols for the elements of the periodic table or names of plant and animal structures, can be taught more efficiently with computerized drill-and-practice packages than with other tutorial methods. If the objective of instruction is to have students produce symbols for element names or name structures of living organisms, then electronic tutorial packages are highly appropriate.

There is, however, a caution in the use of drill-and-practice software with culturally diverse learners and with students who are having difficulty mastering the content of the course. Frequently, culturally and linguistically unassimilated students and low-verbal learners (e.g., mainstreamed special education students)—those who have difficulty in reading, speaking and writing English—are assigned to work independently or in small groups at computer workstations. Sometimes teachers mistakenly think that this will assist students in developing basic skills. Assigning students to work independently at a computer terminal isolates them from their peers. This results in a situation in which children are physically, socially, and educationally separated from the mainstream learning activities in the classroom, a phenomenon sometimes referred to as "electronic segregation." While computers can be powerful tools for learning low-level information, they can also become tools to isolate culturally diverse students from their peers and deprive them of the opportunity to develop oral communication skills.

Retention

Kulik, Bangert, and Williams (1980) also investigated student retention of information in their meta-analytic study. They found that computer-assisted instruction improves retention of information at the lowest levels of Bloom's taxonomy. They reported that four of five studies investigating retention over a period of two to six months showed greater retention of information for students who used computer-mediated instruction. Roblyer's (1985) survey of computer-assisted instruction research indicates a different finding. He reported that although there were differences between the performance of computer-assisted instruction students and "traditionally" instructed students, those differences were not statistically significant.

Although computers can be powerful tools in helping students learn and retain information, care needs to be taken to select software carefully. Culturally diverse learners, indeed all students, learn best and retain what they learn when knowledge is presented in multiple formats, that is, through written words, spoken words, real world objects, pictures or photographs, and icons. While multimedia courseware has the potential to present information in many different formats, there is as yet no substitute for real world objects and hands-on/minds-on learning experiences in the science classroom.

Learning Time

Blaschke and Sweeney (1977) found that computer-assisted instruction has been helpful in decreasing learning time. Their study compared the learning times of students using a computer-assisted electronic training package with a similar programmed booklet. The results from this study indicated that students learn the same information in 10% less time using computer-assisted instruction. A study by Dence (1980) also indicated that students who use computer-mediated instruction learn faster than students who use "traditional" instructional techniques. A study by Lunetta (1972) showed that students using computer-assisted instruction could master physics content in 88% less time than students who used "traditional" physics instruction. Similar findings were reported by Lazarowitz (1984) in a study of middle school students' learning in life science classes.

More recently, studies of multimedia courseware have found that technology can speed learning time. A study by Bergeron (1995) found that level of realism and perceptions of ease of use in multimedia courseware decrease learning time. Dunn (1995) reported that multimedia learning environments decrease students' learning time in activities involving information searches and retrieval. Finally, Recsigno (1988) writes that students' learning time is optimized in self-paced, multimedia learning environments.

Research into instructional time indicates that computer-assisted instruction is highly effective in certain situations, namely low-level learning tasks. Science teachers need to identify those bodies of information that can be learned faster using microcomputer than "traditional" instructional methods. The time saved by learning low-level information on the computer should be used to teach higher-order thinking skills in the multicultural science classroom.

Attitudes

In addition to improving students' achievement, increasing retention, and decreasing instructional time, computer-mediated instruction appears to improve students' attitudes toward learning. Studies of the impact of multimedia instruction on students' attitudes have found that computer-mediated environments improve students' attitudes toward computers and science, while increasing students' sense of efficacy in learning (Arch, 1995; Recsigno, 1988). A meta-analysis conducted by Kulik, Bangert, & Williams (1980) indicated that in eight of ten studies reviewed, students' attitudes toward subject matter were more positive after students had used computer-assisted instruction. A study by Bracey (1984) indicated that students react favorably to the use of the computer for instructional purposes. In fact, Bracey found that students who have worked in electronic learning environments have a more positive attitude toward the subject matter than do students who work in "traditional" learning environments. Other researchers (Fiber, 1987; Foley, 1984) have reported similar findings regarding learning in computer-mediated learning environments.

Computers have endless patience in tutorial situations. Science teachers need to capitalize on the microcomputer's ability to present and repeat information. Electronic learning frees the science teacher from the drudgery of endless drill-and-practice learning situations. Caution needs to be taken in assuming that all computer-mediated learning is equally effective. Although electronic learning environments have been shown to be effective in learning knowledge- and comprehension-level information, this effect has not been noted with higher-order thinking skills.

Beyond Drill and Practice

Although drill-and-practice software is the most commonly used software in the science classroom, it is not the only computer application available to the science instructor in the multicultural classroom. Indeed, other types of software provide for higher levels of questioning skills and for deeper levels of understanding regarding content area information. Graphing packages, instrument interfacing kits, electronic simulations, statistical packages, database simulations, and spreadsheet simulations provide for deeper information processing on the part of the learner and for high levels of user interactivity—interaction between learner, microcomputer, and real world.

Computerized Graphing Packages

Computerized graphing packages such as MECC Graph, Excel, Microsoft Works, and Microsoft Office allow students to rapidly generate bar graphs, line graphs, and pie charts. The primary value of computerized graphics packages is that they change the level of questioning skills in the classroom from the lowest levels of Bloom's taxonomy to higher levels of that taxonomy (application, analysis, synthesis, and evaluation). When graphing packages are introduced into the classroom, they allow students to spend time asking "what if" questions rather than questions about constructing graphs. Graphing packages allow learners in the multicultural classroom to focus on questions such as, What is the relationship between the variables? rather than focusing on how to draw a graph or plot a point. This is not to say that students shouldn't be afforded the opportunity to construct graphs on their own at some point in their educational experience, rather that graphing packages allow teachers to focus on higher-order thinking skills after students have acquired a conceptual understanding of graphic representation of data.

In a study of the effectiveness of graphing packages, Gesshel-Green (1987) found that students who use computerized graphing packages do not differ from traditionally instructed students on immediate-recall scores. However, students using computer graphing packages do show significant positive gains when compared to traditionally instructed students on measures of long-term retention, motivation, and cooperation. Results from a study of the use of computerized graphing packages to teach concept formation indicated that students formulate concepts in significantly less time when using computer graphing packages (Heid, 1988).

Graphing packages focus the attention of teachers and students on the appropriate use of graphs rather than on their construction. Ideas such as the use of pie charts or circle graphs to present information about parts of a whole, the use of line graphs to represent change over time, and the use of bar graphs to represent comparisons are readily taught in an electronic graphing environment.

Instrument Interfacing

Instrument to microcomputer interfacing is the domain of the science teacher. Connecting thermistors (temperature probes), potentiometers (stick pendulums), photoresistors (light probes), and electrically conductive styrofoam (hand grips) to microcomputers allows students and teachers to collect and analyze data in real time. Microcomputer-based laboratory (MBL) activities have been shown to improve students' understanding of science processes (Nachmias & Linn, 1987). While conducting an experiment to compare traditional laboratory activities with computer-based laboratory activities, these researchers discovered that eighth-grade students engaged in computer-based activities showed greater understanding of scientific processes than did students in conventional science labs.

Krendl and Lieberman (1988) report that student motivation, involvement with the laboratory activity, and self-perceptions are improved as a result of computer-based lab instruction. Instrument interfacing allows learners to focus on science processes rather than on data collection and interpretation. Events that occur very rapidly or very slowly, that involve minute changes in temperature or light intensity, or that require extreme care in data recording can be easily observed with instruments interfaced to microcomputers (Barba, 1987). Laboratory activities that have traditionally been left out of the curriculum because they required extreme care in observation (heat of seed germination is one such activity) can be conducted using microcomputer interfaces. Instrument interfacing allows students to work with higher-level thinking skills, to focus on the relationships between variables, rather than to focus on low-level skills such as reading a thermometer or a light meter.

Simulations

Simulation activities are a form of computer-mediated instruction in which the learner assumes a role within a structured environment (Lockard, Abrams & Many 1987, p. 398) and makes decisions based on that role playing. These activities can be conducted in the science classroom with single-use packages (e.g., Oh, Deer!, Island Survivors, and Energy House) or through spreadsheets or simple computer programs. In reporting on the effectiveness of CATLAB, a genetics simulation activity, Krajcik, Simmons, and Lunetta (1988, p. 151) point out that computer simulations facilitate student problem-solving skills by allowing students to (1) generate their own questions, (2) control variables themselves, (3) gather, record, and interpret data, and (4) draw conclusions to support or reject hypotheses. Experiments that are dangerous or very time consuming can be performed quickly and easily by computer simulation.

Spreadsheets also allow students to engage in simulation activities. While investigating the use of spreadsheets as simulation tools, Dubitsky (1986) discovered that sixth-grade students are able to transfer understandings and methods of solutions from one problem to another. In assessing the value of spreadsheets in the science classroom, Pogge and Lunetta (1987) point out that spreadsheets allow students to spend extra time collecting and interpreting data, rather than on routine computational work. The use of spreadsheets allows students in the multicultural science classroom to develop science processes, especially inferring, predicting, and hypothesizing.

Virtual reality software, such as VistaPro's Mars Explorer, is the newest type of simulation software. With this product students can construct and move through artificial worlds of their own creation. Oftentimes, we think of virtual experiences in terms of specialized headgear, gloves, and visors—in fact, virtual reality is accessible in the science classroom through the use of ordinary microcomputers. Experiences in traveling to other planets, available through CD-ROM software such as Mars Explorer and Venus Explorer, provide students the opportunity to investigate other worlds in their own classrooms. This type of virtual experience enlivens instruction.

Multimedia and CD-ROM Technology

Multimedia courseware on CD-ROM disks is among the new advances in instructional software. Typically CD-ROM drives or laser disk readers are connected to computers. Since the storage capacity of these devices is far greater than that of traditional floppy diskettes, computer programs can now feature segments of on-screen movies, on-screen dictionaries, glossaries, embedded electronic notebooks, and on-line encyclopedias. The availability of text screens, embedded graphics, movies, and multiple language channels means that software is better able to address the needs of culturally and linguistically diverse learners (see Figure 10.6).

Multimedia courseware is particularly appealing for use with culturally diverse learners since it allows for multiple means of knowledge representation, including written words, spoken words, line drawings, icons, and movie segments. Multimedia products with multiple sound tracks allow students to

FIGURE 10.6   ■   Frame from A.D.A.M., a Multimedia CD

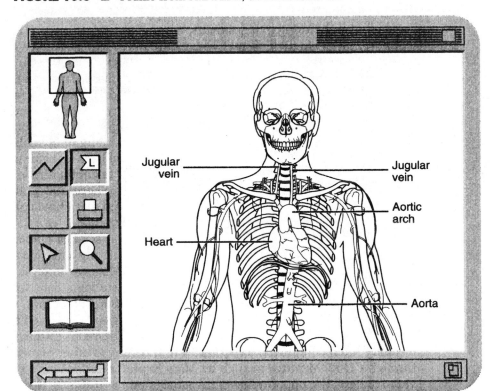

develop language skills and science concepts simultaneously. For students socialized to learn from spoken language or pictorial presentations of information, multimedia products are particularly appropriate.

Multicultural and Multimedia

The effectiveness of multimedia products for culturally and/or linguistically diverse learners may be best explained in terms of visual learning theories. Flory (1978) pointed out that (1) a visual language exists, (2) people can and do think visually, (3) people can and do learn visually, and (4) people can and should express themselves visually. For many students, multimedia products provide instructional richness, in that they provide alternatives to text-based information sources. Moore and Dwyer (1995) have pointed out that successful learning starts with participants understanding their frames of reference as well as the frames of reference of others with whom they are involved.

Pictorial and visual information in multimedia learning environments helps many students establish frames of reference for learning. The increased visualization contained in multimedia products allows students to build conceptual bridges between home learning and school learning. This notion is posited in the Whorf-Sapir hypothesis (Moore & Dwyer, 1995), which holds that (1) thoughts are determined by language, (2) behavior is determined by language, (3) language is strongly related to the culture in which that language is spoken and reflects that culture's values, and (4) language serves as a filter for how one views the world. For many linguistically diverse students, multimedia learning environments provide visual cues that activate prior knowledge and help them append new knowledge to existing mental structures, knowledge that may have been constructed in another language.

Connectivity (World Wide Web and Internet)

Networking or connecting computers from around the world via existing telecommunication channels is another example of computer applications that benefit science teachers. By using electronic connections to the World Wide Web, teachers may access satellite images of weather patterns, stored NASA documents from previous space flights, botanical and zoological data bases, and information about earth resources. Electronic servers such as Ecogopher, the Smithsonian on Line, and the University of Hawaii's Dinosaur Museum provide updated information about a wealth of subjects. Libraries, taxonomic keys, science research reports, and electronic images are a few key strokes away from students and teachers. Even issues of diversity may be addressed by Web sites (see Figure 10.7).

In addition to the resources available from electronic servers, telecommunication allows students to communicate with others in their native lan-

FIGURE 10.7 ■ Web Page That Addresses Diversity

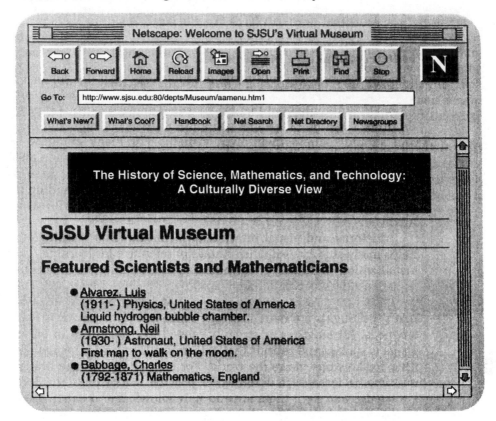

guage. Bulletin boards around the world provide the chance for students to interact in cyberspace, to send messages to others. The Internet or World Wide Web affords students the opportunity to use the entire planet as a classroom, to think globally.

Web-Based Learning

Web-based learning may be differentiated from other telecommunications in that the computer assists the learner in forming new knowledge and new products. From a student-centered perspective, there are three models of interactivity in telecommunication: receiving, selecting, and collaborating. At Level 1, the receiving level, students use telecommunications to receive information from some authority figure. The educational television model developed during the 1950s is still in use as a means of conveying information from an "expert" to an audience of listeners. *Channel One* is the most widely used example of this type of telecommunications. At the receiving level, students do not participate in the conversation, rather they are recipients of the information. In the science classroom, weather services are an example of Level 1 telecommunications. At this level of interactivity, the learner opens the resource and downloads the information for later use.

Level 2 telecommunications, the selecting level, involves the learner in interactive learning. At this level, the student decides what information to receive. On-line bulletin boards, gophers or servers, and electronic museums are examples of Level 2 telecommunications. When using these resources, the learner controls the information that is received. When a student logs on to an electronic museum, such as the Smithsonian Bulletin Board or an electronic NASA Resource Center, the student selects the material to view and the material to download. Electronic bulletin boards represent stored expertise, data base resources that the learner controls but does not alter. Gophers such as Space Science and Engineering Center's Global Satellite Images, Electronic Books from Project Gutenberg, Biodiversity, and Green Peace are resources that enliven learning and that represent selecting-level telecommunications.

Mediated conversations or interactive telecommunications are the product of Level 3 interactions. Level 3, the collaborating level, involves the learner in two-way communications that result in new knowledge and new products. At this level of telecommunications, the student's thoughts and ideas are incorporated into a new entity. Age-appropriate chat rooms, such as those provided by America Online and Prodigy, are examples of commercially sponsored interactive telecommunications. In a science education context, Journey North's Map the Monarchs! project is an example of a mediated communication. This gopher or electronic bulletin board allows students to download information about monarch butterfly migration patterns and to enter their own observations on monarch sightings. Each student has the opportunity to add new knowledge to the existing body of knowledge, thus producing a new whole.

National Geographic's KidsNet is another example of a Level 3 telecommunications resource. With KidsNet, students collaborate with others to engage in problem-solving activities. Reports from McMurdo Station, Antarctica, is another example of collaborative-level telecommunications. In this project, students may send e-mail notes to scientists at McMurdo Station; their conversations with scientists represent collaborative efforts in learning. Levels of telecommunications are differentiated by level of interactivity and by locus of control, that is, by who is allowed to contribute to what is being said. E-mail represents the third level of telecommunications. Some Level 3 Web sites that hold the potential to enhance science education are listed in Table 10.2.

TABLE 10.2 ■ Web Sites for Science Teachers

Site	URL Address	Comments
CIA World Factbook	http://www.odci.gov/cia	Information on countries
CU See Me	http://cu-seeme.cornell.edu	Two-way interactive video
EnviroLink	http://www.envirolink.org	Environmental resources
Galaxy	http://galaxy.eimet.net/galaxy.html	Access to other sites
History of Science & Technology	http://www.sjsu.edu:80/depts /Museum/aamenu.html	Famous scientists
Hubble Telescope	http://www.stsci.edu/public.html	Pictures from Hubble
Infoseek	http://www.infoseek.com	Search Engine
Library of Congress	http://lcweb.loc.gov	Library sources
Lycos	http://lycos.cs.cmu.edu	Search Engine
NASA	http://www.nasa.gov	Space travel resources
National Science Teachers Association	http://www.nsta.org	Professional Organization
National Weather Service	http://thunder.met.fsu.edu	Current weather
Scientific American	http://www.sciam.com	Scientific articles
Shareware	http://www.shareware.com	Free software for teachers
Smithsonian Online	http://www.si.edu	Gems and Minerals
Virtual Hospital	http://indy.radiology.uiowa.edu	Human body images
Virtual Reality	http://www.sgi.com	VR Software
Weathernet	http://cirrus.spri.umich.edu	Satellite images
Webcrawler	http://webcrawler.com	Search Engine
Web Elements	http://chemserv.bc.edu/web-elements	Periodic Table
World Museums	http://cgrg.ohio-state.edu	List of museums
Yahoo	http://www.yahoo.com	Search Engine

CLASSROOM PRACTICE

Technology affords you as a science teacher the opportunity to address the individual needs of culturally diverse learners. Newer technologies such as multimedia and Web-based learning allow information to be presented in writing, orally, pictorially, and iconically. Research has shown that when information is represented in multiple modes, students' understanding and learning are increased. Additionally, the multilinguistic capabilities of newer technologies allow learners to control the instructional language in the science classroom. Multiple language tracks embedded in video disks allow students to use their home language in the science classroom and assist them in connecting their prior learning to new learning.

Evaluating Software

By combining what is known from science education research and language acquisition literature, a picture emerges of the characteristics of quality software for culturally and linguistically diverse learners. From that literature, a rubric may be generated to evaluate software; that rubric includes:

- *Visualization strategies:* How well does the software incorporate extra visuals (pictures, icons, photographs) to support the learning of culturally and linguistically diverse learners?
- *Information processing:* Does the software support the learning of culturally diverse learners by providing a wealth of information-processing strategies, such as computer-assisted instructional materials that contain review sections, paraphrasing, analogies, elaborations, dictionaries, data bases, and rehearsal strategies?
- *Active study strategies:* How well does the software incorporate note taking, underlining, or other active study strategies to facilitate students' processing of new information?

TABLE 10.3 ■ Software Evaluation Form

Name of Software:					
Supporting Learning	**Excellent**	**Good**	**Average**	**Fair**	**Poor/None**
Visualization strategies					
Information processing					
Active study strategies					
Metalearning strategies					
Support strategies					
Second language support					
Culturally familiar objects					

- *Meta-learning strategies:* How would you rate the computer package in terms of its ability to provide for planning instruction (instructional maps, directories, or overview menus), asking higher-order questions, and encouraging students to reflect on their learning?
- *Support strategies:* How well does the software inform students of instructional goals and provide a variety of activities to support student learning?
- *Second language support:* Does the software provide second-language support in that, whenever possible, it provides for multiple language needs and allows students to move from one language to another?
- *Culturally familiar objects:* How well does this software present references to objects, people, and events that are part of the child's milieu?

CHAPTER SUMMARY

We know from research that computerized learning can make a significant difference in students' achievement, retention of information, learning time, and attitudes. Software in the future will feature a strong research base and rationale for pedagogical decisions. Transactional triangles (sets of interactions between learners, microcomputers, and the natural world) will be established within the science courseware of the future. Technology can assist you as a teacher in providing individualized instruction that supports individual learners in the multicultural science classroom.

TOPICS TO REVIEW

- Computer-mediated instruction
- Graphing packages
- Instrument interfacing
- Simulations
- Multimedia
- Visual learning theory
- Networking

REFLECTIVE PRACTICE

1. In your opinion, what impact have computers made in elementary science instruction in public schools? Why do you think this is so?

2. What would you consider the perfect classroom in terms of available technology? Describe this classroom in terms of the type of technology available to teachers, the amount of hardware in the classroom, the

amount of time that students will spend using the technology in learning, your role as a teacher in this classroom, and the types of instructional activities you would undertake in this environment.

3. Much of the early computerized instruction in elementary science classrooms was dominated by a drill-and-practice instructional model. What improvements, innovations, etc., are needed to move teachers and students away from this instructional model?

4. Practice evaluating software using the rubric presented in Table 10.3. After reviewing several pieces, answer these questions: Which piece of software would you most like to use in a classroom with children? Why? What attributes make this piece of software appealing to you?

5. How will you integrate technology in your science classroom? Explain your answer.

6. Construct a data base of web sites. In your data base, record the name of the site, its URL address, and its potential use in the science classroom. As you move from one Web site to another, increase the size of your data base.

CHAPTER 11

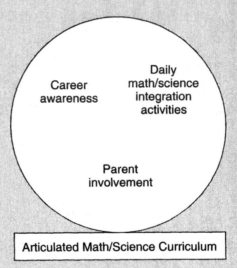

Career awareness

Daily math/science integration activities

Parent involvement

Articulated Math/Science Curriculum

Math/Science Integration in the Multicultural Classroom

![POINTS TO PONDER icon] **POINTS TO PONDER**

- Math/science integration is one approach to thematic teaching. What is thematic teaching?
- How does math/science integration encourage real world learning?
- How does math/science integration involve parents and community members in the educational process?

A friend of mine, Dr. Mae Chen, recently recalled her adventures in taking her daughter to work. Her company had sponsored a "Young Women in Science" day at work. The corporation had urged employees to bring their daughters or other young female relatives to the workplace to provide math/science/technology awareness activities for the young women. During the morning hours the youngsters had been kept occupied learning about products that the company researched and manufactured. They had used the company's computers to download satellite weather maps, had manufactured shaving cream and "super" balls in the company's labs, and had freeze-dried peaches and ice cream.

At lunchtime, the young women had a chance to rejoin their adult sponsors in the company dining room. Mae's daugther had described her morning's activities and her excitement about science careers. She wanted to become a chemist like her mother. As Angie spoke with her mother, she said, "Mom, I really like science, but why do I have to study math?"

Many children share Angie's lack of understanding of the connections between academic disciplines. For a long time, schools have used an "egg carton" instructional model—science here, math there, and language arts someplace else. We teach children in a disjointed fashion. No wonder they don't see the connections between academic disciplines.

THEMATIC TEACHING: MATH/SCIENCE INTEGRATION

In writing of the need to improve science and mathematics instruction in the United States, the National Science Board's Commission on Precollege Education in Mathematics, Science, and Technology stated:

> Alarming numbers of young Americans are ill-equipped to work in, contribute to, profit from and enjoy our increasingly technological society. Far too many emerge from the nation's elementary and secondary schools with an inadequate grounding in mathematics, science and technology. As a result, they lack sufficient knowledge to acquire the training, skills and understanding that are needed today and will be even more critically needed in the 21st century. (1983, p. 3)

The concern for the quality of education expressed by the National Science Board has been echoed in many school reform documents during the past decade. Science instruction should allow students to model the characteristics of scientists and mathematicians, to enjoy the joys of discovery, of creativity, of inquiry, of curiosity, and of striving to obtain a knowledge of the world around them. Effective learners are actively engaged in the learning process, understand the value of what they are learning, and accept responsibility for their own learning throughout their lifetimes (Mullis & Jenkins, 1988, p. 13). Lifelong learning includes the ability to participate as a scientifically literate adult in society. In attempting to provide a knowledge of science, a knowledge of science career opportunities, and an awareness of the role of science in society, many teachers have come to use a math/science integration approach to instruction.

Math/science integration is an inquiry-based, thematic approach to teaching that stresses the real world applications of the study of science and mathematics. In speaking of this approach to teaching, the National Research Council stated that, "since mathematics is both the language of science and a science of patterns, the special links between mathematics and science are far more than just those between theory and applications. The methodology of mathematical inquiry shares with the scientific method a focus on exploration, investigation, conjecture, evidence and reasoning" (1990, p. 44). Modern-day advocates of mathematics and science integration are links in a long chain of educators who have sought to bring a thematic approach to the study of these disciplines. Integrating science and mathematics is not a new idea in education. Modern math/science integration curriculum-writing efforts are an eclectic approach to curriculum design in that they incorporate elements of constructivism, confluentism, humanism, and social reconstructionism.

Historical Foundations

One of the first known attempts at math/science integration appeared in the works of Fredrich Froebel, the inventor of the term *kindergarten.* During the 1840s, Froebel pioneered the use of manipulative materials to teach young children mathematical concepts and scientific principles simultaneously through a thematic, inquiry-based approach to learning. Around 1900, the Central Association of Science and Mathematics Teachers (parent organization of today's School Science and Mathematics Association) was formed in the United States (Breslich, 1936). The purpose of this organization was to establish a closer relationship between mathematics and science teachers. Its founders recommended that "algebra, geometry and physics be combined into a single, coherent course" (Breslich, 1936, p. 58). The 1960s were a time of resurgence of interest in math/science integration in elementary schools in the United States. During this decade several elementary science curriculum projects, including Science—A Process Approach (SAPA), Science Curriculum Improvement Study (SCIS), and Elementary Science Study (ESS), were written using a math/science inquiry-based approach to learning. Modern-day advocates of math/science integration echo the sentiments of their predecessors in stating that it is vital that we teach young children both mathematics and science in an integrated, discovery-based environment. Recent elementary school math/science curriculum-writing efforts have produced Activities that Integrate Mathematics and Science (AIMS), Unified Science and Mathematics for Elementary Schools (USMES), South Central Kansas Elementary Science Math Project (SOCKEMS), and Great Explorations in Math and Science (GEMS) materials.

Finally, the *National Science Education Standards* encourage thematic instruction, in the form of mathematics and science integration. The program standards section of that document states that "science programs should be coordinated with the mathematics program to enhance student use and understanding of mathematics in the study of science and to improve student understanding of mathematics" (National Research Council, 1996, p. 214). The framers of the standards point out that a program of study in science should connect to other subjects in school. They go on to state that such coordination can make maximal use of time in a crowded school schedule (1996, p. 214).

Research Foundations

Math/science integration is used as a pedagogical approach with culturally diverse students because research has shown that it is effective in improving students' science process acquisition. An integrated thematic approach to mathematics and science instruction emphasizes problem-solving skills rather than computational proficiency in mathematics instruction. Thematic teaching of mathematics and science stresses the relevancy of content area knowledge and assists students in making connections between school learning and the real world. Studies have shown that the use of thematic instruction with culturally diverse learners results in greater parent participation in the educational process and in the education of their children. For teachers, math/science integration is an effective way to reduce time spent on lesson planning, in that it reduces redundancy of content area presentations. In writing of the need for an integrated curriculum, Rutherford and Ahlgren state that "science and mathematics have had a long and successful relationship. On the one hand, science continually provides mathematics with challenges, while on the other hand, mathematics was developed as a suitable way to analyze scientific problems" (1988, p. 82).

The Teacher

A search of mathematics and science research literature reveals that an integrated math/science approach to teaching (1) improves teachers' attitudes toward teaching mathematics and science (Lehman & McDonald, 1988), (2) improves teachers' ability to articulate the curriculum (Bomeli, 1991; McGarry, 1986; Milson & Ball, 1986), (3) encourages teachers to teach higher-level thinking skills (Lewis, 1990; Voss, 1980), (4) emphasizes school and business partnerships to improve education (Lewis, 1990), (2) encourages the use of alternative assessment devices (Lewis, 1990), (6) promotes the introduction of technology in the mathematics and science curriculum (Winner & Holloway, 1983), (7) assists teachers in incorporating career awareness in their instruction (Voss, 1980), and (8) increases teachers' motivation to teach mathematics and science (Berlin, 1990; McGarry, 1986). When teachers use an interdisciplinary approach to mathematics and science teaching, they typically feel that their students' excitement for learning is increased, that the number of self-initiated learning activities undertaken by their students increases, and that their students improve in their social interaction skills.

The Student

When mathematics and science are taught in an integrated, thematic manner, students' attitudes toward mathematics and science improve significantly (Dowd, 1990; Friend, 1985; Young, 1990). The use of a math/science approach to teaching improves students' problem-solving abilities in both subjects (Lewis, 1990; Shann, 1977). Math/science integration is highly effective in improving students' mathematical graphing skills and science process acquisition (Kren & Huntsberger, 1977). The acquisition of basic skills in reading comprehension and mathematical computation is fostered by an interdisciplinary, problem-solving curriculum (Shann, 1977). Additionally, an integrated approach to instruction results in an improvement in students' concept acquisition in the two content areas (Friend, 1985; Kren & Huntsberger, 1977). In writing of students' concept acquisition through math/science activities, Kurtz and James stated that "children learn best when they discover concepts through concrete experiences" (1975, p. 258).

The Parents or Guardians

Frequently, parental or guardian involvement is not mentioned in science education literature or in teacher-training activities. Research has shown that parental or guardian involvement is an important variable in children's academic success and in their future career decision-making processes (Useem, 1990). Successful math/science integration activities normally include a home involvement component—an opportunity for parents and guardians to discuss with children their school learning, to assist their children in extending school knowledge, and to advise their children about career options. Research has shown that parents and guardians of culturally diverse learners are willing to become involved in their children's education, given the opportunity (Mucha, 1987). When parents or guardians of culturally diverse learners become involved in their children's education, (1) children's academic performance improves (Allen, 1987; Gibb, 1989), (2) children's interest in sci-

Parental involvement in children's learning is essential in schools.

ence and mathematics increases (Beane, 1990; Gibb, 1989), and (3) children's career awareness increases (Anderson, 1989; Gibb, 1989). Additionally, research has shown that parent or guardian involvement in schools through math/science integration activities produces positive changes in students in terms of decreased referrals for disciplinary reasons and increased school attendance (Sosa, 1986). Students with higher science proficiency are more likely to report home involvement in science projects and activities, access to more types of reading and reference materials in the home, and less television viewing (Mullis & Jenkins, 1988, p. 112). In summarizing the importance of home support for children's learning, Mullis and Jenkins state that "home support for and involvement in student's learning appears to be correlated with proficiency in various subject areas" (1988, p.117).

Social Foundations

Math/science integration addresses the need for relevant curricula in schools by incorporating social reconstructionist sociological foundations (Freire, 1970). Frequently, schools are criticized because school knowledge doesn't seem to be relevant or to have practical value. Although knowledge for the sake of knowledge may be desirable in certain instances, parents sometimes feel that schools are out of touch with the realities of the marketplace. Parents hold high aspirations for their children; they usually expect their children to do better in life than they did. Thus parents anticipate that schools will empower their children to participate in society by providing them with career awareness and job-related skills. Math/science integration incorporates elements of social reconstructionism in helping students to make real world connections between what they are learning and its practical application in the workplace. Math/science integration can be viewed from a sociological perspective as a powerful tool for helping to build bridges between school learning and the world of work and as a means for empowering children to participate fully as scientifically literate adults in a democratic society.

Psychological Foundations

As with the other pedagogical approaches discussed in this book, math/science integration contains many elements of constructivist learning theories. Problem-centered learning, which is central to constructivist instructional models, is also prevalent in math/science integration activities. Working in groups to seek possible solutions to real world problems is a constructivist psychological tenet that has been adopted by math/science integration instructional models. Group work, which accommodates the sociocultural aspect of constructivist learning models, is also indigenous to thematic math/science instructional activities. Sharing, reporting findings in small group and large group settings, reflective learning, and metalearning skills are found in both constructivist and confluent educational traditions.

Philosophical Foundations

While modern math/science integration contains elements of constructivist psychological and social reconstructionist sociological foundations, it is also based on confluent education philosophical foundations. **Confluent education** is the integration of the affective domain and the cognitive domain. The goals of math/science integration from a confluent education viewpoint are (1) to provide students with more alternatives to choose from in terms of their own lives, (2) to assist students in making choices, and (3) to assist students to realize that they can indeed make choices. Inherent in modern math/science integration programs are four confluent education principles: (1) participation, (2) integration, (3) relevance, and (4) social goals (Shapiro, 1972). From a confluent education perspective, math/science integration involves power sharing, negotiation, and joint responsibility for teaching and learning between students and teachers (Friere, 1970). Confluentist ideas of interpenetration (i.e., the mutual sharing of ideas), thematic learning, and the integration of social values into the content areas are inherent in math/science integration. The solving of real world problems and the focus on applications of mathematics and science knowledge address the confluentist concept of relevancy of education. Finally, the social goal of developing a person who is able to function in society is strongly embedded in math/science integrated curriculum programs.

COMPONENTS OF AN INTERDISCIPLINARY CURRICULUM

Math/science integration programs may be viewed as add-on programs in that they add parental involvement, social concerns, and career awareness to the existing mathematics and science courses of study. Four types of activities are common to successful math/science integration projects: (1) articulation of the curriculum to identify opportunities for integration, (2) thematically planned, inquiry-based daily activities; (3) parental involvement; and (4) career awareness.

Articulation

The first step in building an integrated curriculum is articulation. Articulation of the curriculum involves examining the mathematics and science curricula and identifying opportunities for thematic activities. Articulation may be undertaken using concepts, themes, units of study, skills, processes, or a combination of these approaches. One approach to identifying opportunities for math/science integration is to construct a matrix that includes mathematics topics and science disciplines as starting points, such as that in Table 11.1.

TABLE II.I.   ■   Mathematics Topics/Science Disciplines Matrix

	Science Discipline		
Math Topic	*Life Science*	*Physical Science*	*Earth Science*
Measurement	Plant growth	Temperature	Map scale
Equations	Magnification	Work	Relative humidity
Probability & statistics	Population sampling		Hurricane prediction
Ratio/Proportion	Symmetry	Balancing equations	
Graphing		Displaying data	Displaying data
Spatial visualization	Animal drawings	Light	Mineral crystals
Geometry/Angles		Wave theory	Mineral identification
Scientific notation	Growth curves		Geologic time Radioactive decay
Percent		Solutions	
Decimals		Work/force	Specific gravity

The result is a matrix that identifies opportunities for math/science integration activities for the teacher. From this matrix, the teacher can determine when conceptual knowledge is to be duplicated in the two content areas; these occasions become opportunities for thematic instruction. For example, the earth science unit of a particular upper elementary science textbook series presents information on specific gravity at the sixth-grade level. The mathematics curriculum materials at the same grade level present the topic of decimals and decimal notation. Since related concepts are presented in both sets of materials, an integrated approach to learning is possible in this instance. Math/science integration begins when related concepts are presented thematically to students, rather than in a fragmented or compartmentalized fashion.

A second approach to identifying opportunities for math/science integration is based on articulating the broad unifying themes of science and mathematical ideas. In the instance shown in Table 11.2, six science themes form one axis of the integration grid: energy, evolution, patterns of change, scale and structure, stability, and systems and interactions (California State Board of Education, 1990). The other axis of the grid represents five broad ideas of mathematics: dimension, quantity, uncertainty, shape, and change (Steen, 1990). The concepts identified in this process become the basis of math/science integration instruction, the chance to simultaneously fulfill the requirements of the mathematics and science curricula.

It is impossible to integrate mathematics and science instruction every day of the school year. Certain concepts in science and mathematics are domain specific; they have no corresponding concept in the other discipline. Frequently, math/science integration matrices will have holes or empty spaces where no common concepts have been identified. Holes are healthy. They reflect the fact that thematic teaching is not possible every day in all content areas.

TABLE 11.2 ■ Science Content/Mathematics Idea Matrix

Science Content	Mathematical Idea				
	Dimension	**Quantity**	**Uncertainty**	**Shape**	**Change**
Systems, order, and organization	Scientific notation	Laws of motion	Atomic structure	Classification systems	
Evidence, models, and explanation		Formulae	Hypothesis testing	Physical models	Animations of phenomena
Change, constancy, and measurement	Volume and density	Mass and density		Crystal structures	
Evolution and equilibrium			Radioactive dating	Fossil evidence	Chemical reactions
Form and function		Energy flow and food pyramids		Organs and systems	

Thematic Activities

Once a matrix of integration opportunities has been generated, the teacher can identify instructional activities that will build a knowledge of the science and mathematics concepts simultaneously. Math/science integration is predicated on problem solving. For example, suppose Mr. Son, a fifth-grade teacher, had discovered that he taught map construction in his science curriculum and ratio and proportion in mathematics to the same students. He could begin by stating a problem to his students: "Next week is PTA Open House, and let's assume your grandfather will be coming to meet me. Can you help him find my classroom?" After a period of discussion, Mr. Son could ask the students to draw a map of the school in their small groups. The students could measure the building and construct a map to scale showing their findings. This activity teaches map skills and ratio and proportion simultaneously in a meaningful manner. There is an inherent career awareness component built into this instructional activity. Surveyors, cartographers, and geologists in their everyday work use the same concepts and skills that the students are learning. Daily integration activities build science and mathematics concepts and skills and their real world connections in a unified, thematic fashion.

Parental Involvement

Successful math/science integration programs actively involve parents and guardians in children's learning. Sometimes parents may be directly involved in school activities by serving as resource persons to the class, that is, parents may be guest speakers who visit with children in the classroom and tell them about their jobs and their careers. At other times, parents or guardians may serve as mentors and tutors assisting students at home with math/science projects, such as the bridge-building or aluminum boat–building contests mentioned in the classroom practice section of this chapter. A problem-solving approach allows children to bring their home knowledge to school while encouraging students to use their home as a resource in the learning process.

Career Awareness

Career awareness is the final component of successful math/science integration activities. A knowledge of when and where science and mathematics concepts are used in adult life is vital for every student. Career awareness may be undertaken daily as well as through the use of occasional guest speakers and visitors to the classroom or through field trips to job sites. Successful math/science integration activities assist students in making connections between classroom learning and adult work in the real world. Expanding every student's knowledge base regarding preparation for various mathematics, science, and related technology careers is a primary focus of integrated instruction.

CLASSROOM PRACTICE

Four components are typically found in successful math/science integrated programs: an articulated curriculum that identifies opportunities for math/science integration, thematic daily lessons, parental involvement, and career awareness. One way to include these components is through the use of daily math/science instructional activities, monthly guest speakers or field trips to the community, and monthly contests to be used as motivational devices and to build career awareness. Daily lesson plans should provide students with a knowledge of mathematics and science concepts as well as a knowledge of when this information is useful in the real world. Guest speakers (e.g., parents, community members) and field trips to business and industry in the immediate geographic area give students an awareness of the connections between school learning and adult work in society. Finally, motivational contests on a weekly, monthly, or quarterly basis give students the opportunity to engage in problem solving while involving parents and guardians in children's learning.

Daily Math/Science Activities

Foundational to the teaching of math/science integrated curricula are daily lessons that incorporate mathematics and science concepts, or concepts common to the two disciplines. Daily activities also lend themselves to building career awareness in each student. Wheatley's (1991) instructional model involving tasks, groups, and sharing should be central to math/science instruction. Math/science integrated instruction involves problem solving; thus the task or the problem is the beginning of instruction. As problems are presented to students, students should be encouraged to work in cooperative groups in the classroom. Finally, students should be encouraged to share their solution paths with others in the class. Activities 11.1 through 11.3 show math/science lesson plans.

ACTIVITY 11.1 ■ Bouncing Ball

Science Concept:	Energy can be converted from one form to another.
Mathematics Concept:	Function
Materials:	Rubber ball (tennis ball), meter stick
Student Directions:	1. What will happen if a ball is dropped and allowed to continue bouncing? Make a prediction.

2. Drop a tennis ball or similar ball from a height of about 2 meters. Measure the height of each of four rebounds.
3. Make a table of data of the results.

Rebound heights of tennis ball

Rebound Number	Height of Bounce
0	2.0 meters
1	
2	
3	
4	

4. Make a line graph of your results.
5. What happens to the height of the ball as it continues to bounce?
6. What would happen with other types of balls?

ACTIVITY 11.2   ■   Springs

Science Concept:	Elasticity
Mathematics Concept:	Mass
Materials:	Springs (from old ballpoint pens), washers or metric weights
Student Directions:	1. Attach a spring to a hook (attached to a table, wall, etc.). Measure the length of the spring.
	2. Add one washer or weight to the spring. Record its length.
	3. Repeat for ten or eleven washers. Make a table of data and line graph from your results.

Measuring springs

Number of Washers	Length of Spring
1	
2	
3	

4. What happens to the length of the spring as the mass increases?
5. What is the independent variable? Dependent variable?
6. What would happen if another spring were used?

ACTIVITY 11.3 ■ Sugar Cubes (Pentaminoes)

A C T I V I T I E S

Science Concept:	Isomers
Mathematics Concept:	Spatial visualization
Materials:	Five sugar cubes
Student Directions:	1. Determine how many different ways you can arrange the sugar cubes so that at least one side of a cube touches another cube.
	2. Draw each arrangement that you make.

Pentaminoes

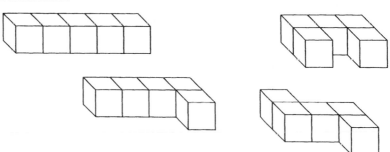

3. How many different arrangements can you make with six sugar cubes? Four cubes? Three cubes?

Math/Science Contests

Contests are motivational activities based in problem-solving activities that should foster an interest in mathematics, science, or related technology fields in students. Typically, classroom contests should be used in lieu of other homework assignments and should encourage parental involvement. Contests are most effective when equity issues (especially those associated with socioeconomic status) are addressed. Simple, readily available materials should be used to insure that all students have the opportunity to participate. Contests that foster career awareness in elementary aged students and build parental involvement in the process of schooling are illustrated in Activities 11.4 through 11.7

ACTIVITY 11.4 ■ Tower Building Contest

Materials: Twenty-five soda straws, 100 straight pins

Problem: The objective of this contest is to build the tallest "building" possible that will withstand hurricane force winds (an electric fan).

Teacher Materials: Electric fan, meter stick

Conducting the Contest:
1. Allow students to construct their towers at home with parental or adult assistance (if available). Address equity issues by encouraging students to use very simple materials (regular soda straws available at stores, school cafeterias, and fast-food restaurants).
2. On the day of the contest, have the students "bolt" their towers to a sheet of cardboard on the floor of the classroom.
3. Allow a student to hold a corner of the cardboard (not the building) to keep it from flying across the room.
4. Using a window fan, create a "hurricane" by setting the fan on its highest setting. Allow the hurricane to rage for 30 seconds before turning off the fan. If the tower doesn't fly apart during the hurricane, measure its height in meters.
5. Place each child's tower in the same starting position—the same distance from the wind source. Measure each tower in the same manner.

Follow-Up Activities: As each tower is measured have the students record their peers' names and the heights of their successful towers. Make a table of data and/or accompanying histogram or bar graph showing the heights of the towers.

Guest Speakers: Architects and engineers who work with concepts related to this activity

ACTIVITY 11.5 ■ **Aluminum Boat Contest**

Materials: One sheet of aluminum foil per student (20 × 20 cm.)

Problem: The objective of this contest is to build an aluminum foil boat that will hold the greatest mass before sinking.

Teacher Materials: Metric stacking masses or a set of weights, container for water (plastic pan if inside or small wading pool if outside)

Conducting the Contest:
1. Allow students to construct their boats at home with parental or adult assistance (if available). Address equity issues by encouraging students to use simple materials. Aluminum foil is inexpensive. One roll of foil is sufficient for an entire class of children and is a material readily available to all children.
2. On the day of the contest establish ground rules for adding "weights" or masses to the boats. With younger children, you may wish to have them add marbles to their boats and count how many marbles were needed to sink the boats rather than using metric weights or stacking masses.
3. The aluminum boat activity is a little messy; it is difficult not to have some spilled water when children float an object in a container of water. This activity is most appropriately done outside, on a tiled floor, or on flat-topped tables that can be mopped up with a sponge or paper toweling.

Follow-Up Activities: As each boat sinks have the students record their peer's name and the maximum mass that the boat held prior to sinking. Have the students make a table of data and/or accompanying histogram or bar graph showing the masses that the boats held. For older students, computational work with determining the average mass is appropriate; calculators can be integrated into this activity.

Guest Speakers: Container design engineers, boat captains, architects, and expeditors who deal with concepts covered in this activity

ACTIVITY 11.6 ■ **Bean Growing Contest**

Materials: Three bean seeds per student

Problem: The object is to grow a plant that has the greatest biomass during a one-month growing period.

Teacher Materials: Provide seeds for the students at the beginning of the contest period—bean seeds are sold relatively inexpensively in bulk in the grocery store. On the day of the contest a metric balance is needed to determine the plant's biomass (the mass of the living material)—cut the plant at the soil level and determine its weight or mass.

Conducting the Contest:

1. Allow students to plant their seeds in any manner that they choose. Have students adjust soil, fertilizer, water, etc., on their own. Address equity issues by providing seeds for the students. By allowing students to select their own container (e.g., paper cups, pots, cans, etc.) and soil for the containers, the contest becomes open to all students.
2. On the day of the contest instruct the students to bring their growing plants to class. Allow the student to select their largest plant.
3. Using scissors, cut off the largest plant at the surface of the soil and weigh each plant on a metric balance. The use of biomass rather than plant height discourages the use of expensive plant-growth lamps and makes this a fair contest for all students.

Follow-Up Activities: As each bean plant is weighed, have the students make a table of data and/or accompanying histogram or bar graph showing the biomass of each person's plant. With older students, determine the average biomass for the class; calculators are appropriate for averaging procedures. Computer graphing is also easily integrated into this activity.

Guest Speakers: Agricultural extension agents, feed store operators, farmers, gardeners, horticulturists, and those engaged in agribusiness careers who work with concepts related to this contest

---

ACTIVITY 11.7   ■   Bridge Building Contest

Materials: Twenty-five soda straws, 100 straight pins

Problem: The object is to build a bridge that will span a distance of 30 centimeters and hold the greatest mass possible before collapsing.

Teacher Materials: Metric weight set

Conducting the Contest:

1. Allow students to construct their bridges at home under adult supervision and guidance.

2. On the day of the contest, place two stacks of books 30 centimeters apart on the floor of the classroom or on a table. Place one bridge at a time over this span.
3. Hang weights under the bridge until the bridge breaks.

Follow-Up Activities: As each bridge is tested, have the students record the name of each of their classmates and the mass that their bridge held when it broke. Make a table of data from the findings. You may also wish to have the students construct a bar graph comparing the results of their classmates. For older students, simple univariate statistics are appropriately used with this activity. Students can determine the mean, median, mode, range, and rank of the "strength" of the bridges. Calculators are especially useful in this type of activity with older elementary students.

Guest Speakers: Civil engineers, structural designers, cargo storage personnel, and container designers who work with concepts related to this contest

Guest Speakers and Field Trips

Every community, no matter how large or how small, contains resources in the form of people willing to assist teachers with building career awareness in children. Guest speakers bring career awareness alive for students. Contact

Career awareness is vital to math/ science integration activities.

TABLE 11.3 ■ A Career Awareness Plan

Month	Topic	Career Emphasis
September	Energy	Power plant worker
October	Simple machines	Engineer
November	Magnetism and electricity	Recycling attendant
December	Rocks and minerals	Jeweler
January	Landforms	Geologist
February	Tissues and organs	Physician
March	Human body	Exercise therapist
April	Simple plants	Farmer
May	Flowering plants	Florist
June	Ecosystems	Fish and wildlife worker

with successful role models is a strong and powerful device for stimulating students' interest in mathematics, science, and related technology careers. One schedule of math/science concepts, guest speakers, and related motivational contests is shown in Table 11.3.

CHAPTER SUMMARY

Math/science integration is a thematic approach to teaching based on confluentist philosophical, social reconstructionist sociological, and constructivist psychological foundations. Successful math/science integration programs share four components: articulation of the mathematics and science curriculum, parental involvement, career awareness, and daily math/science integration activities. Research has shown that this thematic approach to learning improves students' mathematics and science concept acquisition, improves students' science processes, and improves students' attitudes toward mathematics and science. Thematic teaching of science and mathematics is a problem-solving approach to teaching and learning that fosters tasks, groups, and sharing.

▒ TOPICS TO REVIEW

- Underrepresentation in science careers
- Math/science integration
- Thematic teaching

- Role of teachers
- Role of students
- Role of parents

REFLECTIVE PRACTICE

1. Dr. Peg House of the University of Minnesota is quoted as saying that "math/science integration has always made good sense." What do you suppose she means by this?

2. Successful math/science integration activities typically contain four components: (1) an articulated curriculum, (2) thematically planned daily activities, (3) parental involvement, and (4) career awareness. In your opinion, why is each component necessary for a successful program?

3. Why do you think math/science integration is not more widely used in elementary science and mathematics instruction? Justify your answers.

CHAPTER 12

Role of the Learners

Constructing
a knowledge
of science
from text

Qualities of the text

1. Organization
2. Cohesion
3. Explication
4. Conceptual density
5. Metadiscourse
6. Writeability
7. Instructional
    devices

Role of the teacher

1. Selecting passages
2. Providing study guides
   TRICA
   QUEST
   ITM
3. Establishing
   environment
4. Reciprocal teaching

Constructing a Knowledge of Science from Text in the Multicultural Science Classroom

POINTS TO PONDER

- How do students construct a knowledge of science from text?
- What is a constructivist view of reading in the science classroom?
- How do "friendly texts" differ from traditional science texts?
- What strategies may teachers use to make reading in the science classroom an interactive experience?

*R*eading in the science classroom is not simply a matter of the teacher instructing students to "read the book and answer the questions at the end of the chapter." Learning from text is not a passive act. Children are not tree roots; they do not learn by the process of osmosis, nor do they take in knowledge in the manner that trees take in water. A child's conceptual knowledge of science is constructed over time. Children construct knowledge through their interactions with written material, through their experiences in the real world, and *through their interactions with others. Students append new knowledge to what they already know. Wheatley has written that "knowledge is not disembodied but is intimately related to the action and experience of the learner—it is always contextual and never separated from the knower" (1991, p. 10).*

In the past, emphases in content area reading have included reading skills, word recognition, reading comprehension, and study skills. This "traditional" approach to content area reading has been based on two assumptions: (1) that the major way to learn an academic subject is to read about it, and (2) that the textbook is the major source of content area knowledge. This perspective on reading is based on theories and philosophies of education that view textbooks as sources of authoritative information that may somehow be transmitted to children.

There has arisen a belief among some segments of the science education community that reading in the science classroom is counterproductive and is not "real science." Proponents of this viewpoint suggest that reading is not the domain of the science teacher and that teachers who encourage reading in the science classroom are somehow "bad" teachers. The reverse is actually true. Writing and reporting the findings from scientific investigations are part of the job of every scientist. Reading the research of others, wrestling with the theories and hypotheses of others, is part of every scientist's job. If we view reading as part of the everyday life of a scientist, and if we assume that children can construct meaning from verbal materials, then we find that indeed reading has a very valuable role in the science classroom. Textbooks, journal articles, newspaper articles, pamphlets, trifolds, infobrochures, and Web-based communications are sources of information that cannot in many instances be accessed by hands-on activities. Historically, textbooks in the science classroom have been used as encyclopedias, not as tools to facilitate the learning process. The framers of the National Science Education Standards *emphasize the relationship between science and the language arts when they write that there needs to be "more emphasis on communicating science explanations and a management of ideas and information" in the science classroom (National Research Council, 1996, p. 113).*

LEARNING FROM TEXT

Problem-centered learning, according to Wheatley (1991), has three components: tasks, groups, and sharing. Reading in the science classroom should be a problem-centered activity. If we use Wheatley's model, then selecting **friendly texts** (prose accessible by all students) and developing accompanying study guides is the first component in a problem-centered reading approach in the science classroom. When presenting reading materials to students, teachers should emphasize the task, that the purpose of the reading

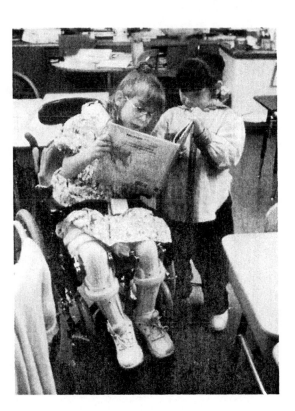

Group reading or reciprocal teaching is a highly effective strategy for culturally diverse learners.

materials is to allow students to construct knowledge of scientific phenomena. Social interactions (e.g., reading and discussing together in small and large groups) are the second component of a problem-centered reading process. Group reporting or reciprocal teaching (in which teachers and students share the responsibility for teaching) is the final component of a problem-centered approach to reading.

Constructivist theory holds that knowledge is not transmitted to children but is constructed by children. The process of understanding written text is one in which readers combine what is written, what they already know, and various general metacognitive processes to construct a plausible representation of what the author presumably had in mind. In addressing the linguistic needs of learners in the multicultural science classroom, three main concerns arise: (1) the role of the textbook, (2) the means by which children construct meaning from that textbook, and (3) the role of the teacher.

The Role of the Textbook

Science textbooks historically have been described at best as packed with facts but lacking in concepts, and at worst as inaccurate, poorly organized, and uninteresting. Nevertheless, surveys repeatedly show science teachers relying heavily on textbooks as both pedagogical guides and subject matter authorities in the modern science classroom. In addition, teachers believe the reading level of science textbooks is "too hard" for their students. Difficulties students encounter in comprehending modern science textbooks, however, may be attributable more to their being reader unfriendly than to their being too difficult for the age group intended. Low-verbal learners, students with limited English proficiency, and students from culturally diverse backgrounds find science textbooks difficult to understand even when those students have a basic mastery of the English language. Singer and Donlan (1990), in studying science textbooks, found that the writing style was more an impediment to student learning than was the science content.

Friendly textbooks assist the learner to recall background information, perceive relationships among ideas, make inferences, and draw conclusions. Textbooks should assist the student in constructing declarative knowledge of science facts, concepts, and rules and principles. Most currently used science textbooks are not friendly, in that they do not assist learners in structuring new knowledge. Friendly textbooks reflect consideration of text organization, cohesion, explication of material, conceptual density, elements of metadiscourse, writability, and instructional devices that increase students' overall comprehension of the reading material.

Text Organization

A text's organization includes not only the purpose and arrangement of textual materials, but also the choice of rhetorical patterns used to show the relationship among ideas. The five rhetorical patterns commonly found in textbooks are (1) the question-and-answer format (response pattern), (2) the cause-and-effect relationship (covariance pattern), (3) the sequencing of events in chronological order (temporal pattern), (4) the comparison and contrasting of characteristics (adversative pattern), and (5) the listing of characteristics to define concepts and ideas (attribution pattern). According to textbook surveys, the most common patterns for science textbooks are two: comparison and contrast, and cause and effect. Most students in the elementary multicultural classroom have difficulty constructing meaning from textual materials that use the adversative and covariance patterns of text organization. Science textbooks and trade books that use the response, temporal, or attribution rhetorical patterns have been shown to increase student comprehension and thus are reader friendly.

Cohesion

Cohesion refers to how writers tie information together from sentence to sentence, paragraph to paragraph, and chapter to chapter. *Cataphora* is a cohesion pattern in which cited elements point to a later referent in the text, whereas *anaphora* denotes a pattern in which elements point to a prior referent. Five cohesive patterns are commonly used in textual materials: (1) constructing sentences or phrases such that a word's meaning depends on a previous word (reference), (2) repetition of words or the use of synonyms (lexical cohesion), (3) deletion of previously stated words or ideas (ellipsis), (4) substitution, and (5) conjunction. Research has shown that their relative lack of cohesion makes science textbooks boring, slows the reading rate of students, lowers reading comprehension rates, and reduces student recall. Friendly textbooks employ all types of cohesive devices to tie together sentences, paragraphs, and chapters. Cohesion increases student comprehension of the written material. Writers of science textbooks particularly need to include reference, lexical, and ellipsis patterns of cohesion to benefit students who have difficulty comprehending verbal materials.

Explication

Writers use explication when they state facts, ideas, and their relationships directly instead of requiring readers to infer, organize, or construct the relationships themselves. Textbooks, especially science textbooks, tend not to explicate information systematically. Explication devices include: (1) vocabulary (defining new terms using language familiar to the student), (2) background knowledge (relating new ideas to students' prior knowledge), and (3) organizing ideas with real world applications. Friendly science textbooks activate students' prior knowledge, use common analogies or analogies that are part of the child's milieu, and present students with real world applications of new knowledge. The use of real world knowledge, culturally familiar or culturally syntonic examples, and everyday vocabulary is especially important for students in the multicultural science classroom.

Conceptual Density

Conceptual density refers to the number of new ideas and vocabulary words contained in a textbook. According to Singer and Donlan (1990), Mary Budd Rowe has determined that the average high school textbook introduces 7 to 10 new concepts per page and between 2,400 and 3,000 terms and symbols overall during a one-year course. This is an average of 20 concepts per class period or 1 concept every 2 minutes. Research shows that friendly textbooks use wordier text, while controlling the introduction of new concepts. Explication helps students bridge the gap between their own knowledge and experience and the new knowledge contained in the textbook.

Metadiscourse

Metadiscourse is like a conversation between the author and the reader. It occurs when the author of a text talks directly to the reader about the information in the textbook. This book uses elements of metadiscourse in the classroom practice section of each chapter. Research studies have shown that the use of metadiscourse improves a reader's comprehension of the information that the author is attempting to convey. Metadiscourse may include statements of textual goals such as, "You will learn . . ." Metadiscourse may assist the learner in previewing or recalling prior knowledge: "You recall in the first chapter that you learned . . ." or "When you were a child . . ." Stressing the importance of an idea to the reader ("You realize that this is important . . .") is a form of metadiscourse. Finally, stressing an attitude toward a fact or an idea ("Your attitude toward . . .") is metadiscourse. Research indicates that readers prefer textual materials that reflect this interaction between the author and the reader, that is, material that helps them to negotiate and personalize meaning. Research also indicates that metadiscourse increases students' declarative learning.

Writeability

Writeability (Fry, 1982) is the reverse side of the readability coin. Writeability answers such questions as, Are sentences long enough to adequately explicate cause/effect relationships? Are sentences sufficiently long enough to define new terms? and Are sentences long enough to compare and contrast ideas? Two hundred twenty common words (such as; *a, the, and, some, but, to, from*) make up 75% of the textual material in elementary school science textbooks. Including these common words in readability formulae does not give an accurate picture of the level of difficulty of textual materials.

How does sentence complexity affect the friendliness of a reading passage? Psycholinguistic research has shown that "kernel" sentences (those that contain only a noun and a verb) are more easily understood by students than are complex sentences. Clauses that contain cause-and-effect relationships should be used after the kernel portion of the sentence. Less punctuation makes textual passages easier for children to understand. Additionally, variation of paragraph format makes for friendlier text.

Instructional Devices

Instructional devices are reading strategies that help the reader to focus attention on shifts in topic, the relative importance of ideas, and the relationship among elements. Such conventions as headings and subheadings, glossaries, and visualization strategies (e.g., diagrams, tables, graphs, and flow charts) are commonly used instructional devices. Research has shown that embedding instructional devices or strategies in the text supports the learning of all students and proportionally benefits bilingual/bidialectic students. Photographs, diagrams, charts, and tables of data that illustrate textual material increase the learning of students, especially low-verbal students and students for whom English is a second language. There is a strong aptitude-by-treatment interaction favoring low-verbal learners that supports the enhancement of textual materials with visual and graphic displays.

Summaries of textual information embedded in written materials benefit all learners. Since transferring knowledge from one situation to another is a major purpose in learning, friendly textbooks or passages written in considerate prose facilitate this objective by providing suggestions for applying the text's knowledge to new situations. No matter how friendly the textbook, how that textbook is used is vital in the learning of children in the multicultural science classroom. Science textbooks are heavily used as the primary source of science instruction in many classrooms. Although the quality of those textbooks could be greatly improved through the addition of the elements of friendly text or friendly prose, that the textbooks are used at all is the vital concern in the reading process.

The Role of the Learner

Learners in multicultural classrooms construct meaning or a knowledge of the physical world through what they do and what they read. Constructing new knowledge of the physical world from verbal materials depends in large part on the knowledge that the reader brings to the text. Guided by one's purpose in reading and the sociocultural conditions that apply, one builds a personal rendition of the message intended by the author. Activity-based instruction, which is the hallmark of good science instruction, is also the hallmark of good reading instruction in the science content area. Reading in the science classroom should involve active mental processing in the same way that laboratory investigations involve active information processing. Students construct a knowledge of science concepts from verbal materials or from prose passages when they are actively involved in reading at the literal, interpretive, and applied levels of comprehension. Reading, like all inquiry in the science classroom, involves identification of a task and the interactions that students experience while doing the task.

Reading is a form of inquiry learning.

The Role of the Teacher

The teacher, not the textbook, is responsible for guiding the process of learning. In orchestrating the use of printed materials for science instruction, the teacher performs four vital roles: (1) selection of textbook passages and/or other printed materials that will enhance students' understandings of the concepts, (2) preparation of study guides or of questioning procedures that actively involve all students in interacting with the verbal material, (3) establishing the physical environment, and (4) assisting students in constructing meaning. In establishing a classroom atmosphere in which students can actively construct meaning from verbal materials, the teacher first needs to select passages that reflect the characteristics of friendly text. Second, the teacher should prepare study guides or question procedures that will actively engage students in questioning, evaluating, criticizing, and in general "worrying about" the knowledge that the authors are trying to convey. Third, teachers should place children in cooperative reading groups in which children are required to explain, elaborate, or defend their positions to others (as well as to themselves). Striving to explain a text passage forces the learner to integrate and elaborate knowledge in new ways. Finally, teachers need to engage in reciprocal teaching, that is, to allow students to assist in the teaching process. Within cooperative groups, students should question each other: "Where does the author say that?" "How do you know that?" Additionally, the teacher should assist students by asking clarifying or focusing questions that encourage students to collect data from textual passages and to construct new knowledge based on those data. Teachers can actively engage students in the act of reading through three-tiered study guides, QUEST (QUEstions that Stimulate Thinking) techniques, or inductive thinking methods, also referred to as ITM (Singer & Simonsen, 1989).

Reflective Reading

When assisting children in the learning process, a **TRICA** (Teaching Reading in Content Areas) technique is especially useful in the science classroom. One of the most widely used reflective reading techniques was developed by Harold Herber. Herber's (1978) technique allows students and teachers to construct meaning from textual passages at literal, interpretive, and applied levels. When working with literal-level reading activities, teachers should ask students, "What does the author say?" At the interpretive level, teachers should encourage students to consider the question, "What does the author mean?" Finally, at the applied level of reading comprehension, teachers should encourage students to think in terms of "How does this new information relate to what you already knew about the subject?" The use of reflective reading techniques (discussed in depth in the classroom practice section of this chapter) allows students to construct a knowledge of science concepts from prose passages.

QUEstions that Stimulate Thinking (QUEST)

While the use of Herber's technique is a powerful tool in assisting students to construct meaning from prose passages, it is not the only technique for assisting culturally diverse students in the elementary classroom. The QUEST technique is also a powerful device for guiding students in constructing meaning from verbal information sources. Most classroom discussion of prose material is conducted at a literal level. QUEST techniques attempt to raise the questioning levels to the inferential and interpretive and finally to the generalized, applied, and evaluative levels of thinking (Singer & Simonsen, 1989, p. 45).

To use QUEST in a science lesson, a teacher first has students read the text to obtain information. For example, the teacher could supply the students with a textbook chapter that describes the kingdoms of living things. Next, the teacher conducts a discussion that leads the students to recall information that they have just read about organisms in each kingdom. This discussion is stimulated by a *focusing question*, such as, "Would someone summarize the characteristics of plants?" The teacher may subsequently ask an *extending question*: "Who can give us some more information about plants?" The teacher repeats this process for animals, protists, moneran, and fungi.

After the relevant literal-level information has been reviewed, the next step is to get students to abstract the common properties or attributes of each of the kingdoms of living things. A *lifting question* is then posed for the students, such as, "What do all living things have in common?" or "How are all living things alike?" After extending questions have led to a definition of *living things*, the teacher can then have students evaluate the quality of their answers by asking, "Is a tomato a living thing? How do we know?" "Is a bacterium a living thing? Explain your answer." As with TRICA techniques, QUEST techniques encourage students to work at literal, interpretive, and applied levels of reading, to construct meaning from prose materials at many different levels.

Inductive Thinking Method (ITM)

The Inductive Thinking Method (ITM) is another tool to assist children in constructing meaning from verbal materials. In using this procedure, the teacher asks a series of hierarchically arranged questions to facilitate students' thinking about what they have read. The ITM technique moves students from concrete discussions of facts to abstract discussions of principles. The following is a list of the nine stages in the ITM procedure with sample questions:

1. *Enumeration and listing:* What were the . . .? What did you notice?
2. *Grouping:* What belongs together?
3. *Labeling and categorizing:* What are good names for these groups?
4. *Identifying points:* What did you notice?
5. *Explaining items of identified information:* Why did this happen?

6. *Making inferences:* What does this mean?
7. *Predicting consequences and hypothesizing:* What would happen if . . .?
8. *Explaining and/or supporting the prediction:* Why do you think this would happen?
9. *Verifying the prediction:* What could show this prediction to be true? Is there anything that you have seen that might support what you have predicted? (Singer & Simonsen, 1989, p. 46)

The first three stages of the inductive teaching method involve describing and categorizing information found in text passages. The middle stages involve interpreting information, and the final stages involve hypotheses formation and testing. The ITM method is a procedure that systematically leads students to think about information that they are acquiring or structuring from prose passages.

CLASSROOM PRACTICE

The TRICA technique advocated in this chapter is a cooperative learning model in which you, as a teacher, construct a three-tiered study guide for use by your students. The purpose of the study guide is to encourage your students to work together to construct meaning from verbal materials. The three-tiered study guide allows you to use reciprocal teaching in the science classroom. In reciprocal teaching, you and your students take turns in leading discussions of text passages as together you attempt to understand what the author is saying.

Constructing a Study Guide

In using a TRICA technique, you first construct the guide to accompany the reading material. Your students should be placed in cooperative groups of three or four, with stronger and weaker readers in each group. Cooperative groups should be constructed so that limited English proficient students have the opportunity to interact with those who possess stronger English language skills. Begin the reading process by setting the task. Explain to your students that the textual passage they are about to read contains information about the current unit of study and that all students in the class should work together to understand what the author is saying.

Guiding Literal Comprehension

When using a three-tiered study guide, begin by instructing the students to read the statements written at the **literal level** in the study guide. Literal-level comprehension, according to Herber, "is determining what the author(s) are saying, what information their words convey" (1978, p. 43). Tell the students that their job in reading is to find the specific passages of text in the article, book, or chapter that were mentioned in the study guide. Next, instruct the students to read the text passage together in groups. Allow your students to read aloud to each other. After reading aloud, ask the students to work cooperatively to find the specific place in the text in which the author(s) used the statements mentioned in the guide. Some of your students have difficulty reading at this level of comprehension because they do not understand the definitions of words; therefore, the information is temporarily unobtainable. Guided practice in reading selections at the literal level with others in their class will reinforce vocabulary development skills and will assist these students in making sense of the textual information.

After your students have concluded their discussion of the literal-level passages, allow for group reporting, for reciprocal teaching. Have your students read aloud the literal-level passages to the class and state whether they did or did not find the passage in the text. Have your students justify their answers. Ask your students clarifying questions, such as, "Where specifically did you find the textual passage or statement?" and "Cite the page and paragraph." Allow your students to evaluate their responses and the responses of other groups in the classroom.

Guiding Interpretive Comprehension

The second stage of the reading process involves developing skills at the interpretive level. According to Herber (1978, p. 43) when "reading at the **interpretive level** of comprehension the readers determine what the author(s) mean by what they say." It is at this level that your students develop **intrinsic concepts** from the relationships that they perceive in the authors' information or the textual passage. The concepts at this level are intrinsic because they are formulated from information presented in the information source. As with literal-level learning, have your students begin by reading the statements in the study guide and then have the students work cooperatively in groups to address each statement. Your students should be guided by the question, Is this what the author means? As with literal-level information, have your students read cooperatively at this level and find instances of support for their statements in the textual material. Interactions between your students in their small groups should focus on formulating answers and justifying those answers based on the textual material. As you lead a full class discussion of the findings, focus not only on the content of the reading passage, but also on the basic strategies of questioning, clarifying, and summarizing. Throughout this process, you should transfer the responsibility for comprehending the textual material to your students so that they take charge of their own learning.

Guiding Applied Comprehension

Prior knowledge and experience have a bearing on the relationships perceived in the information provided by the author(s) and on the meaning constructed by the learner. According to Herber, **applied-level** knowledge "involves the way that prior knowledge and experience relate to what the student has just read, that is, what the child sees in a relationship between the ideas acquired from other sources and the ideas derived from the reading selection" (1978, p.

47). Out of the perceived relationships, children evolve broad generalizations or principles that embrace both sets of ideas, representing something more than just the sum of the two. The applied level of comprehension is the process of taking what one knows and applying it to what one has just learned, then evolving ideas that encompass both but extend beyond them. These ideas, according to Herber, can be called **extrinsic concepts;** they are external to the text, even though they embrace ideas in the text.

When working at the applied level of reading, you should encourage children to read statements in the study guide and then ask them, "Does what you have just read and what you already know support this statement?" As you work at this level of the three-tiered study guide, focus on constructing meaning, linking new learning to what students already know. Reading at this level results in a conscious awareness of what is being learned, when it will be useful, and how to use it effectively in the future. At this level, your students should be applying the new knowledge that they have gained to what they already know.

Developing Vocabulary

Vocabulary development may be operationally defined as the ability to sort out one's experiences and concepts in relation to words and phrases in the context of what one is reading. For the vast majority of students, experience with building science concepts is much more critical than experience in pronouncing words. By the time students enter fourth grade, most have acquired the basic word-recognition skills that allow them to pronounce words they encounter in print (Vacca & Vacca, 1989).

Vocabulary development in the science classroom involves four hierarchical areas of responsibility for the teacher assisting students in: (1) developing new words for new concepts, (2) applying old words for new concepts, (3) acquiring new words for old concepts, and (4) using old words more broadly to describe old concepts already held in memory. The most time-consuming vocabulary development activity is assisting students in developing new concepts and attaching new labels or words to those concepts. For example, if you wish to have students develop a knowledge of the ecological concept of interdependence, you need to expose students to a variety of experiences that will allow them to develop a framework for themselves. Within this framework, students will be able to operationally define *interdependence* as meaning "depending on each other." Science vocabulary development is not simply a matter of using a glossary or a dictionary and looking up the meaning of a word; rather it is a process of constructing meaning regarding objects and phenomena in the natural world. Reading activities should be part of an integrated thematic whole. Laboratory and hands-on activities that provide multiple modes of knowledge representation should be used in conjunction with reading activities. Writing and reporting activities should also be used to present students with a unified thematic approach to learning about the physical world.

Providing After-Reading Activities

After-reading activities provide students assistance in developing background knowledge that they will need for subsequent learning. Additionally, after-reading activities should provide the opportunity for students to integrate, consolidate, and synthesize new information with prior knowledge (Anders & Lloyd, 1989, p. 269). Syllabification activities, developing analogies, concept mapping or word webbing, preparing electronic presentations of learning (e.g., using PowerPoint, More, Astound, and Acrobat), constructing poster presentations, preparing multimedia presentations (e.g., using HyperStudio, the Digital Chisel, HyperCard), constructing videos, and writing journals, diaries, or poetry are activities that extend the reading activity and assist students in developing competency in using the English language.

■ THE ENERGY CRISIS
A Reflective Reading and Science Activity

PREREADING CHECK

What Do I Know about the Energy Crisis?

Directions: Draw a word web or concept map which shows your knowledge of the energy crisis.

What Do I Want to Learn about the Energy Crisis?

Target Objectives:

1. T.O.   Am I able to define the term *energy crisis*? How likely am I to define the word *energy*?

Highly Unlikely   Highly Likely

2. T.O.   Am I able to name 10 ways that gasoline-powered automobiles directly and indirectly impact the environment? How many ways can I now name?

1	2	3	4	5	6	7	8	9	10

3. T.O.   Am I able to name 3 alternate energy sources? How many alternate energy sources am I able to name?

1	2	3	4	5	6	7	8	9	10

4. T.O.   Am I able to construct a model of a wind-powered vehicle? How likely am I to construct a model of a wind-powered vehicle?

Highly Unlikely   Highly Likely

5. T.O.   Am I able to identify possible solutions to the energy crisis? How likely am I to identify solutions to the energy crisis?

Highly Unlikely   Highly Likely

6. What new information would I like to learn about the energy crisis?

READING MATERIALS

ECOGOPHER NEWS: Alternate Energy Sources

WASHINGTON, DC—April 21, 1993—Secretary of Energy Hazel R. O'Leary today said President Clinton's Executive Order on Alternative Fuels will make the federal government a "driving force behind efforts to increase the availability of both alternative fuel vehicles and fuel supplies." President Clinton signed the order today, which calls for federal purchases of alternative fuel vehicles in numbers over the next three years at least 50 percent higher than those called for in the Energy Policy Act of 1992. President Clinton also announced that Texas Land Commissioner Gary Mauro will head up the Federal Fleet Conversion Task Force to advise O'Leary on implementation of the Executive Order. "I am delighted that I will be working with Gary Mauro to make this happen," O'Leary said. "As Land Commissioner, Gary Mauro has helped make Texas a national leader in converting the state fleet to alternative fuels, and has been a tireless proponent of natural gas vehicles in speeches across the country." The task force is to issue a report within 90 days recommending a plan and schedule of implementation. "The Department of Energy and all of us in government must lead by example if the option of alternative fuels is going to become a practical, affordable choice for fleet owners across the country," O'Leary said. "Increased use of domestically produced alternative fuels means reducing pollution while creating jobs. We believe that energy efficiency, protecting the environment, and a healthy economy are complimentary goals."

O'Leary said that plans call for the Department of Energy to coordinate the agencies' five-year purchase plans, help with funding for extra purchase

Smaller cars are usually more fuel efficient

or conversion costs, and work with GSA to encourage development of the fuel infrastructure needed to make fleet conversions practical. Under the order, the Department of Energy will also be working with states, local governments and industry to coordinate vehicle purchases and encourage manufacturers and fuel suppliers to make alternative fuel vehicles and alternative fuels more widely available.

A Fact Sheet Brought to You by EcoGopher at the University of Virginia

This fact sheet was prepared with the assistance of the Worldwatch Institute. Lester Brown, Project Director of the Worldwatch Institute, is a member of Earth Day 1990's Board of Directors. This reading is available on the public domain EcoGopher and was downloaded from EcoGopher by the author.

How Do Cars Affect the Environment?

1. America's love affair with the automobile has a heavy impact on the environment. Burning gasoline emits pollutants into the air we breathe; chlorofluorocarbons (CFCs) from leaky car air conditioners deplete the ozone layer; oil and other automotive fluids contaminate water and soil; and large tracts of land are lost as they are covered with asphalt to make roads and parking lots. Despite the magnitude of these problems, more people are driving greater distances. The problem will only get worse unless changes are made in our transportation priorities. We desperately need better public transportation, improved carpooling programs, increased interest in biking and walking, and higher gas mileage standards for automobiles.

2. Automobiles use approximately half of all the oil consumed in the United States. To keep up with this demand, oil companies are drilling in sensitive natural areas, such as in offshore waters and in the pristine wilderness of Alaska. With the Earth's known usable oil reserves expected to be depleted by the year 2040, oil is becoming harder to extract and the process is inflicting greater damage to the environment. As the US supply dwindles (it is expected to run out by 2020), more oil will be imported from foreign sources across great expanses of water, leading to increased oil spills. The recent Exxon Valdez oil spill in Alaskan waters clearly illustrated the scale of the risks involved. When oil is burned, large amounts of carbon dioxide, the major "greenhouse gas," are released into the air. Greenhouse gases trap heat from the sun in the Earth's lower atmosphere, causing temperatures to rise, a process known as global warming. Automobiles are responsible for about 20 percent of carbon dioxide emissions in the United States, with the average car releasing about five tons every year. Automobiles also emit about 40 per-

cent of the nitrogen oxides that contribute to acid rain, as well as poisonous carbon monoxide and hydrocarbons that cause smog. 158 million Americans live in areas that violate the Clean Air Act standards.

3. Automobile air conditioners use CFCs (Freon) that, when discharged into the atmosphere, destroys the Earth's protective ozone layer that shields us from cancer-causing ultraviolet light. In 1985, a hole the size of the continental United States was discovered in the ozone layer over Antarctica. CFCs also are responsible for as much as 25 percent of the global warming trend. Although there are far fewer CFCs than carbon dioxide molecules in the atmosphere, each CFC molecule is up to 15,000 times more efficient at trapping heat. One charge of CFCs from an automobile air conditioner contributes as much to global warming as the carbon dioxide emitted from an average new car driven 20,000 miles.

4. More than 60,000 square miles of land have been paved in the lower 48 states to accommodate America's 135 million cars. This amounts to 2 percent of the total land surface—an area the size of Georgia. Close to half of the land area in most cities goes to providing roads, highways and parking lots for automobiles, and two-thirds of Los Angeles is paved.

Transportation Facts

5. Fact: Transportation consumes 63% of all oil used in the U.S.

   Fact: In 1989, imported oil accounted for $45 billion of our $101 billion annual trade deficit, more than 40% of the total.

   Fact: In 1989, the U.S. consumed 17.2 barrels of oil a day, 27% of the worldwide consumption.

   Fact: Motor vehicle transportation accounts for 22% of all energy use in the U.S. and half of all oil.

   Fact: More than 85% of all American workers commute to work by private automobiles.

   Fact: Transportation is the only sector of the economy in which oil use grew from 1979 to 1989.

Energy Production

6. It is often difficult to grasp the importance of energy in our lives. On any given day, we may drive to work, turn on a heater, store food in a refrigerator, take a warm shower, watch TV, turn on lights and cook dinner. All of these actions use energy. Americans use more energy per person than any other people on Earth, yet we also have a deep appreciation of nature. Unfortunately, our energy practices often harm the environment. Acid rain, global warming, oil spills, and nuclear waste are all directly related to the way each of us uses energy.

7. When fossil fuels (oil, coal and gas) are burned to power vehicles and machines or to produce electricity, they release "greenhouse" gases (most notably carbon dioxide) and pollutants that cause acid rain and smog. Greenhouse gasses are changing the Earth's climate, a process that scientists believe will lead to increased droughts and flooding, a rise in sea levels and mass extinctions of plants and animals. Acid rain, also caused by fossil fuel use, is destroying rivers, lakes, and forests.

8. Nuclear energy produces between 15 and 20 percent of our electricity. But in the process of producing energy, nuclear power creates plutonium and other radioactive wastes that remain dangerous for tens-of-thousands of years.

Energy Efficiency

9. By using energy more efficiently we can reduce the negative impacts of energy production without sacrificing our standards of living. For example, there are now compact fluorescent light bulbs that screw into standard sockets and are easy on the eyes, but they use only a quarter as much energy as conventional incandescent bulbs. They cost more initially, but last about ten times as long, and save up to $40 apiece in energy costs over their lifetimes. For every incandescent bulb that is replaced with a compact fluorescent bulb, about half a ton of carbon dioxide is kept out of the atmosphere.

10. Other measures, such as insulating homes and buildings and insisting on higher gas mileage from our vehicles, have the potential to reduce our energy use significantly. In response to the oil shortage of 1973, the U.S. took measures to greatly improve its energy efficiency, and as a result was able to cut its oil use by 13 million barrels per day. Between 1973 and 1986 our economy grew 35 percent while energy use remained at the same level. Despite past improvements, the U.S. still uses twice as much energy as Japan per unit of economic output. If the U.S. reached Japanese levels of efficiency, we would save $220 billion annually.

Renewable Energy

11. Renewable energy resources, most notably solar, geothermal, and wind, are abundant and cause little harm to the environment. Using renewable energy can be as simple as designing a building to face south to take advantage of heat from the sun.

12. Solar energy can be used for heating or to convert sunlight directly into electricity—a technology called photovoltaics. Photovoltaics are now commonly used to produce electricity in remote areas that lack power lines and for powering space satellites. Another form of solar energy, called solar thermal, produces heat and electricity by concentrating sunlight on a receiver containing fluid. The heated fluid runs through pipes

that are submerged in water, creating steam to power an electric turbine. Improvements in solar technology over the past 15 years have greatly reduced its cost, and solar may soon be competitive with conventional energy sources, especially if environmental costs are included.

13. Geothermal energy uses natural steam from the Earth to produce electricity. According to the Department of Energy, there could be more domestic energy potential in geothermal resources than in either oil or gas. Over 250 geothermal plants are in operation worldwide with a total and planned capacity of 13,000 megawatts. Natural steam resources provide California with almost seven percent of its electricity needs. California Energy Company's Coso Geothermal Project currently produces 240 megawatts—enough electricity to meet the needs of 240,000 Southern California households.

14. In California, where most of the country's wind turbines are located, wind generates nearly 2 billion kilowatt hours of electricity per year—enough to meet the needs of a city the size of San Francisco. Every year, wind energy in California keeps 11 million pounds of air pollutants and 1.8 billion pounds of greenhouse gasses from passing into the atmosphere.

15. Renewable energy and energy efficiency are the only solutions to pollution caused by energy production. As energy consumers, each one of us can contribute to a healthier planet by using energy more wisely.

    ■ Our currently used energy sources are resulting in many of our greatest environmental problems. These include: acid rain, global warming, air pollution, oil spills, radioactive waste and more.

    ■ Energy produced by the wind does not contribute to any of these problems and is renewable.

    ■ The United States consumes one fourth of the world's energy each year. Experts say wind power could eventually produce 10 percent of this vast consumption.

    ■ California's 17,000 wind turbines provide enough electricity to meet all the residential needs of a city the size of San Francisco.

    ■ Since 1980 the cost of wind power in the U. S. has dropped quite considerably, from 25 cents per a kilowatt hour to about 7–9 cents a kilowatt hour.

    ■ Sweden has begun to harness the strong ocean winds over the Baltic Sea with ocean-based windmills.

The Solution

16. Raising the fuel efficiency standards for automobiles will cut down on air pollution by requiring less gasoline to be burned per mile driven. There are already cars on the market that get 50 miles per gallon or more. Converting segments of our transportation system to cleaner burning

fuels, such as compressed natural gas, methanol and ethanol, may also improve air quality. However, methanol is a questionable fuel because when it is derived from coal it releases twice as much carbon dioxide as oil. Furthermore, alternative fuels do not address the problems of traffic congestion and highway expansion. The true solution to our transportation problems lies with improvements in public transportation and carpooling programs, and increased interest in biking and walking.

17. According to the American Public Transit Association, commuting on mass transit in place of driving cuts hydrocarbon emissions that produce smog by 90 percent, carbon monoxide emissions by more than 75 percent, and nitrogen oxide emissions by up to 75 percent. Despite these impressive figures, only one penny of the nine cents per gallon federal gasoline tax is used to improve mass transit.

18. *Railway Age Magazine* points out that a single highway lane can accommodate 2,250 people per hour in automobiles, 9,000 in buses, 15,000 on a light rail line and 34,000 people on a heavy rail line. The newest French train is capable of traveling at a speed of more than 180 miles per hour while saving energy and providing a safe comfortable ride.

What You Can Do

19. ■ Walk or bike for close errands.
   ■ Arrange for a carpool with your co-workers.
   ■ Use public transportation whenever possible.
   ■ If it's reasonable, ask your employer to allow you to work at home one or two days a week.
   ■ Encourage your employer to offer financial incentives in place of a parking permit.
   ■ Take a job close to your home or move closer to your place of work.
   ■ Enjoy local recreational activities rather than traveling long distances for entertainment.
   ■ Urge your local officials to improve and promote public transportation, carpooling programs and bicycle lanes.

Alternate modes of transportation

- Write your elected officials and urge them to support legislation to raise the fuel efficiency standard for automobiles and to put funding towards public transportation rather than highway expansion.
- If you are buying an automobile, consider a model that:
  —Gets good gas mileage (at least 35 miles per gallon).
  —Doesn't have an air conditioner.
  —Has radial tires with a high tread rating for longer use.
- For proper driving and maintenance:
  —If your car has an air conditioner, make sure the CFCs are recycled anytime it is serviced and before the car is scrapped.
  —Have your car smog checked and install pollution-control equipment if necessary.
  —Keep your car tuned up and the tires properly inflated.
  —Call ahead before shopping and consolidate errands.
  —Avoid quick acceleration and deceleration and keep your speed under 60.
  —Avoid "drive through" where your car engine idles for long periods.
  —Recycle used motor oil, transmission fluid, brake fluid, and antifreeze.
  —Turn in your old battery when you buy a new one.

Three-Tiered Study Guide

Part I. Literal Level   Reading Comprehension Skills—Accreting

Directions: Read the first statement with others in your group. Place a check on the numbered line if the statement contains information from the text (exact words or a paraphrase). You must be able to give evidence to support your opinion. If any person in the group has a problem with words in either the statements or the reading selection, be certain to help them develop an understanding of those words. React to all ten statements.

_____ 1. Burning gasoline emits pollutants into the air we breathe.
_____ 2. Two-thirds of Los Angeles is paved.
_____ 3. The *Exxon Valdez* oil spill provided work for many Native Americans.
_____ 4. Americans use about the same amount of energy per person as others on planet Earth, yet we also have a deep appreciation of nature.
_____ 5. Nuclear energy produces between 15 and 20 percent of our electricity.
_____ 6. Renewable energy resources, most notably solar, geothermal and wind, are abundant and cause little harm to the environment.
_____ 7. Geothermal energy uses natural chemical reactions in the Earth to produce electricity.

_____ 8. Sweden has begun to harness the strong ocean winds over the Baltic Sea with a large series of dikes and cranes.

_____ 9. Use public transportation whenever possible.

_____ 10. Have your car smog checked and install pollution-control equipment if necessary.

Part II. Interpretive Level   Reading Comprehension Skills— Establishing Relationships/Structuring

Directions: Place a check on the numbered line before each statement that expresses an idea that can be reasonably supported with information from the reading selection. Be ready to discuss the supporting evidence with others in your group.

_____ 1. Public transportation, carpooling, biking, walking, and higher gas mileage standards for automobiles would help ease the energy crisis.

_____ 2. Within most of our lifetimes planet Earth will run out of oil reserves.

_____ 3. Automobile air conditioners that use CFCs help to cool the ozone layer, thus protecting us from ultraviolet light.

_____ 4. Paving helps to prevent soils from eroding and washing into the sea.

_____ 5. Carbon dioxide is a "greenhouse" gas.

_____ 6. Photovoltaics are commonly used to produce electricity in remote areas and in space satellites.

_____ 7. California has more wind turbines than many other areas.

_____ 8. Burning natural gas (methanol and ethanol) may improve air quality.

_____ 9. Less than 10% of the federal gasoline tax is used to improve mass transit.

_____ 10. We should recycle motor oil, transmission fluid, brake fluid, and antifreeze.

Part III. Applied Level   Reading Comprehension Skills— Generalizing/Tuning

Directions: Read through the statements. Think about the ideas and experiences that you have had that are similar in principle to what you found in the reading selection. Check each statement that you think is reasonable and that you can support by combining ideas contained in the reading selection with your own related ideas and experiences. Be ready to present evidence from both sources to support your decisions.

_____ 1. Everything must go someplace.

_____ 2. The oceans are nature's trash cans.

_____ 3. A stitch in time saves nine (B. Franklin).

Problems of energy usage are universal

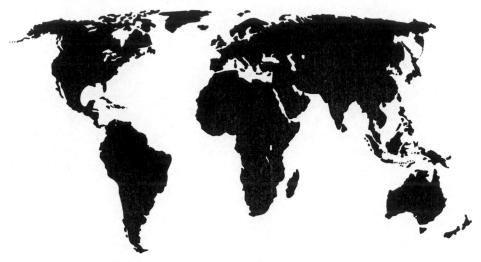

_____ 4. Plants and animals depend on each other; we say they are interdependent.

_____ 5. Humans are part of the natural environment.

Related Vocabulary Activities

1. Divide each word into syllables.
   automotive   fossil   megawatts   chlorofluorocarbons
2. Define each term.
   geothermal   solar   nuclear   pollutants
3. Write the plural of each word.
   automobile   gas   drought   activity
4. Write the singular of each word.
   rivers   barrels   megawatts   turbines
5. Write a rhyming word for each word.
   rely   bog   lithosphere   haste
6. Write a word that sounds the same but is spelled differently.
   too   waist   rein   kneed
7. Below you will find sets of two words. In the first set the two words have a definite relationship. Under the first two words in each set is a single word and then a blank. Next to the blank are three words; write on the blank the one that relates to the single word in the same way the first two relate to each other.
   a. people/carbon dioxide
      automobiles/_____ (oxygen, carbon monoxide, fluorine)

   b. shell/turtle

     ozone/_____ (Earth, gas, automobiles)

   c. solar/sun

     geothermal/_____ (California, waste, Earth)

8. Circle the word that is not related.

    acid rain   global warming   oil spills   recycle   radioactive waste

9. Solve this puzzle.

   a. E _ _ _ _ _ _ _ _ _

   b. N _ _ _ _ _ _ _ _ _ _

   c. E _ _ _ _ _ _ _

   d. R _ _ _ _ _ _ _ _

   e. G _ _ _ _ _ _ _

   f. Y _ _ _

   a. Nuclear energy produces 15 to 20% of our _____.

   b. Emission produced by automobile engines.

   c. When automobiles burn less gasoline, we say they are energy _____.

   d. Plutonium is considered _____ waste.

   e. Energy produced by natural steam.

   f. 365 days.

Related Science and Language Activities

1. Make a poster showing alternate energy sources.
2. Calculate the number of calories in a peanut (laboratory investigation).
3. Draw a cartoon about depicting a way to save energy.
4. Conduct a survey and determine ways that others in your class or group are saving energy.
5. Write a letter to your representative or senator asking them about their efforts to help save energy.
6. Gather information on the "greenhouse" effect and report your findings to others.
7. Survey your home and/or school and identify energy-saving devices.
8. Determine the air quality in your neighborhood (laboratory investigation).
9. With a group of friends, brainstorm a design for a car to be used in the year 2100 A.D.

Van pooling saves energy

Finding Out Activity: Puffmobiles

Materials: Ten straws, 25 straight pins, four macramé beads, one sheet 8½" × 11" paper

Procedure: Using the materials provided construct a "Puffmobile." A puffmobile is a wind-propelled vehicle. All materials must be affixed to the puffmobile. One straw must be reserved for the propulsion system.

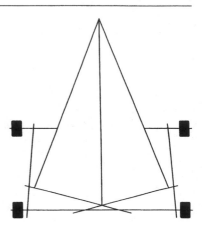

Puffmobiles—alternate energy vehicles

SELF-EVALUATION

What Have I Learned about the Energy Crisis?

Target Objectives:

1. T.O.   Am I able to define the term energy crisis? How likely am I to define the word energy?

Highly Unlikely   Highly Likely

2. T.O.   Am I able to name 10 ways that gasoline-powered automobiles directly and indirectly impact the environment? How many ways can I now name?

1	2	3	4	5	6	7	8	9	10

3. T.O.   Am I able to name 3 alternate energy sources? How many alternate energy sources am I able to name?

1	2	3	4	5	6	7	8	9	10

4. T.O.   Am I able to construct a model of a wind-powered vehicle? How likely am I to construct a model of a wind-powered vehicle?

Highly Unlikely   Highly Likely

5. T.O.   Am I able to identify solutions to the energy crisis? How likely am I to identify solutions to the energy crisis?

Highly Unlikely   Highly Likely

6. What new information have I learned about the energy crisis?

CHAPTER SUMMARY

Reading is a vital part of science instruction. Children can construct knowledge of the physical world through their interactions with prose passages as well as through hands-on learning activities. In the multicultural classroom, interactions among children during the reading process are vital as children talk about ideas and negotiate meaning with each other. Teachers may facilitate the learning of culturally diverse students by providing (1) the task (friendly text passages), (2) the opportunities for social interactions in which children discuss those passages, and (3) the opportunity for group reporting as students work at the literal, interpretive, and applied levels of reading.

 TOPICS TO REVIEW

- Characteristics of friendly text
- Role of text in science learning
- Role of learner in science learning
- Role of teacher in science learning from text

 REFLECTIVE PRACTICE

1. How is it possible for students to construct a knowledge of science from prose passages? Explain your answer.

2. What is meant by the concept of "reading as an interactive process"? Explain your answer.

3. Traditionally, reading instruction has frequently been conducted in homogeneous groups. How does that teaching strategy complement the reading strategies proposed in this chapter? How does it conflict with the reading strategies proposed in this chapter?

4. In your opinion, what characteristics of text are important in terms of the learning of culturally diverse students? Why?

5. The reading strategies discussed in this chapter are thematic reading strategies designed to foster the learning of culturally diverse students. Explain why thematic teaching might be useful for culturally diverse students. For *all* students.

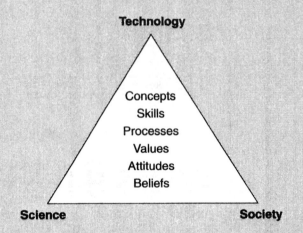

CHAPTER 13

Science/Technology/Society in the Multicultural Classroom

![icon] **POINTS TO PONDER**

- How can students become engaged in taking action on social issues?
- Why is the integration of science technology and society important?
- How does STS education fulfill the need for "real world" applications of science?

"*P*aper or plastic?" is the weekly refrain of the bag person at my grocery store. Should I have my groceries encased in a plastic bag or a paper bag? Everyone else seems to have a rapid answer for this dilemma. I don't. Much to the annoyance of those in line behind me, I mentally go through a checklist to evaluate the pros and cons of each type of wrapping. If it is August, I normally take a paper wrapping, because I know my children will soon need paper covers for their school books. During the winter months, I opt for paper bags because I know that we will recycle them when we start our fireplace burning. The rest of the year, I anguish over this decision.

I know U.S. landfills are clogged with paper products, that paper is more a source of pollution than plastics. I also know that I don't assume enough personal responsibility for recycling either product. If I were environmentally correct, I would carry my basket or cloth bags to the store and wouldn't use either paper or plastic to carry my groceries home. Indeed, I have a stack of cloth *bags in the trunk of my car, but I keep forgetting to carry them into the store. Like many members of our society, I am aware of the issues involved with recycling our natural resources, but I don't take personal action frequently enough.*

On recycling days, I separate my glass, aluminum, and paper at curbside, but I shouldn't have all that waste in the first place. I know I should carry my vegetable scrapings out to the compost pile in the backyard, but I often churn them up in the garbage disposal. Although my family recycles their cans and bottles, I sometimes toss mine in the kitchen trash can. Instead of donating used clothing to an agency that can use it, I sometimes toss out old garments. I remember to add grass clippings to our compost pile on the days we cut the lawn, but during the rest of the week I fall into bad habits. I'm afraid that I add to the problem of solid waste management more often than I help. At various times in my life, I've been a water hog, a litter bug, and just plain socially irresponsible in my environmental awareness and behavior. Building an awareness of environmental issues, helping children to become responsible citizens in a democracy, involves the integration of science and social living skills.

SCIENTIFIC LITERACY THROUGH STS

The American Association for the Advancement of Science began Project 2061 in 1985, when Halley's comet was in the vicinity of the earth. At that time, there was a realization that children who were just starting school would live to see the return of the comet. One of the documents produced in conjunction with Project 2061 dealt with scientific literacy for children; it was entitled *Science for All Americans.* According to this document, the goals of scientific literacy should include:

- Being familiar with the natural world and recognizing both its diversity and its unity;
- Understanding key concepts and principles of science;
- Being aware of some of the important ways in which science, mathematics, and technology depend upon one another;
- Knowing that science, mathematics, and technology are human enterprises and knowing what that implies about their strengths and limitations;
- Having a capacity for scientific ways of thinking; and
- Using scientific knowledge and ways of thinking about individual and social purposes (Rutherford, 1991, pp. 406–407).

Similar goals are echoed in the *National Science Education Standards.* The standards place less emphasis on broad coverage of unconnected factual information and more emphasis on curricula that include natural phenomena and science-related social issues that students encounter in everyday life (National Research Council, 1996, p. 234). They deemphasize textbook- and lecture-driven curricula and emphasize laboratory activities that feature inquiry and connections to field-based learning. Finally, the content standards at all grade levels emphasis an understanding of the relationship between science and technology.

Actualization of these goals will entail an integrated, thematic approach to teaching and learning, a science/technology/society (STS) world view. Indeed, at the elementary school level, STS is frequently thought of as the integration of social studies or social living with science. Science, technology, and society issues are frequently the same as social studies issues in that they both speak to the relationship between humans and their environment.

What Is STS?

Science/technology/society (STS) may be defined as an integrated approach to teaching that seeks to (1) prepare students to use science for improving their own lives and for coping in an increasingly technological world, (2) teach students to deal responsibly with technology/society issues, (3) provide students with a fundamental knowledge of STS issues, and (4) give students a knowledge of career opportunities in STS-related fields (Yager, 1990, p. 52). Wraga and Hlebowitsh (1991) have defined STS as a topical curriculum that addresses a broad range of environmental, industrial, technological, social, and political problems. STS topics may include acid rain, air quality, deforestation, drugs, erosion, euthanasia, food preservatives or additives, fossil fuels, genetic engineering, greenhouse effect and global warming, hazardous waste, hunger, land usage, mineral resources, nuclear power, nuclear warfare, overpopulation, ozone layer, pesticide usage, rainforest preservation, and water quality/water usage.

Collette and Chiappetta (1989) have stated that individuals do not understand how science and technology influence society, or, conversely, how much of an influence society exerts on science and technology. Science, ac-

FIGURE 13.1 ■ Science/Technology/Society Interactions

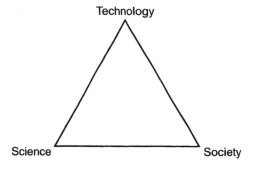

cording to these authors, is a way of knowing that involves the pursuit of understanding of the natural world. Additionally, these authors define science as a way of thinking that promotes an attitude of objectivity, a search for evidence, and self-examination. Technology is defined as applied science. Technology is the translation of scientific knowledge into practical, everyday applications that benefit humankind. The board of directors of the National Science Teachers Association in January 1990 adopted the policy that it was vital to include opportunitites for all students to study real life, personal, and societal science and technology problems in schools' curricula.

Science and technology are highly related, relying on each other. Both technology and science have profound effects on society. Scientific knowledge has both positive and negative influences on individuals in our society. The products of technology have the capacity to improve our daily lives or to negatively impact them. New technologies are frequently accepted in human society because there is a demonstrated need for them. Society, therefore, passes judgments on the relative worth or merit of scientific discoveries and technological developments.

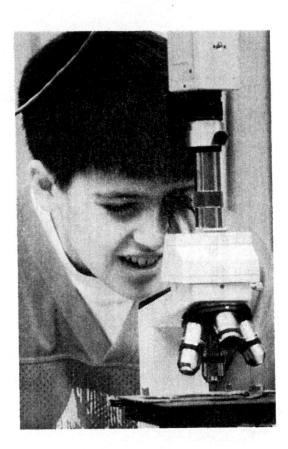

Science, technology, and society
are interrelated in our lives.

Ramsey, Hungerford, and Volk (1990) point out that science, technology, and society instruction involves a consideration of four levels of educational goals: (1) foundation (2) issue awareness, (3) investigation and evaluation, and (4) citizenship responsibility. At the foundation level, the goal of STS instruction is to provide learners with the knowledge needed to understand STS issues. This knowledge could include basic science content associated with the issues and the nature of science, technology, and society and the interrelationships between the three. At the second level—issue awareness—the goal of STS instruction is to foster the conceptual understanding of science-related social issues originating from the interactions of science, technology, and society. Additionally, issues awareness focuses on developing students' expertise in investigation; evaluation; analysis of personal beliefs, attitudes, and values; decision making; and citizenship in action. The third level of educational goals associated with STS instruction—investigation and evaluation—provides for the development of the skills and knowledge necessary to permit students to inquire into social issues and to generate and evaluate possible solutions to these problems. The fourth level of educational goals is concerned with the responsibilities of citizens in a democracy. Citizenship responsibility educational goals involve the development and application of those skills necessary for students to make informed decisions in a democracy. At this final level of educational goals for STS instruction, students are encouraged to take positive action to resolve science-related issues.

STS as Thematic Teaching

In writing of the need for science/technology/society instruction, Ramsey (1989) points out that all students will become citizens in a democracy. He also points out that students will be consumers of the products and services of science and technology. "All will assume and be responsible for the benefits and risks of scientific and technological decision-makers concerning matters of science and technology, either willfully via participation in democratic decision making or apathetically via the lack of such participation" (Ramsey, 1989, p. 40). STS education is distinguished from "traditional" environmental education in that STS focuses on the societal issues involved with science and technology. This connection with students' values, attitudes, and beliefs involves teachers in decisions about how best to address value formation with young children.

From a science education perspective, STS instruction focuses on issues that involve the interaction of people and the environment. Concepts such as interdependence, food chains, food webs, limiting factors, population growth, geochemical cycles, and resource management typically are incorporated into STS instruction. Additionally, STS instruction tends to develop a knowledge of science processes in students. From a social studies perspective, STS instruction focuses on the human experience, on the development

FIGURE 13.2 ■ STS (Science, Technology, and Society) Issues

STS Issues

■ Should scientists be permitted to exhume the bones of deceased Native Americans for scientific research?

■ Should scientists be able to create and patent new organisms?

■ Should laws be enacted to enforce mandatory water conservation?

■ Should people be allowed to burn household paper waste on their own property?

■ Is the burning of garbage in city incinerators a risk to public health?

■ Should insect vectors (insects that feed on other insects) be imported into the United States to control insect pests?

■ Should the use of herbicides (weed killers) be banned from farms?

■ Should sport hunting of deer be allowed?

■ Should animals be used in medical research? If not, why not? If so, should controls be used?

■ What controls, if any, should be used on liquid waste poured into streams and rivers?

■ What efforts should be made to preserve species on the endangered species list? Why?

■ Are adequate efforts being made to preserve wetlands in your area? Why are wetlands important? Should they be protected? If so, how? If not, why not?

---

of critical thinking, and on values education. Writing, reading, collecting and analyzing data, and reporting, competencies developed in language arts and reading and in mathematics classes, are also incorporated into elementary school's STS instruction. STS is thematic teaching in that it incorporates concepts, processes, and skills from many content area domains. Some examples of science/technology/society issues are listed in Figure 13.2.

STS Values and Education Approaches

Societal issues associated with STS instruction involve teachers and students in values identification, formation, and clarification. Values education encourages students to examine their personal points of view (which are based on their attitudes, beliefs, and values) and the viewpoints of others. Science, technology, and society issues involve students in becoming informed citizens in a democracy, citizens who will use their decision-making abilities in a real world setting. Superka, Ahrens, Hedstrom, Ford, and Johnson (1976) have identified a continuum of values formation activities, ranging from inculcation to action learning (see Figure 13.3).

FIGURE 13.3 ▓ Values Education Continuum

Inculcation   Clarification   Analysis   Moral   Action
                                            development   learning

Inculcation

Inculcation exists at one pole of the continuum of values formation activities. Inculcation may be defined as the instilling of values in students. This implies that teachers identify a belief system, value that belief system, and attempt to impose the belief system on students. Inculcation may involve expository teaching and persuasive communication. In the extreme case, inculcation may be labeled propaganda. Often, inculcation is not an attempt to warp young minds, but rather the result of a teacher being overly zealous about an environmental cause. Most teachers do not mean to stand on a soap box as they instruct students.

An example of inculcation may be seen in a hypothetical teacher who feels very strongly that the tuna fishing interferes with the welfare of dolphins. The teacher may lecture students about the problems of tuna fishing and how dolphins die when they are trapped for prolonged periods in fishing nets. This teacher may frequently refer to how the fishing is "killing" the dolphins and how this is a cruel and inhumane act. At every possible opportunity, the teacher speaks about the horrors of tuna fishing, about not buying tuna from certain companies that engage in ecologically offensive fishing practices. If the teacher also assigns the students to draw a poster showing cruel fishers killing Flipper, we would say that this teacher is engaging in inculcation. The teacher is attempting to indoctrinate students with his or her personal environmental attitudes, values, and beliefs. Inculcation is an extreme attempt to deliberately influence children's values, attitudes, and beliefs.

Critics of inculcation frequently refer to it as the "hidden curriculum." In writing of the hidden curriculum, Welton and Mallan (1992) point out that the term refers to a multitude of things that schools and teachers convey to children but that are not part of the formal school curriculum. Inculcation may involve relatively harmless values such as indoctrinating students to such school rules as "Line up when leaving the room," "Take off your hat when entering the building," and "Don't chew gum in rooms with carpeted surfaces." The hidden curriculum may also take on a more sinister cast as teachers convey or confer attributes on students: "I need some strong boys to move the chairs" or "When your father goes to work . . . ." Welton and Mallan point out that some teaching materials, especially textbooks, try to emphasize only positive virtues, such as honesty or truthfulness, and downplay or exclude any mention of nonvirtuous behaviors such as lying or cheating. These authors assert that, although such approaches are well intentioned, even young children know that not everyone is honest or truthful. In terms of science education's hidden curriculum, values associated with protecting the natural environment are treated in the same nonbalanced manner when inculcation is used in the classroom.

Clarification

Clarification is the second method or approach for addressing values education. Clarification is a method of providing students the opportunity to become aware of their personal beliefs and those of others through large group discussion techniques. Values clarification is an easy-to-use approach for increasing students' awareness of science, technology, and society issues. This approach is often initiated with a survey. One such survey, typical of those used in California during the last drought, appears in Figure 13.4; it may be used to initiate discussions about water usage and the rights of individuals to use water resources.

After completing the survey, students share their findings with others in the class. Values clarification serves to inform students that there are many points of view on STS issues, that not everyone thinks or feels the same about them all.

Brinckerhoff (1986) suggested the use of vignettes as a means of facilitating values clarification. When a vignette (see Figure 13.5) is used, the teacher normally will allow students the opportunity to read the vignette and react to it. Students' reactions may be shared during large group discussions or through entries in written journals or diaries. The purpose of the vignette

FIGURE 13.4. ■ Values Clarification Survey

Water Usage Survey

1. Are you a "water hog"? (Do you waste water?)
2. Are members of your family "water hogs"?
3. What efforts does your family make to conserve water?
4. What efforts is your community making to conserve water?
5. Do you think that people should be allowed to use water as they choose?
   - Growing lawns?
   - Growing gardens and fruit trees?
   - Washing cars?
   - Washing driveways?
   - Filling swimming pools?
   - Operating outdoor fountains?
6. Do you think there should be penalties for those who waste water?
7. How do you feel about laws that regulate the amount of water that each family can use per month?
8. How do you feel about laws that require home owners and hotel businesses to buy low-flow shower heads and low-flush toilets?

FIGURE 13.5 ■ STS Vignette

Earthquake Problem

Scientists at a large California university are proposing to set off a series of minor earthquakes to preclude a large earthquake from occurring. The scientists have theorized that if they remove stress along an earthquake fault, they might be able to prevent a large earthquake from occurring. The scientists at the university propose drilling a series of dry test wells on both sides of an active earthquake fault. The scientists will then pump water into the wells and "lubricate" the fault. It is the feeling of the scientists that this will allow minor slippage along the fault, resulting in minor earth tremors or small earthquakes. The minor earthquakes will cause some shaking and earth movement but should be far less severe than a major earthquake. Residents in the town near the fault object to the scientists' causing earthquakes. They fear that their homes and businesses will be damaged by a series of minor earthquakes. They want to obtain a court injunction to prevent the university from drilling the test wells. What is the point of view of the scientists? What is the viewpoint of the residents?

is to allow students to state their own values regarding a particular subject and then to share those with others. Vignettes are meant to be springboards to discussions.

Opponents of values clarification point out that some values clarification activities have generated enough controversy that their use has been restricted or banned in some school systems. Some of the criticism of values clarification centers on students' right to privacy. Many parents and school boards believe that students shouldn't be required to state their beliefs publicly, that to do so is to violate students' right to privacy. It is nearly impossible for students to reveal their beliefs about controversial topics without revealing personal information about themselves and their families. Values clarification has also been criticized for its failure to distinguish between moral and ethical values and nonmoral and esthetic values.

Analysis

Values analysis goes beyond values clarification in that it stresses the gathering and organizing of factual information so that students may be better informed about issues involving science, technology, and society. This third approach to values clarification involves students in library research, in field studies, and in determining other people's beliefs, attitudes, and values. The analytical approach encourages scientific inquiry on the part of students; it encourages students to separate facts from opinions.

Values analysis involves students in social moral issues associated with science, technology, and society topics. For instance, to analyze an environmental issue, they might (1) identify the environmental question, (2) gather information about the issue, (3) evaluate the data, (4) evaluate the worth or significance of the data, (5) propose tentative solutions, and (6) determine acceptable solutions.

Suppose a company in a small town petitions the city council to allow it to treat its own industrial waste and to discharge the treated effluent into a stream passing through the town. Students in the class have heard about the petition from their parents and are concerned that this might cause pollution and damage the stream. Students would begin by identifying the environmental question. Will treating and discharging waste pollute the stream? Next the students need to gather data. What type of treatment will the company use for its industrial waste? What is a standard way of treating waste products? As part of the process, students will need to identify salient variables and separate facts from opinion. They will need to compare the company's plan to what is known of good waste management plans and to what is already being done in the community. The students will need to determine the impact of a second sewage treatment plan on their community, and they will need to determine the quality and quantity of the effluent to be produced by the company. Next the students will need to compare plans of action. Will the company's plan be better than what is already being done? Are there other options available for waste treatment? Has the company considered all of the options? Finally, students will need to make a judgment. Is the company's plan in the best interests of the community?

Students may determine that their city's former waste disposal procedures were inadequate and that the company's plan is better than past practice. They may also determine that the waste treatment might affect the town's water table and may pollute drinking water supplies. Analysis involves students in gathering and interpreting data. It engages students in real world problem solving, in generating alternative solution paths, and in judging between solution paths. An analytical approach to values clarification prepares students to be participating citizens in a democracy. It encourages students to use science practices and procedures to gather data, to evaluate data sources, to form working hypotheses, and to generate solutions to problems. Analysis involves students in an inquiry approach, that is, a problem-solving approach, to issues involving science, technology, and society.

Critics of the analysis approach to values education point out that teachers need to be sensitive to students who are not participating in the activity either because they are not interested in the topic or because they lack the verbal proficiency to participate. Typically, values analysis instruction relies heavily on teacher-directed questioning. Such instruction may be difficult for children who lack English language proficiency.

Moral Development: The fourth type of values education approach identified by Superka, Ahrens, Hedstrom, Ford, and Johnson (1976) is moral development. A moral development approach to education involves students in reasoning and thinking; however, moral development focuses on personal moral values such as justice, equality, and fairness. Moral development is differentiated from analysis in its focus on the individual's reasoning and thinking; analysis focuses on society's needs. Typically, the moral development approach to values education uses a vignette that represents a moral dilemma, which causes students to examine their personal belief structures.

Kohlberg (1980) developed a five-stage model for moral development. At the lowest levels, students are concerned with external, concrete consequences for themselves. At the middle stages of Kohlberg's model, students are concerned with external social expectations. Finally, at the highest stages of moral development, students are concerned about questions of "conscience," about respect for the rights, life, and dignity of other persons. Kohlberg points out that most people do not achieve the final stage of moral development, that is, a concern for the fundamental moral principles on which this nation was founded.

Moral-dilemma vignettes cause students to choose between two alternatives, each accompanied by a difficult consequence. Vignettes used in moral development may include readings, films, plays, and so forth. The moral reasoning level of students will influence how they respond to moral issues and social problems. Here is a vignette appropriate for elementary school children:

> Your mother works for a large lumber company. Her company is currently clear cutting a large wooded area north of your town. As the lumber company has worked in the area, they have come upon nests of a new species of woodpecker. Lumbering in the forest has temporarily stopped while the plight of the woodpeckers is being investigated. Scientists from a local university have stated that this is the only known habitat of the woodpecker and that removing more trees from the area will cause the extinction of the species. If the lumbering operations are stopped, your mother will lose her job. If the lumbering resumes, the woodpecker will become extinct. What do you feel should be done? Why?

In this vignette, students are forced to think about their family's economic situation and also the plight of an endangered species. The student must choose between two equally unattractive yet viable alternatives. This vignette forces the student to think about personal moral values. This situation is very real in many communities, as choices need to be made between people's jobs and the survival of endangered plant and animal species.

Critics of the moral development approach to values education point out that the approach has been challenged because of the questionable adequacy of Kohlberg's theory or because of the assumption that higher-stage reasoning is better than lower-stage reasoning. Some critics additionally point out that the development of moral reasoning is a slow process and requires a great deal of instruction before students actually move from one stage to another. Most instruction in school is too shallow to bring about significant changes in students' levels of moral reasoning.

Action Learning

The final approach to values education is action learning. Action learning involves more than clarification, thinking, reasoning, and decision making; it calls on students to take personal action regarding science, technology, and society issues. Action learning extends learning beyond the walls of the classroom into the community. The North American Association for Environmental Education states that action learning stresses the need for active participation in solving environmental problems and preventing new ones (Tanner, 1987). Action learning helps students to become active in solving local environmental problems.

Action learning involves students in their communities. It empowers students to take action on local environmental issues. Suppose Mr. Johnson, a fourth-grade teacher, wants his students to learn about pollution in their local community. A small arroyo runs through the school grounds. On rainy days, the arroyo overflows onto the school grounds and for several days afterwards students need to remain inside during recess periods, as the playground is flooded.

During the next rain storm, the students notice that the old tires, metal cans, and scrap metal in the arroyo are damming the waters, causing the stream to flow onto the school grounds. When the arroyo dries out, Mr. Johnson and his students begin to remove the litter clogging the stream channel. They arrange with the school's trash removal service to cart away the old debris. The students volunteer to clean the arroyo during their recess periods. As the students clean the arroyo, they notice that some local businesses are using the arroyo as a landfill area. Mr. Johnson's students write letters to the city council asking for city help in keeping the arroyo free from debris. The city arranges to have dumpsters installed for the merchants to use, thus eliminating the source of the litter. In this scenario, the students have learned that they can take action to improve the quality of their school grounds and that they can also influence others in the community to take part in efforts to improve the quality of the environment.

Although values education approaches to STS issues range from inculcation to action learning, Rubba and Wiesenmayer (1991) point out that effective STS instruction empowers citizens with the knowledge, skills, and affective qualities needed to make responsible decisions and take action on science- and technology-related societal issues. Wraga and Hlebowitsh (1991) state that STS education stresses the interaction of personal and social goals within a problem-focused framework. Finally, Mayer (1990) points out that future leaders and voters (today's students) must understand our interrelationships with peoples around the world and how our daily activities affect our planet and its resources.

STS Issues

Science, technology, and society instruction focuses on values formation. Within this context, the selection of appropriate issues is of vital importance. In writing of this concern for selecting appropriate STS issues, Rhoton (1990) points out that there needs to be a focus on the needs of students to understand and make decisions on STS issues that impact their lives. Some STS topics are more appropriate for older students than for younger ones.

A discussion of the implications of genetic engineering and surrogate mothers that may be appropriate for high school students is probably not appropriate for elementary school students. If Rhoton's criterion is used, genetic engineering is probably not appropriate for young children because it is not readily understood by most elementary-aged children. Other topics, such as land management, water pollution, and recycling, are more likely to be of interest to younger children. Good STS issues for elementary classrooms are understandable by younger children and are matters that directly impact the lives of children.

STS issues exist in all American communities.

What Does the Research Say?

In writing of the impact of science, technology, and society instruction, Yager (1990) points out that STS instruction improves students' abilities in five areas: (1) connections and applications, (2) creativity, (3) attitudes, (4) science processes, and (5) content area knowledge. In the area of connections and applications of science knowledge, Yager points out that STS instruction assists students in relating classroom knowledge to their daily lives, in connecting classroom learning to real world situations. Students participating in science, technology, and society instruction become involved in identifying and resolving social issues, and they come to see science as a way of fulfilling their responsibilities as citizens (Yager, 1990). STS instruction provides students with a knowledge of the real world value and worth of technological developments and of the importance and relevancy of science instruction.

In the area of creativity, STS instruction encourages students to ask more questions that reflect their own interests in science and technology. STS instruction encourages students to engage in inquiry learning, to propose possible solutions to real world problems. Science, technology, and science instruction assists students in identifying possible causes and effects of certain observations and actions.

STS instruction results in students seeing science as a way of dealing with problems. It encourages students to become curious about the real world, to become personally involved in solutions to real world problems. Additionally, STS instruction involves students in identifying local problems and resources to solve those problems—it helps students to act locally. Finally, STS instruction helps students to become aware of their rights and responsibilities as citizens as they attempt to resolve issues that they have personally identified in their local communities.

In terms of science processes, STS instruction assists students to view science processes as skills they can use in problem-solving situations. Students readily see the connection between the processes they have learned in the classroom and action needed to solve problems. STS instruction encourages students to connect school learning to real world problem solving.

From the perspective of science content knowledge, an STS approach encourages students to view science knowledge as personally useful learning. Students who learn by experience readily retain information and are able to relate existing knowledge to new situations. Science, technology, and society instruction encourages students to view science content knowledge as more than a dead body of information to be stored in books and memorized. STS instruction encourages students to enjoy what they are studying.

Researchers have asserted that STS instruction improves students' learning. In a study of the effectiveness of STS instruction, Pederson (1992) found that STS instruction, while not impacting students' learning of science concepts, does reduce students' anxiety toward learning science. Pederson also concluded that when students are placed in a situation in which they study issues relevant to them, share information cooperatively, present their perspective of the issue being studied, and cooperatively come to a group consensus on the issue, anxiety toward science is reduced. He also pointed out that the goal of scientific literacy for all students is best met when students overcome their anxieties associated with the study of science.

CLASSROOM PRACTICE

As a teacher, one part of your job is to identify appropriate instructional activities for students. Science, technology, and society instruction is most effective when the topic is of local concern, impacts the lives of all of your students, and offers your students the chance to take personal action. Pizzini, Bell, and Shepardson (1990) developed a four-step method for developing science, technology, and society lessons called Search, Solve, Create, and Share. In this method, students seek out a local problem, use research methods to gather information, create possible solution paths, and share their findings with others.

This section presents a series of activities that can be used to consider issues associated with land use. The activities are meant to be personalized or localized to the needs of your students. They may be used to encourage students to find a local problem they can solve using commonly available classroom resources. After finding a local problem concerned with land management, students may establish a research agenda to investigate the problem and then seek solutions within the local community. Finally, students should be encouraged to share their findings with others. Before beginning the activities, collect three soil samples from your area (preferably sandy soil, loam, and clay). Also assemble topographic maps, land-use maps, street maps, and so forth to assist students with the problem. Localizing this problem to your geographic location will assure that students connect classroom learning to their community.

■ Preparation for Soil Consultation Project Activities

Teacher Preparation: Before beginning the activity, locate three possible locations for the imaginary housing development in your geographic area. Provide students with maps showing the proposed locations. Also locate three buckets of local soil samples typical of the areas in question.

Problem: A national building company has proposed building a 300-unit housing project in your area. The company is attempting to decide among three locations. Adequate water resources have been found for the housing development. Additionally, it has already been determined that there are adequate roads and streets to reach the houses. A survey of local city, county, and state government agencies indicates that there will be adequate sewers, electrical services, and garbage removal for the area. The only remaining problem is a soil analysis. Your group is to serve as a consulting team in helping the city council decide where to place the development. Keep a log of your investigations of the soil samples. If a soil-testing kit is available, investigate the physical and/or chemical properties of the soil. Prepare a report to the community (or your class) on your findings. As you write your final report, consider the following question: Should houses be built on the best land (the land that grows plants best)? Why or why not?

Note: If resources are available, have students prepare their reports as video tapes or electronic presentations (i.e., done in PowerPoint, HyperStudio, Astound, More, Publish It!, or similar electronic presentation package).

ACTIVITY 13.1   ■   Soils and Plant Growth

Materials: Nine bean seeds, three containers for plants (paper cups, pots, etc.), three soil samples, metric ruler, balance, graduated cylinder or measuring cup

Teacher Notes: This project requires approximately 4 weeks to complete.

Student Directions: 1. Fill each container with soil. Plant the bean seeds in each container (at a depth of about 1 centimeter).

Plant growth studies

2. Water the plants every other day. Be sure to place the same amount of water in each cup (for example, 20 ml. every 2 days). Measure the height of each plant each week. Record the average height of the three plants on a plant growth chart.

Plant growth chart

Week Number	Sandy Soil	Clay Soil	Loam
1			
2			
3			
4			

3. Make a line graph showing the average plant growth in each soil.

ACTIVITY 13.2 ■ Biomass

Materials: Three containers of plants, balance

Conducting the Activity:

1. At the end of the 4 weeks of plant growth activities (Activity 13.1), have the students cut off the plants at soil level (where the plant touches the soil). Using a balance, weigh all the plants at one time. This is the biomass, the weight of living plant material that has grown in 4 weeks in the soil sample. (Biomass is the weight of living material.)

Biomass recording sheet

	Sandy Soil	Clay Soil	Loam
Biomass (in gms.)			

2. Ask students: Which soil supported the greatest amount of biomass? Why is biomass an important measure of a soil's vitality?

ACTIVITY 13.3   ■   The Living Soil

Materials: Three fresh soil samples (not dried out), three ring stands and ring clamps, three funnels, three flasks, alcohol, wire mesh (large enough mesh so that soil organisms may pass through yet small enough to hold soil in the funnel), three light sources, dissecting microscopes, eye droppers, and petri dishes

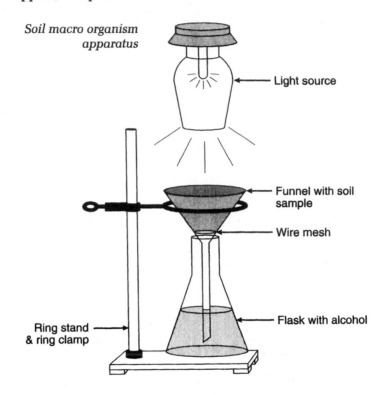

Soil macro organism apparatus

Light source

Funnel with soil sample

Wire mesh

Flask with alcohol

Ring stand & ring clamp

Conducting the Activity:

1. Set up the apparatus as shown. Place about 50 grams of soil on top of a piece of wire mesh in the bottom of the funnel. Place the funnel so that the bottom is immersed in alcohol in the flask. Place a light source over the funnel. Allow the apparatus to sit for 1 or 2 days. Macro organisms in the soil will migrate from the soil into the alcohol, where they will be captured. Remove the organisms from the alcohol with an eye dropper, place them in a petri dish, and view them under the microscope.

2. What organisms do you find in each soil sample? Draw and describe the organisms. Which soil has the most organisms? Which soil has the fewest organisms? From this activity, which soil is best for supporting living things?

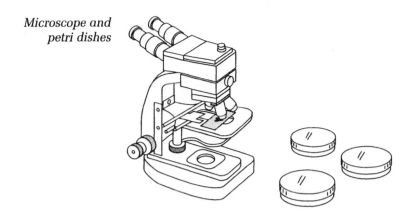

Microscope and petri dishes

ACTIVITY 13.4 ■ Holding Capacity

Materials: Three soil samples (dried out), three ring stands and ring clamps, three pieces of filter paper, graduated beaker or graduated cylinder, three flasks, three funnels, balance

Student Directions: 1. Weigh out 100 grams of each soil sample. Place each sample in a piece of filter paper in the holding capacity apparatus.

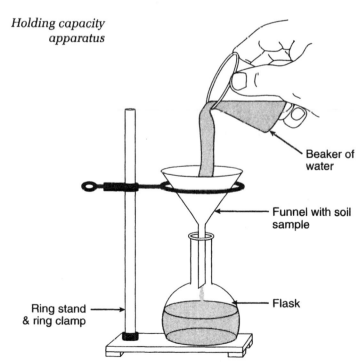

Holding capacity apparatus

Beaker of water

Funnel with soil sample

Flask

Ring stand & ring clamp

2. Pour 50 milliliters of water into each soil sample. Measure the amount of water that runs off the soil. The water that is retained by the soil is a measure of its holding capacity. Soils that hold more water have a greater holding capacity and greater capacity to provide water to plant roots (remember that if drainage is poor, plant roots may rot). Use the chart to record your data.

Holding capacity data sheet

Type of Soil	Amount of Runoff (in milliliters)	Amount of Water Held (50 – runoff)	Percent of Water Held ([Water held/50] × 100)
Sandy soil			
Clay soil			
Loam			

ACTIVITY 13.5   ■   Soil Composition

Materials: Three soil samples, three jars with lids, balance, graduated cylinder, metric ruler

Conducting the Activity: Place 100 grams of each soil sample in a jar (mayonnaise jars work well). Add 200 milliliters of water. Cap the jar and shake vigorously. Allow the sample to sit overnight. The next day, measure the amount of gravel, sand, silt, clay, and organic matter in each soil sample. Record your results. Older students should compute the percentage of each of these components. Younger students should construct bar graphs comparing the amounts of each soil component.

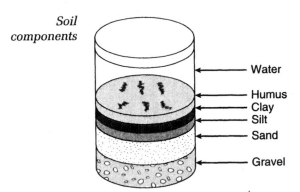

Soil components

Water
Humus
Clay
Silt
Sand
Gravel

Soil composition data sheet

Soil Component	Sandy Soil	Clay Soil	Loam
Organic matter			
Clay			
Silt			
Sand			
Gravel			

ACTIVITY 13.6 ▦ Soil Food Chains

Materials: Soil organisms picture and soil organisms chart.

Soil organisms

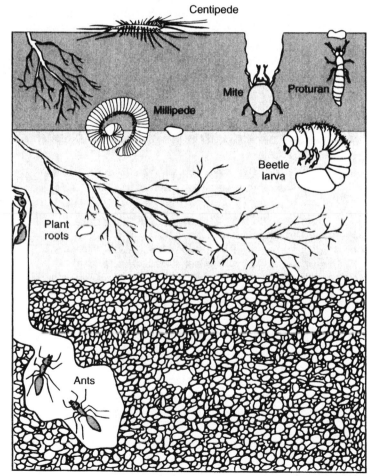

Forest food chains (soil organisms food chart)

Producer	*Primary* *Consumer*	*Secondary* *Consumer*	*Decomposer*
Oaks	Termites	Centipedes	Bacteria
Maples	Beetle larvae	Beetles	Fungi
Grasses	Mites	Ants	Earthworms
Algae	Proturans		Millipedes
	Thrips		
	Springtails		

Conducting the Activity: Construct five food chains using the information contained in the soil organisms picture and the soil organisms chart. Each food chain should begin with a producer. Producers are green plants that make the food. Producers are eaten by primary consumers or herbivores (plant eaters). Primary consumers are eaten by secondary consumers or carnivores (animal eaters) and/or omnivores (animals that eat plants and animals). Decomposers (bacteria and fungi) feed on dead plant and animal materials. Sample food chain: oak tree—termites—beetle larvae.

■ Sharing on Soil Consultation Project Activities

Presentation: Using a written report, an oral presentation, posters, or other medium, share your findings with others in your class. Based on what you have learned of soils, where would the best location be for a housing development in your neighborhood? Why?

Constructing a Presentation: Use available media materials to present your findings to others. Some means of reporting might include:
- Electronic slide show constructed with PowerPoint, Astound, More, HyperStudio, and so on.
- Poster sessions. Construct posters and present findings to others in a traditional science poster set-up.
- Video. Construct videos that summarize your findings.
- Panel presentation. Divide up into your areas of expertise and report in a panel format.
- Newspaper. Use computer applications to construct a newspaper or newsletter to present your findings.
- Trifold or infobrochure.
- One-page flier to inform parents of the results of the study.
- Formal debate for other students in the grade or school.

CHAPTER SUMMARY

Science, technology, and society instruction takes a thematic approach to teaching science that incorporates a knowledge of science, technological applications of science, and a concern for the societal implications of scientific endeavors. STS instruction incorporates values education. Frequently, at the elementary school level STS instruction is regarded as combining social studies and science instruction. A study of science, technology, and society involves students in problem solving in the real world. One purpose of STS instruction is to prepare students to participate as scientifically literate adults in a democratic society.

 ## TOPICS TO REVIEW

- STS (science/technology/society)
- Values education approaches

 ## REFLECTIVE PRACTICE

1. Based on your experience, which approach to values education might be best? Why?

2. Explain what is meant by the interrelatedness of science, technology, and society.

3. Based on your experience, what STS unit of study would you feel most comfortable teaching at the elementary school level? Why?

4. Why is STS instruction vital for culturally diverse learners? Justify your answer.

5. STS instruction is referred to as thematic instruction. How are science, social studies, language arts, reading, and mathematics incorporated into STS units?

6. Based on what you have read in this chapter and on your experience, why is STS instruction more valuable than "traditional" science instruction to culturally diverse learners? Justify your answer.

CHAPTER 14

What do they want to know?

What do they know?

What have they learned?

How will they find out?

Guiding Learning in the Multicultural Science Classroom

POINTS TO PONDER

- What type of lesson planning best addresses the needs of culturally diverse learners?
- How should you go about planning for learning?
- How do all the parts and pieces about teaching and learning fit together?

If I have one admonition to give teachers, it is this: Whenever you teach, teach well. You never know when the product of your efforts will come into your life again. This realization hit me the night my first son was born. At around 5 o'clock A.M. I lay on a stretcher in a hospital delivery room about to give birth. I had entered the hospital around midnight. After five hours of labor, I was ready for the great event. A nurse appeared at my bedside and announced that my doctor had been called away to perform an emergency delivery for a woman who had been in an automobile accident. She assured me that I needn't worry, that all was progressing nicely, and that his resident would be with me momentarily.

I lay back on the stretcher as a labor pain moved from my back to my front. When I looked up, I saw a familiar face. "Carlton, what are you doing here?" I yelled. Carlton had been a student in the first advanced biology class that I ever taught. The last I had seen him was at his high school graduation ceremony. He smiled and announced that he was now a doctor and would be my attending physician. Suddenly, I remembered that he couldn't distinguish between dorsal and ventral in biology class and that he had dissected his frog upside down. "Did you do well in medical school?" I inquired. I'll never know how well Carlton did in medical school because at that moment my regular doctor walked into the room. The experience did, however, teach me the value of teaching well. And planning is prerequisite to all good teaching. This chapter is designed to help you put into practice the topics that have been discussed throughout this book.

PUTTING THE PIECES TOGETHER

An effective program of science instruction for culturally diverse learners requires attention to scope-and-sequence documents, state frameworks, and local curriculum guides. Additionally, science instruction for culturally diverse learners should combine assessment, thematic teaching, experiential learning, language acquisition, and a consideration of the needs of individual learners, as mentioned previously in this text.

Effective Science Teaching

The authors of the *NSTA Pathways to the Science Standards* point out that teachers of science design and manage learning environments that provide students with the time, space, and resources needed for learning science (Texley & Wild, 1996). In doing this, teachers (1) structure the time available so that students are able to engage in extended investigations, (2) create a setting for student work that is flexible and that supports science inquiry, (3) ensure a safe working environment, (4) make science tools, materials, media, and technological resources accessible to students, (5) identify and use resources outside the school, and (6) engage students in designing the learning environment (Texley & Wild, 1996, p. 17).

In describing the characteristics of effective science instruction in the multicultural classroom, Atwater (1993) identifies classroom climate, creative curricula, multiple modes of communication, planned progress, and reflective teaching as some of the elements necessary for successful planning. Planning for culturally diverse students involves orchestrating elements in the learning environment to provide each child the opportunity to acquire a knowledge of science concepts and processes.

The broad goal of producing a scientifically literate society carries implications for multiple levels of planning and implementation. As far as possible, elementary science programs for culturally diverse learners should (1) provide a balanced curriculum of physical, earth, and life sciences, (2) show students that science is enjoyable, (3) reinforce conceptual understanding rather than rote learning, (4) present an articulated scope and sequence at the school level, (5) arrange classroom settings that encourage positive attitudes for learning science, (6) integrate science with other subject areas, and (7) use community resources (California State Board of Education, 1990).

Providing a Balanced Curriculum

Just as a balanced diet is necessary for physical health, a balanced science curriculum is necessary for the healthy academic development of children. Each year, children should have experiences in physical, earth and space, and life sciences. Each of these disciplines lends itself to activities that involve students in "doing science." When teaching science, teachers should encourage students to make connections between the disciplines of science. For example, energy is transferred during chemical reactions; it is also transferred during metabolism in living things and during earthquakes. The concept of energy transformation is a basic science theme that is found in physical, life, and earth and space sciences. Thematic teaching breaks down the divisions between sciences, encourages lifelong learning, and develops conceptual understandings in all children. A balanced curriculum, in which all science disciplines are taught every year, provides for the varied science interests of young learners. Finally, balanced science programs consider the development of the affective and psychomotor domains as well as the cognitive domain.

Making Science Enjoyable

Too often in the past, especially when science has been taught to limited English proficient children, it has been taught as a vocabulary activity, as a list of words and definitions to be committed to memory. When science is taught as a list of words, the joy of learning—the adventure of exploring the natural world—is frequently lost. Science is a way of doing. It is a way of exploring the physical world. When science is taught as a hands-on/minds-on, laboratory-based investigative activity, children become actively involved in their own learning. If science is an enjoyable experience, students will continue to learn after the instructional period ends. A desire to learn science begins with teachers who model a fascination with science and its dynamic presence in our daily lives (California State Board of Education, 1990). Effective science instruction ought to encourage all students—particularly children from underrepresented groups—to take more science in the future.

Encouraging Conceptual Understanding

When the science curriculum focuses on higher-order thinking skills and a problem-solving approach to learning, children tend to learn more readily than if it is presented as low-level learning replete with drill-and-practice activities. Conceptual understanding of science is strengthened when students relate what is being learned in school to that which they have learned at home and in the community. The focus on open-ended questioning, questions with multiple solution paths, encourages students to use their existing knowledge to solve new problems. In the process, students expand their vocabularies and their understanding of the natural world. Students should increase their conceptual understandings of science, as well as their knowledge of science processes.

Articulating Scope and Sequence

Teachers, in conjunction with parents, school administrators, and the community as a whole, should plan and sequence science instruction in order to meet the unique needs of children in the neighborhoods they serve. Successful science programs are tailored to meet the unique science education needs of the entire community. The process of articulating a curriculum involves identifying prior learnings as well as future learnings. Typically, district and/ or building curricular committees divide units of instruction among grade levels. This insures that students do not repeatedly study some topics while ignoring others. Working with colleagues, parents, and administrators provides teachers the opportunity to mesh their instructional programs with the efforts of others, to develop a unified instructional program.

Classroom Setting

Most science curricula today require the space and opportunity for hands-on learning activities. The physical environment of the classroom needs to be arranged so that small group work is easily undertaken by students. Resources necessary for science learning should be within easy reach of all students. Laboratory equipment, computer software, library books, bulletin

Effective planning is the first step in effective instruction.

boards, learning centers, reference materials, and so forth, need to be readily accessible. Additionally, classroom setting considers the unique needs of culturally diverse learners. When students feel at ease in the classroom, learning is maximized. Part of effective planning is a consideration of the resources and classroom climate necessary to implement instruction.

Integrating Content

Science instruction does not occur in isolation. Effective science programs incorporate concepts, skills, processes, and affective appreciations from the domains of language and literature, mathematics, social studies, music, and art. Scientific literacy could receive a considerable boost if science were used as a vehicle to enhance reading, mathematics, and the arts. The integration of content from many disciplines leads to exemplary science teaching and learning. Math/science integration, Teaching Reading in the Content Area (TRICA), and Science/Technology/Society (STS) are examples of thematic approaches to the teaching of science that integrate traditional disciplines.

Marshaling Resources

No project manager would go into a project without knowing the objective and the resources available, and without a plan to achieve the objective. Teaching requires a similar level of preparation. Teachers need to know their students, their community, and the objectives of instruction. In terms of culturally diverse learners, a knowledge of the community and the community's expectations is perhaps the most important advance preparation a teacher undertakes. Effective science curricula capitalize on the wealth of resources of the local community. Resources may include tangible items such as laboratory equipment; access to parks, fields, and streams; museums; and human resources in the form of guest speakers and community experts. Effective science instruction involves components of career awareness as well as a conceptual understanding of science. Additionally, access to resources frequently controls the depth and breadth of science instruction that is afforded students. Community support, including parental involvement, is necessary to insure the vitality of science education programs.

Translating Curriculum into Practice

One job of the classroom teacher is to translate existing scope-and-sequence documents, standards, frameworks, and curricular guides into classroom practice. Most school districts assign units of study or topics to particular grade levels. Typically, textbooks are purchased or adopted at the state or district level. Teachers function within these constraints when planning activities for children's science learnings.

Science units are normally organized around broad themes, questions, topics, or problems. Units typically range in length from two weeks to several months. Normally, units contain broad unifying concepts as well as grade-level concepts and subconcepts. Four broad reflective questions should guide teachers in the planning, implementation, and assessment process: (1) What do they know? (2) What should they know or want to know? (3) How will they find out? and (4) What have they learned? Planning involves a consideration of children's prior knowledge, their interest and curiosity, their learnings or understandings, and available educational resources. One effective means of planning is with a vee map (Roth & Bowen, 1993, Roth & Verechaka, 1993). This reflective teaching model encourages teachers to consider students' entry-level knowledge, interests, existing resources, and educational outcomes.

What Do They Know?

What do they know? is a question dealing with children's prior knowledge. Chapter 6 deals with ways of assessing or measuring children's understandings of science. Before beginning any unit of study, teachers will want to assess children's knowledge in the cognitive, affective, and psychomotor domains. Concept mapping, word webbing, brainstorming, semantic mapping, journal writing, and pretesting are means to get a handle on children's prior knowledge in the cognitive domain. Task tests may be used to assess children's motor skills. Attitude instruments and writing exercises may be used to assess children's attitudes.

What do they know? also considers the conceptual knowledge children have acquired and the way that those ideas or notions are connected and related. Additionally, assessment of children's knowledge includes related or associated knowledge children may hold and the way that knowledge is interrelated. Assessment of prior knowledge may include measurements of

FIGURE 14.1 ■ Vee Map Planning

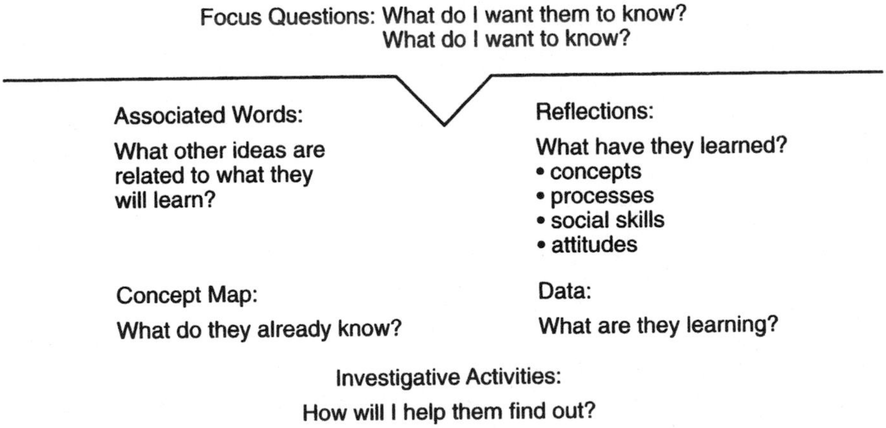

Focus Questions: What do I want them to know?
What do I want to know?

Associated Words:

What other ideas are related to what they will learn?

Reflections:

What have they learned?
• concepts
• processes
• social skills
• attitudes

Concept Map:

What do they already know?

Data:

What are they learning?

Investigative Activities:

How will I help them find out?

children's intellectual skills, cognitive strategies, verbal information, motor skills, and attitudes. Planning involves teachers in addressing the question, What do they know? at a yearly, unit, and daily level.

What Should They Know or Want To Know?

The question, What should they know or want to know? may be answered at an individual, collective, or comparative level. At the individual level, each child may provide a blueprint for learning, that is, a list of questions each wants to have answered during a unit of study. At a collective level, through talking with one another and by talking with others in their school, family, and community, children should be encouraged to formulate a set of questions that they desire to answer as they discuss and study a particular topic. Finally, anticipation of future learning may be addressed at a comparative level by the teacher. How do my students compare with a standard set by my school district? By my state?

What should they know or want to know? may be addressed in terms of long-range aims, goals, and target objectives, as well as short-term or daily objectives. Aims are typically broad, long-range educational outcomes that are anticipated by school districts, states, or both. One aim of science instruction is to produce a scientifically literate society. This aim of science teaching may require years to achieve. Goals, on the other hand, are typically narrower in scope and may be defined as statements of the outcomes of education (Gagné, Briggs, & Wager, 1988). The ability to read on grade level may be seen as a goal of education. Frequently, district curricular guides translate goals into grade-level objectives.

The question, What does my school district or state say that children ought to know about this topic or unit or concept? involves a comparison of students' knowledge against a particular existing curricular standard. At this comparative level, teachers are actually identifying educational needs of their students. An educational need may be defined as a discrepancy or gap between a desired state of affairs (goal) and the present state of affairs (Gagné, Briggs, & Wager, 1988).

Instructional objectives are the teachers' objectives for student learnings. Instructional objectives speak to the gap between what students know and what the district or state curriculum guide or framework suggests that they should know. In formulating instructional objectives teachers typically include objectives that reflect students' concerns for new learnings. Instructional objectives serve as guideposts for teachers' planning, as road maps for selecting activities that will attend to students' educational needs. One instructional objective might be that students will be able to measure the mass of an object using a pan balance. Another instructional objective might be that students will be able to operationally define the terms *potential* and *kinetic energy*. Unit planning is guided by instructional objectives, that is, by teachers' expectations for students' learnings.

Teachers' instructional objectives eventually become **target objectives.** That is, instructional objectives are also instructional outcomes by which students monitor their progress in learning. A target objective may be thought of as an objective that students and the teacher share and that all are working to achieve. Target objectives are guideposts for student learnings. These objectives serve to inform students of the goals of instruction, of the anticipated learning outcomes that the student should achieve, and of students' progress in learning. Suppose that a school district's elementary science curriculum calls for students to compare and contrast producers, consumers, and decomposers as an outcome of a unit of ecology studies. This goal may be translated into a series of target objectives for students: Am I able to define producers, consumers, and decomposers? Can I identify ways that producers, consumers, and decomposers are alike? Different? How likely am I to do these things? Target objectives not only inform students and their teachers of what is to be learned, they also encourage students to reflect on their learning and on their need for additional learning. The relationship between instructional objectives and target objectives is shown in Figure 14.2.

In addition to guiding learning, target objectives serve as a basis of student assessment. At the end of a particular unit of study, teachers may ask students if they have in fact mastered a particular set of target objectives. Target objectives become "test stems" or assessment items for measuring students' knowledge, as a means for students to convey what they have learned.

FIGURE 14.2   ■   Relationship of Instructional Objectives and Target Objectives

Instructional Objective:	By the end of the unit students will be able to operationally define the term *erosion*.
Target Objective:	■ Am I able to define the term erosion?
Instructional Objective:	The students will be able to compare and contrast the characteristics of beetles and true "bugs."
Target Objective:	■ Am I able to compare and contrast beetles and true "bugs"?
Instructional Objective:	The students will be able to construct a wet mount of a plant stem.
Target Objective:	■ Am I able to construct a wet mount of a plant stem?
Instructional Objective:	The students will be able to measure linear distance using a meter stick.
Target Objective:	■ Am I able to measure distances using a meter stick?

How Will They Find Out?

How will they find out? is the third question guiding planning for both teaching and learning. This question encourages teachers to identify available educational resources and activities to initiate student investigations of the natural world. When planning instructional activities for students in the multicultural classroom, teachers need to consider the characteristics of the learners and the ways that children learn. Additionally, teachers need to identify the means by which students will learn science concepts and processes.

The question How will they find out? engages the teacher in brainstorming. What materials, activities, and resources are available to me as I plan? What instructional strategies will I use? What conceptual knowledge will be included in this unit? What science processes will be highlighted during this unit of study? What accommodations will be made for children with special needs? Have I attended to the instructional needs of all students? Planning engages the teacher in identifying available resources to meet children's educational needs. When planning, teachers consider the nature of the learning situation, the type of learning outcome that is expected, the environment or climate for learning, the conditions under which children will receive instruction, and practical considerations such as cost, feasibility, and access to materials.

After activities, resources, and materials are identified, the teacher wrestles with the question of the instructional approaches to be used. Will this be a thematic unit or a stand-alone unit? If the unit is a thematic unit, what subject or content areas will be included? What activities will be used to teach or illustrate the concepts in the unit? Are the materials and resources readily available? What materials and resources need to be gathered? Where will they be obtained?

Once the instructional activities have been selected, the next issue is sequencing. Do some of the activities require prerequisite skills or knowledge? If so, which activities should be first, second, third, and so forth? How should the unit be structured? Suppose a teacher desires that students record data on mold growth as part of a unit of studies of fungi.

The teacher should begin by examining this activity to determine what types of prior knowledge are required. In this instance, the activity requires students to record data on a table of data, control variables, and make measurements of the size of colonies of fungi. If the students have not had previous experience using these science processes, these should be taught as the students work through the activity.

Additionally, teachers should reflect on the total unit of study. Is there a variety of learning activities? Have the needs of all students been met? Does the unit include at least one activity that will appeal to every child? Are students encouraged to bring their home learning to school and to combine that with new information to be presented in class? At this level, planning involves integrating parts to make a unified whole. Translating units into daily instruction involves teachers in identifying prerequisite concepts, skills, and processes and in sequencing instruction so that students acquire a knowledge of science gradually over time.

What Have They Learned?

The final question in the planning process involves evaluation and reflection on what has been learned. What have they learned? is a question that teachers wrestle with daily as well as on a unit basis or yearly. In addition to daily assessment of learning, students may be evaluated using teacher-made or publisher-made tests. They may also be evaluated by entries in journals, task tests, posters, and so forth.

Not only should teachers evaluate students' learnings, they should also reflect on their own teaching. What things have I done well? What things might I do better in the future? What types of learning activities worked well with this group of students? What types of learning activities might work better? Planning involves teachers not only in planning and implementing instruction but in reflecting on what students have learned and on what might have been done better.

Finally, as part of the reflection on planning, teachers should check to be sure that there is congruency and consistency among the objectives, the instruction, and the assessment. If the instructional objectives were to provide students with a knowledge of the characteristics of fungi and the conditions necessary for fungal growth, then the teacher would evaluate the instruction to be sure that the activities met these objectives. Did I provide students the opportunity to learn the characteristics of fungi? Did I provide students the opportunity to learn about the conditions necessary to grow mold or fungi? Finally, did I measure students' learnings in accordance with the objectives? If the objective was to identify the characteristics of fungi, did I design an assessment question that measured students' progress in mastering this objective? Did I measure students' knowledge of the conditions necessary for mold growth? Objectives, instruction, and assessment should match. In other words, teachers should teach to the objectives, and teachers should measure how well the objectives were achieved.

CLASSROOM PRACTICE

Suppose you want to prepare a unit of instruction on sound for a second-grade class. Your school district science curriculum guide requires that second graders in your district engage in a unit of study on sound. You might begin by administering a pretest on sound or by asking your students to make a concept map or word web that shows what they know about sound. This provides information not only about students' notions of sound, but also about their knowledge of associated or related concepts.

As you prepare to write a unit on sound, you would compare your students' knowledge of sound with the criteria that have been established by your school district. What does the district suggest that students know about sound? What do my students already know about sound? Once you have determined what your students already know about sound, you should determine what they need to know. Additionally, you should ask your students, What do you want to know about sound? What new information would you like to gain as we study sound? Planning begins by assessing gaps in your students' knowledge base and by identifying gaps between what they already know and what they need to know (see Figure 14.3).

FIGURE 14.3 ■ Vee Map for a Unit on Sound

Focus Questions: What do I want them to know?
What do they want to know?

District objectives: Concept – Sound is a form of mechanical energy.
– Pitch is the highness or lowness of sound.
– Sound is caused by a vibration of matter.

Processes – Observing, recording data, predicting, using
cause and effect relationships

Students' desired learnings: What causes sounds?
What kinds of sounds are there?
(Brainstorming session) How can I make sounds?

Associated Words:

What other ideas are
related to what they
will learn?
- pitch
- music
- loudness
- vibration
- energy
- hearing

Reflections:

What have they learned?
(Teacher reflections after the unit)

- concepts — assessed on posttest
- processes — assessed in journals
- social skills — checklist
- attitude — assessed on library day

Concept map:

What do they already know?
- Word web for preassessment

Data:

What are they learning?
- Laboratory journal — record
  of activities and reflections
  on learnings
- Additions to word webs

Investigative activities:

How will I help them find out?

- Textbook readings on sound —
  three-tiered study guide
- Video on sound from library
- Beaker and tuning fork activity
- Ping pong ball and tuning fork activity
- Bleach bottle banjo
- Meter stick activity
- Bottle flute
- Straw flute

- Shoebox activities on sounds
  (rubber bands, plastic
  instruments)
- Guest speaker — band director
- Reading corner — library books
- Poster on musical instruments
- Paper cup phone
- Computer disk on sound

The next step involves identifying resources. What textbook chapter, tradebooks, and readings will assist my students in constructing a knowledge of sound? What activities will I plan to help students add to their conceptual knowledge of sounds? What science processes will I emphasize as we study sound? What social skills will I encourage students to work on? How will I evaluate those skills? What attitudes will I stress during the unit?

In the unit plan shown in Table 14.1, a series of hands-on science activities may be integrated with TRICA (Teaching Reading in the Content Areas) activities, guest speakers, and cooperative tasks. The overall unit includes textual passages, videos, computer software programs, hands-on manipulative activities, guest speakers, and individual learning activities. Information on sound is presented to students by a variety of methods. The unit emphasizes the acquisition not just of conceptual knowledge of sound, but of science processes, attitudes, and social skills. Planning is a road map; the activities illustrated in the unit plan "schedule" indicate approximate time periods. Most teachers recognize that activities sometimes go according to schedule and sometimes require adjustments in timelines. Students' rate of acquisition of conceptual knowledge is frequently difficult to gauge in advance.

Students' conceptual knowledge of sound is evaluated through traditional posttesting, times of sharing learning, journal writing, and poster sessions. Acquisition of science processes is to be evaluated in this unit through an examination of students' laboratory journals. Attitudes toward sound are assessed through unobtrusive observation of students' reading preferences during library periods. Finally, students' social skills are evaluated through an observation checklist. Evaluation is an ongoing process. Daily sharing of what students are learning and daily reflection on students' written work pro-

Sharing is part of learning.

TABLE 14.1 ■ Instructional Plan for a Unit on Sound

	Monday	Tuesday	Wednesday	Thursday	Friday
Week 1	■ Word webs on sound 14.1 ■ Brainstorming—What do we want to know about?	■ Assess attitude during library period (books on sound checked out) 14.2	■ Reading on sound ■ Introduce shoebox corner 14.3	■ SCALed lesson—tuning fork and water 14.4 ■ Journal writing 14.5	■ Video on sound ■ Minilecture on sound
Week 2	■ SCALed lesson—Paper cup phone 14.6 ■ Add to word webs 14.1	■ Finish sound readings—three-tiered study guides	■ Ping-Pong ball activity 14.7 ■ Sound vocabulary activities	■ Meter stick activity 14.8 ■ Bleach bottle banjo 14.9	■ Straw flute activity 14.10
Week 3	■ Computer program on sound	■ Reading study guide on sound	■ Bottle flutes 14.11	■ Guest speaker—band director	■ Playing home-made instruments 14.12
Week 4	■ Begin adopting an instrument activity—Jigsaw 14.13	■ Complete jigsaw activity on sound ■ Use checklist to evaluate students' group skills	■ Postassessment on attitudes—library check ■ Sharing on musical instruments 14.14	■ Make a poster—share what you've learned about sound 14.15	■ Posttest on sound

vides teachers with an understanding of the ways that students are construct-ing a knowledge of sound. Activities 14.1 through 14.15 are associated with the sound unit.

ACTIVITY 14.1   ■   Word Webbing Sound Concepts

Type of Activity: Conceptual assessment: pretest and reflective learning

Student Directions: Draw a word web that shows your understanding of sound. Show all of the words that you can think of that are related to the concept of sound. Draw lines to show the ways that the ideas are related. As you work through the unit, your teacher will ask you to look at your word web and to add new ideas.

ACTIVITY 14.2   ■   Attitudes toward Sound

Type of Activity: Attitude assessment

Conducting the Activity: Observe the students during their regular library period. As students leave the library, count the number of students who voluntarily select books on sound. The difference between the number of students who select a book on sound before beginning a unit of study and those who select such a book after the unit is a crude indicator of change in inter-est toward the subject.

ACTIVITY 14.3   ■   Sound Shoebox

Type of Activity: Self-directed learning

Materials: Rubber bands (different sizes), small box

Shoebox thumb harp

Student Directions: Make a musical instrument by stretching the rubber bands across the top of a box. Pluck the rubber bands. Arrange the bands in order from the one that makes the lowest pitch to the one that makes the highest pitch.

Record Your Observations:

Focus Questions:

1. Can you change the pitch of a rubber band? If so, how?
2. Does a thick rubber band make a different sound from a thin one? If so, how?
3. What happens when you pluck the rubber band quickly? Slowly?
4. What happens to the pitch when you stretch a rubber band? Let it sag?
5. How is a rubber band like a stringed instrument?

ACTIVITY 14.4 ■ Investigating Sound Waves

Type of Activity: SCALed lesson (discrepant event)

Activation Stage

Materials: Tuning fork, beaker of water

Focus Question: What happens when a tuning fork is placed in a container of water?

Student Directions: Fill a container with water. Tap a tuning fork against the edge of a table or chair. Place the vibrating fork in the water. What happens?

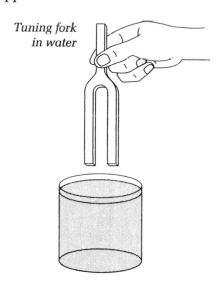

Tuning fork in water

Actualization Stage

> **Materials:** Tuning fork, beaker of water
>
> **Student Directions:** Change some of the variables and record what happens on the following data sheet.

> *Tuning Fork Variables*

Conditions	Observations
Beaker filled to top	
Beaker half filled	
Beaker nearly empty	
Tuning fork added quickly	
Tuning fork added slowly	

Application Stage

> **Focus Questions:** Based on what you have observed, what would you say about sound? Explain your answer in your journal.

ACTIVITY 14.5 ■ Journal Writing

Type of Activity:	Thematic: language and science activity
Materials:	Outline of vee map or a science journal
Student Directions:	As you work through the investigations of sound, keep a record of your investigations. Describe the materials and the procedures you are using and keep a record of your findings. As you do each activity, explain what new information you are adding to your knowledge base about sound.

ACTIVITY 14.6 ■ Paper Cup Phone

Type of Activity:	SCALed Lesson

Activation Stage

> **Materials:** Paper cups, string
>
> **Procedure:** Construct a paper cup phone like the one shown.

Paper cup phone

Actualization Stage

Focus Questions:

1. What happens when you speak into the paper cup?
2. What happens when someone else speaks into the paper cup phone and you hold your cup at your ear?
3. What happens when the string is tight?
4. What happens when the string is loose?
5. How far can you stretch the phones apart and still have them work?
6. Does your phone work around corners? Why or why not?

Application Stage

Focus Questions:

1. How is your paper cup phone like a real phone?
2. How is your paper cup phone different from a real phone?
3. How does a paper cup phone work? Explain your answer.

ACTIVITY 14.7 ■ Ping Pong Magic

Type of Activity: SCALed lesson

Activation Stage

Materials: Tuning fork, Ping-Pong ball glued to a piece of thread

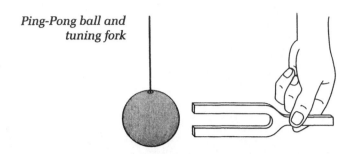

Ping-Pong ball and tuning fork

Procedure: Hold the Ping-Pong ball (glued to a thread) very steady. Touch the ball with a vibrating tuning fork.

Actualization Stage

Materials: Tuning fork, Ping-Pong ball on a string, Ping-Pong ball

Focus Questions:
1. Touch a vibrating tuning fork to a Ping-Pong ball sitting on a table. What happens?
2. Touch a vibrating tuning fork to a Ping-Pong ball suspended on a thread. What happens?
3. Do the two balls behave in the same manner? Why or why not?

Application Stage

Focus Questions:
1. Explain why the suspended Ping-Pong ball moves so much when it is touched by the vibrating tuning fork.
2. After this activity, how would you describe sound?

ACTIVITY 14.8 ■ Moving Metric Ruler

Type of Activity: SCALed learning

Activation Stage

Materials: Metric ruler or meter stick

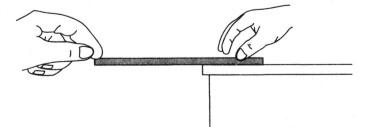

Metric ruler activity

Focus Question: What happens when a meter stick is pressed down and released?

Actualization Stage

Materials: Metric ruler or meter stick

Focus Questions:
1. What happens to the meter stick when it is released?
2. What happens if you press harder on the meter stick?
3. What happens if you press lightly on the meter stick?
4. What happens if you move the vibrating meter stick onto the table?
5. What happens if you move the vibrating meter stick off the edge of the table?
6. As you hear the sound, can you see something happening to the meter stick? What?

Application Stage

Focus Question: Based on what you have observed, what do you think "causes" sound?

ACTIVITY 14.9 ■ Bleach Bottle Banjo

Type of Activity: SCALed learning

Activation Stage

Materials: Empty bleach bottle (cleaned out with bottom removed), paper fasteners, rubber bands of varying thicknesses

Procedure: Assemble the banjo as shown. Can you play a tune on the banjo?

Bleach bottle banjo

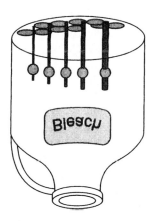

Actualization Stage

Focus Questions:
1. Do the rubber bands make different sounds? Why do you think this happens?
2. What is another name for the highness or lowness of sound?
3. What causes rubber bands to make different sounds?
4. What would happen if you had a thicker rubber band? A thinner band?

Application Stage

Focus Questions:
1. How is your bleach bottle banjo like a real banjo or guitar?
2. How is your bleach bottle banjo different from a real banjo or guitar?

ACTIVITY 14.10 ■ Straw Flute

Type of Activity: SCALed learning

Activation Stage

Materials: Plastic straw, scissors

Procedure: Make a straw flute by cutting the straw as shown. Press your teeth lightly in front of the cut portion of the straw and blow.

Focus Question: What happens?

Straw flute

Side view of straw flute

Top view of straw flute

Actualization Stage

Focus Questions:
1. Can you make a high pitched sound with the flute? If so, how?
2. Can you make a low pitched sound with the flute? If so, how?
3. Could you do something to the flute so that you could make high and low sounds one after the other? What could you do?
4. Could you play a tune on the straw flute? Describe how you would do this.

Application Stage

Focus Questions:
1. How is the straw flute like a real flute?
2. How is the straw flute different from a real flute?

ACTIVITY 14.11 ■ Bottle Flute

Type of Activity: SCALed lesson

Activation Stage

Materials: Empty soda bottles, water

Procedure: Fill the bottles with different amounts of water. Blow across the top of each bottle.

Focus Question: What happens to the sound when different amounts of water are in the bottles?

Actualization Stage

Focus Questions:
1. If sound is caused by a vibration of matter, what is vibrating in the bottles?
2. Which bottle makes the highest sound?
3. Which bottle makes the lowest sound?

Application Stage

Focus Questions:
1. Is there some instrument in a band that works in the same way that a bottle flute works? If so, which one?
2. Why do you think different pitches of sound are produced?
3. From your experiences in working with different homemade instruments, what can you conclude about sound?

Soda bottle flute

ACTIVITY 14.12   ■   Homemade Instrument Orchestra

Type of Activity: Cooperative learning

Conducting the Activity: Tell the students that their group is to use their homemade instruments to play a simple tune. This might be follow-up for a guest speaker (such as a band director or an older student who plays a musical instrument). Ask the students to arrange the pitches of the strings or sounds of their instruments in order from the lowest to the highest. Pass out music sheets to the students. Allow them to select a conductor in each group and to practice briefly playing a selection.

Music scores for homemade instruments

Mary Had a Little Lamb
(Music for soda bottle flute)

Mary had a   little   lamb,   little   lamb,   little   lamb
3 2   1   2 3   3   3   2 2   2   3 5   5

Mary had a   little   lamb,   its fleece   was   white as   snow.
3 2   1   2 3   3   3   2   2   2   3   2   1

ACTIVITY 14.13   ■   Adopt an Instrument

Type of Activity: Cooperative learning: jigsaw

Materials: Library books, filmstrips, and videos on musical instruments, records, etc.; art supplies—poster paper, markers, paints, glue, scissors, etc.

Conducting the Activity: Allow students to form cooperative or familia working groups. Place pictures of musical instruments in a container and allow students to randomly draw an instrument. Ask each group of students to become experts on one musical instrument. Have the students research their instrument and prepare an oral presentation to tell the class about their instrument. Students may share with posters, songs, playing instruments, playing recordings of instruments, and so forth.

Adopt an instrument

Piano   Trumpet   Flute

Drums   Harp   Guitar

ACTIVITY 14.14 ■ Social Skills Checklist

Type of Activity: Student evaluation

Conducting the Activity: As students work in groups constructing a project to share what they have learned with others, circulate from group to group and evaluate students on their social interactions with others, using a checklist like the one following.

Social Skills Checklist

Social Skills	*Never*	*Some*	*Often*	*Always*
How often does student listen when others speak?				
How often does the student contribute ideas to the group project?				
How often does the student share manipulative materials?				
How often does the student hand materials to others?				
How often does the student get materials for the group?				
How often does the student lead the discussion?				

ACTIVITY 14.15 ■ Sharing What You've Learned

**Type of
Activity:**   Authentic assessment

Materials: Poster paper and art supplies (markers, glue, scissors)

**Student
Directions:**   Make a poster and report that describe what you have learned about sound as you have worked through the activities in this unit of study.

CHAPTER SUMMARY

Lesson planning involves teachers in putting it all together, developing a road map to guide students' learning. Reflective planning addresses the questions What do they know? What should they know or want to know? How will they find out? and What have they learned? Lesson planning involves the teacher in assessing children's prior knowledge, involving children in planning for future learning, sequencing activities that may help students acquire new knowledge, and evaluating instruction and that which has been learned.

TOPICS TO REVIEW

- Target objectives

REFLECTIVE PRACTICE

1. In this chapter, planning is viewed as constructing a road map. Do you agree or disagree with this analogy? Why or why not?

2. In your opinion, what is the purpose of scope-and-sequence documents and district curricular guides? Explain your answer.

3. The author points out that planning is a guide and that teachers are rarely able to carry out unit plans as they were first written. Why do you think this happens?

4. In your opinion, why is it important that objectives, instruction, and assessment exhibit "congruency and consistency"?

Safety in the Multicultural Science Classroom

Introduction

Safety in the science classroom is a concern that touches all students. A safe working environment for children includes consideration of classroom management and planning, laboratory equipment, and safety awareness.

Managing and Planning for Safety

If it can go wrong, it will go wrong. This motto ought to guide our planning for children. Young children especially lack the muscle coordination and hand-and-eye coordination of adults. Children will spill, drop, and break things. "Safety First" is the motto of the Santa Fe Railroad; the same motto ought to apply to the classroom.

- Before conducting an activity in the classroom make sure that you have tried it yourself. Identify the potholes in the road, and try to find ways of avoiding these potholes in your activities.
- The activities in this book have all been field tested with real children in real classrooms. They were designed with a consideration of children's safety. Whenever possible plastic containers have been substituted for glassware. Chemicals used in this text are designed to be noncaustic and noncorrosive.
- Plan for the little disasters of life. Remember that children typically lack the hand and eye coordination of adults. Provide sponges, mops, and paper towels for activities involving liquids. Provide brooms and dust pans so that children may clean up after themselves.
- Make sure that proper safety equipment is available. If flames are used, be sure that you have a fire extinguisher on hand. Provide children with protective eyewear and insist that children use the eyewear appropriately. If caustic chemicals are used, provide protective eyewear and protective aprons. Safety shields should be used in classroom demonstrations involving flames or caustic substances. Remember to model the correct use of safety gear at all times.

- Use flat-topped tables or desks or floor space for science activities. Tilt-topped desks are difficult to use in the science classroom.
- Select plant specimens with care; some plants are poisonous and some children suffer allergic reactions to some plants.
- Plan carefully for students' interactions with animals. Be sure to apprise yourself of the Humane Society regulations and recommendations in your geographic area.

Laboratory Supplies and Equipment

- Whenever possible, use nonbreakable containers.
- Whenever possible, use nontoxic chemicals. Children have a habit of tasting and smelling everything, regardless of teacher instructions.
- Make sure that all equipment is in good working order prior to instruction. Don't use defective equipment in the classroom. Frayed electrical cords, chipped glassware, and exposed metal objects are never appropriate in the classroom.
- Test all electrical equipment prior to allowing children to use it. Make sure that ground wires are properly connected and that children use appropriate care when working with electrical equipment.
- Dilute caustic chemicals as much as possible to avoid injury.

Safety Awareness

- Be sure to cue children about potential hazards as part of preactivity orientation. Daily cautions about safety should be part of your planning process.
- Enforce the wearing of safety goggles and protective clothing whenever hazardous chemicals or flames are used in the classroom.
- Be consistent in enforcing safety regulations and model "best practice" in your personal behavior in the classroom.
- Provide safety instructions in native languages if students are not proficient in English.
- Whether working in a monolingual or bilingual classroom, provide safety posters in the child's native language.
- Involve children in planning a safe working environment.

Critters in the Science Classroom

Introduction

The presence of living organisms in the classroom enhances the quality of science instruction. Teachers need to provide adequate food and shelter for "critters" brought into the classroom. In certain areas of the country, school boards, animal protection agencies, and local statutes prevent the use of certain living organisms in classrooms. Common sense also dictates that certain organisms are not appropriate for use in science classrooms. For example, rattlesnakes would not be appropriate guests in a public school setting. Generally, the quality of instruction is vastly improved through the use of living specimens. This is a thumbnail guide to the care, feeding, and use of animals appropriate for most instructional settings.

Ants

Ants make fascinating additions to any elementary science classroom. Stock for ant colonies may be obtained from scientific supply houses or from the natural world. If obtaining ants from the natural world, extract the queen from the anthill first. Colonies may be started without a queen, but all of the eggs laid by the workers will hatch into males.

Ants in the classroom

While homemade ant housing constructed out of wide-mouthed jars is acceptable for most ants, ant houses available from commercial supply houses afford students a better opportunity to view the life history of the ant. Soil in the ant colony should be kept moist (by the insertion of a few drops of water each day). Suitable food for ants includes sugar granules, small pieces of vegetables (lettuce, carrots, potatoes), stale bread crumbs, dried fruits, and small pieces of raw ground meat.

Butterflies

Lepidoptera specimens are easily raised in the classroom and provide hours of observational opportunities for children. The easiest way to begin raising butterflies is to obtain eggs or newly hatched larvae from the natural world. Summer and early fall are the best times of the year to obtain specimens.

Larvae should be kept in a clean, dry, well-ventilated container. Food should be changed once or twice a day. Droppings should be removed daily to prevent mold growth. If leaves are moistened before being placed in the container, the moisture needs of the insects will be met. Toward the end of the larval stage, small sticks should be placed in the container to provide a place for pupation to occur.

After the period of pupation, the chrysalises will hatch into mature butterflies. At this time, the newly emerged butterflies will need several hours to "blow up" their wings. Blood is pumped through the wings and the wings harden before the butterflies take their maiden voyage. Finally, release organisms back into the environment when your study is completed.

Butterflies enliven classroom instruction

Crayfish

Crayfish are readily raised in the classroom in standard aquariums. As with fish, the aquatic environment should be well aerated. Crayfish are regarded as shellfish in some states, and the season to collect specimens may be limited. After specimens are caught in a net, they should be placed in a moist environment for transportation to the classroom.

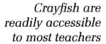

Crayfish are readily accessible to most teachers

If an aquarium is used, the bottom should be covered with gravel. Additionally, plastic flower pots or simulated rock caves should be placed in the bottom of the aquarium to serve as "houses" for the crayfish.

Crayfish are scavengers and eat a variety of fresh and/or frozen meats. Frozen or canned fish is a favorite food of crayfish. Be certain to release the crayfish back into the environment once your study is completed.

Fish

Fish (especially guppies and goldfish) make wonderful additions to the elementary science classroom. Well-oxygenated aquariums with gravel bottoms make fine habitats for these critters. As a rule of thumb, about 4 liters of water is needed for each small fish.

Appropriate water temperatures vary with the species housed in the aquarium. Goldfish typically prefer water that is 20 to 24 degrees C. Some tropical species may require higher temperatures.

Adult fish typically need to be fed daily. Commercially prepared fish foods are best for meeting the nutritional needs of your fish. Be certain that filters and tanks are cleaned regularly and maintain a feeding record on the side of the tank.

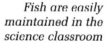

Fish are easily maintained in the science classroom

Mealworms

Mealworms are the larval form of *Tenebrio* beetles. Commercial supply houses are the best source of stock to begin a beetle colony. Tenebrio larvae are comfortably accommodated in the classroom in plastic, glass, or enamel containers. Wheat middling or bran flakes are standard food for mealworms.

Mealworms are easily raised in the classroom

The addition of carrot or apple slices into meal will supply beetles' moisture needs. Springtime is the best season for beginning mealworm cultures. Once established, colonies can last many years, as long as the food supply is periodically recharged.

In addition to providing endless hours of observation, mealworms may serve as food for fish and crayfish being raised in the classroom.

Snails

Land snails make excellent pets for the classroom. They are easily maintained and provide students with a wealth of information about mollusks. Land snails are most easily collected during the early morning hours after a soaking rain. Typically, snails are found in dark damp places.

Snails require a very moist environment to survive. Glass containers, including discarded aquariums, make excellent snail housing. The bottom of the aquarium should be covered with soil. Rotted leaves, decaying tree branches, and moss provide appropriate fauna for the environment. A shallow container of water placed in a corner of the aquarium will supply the moisture needs of the snails. Additionally, a glass cover on the top of the container will keep the humidity level high.

Decaying lettuce leaves and similar rotting vegetation provide an adequate food source for land snails.

Snails teach students the role of decomposers in ecosystems

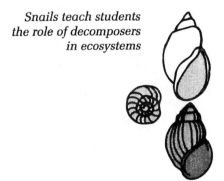

Frogs

The life cycle of the frog is a source of fascination for young children. Frog eggs may be obtained from ponds and slow-moving areas of streams in the early spring. Eggs should be placed in a shallow container. Roughly one liter

Frogs should be released into the wild once studies have been completed

of water is required for each 8 to 10 tadpoles. Water should be maintained at about 20 degrees C.

Tadpoles may be fed dried yeast or small amounts of boiled lettuce. If the tadpoles become sluggish, or if the water becomes cloudy and foul smelling, you are overfeeding the tadpoles. Foul water should be changed. Typically, water should be changed every other day to maintain a clean and hygienic living environment for the tadpoles. Be certain to release the tadpoles back into the environment once your study is completed. Also be certain to maintain a clean environment and a feeding record on the side of the container.

Vertebrates

Mice and gerbils make excellent classroom pets. Specimens should be purchased from a local pet store or a reputable supplier to avoid bringing diseased animals into the classroom. Due to a risk of Hantavirus infection, wild mice should never be used in the classroom. Animals should be housed in soundly constructed wire mesh cages.

The bottoms of cages should be covered with newspaper and cedar chips. Water bottles should be filled daily and animals should be provided with clean food daily. A feeding, cleaning, and watering schedule should be

Mice and gerbils provide a means to teach students about animal care

kept attached to each cage. Be certain to consult with your local Humane Society before setting up a colony of vertebrate animals in the classroom. Local ordinances and school board regulations may provide additional constraints on the maintenance of animals in the classroom.

 **A P P E N D I X   C**

Equipment and Materials for the Science Classroom

Throughout the United States there are hundreds of corporations that supply equipment, supplies, and materials for science instruction. The listing provided on these pages is meant to introduce teachers to some of those companies. The list is in no way meant to be inclusive of all sources of supplies. Updated lists of science education suppliers may be obtained annually from the National Science Teachers Association.

Equipment/Supplies

AccuLab Products Group
200 California Ave., Suite 217
Palo Alto, CA 94306

SensorNet and "Plug & Go" interfacing materials

AIMS Education Foundation
P.O. Box 8120
Fresno, CA 93747

Supplier of AIMS labs

American Geological Institute
4220 King St.
Alexandria, VA 22302

Aquarium and Science Supply Co.
P.O. Box 29726
Elkins Park, PA 19117

Supplies for classroom animals

Arbor Scientific
P.O. Box 2750
Ann Arbor, MI 48106

General lab supplies

Brock Optical
P.O. Box 940831
Maitland, FL 32794

Labware

Carolina Biological Supply Co. 2700 York Rd. Burlington, NC 27215	25,000 items for science teaching
Center for Multisensory Learning Lawrence Hall of Science University of California Berkeley, CA 94720	SAVI/SELPH Program
CHEMPAC E & L Instruments P.O. Box 1942 New Haven, CT 06509	Hardware, software, and laboratory manuals
Connecticut Valley Biological 82 Valley Rd. P.O. Box 326 Southampton, MA 01073	General science supplies
Creative Publications 788 Palomar Ave. Sunnyvale, CA 94086	Elementary science supplies
Cuisenaire Company of America 12 Church St. New Rochelle, NY 10801	General science supplies
Dale Seymour Publications P.O. Box 10888 Palo Alto, CA 94303	Calculators and spatial visualization materials
Delta Education Inc. P.O. Box 915 Hudson, NM 03051	Supplies and lab equipment—SCIS, ESS, SAPA
Edmund Scientific Co. 101 E. Gloucester Pike Barrington, NJ 08007	General science supplies
Educational Rocks & Minerals P.O. Box 574 Florence, MA 01060	Rocks and minerals for ESS, SCIS, ISCS, & ESCP
EME P.O. Box 2805 Danbury, CT 06813	Videodiscs and CD-ROM technologies

Encyclopedia Britannica
Educational Corp.
310 S. Michigan Ave., 6th Floor
Chicago, IL 60604

Videodiscs and CD-ROM
technologies

Estes Industries
1295 H St.
Penrose, CO 81240

Rocket model kits

Fisher Scientific
Educational Materials Division
4901 W. LeMoyne St.
Chicago, IL 60651

General science supplies

Flinn Scientific
131 Flinn St.
P.O. Box 219
Batavia, IL 60510

Chemistry supplies and laboratory
chemicals

Forestry Suppliers Inc.
205 West Rankin St.
P.O. Box 8397
Jackson, MS 39284

General science supplies

Frey Scientific Co.
905 Hickory Ln.
Mansfield, OH 44905

General science supplies

Genesis
P.O. Box 2242
Mt. Vernon, WA 98273

Owl pellet kits

HEMCO Corporation
111 North Powell
Independence, MO 64056

Hoods and laboratory furniture

Hubbard Scientific
3101 Iris Ave., Suite 215
Boulder, CO 80301

General science supplies

Ken-A-Vision Mfg. Co., Inc.
5615 Raytown Rd.
Raytown, MO 64133

Microprojectors and microscopes

Lab-Aids, Inc.
249 Trade Zone Dr.
Ronkonkoma, NY 11779

Science modules

Lab Safety Supply, Inc. 401 S. Wright Rd. P.O. Box 1368 Janesville, WI 53547	Safety equipment and supplies
LaMotte Company P.O. Box 329 Chestertown, MD 21620	Test kits for water and soil
Learning Spectrum 1390 Westridge Dr. Portola Valley, CA 94025	Science on a Shoestring kits
Learning Technologies, Inc. 59 Walden St. Cambridge, MA 02140	Starlab portable planetarium
LEGO DACTA 555 Taylor Rd. Box 1600 Enfield, CT 06083	Lego Technic I and II
Magnet Source The Master Magnets, Inc. 607 S. Gilbert Castle Rock, CO 80104	Magnets in kits
Meiji Techno America 500 W. Cummings Park, Suite 2350 Woburn, MA 01801	Microscopes
Merlan Scientific Ltd. 247 Armstrong Ave. Georgetown, Ontario Canada L7G 4X6	Computer interfaces
Midwest Products Co, Inc. School Division P.O. Box 564 Hobart, IN 46342	Kits for bridge building, airplanes, air balloons
Museum Products Company 84 Route 27 Mystic, CT 06355	Toys in Space, Repli Tracks
Nasco 901 Janesville Ave. Fort Atkinson, WI 53538	General science supplies

National Teaching Aids, Inc.
1845 Highland Ave.
New Hyde Park, NY 11040

Models, micro-slide viewers, micromounts

Nebraska Scientific, a Division
of Cyrgus Co., Inc.
3823 Leavenworth St.
Omaha, NE 68105

Biological specimens

The NightStar Company
1334 Brommer St.
Santa Cruz, CA 95062

Astronomy teaching tools

Norris Science Labs & Kits
P.O. Box 61281
Las Vegas, NV 89160

Science labs and kits

Northwest Laboratories Inc.
#20 - 225 Great Arrow Dr.
Buffalo, NY 14207

General science supplies

Nurnberg Scientific Co.
6310 S.W. Virginia Ave.
Portland, OR 97201

Microscopes and videomicroscopes

Ohaus Corporation
29 Hanover Rd.
Florham Park, NJ 07932

Balances

Optical Data Corp.
30 Technology Dr.
Warren, NJ 07059

Videodisc players and monitors

Parco Scientific Co.
316 Younstwon-Kingsville Rd.
P.O. Box 189
Vienna, OH 44473

Microscopes

PASCO Scientific
10101 Foothills Blvd.
P.O. Box 619011
Roseville, CA 95661

Physics demonstration equipment

Sargent-Welch Scientific Co.
P.O. Box 1026
Skokie, IL 60076

General science supplies

Schoolmasters Science
745 State Circle
P.O. Box 1941
Ann Arbor, MI 48106

General science supplies

Science Inquiry Enterprises 14358 Village View Ln. Chino Hills, CA 91709	Discrepant events
Science Kit and Boreal Laboratories 777 East Park Dr. Tonawanda, NY 14150	General science supplies
Skulls Unlimited P.O. Box 6741 Moore, OK 73153	Osteological specimens
Spectrum Educational Supplies Limited 125 Mary St. Aurora, Ontario Canada L4G 1G3	General science supplies
Swift Instruments, Inc. P.O. Box 562 San Jose, CA 95106	Microscopes, telescopes, and optical instruments
Ward's Natural Science Establishments Inc. 5100 West Henrietta Rd. P.O. Box 92192 Rochester, NY 14692	General science supplies
Young Naturalist Co. 614 East 5th St. Newton, KS 67114	Kits for elementary science

Computer Software

AccuLab Products Group 200 California Ave., Suite 217 Palo Alto, CA 94306	Macintosh products
Addison-Wesley Publishing Co. 2725 Sand Hill Road Menlo Park, CA 94025	Apple II, Macintosh, IBM
Apple Computer Inc. 20525 Mariani Ave. Cupertino, CA 95014	Apple
Arbor Scientific P.O. Box 2750 Ann Arbor, MI 48106	Apple II, IBM

Carolina Biological Supply Co. 2700 York Rd. Burlington, NC 27215	Apple, TRS-80, Macintosh, Commodore, IBM
Central Scientific Co. 11222 Melrose Ave. Franklin Park, IL 60131	Apple, Commodore, IBM
Children's Television Workshop Schools and Technology 1 Lincoln Plaza New York, NY 10023	Apple, Macintosh, Tandy, IBM, Commodore
CONDUIT The University of Iowa Oakdale Campus Iowa City, IA 52242	Apple, IBM
Connecticut Valley Biological Supply 82 Valley Rd., Box 326 Southampton, MA 01073	Apple, IBM
Cross Educational Software 504 E. Kentucky Ave. P.O. Box 1536 Ruston, LA 71270	Apple, IBM, Commodore, Macintosh, Tandy
Daedalon Corporation P.O. Box 2028 Salem, MA 01970	Apple, Macintosh, Atari
EME P.O. Box 2805 Danbury, CT 06813	Apple, Macintosh, IBM
Fisher Scientific 4901 W. LeMoyne St. Chicago, IL 60651	Apple, IBM
Holt, Rinehart and Winston 1627 Woodland Ave. Austin, TX 78741	Apple, IBM
Houghton Mifflin Co. One Beacon St. Boston, MA 01208	Apple II

IBM Educational Systems   IBM
P.O. Box 2150 - Ho6L1
Atlanta, GA 30301

Intellitool, Inc.   Apple, IBM
P.O. Box 459
Batabia, IL 60510

Knowledge Revolution   Macintosh
497 Vermont St.
San Francisco, CA 94107

LEGO DACTA   Apple, MS-DOS
555 Taylor Rd., Box 1600
Enfield, CT 06083

Macmillan School Publishers   Apple II
4635 Hilton Corporation Dr.
Columbus, OH 43232

Merlan Scientific Ltd.   Apple II, Commodore 64, PET, IBM
247 Armstrong Ave.
Georgetown, Ontario
L7G 4XG Canada

Milliken Publishing Co.   Apple II
1100 Research Blvd.
P.O. Box 21579
St. Louis, MO 63132

Modern Talking Picture Service   Macintosh, Tandy, IBM
5000 Park Street North
St. Petersburg, FL 33709

Nasco West, Inc.   Apple, TRS-80, Commodore, Atari,
P.O. Box 3837   IBM
Modesto, CA 95352

National Geographic Society   Apple, IBM, Macintosh
17th & M Sts. NW
Washington, DC 20036

Ohaus Scale Corporation   Apple
29 Hanover Rd.
Florham Park, NJ 07932

Powell Laboratories   Apple, IBM, TRS-80, Macintosh,
Box 187   Commodore 64
Gladstone, OR 97027

Prentice Hall School Group
113 Sylvan Ave.
Englewood Cliffs, NJ 07632

Apple, IBM, Macintosh

Sargent-Welch Scientific
P.O. Box 1026
Skokie, IL 60076

Apple, TRS-80, IBM

Scholastic Software
730 Broadway
New York, NY 10003

Apple, IBM, Macintosh

Science Kit and Boreal Labs
777 East Park Dr.
Tonawanda, NY 14150

Apple, Macintosh, IBM, Commodore

Scott, Foresman and Co.
1900 E. Lake Ave.
Glenview, IL 60025

Apple, IBM

Silver Burdett & Ginn
250 James St., CN 1918
Morristown, NJ 07960

Apple, IBM

Sunburst Communications
1600 Green Hills Rd.
P.O. Box 660002
Scotts Valley, CA 95067

Apple, Tandy, IBM

Tandy/Radio Shack
1600 One Tandy Center
Fort Worth, TX 76102

Tandy, MS-DOS

Texas Learning Technology Group
7703 N. Lamar
Austin, TX 78752

IBM, Sony

Vernier Software
2920 S.W. 89th St.
Portland, OR 97225

Apple, IBM, Macintosh, Tandy

Videodiscovery, Inc.
1515 Dexter Ave., N, Suite 400
Seattle, WA 98109

Apple, Macintosh, IBM

Wadsworth Publishing Co.
10 Davis Dr.
Belmont, CA 94002

Apple, IBM, Macintosh

Ward's Natural Science Est.
5100 W. Henrietta Rd.
P.O. Box 92912
Rochester, NY 14692

Apple, IBM, Macintosh

Media and Visual Materials and Products

Acid Rain Foundation
1410 Varsity Dr.
Raleigh, NC 27606

Transparencies, pictures

Addison Wesley Publishing
2725 Sand Hill Rd.
Menlo Park, CA 94025

Videodiscs, overheads, charts, maps

American Chemical Society
1155 16th Street, NW
Washington, DC 20036

Videotapes

American Association of
Physics Teachers
5112 Berwyn Rd.
College Park, MD 20740

Films, videodiscs, slides, cassettes

American Gas Association
1515 Wilson Blvd.
Arlington, VA 22209

Filmstrips

American Geophysical Union
2000 Florida Ave., NW
Washington, DC 20009

Overheads

American Institute of Physics
335 E. 45 St.
New York, NY 10017

American Nuclear Society
555 N. Kensington Ave.
LaGrange Park, IL 60525

Films, cassettes, slides, videotapes,
charts

American Water Works Assoc.
6666 W. Quincy
Denver, CO 80235

Films, videotapes, charts, pictures

Astronomical Society of the Pacific
390 Ashton Ave.
San Francisco, CA 94112

Videodiscs, cassettes, charts,
pictures, games

Captioned Films/Videos for the Deaf
Modern Talking Picture Service
5000 Park St. N.
St. Petersburg, FL 33709

Films, videotapes

Carolina Biological Supply
2700 York Rd.
Burlington, NC 27215

Films, cassettes, videodiscs, games, dittos

Central Scientific Co.
11222 Melrose Ave
Franklin Park, IL 60131

Films, cassettes, videodiscs, slides, dittos

Children's Television Workshop
One Lincoln Plaza
New York, NY 10023

Cassettes, games, dittos

Connecticut Valley Biological
82 Valley Road
Southampton, MA 01073

Filmstrips, slides, overheads, charts, tapes

Coronet/MTI Film & Video
108 Wilmont Rd.
Deerfield, IL 60015

Films, cassettes, videotapes

Cross Educational Software
P.O. Box 1536
Ruston, LA 71270

Software

Delta Education
P.O. Box 915
Hudson, NH 03051

Filmstrips, slides, overheads, charts

EME
P.O. Box 2805
Danbury, CT 06813

Filmstrips, videodiscs, slides, overheads

Encyclopedia Britannica Corp.
310 S. Michigan Ave., 6th Floor
Chicago, IL 60604

Films, videodiscs, cassettes

Entomological Society of America
9301 Annapolis Rd.
Lanham, MD 20706

Slides

Foundation for Biomedical Research
818 Connecticut Ave., NW Suite 303
Washington, DC 20006

Videotapes, charts

Jeppesen Sanderson 55 Inverness Dr, E. Englewood, CO 80112	Filmstrips, overheads, charts, dittos
MECC 6160 Summit Drive North Minneapolis, MN 55430	Filmstrips, software
MMI Corporation 2950 Wyman Pkwy. Baltimore, MD 21211	Films, videodiscs, slides, overheads
Modern Talking Picture Service 5000 Park St. N. St. Petersburg, FL 33709	Films, videos, overheads, software
Nasco 901 Janesville Ave. Fort Atkinson, WI 53538	General media supplies
National Association of Conservation Dist. 408 E. Main St. League City, TX 77574	Videotapes
National 4-H Council 7100 Connecticut Ave. Chevy Chase, MD 20815	Slides
National Geographic Society 17th & M Sts. NW Washington, DC 20036	Films, videos, charts, software
National Wildlife Federation 1400 Sixteenth St. NW Washington, DC 20036	Films, videodiscs, overheads, charts
PBS Video 1320 Braddock Place Alexandria, VA 22314	Videotapes
TOPS Learning Systems 10970 S. Mulino Rd. Canby, OR 97013	Media modules

![] Glossary

Accommodation   Something supplied for convenience or to satisfy a need, to take in new information, to accept new knowledge, to become aware of new learning

Accretion   First step in taking in new knowledge, according to Norman's theory of learning; to cause to adhere or to become attached

Activation stage   First step in SCALing, activation of prior knowledge or recall of prior knowledge

Actualization stage   Second step in SCALing, appending new knowledge of science concepts to existing mental structures, conceptualizing new knowledge

Adaptation level   Third and final level of psychomotor skills, adapting or modifying existing knowledge to new uses

Additive model   A way of accommodating diversity by appending the names of culturally diverse individuals and white females to exisiting information, normally in footnotes or endnotes

Advance organizer   Derived from work of Ausubel, an activity or word or symbol that prepares a student for new learning

Adversative pattern   Text organization pattern expressing antithesis, opposition, or adverse conditions

Affective domain   The part of human knowledge that deals with human feelings and emotions, values, attitudes, and beliefs

Analogies   Inferences formed if two or more things agree with one another in some respect; similarities; correspondence in function; correspondence between the members of pairs or sets of linguistic forms that serves as a basis for creation of another form

Analysis   Fourth level of Bloom's taxonomy, involves breaking knowledge into its component parts, questioning that examines complexity in terms of elements and functions

Androcentric   Man centered as opposed to woman centered; also having to do with one individual rather than a group of individuals

Application   Third level of Bloom's taxonomy, involves breaking knowledge into its component parts, questioning that examines complexity in terms of elements and functions

Application stage   Third stage of SCALing, to apply new learning or conceptualizations

Applied level   Practical application of new knowledge; to use a real world application of knowledge

Articulation   To utter distinctly, to be able to speak, to discuss, to present one's viewpoint

Assessment   The act or instance of assessing or measuring, appraisal; to make a determination of size or value or importance

Assimilation   To take in, to incorporate, as in to append new knowledge to existing knowledge structures

Attribution pattern   Text organization pattern, to list the characteristics or attributes of an object, concept, or event in a textual passage

Attribution theory   To assign characteristics to mental processes

Attrition rate   Drop-out rate; reduction in size

Authentic assessment tools   Portfolios, task tests, pictorial tests, journal writing activities, concept maps, word webs, semantic maps, when used to assess cognitive knowledge

Automaticity   To perform automatically, without conscious thought

Axiological   The study of nature, types, and criteria of values and of value judgments, especially in ethics

Behavioral psychology   Branch of psychology based on theories of stimulus and response learning, includes programmed instruction and training modules

Bidialectic   Use of two dialects of the same language, e.g., Appalachian English and standard English

Bilingual/bicultural   Possessing two or more languages and/or cultures

Camaraderie skills   Social skills involved with group dynamics

Career awareness   Awareness of adult work experiences, opportunities for employment

Cataphora   Linking of textual passages that involves linking to a future or predicted referent

Characteristics of science   Amoral, creative, developmental, parsimonious, testable, and unified

Chunking   Treating increments of knowledge as a single unit

Classifying   Science process of arranging in groups by some common attribute, assigning to a category

Cluster skills   Social skills involved in group work

Coach   A function of the teacher in the classroom that involves training intensively by instruction, demonstration, and practice

Cognitive disequilibrium   State of temporary mental confusion that results when new knowledge does not fit with existing mental structures

Cognitive dissonance   State of temporary mental confusion about information; psychological conflict

Cognitive domain   Knowledge that deals with elements of perception; process of knowing including both awareness and judgement

Cognitive psychology   Branch of psychology that deals with learning, based on medical models of brain function and human perception of environmental stimuli

Cohesion   The mutual attraction by which the elements of a body are held together or joined

Communicating   Science process that involves disseminating information to others via written and spoken words and through the use of language

Comprehension   Second level of Bloom's taxonomy, involves understanding

Computer assisted instruction   Electronic means of communicating information, typically drill-and-practice software or tutorials

Concept application phase   Learning to classify stimuli according to an appropriate principle; applying newly gained conceptual knowledge to a new situation

Concept invention phase   Part of learning cycle in which students construct a mental representation for a concept

Concept map   Visual organizer that shows declarative knowledge a student holds and how it is organized

Conceptual density   The number of concepts introduced during a textual passage

Concrete concept   Second level of Gagné's taxonomy of cognitive knowledge

Confirmatory feedback   A knowledge of results in which the child is apprised of the "correctness" of the answer

Confluent education   Educational philosophy that incorporates social action into educational foundations

Congruency   The quality or state of agreeing or corresponding

Connectionism   The theory that all mental processes can be described as the operation of inherited or acquired bonds between stimulus and response

Consistency   Agreement or logical coherence among things or parts; compatibility or agreement among successive acts, ideas, or events; the condition of holding together; firmness; the degree of firmness or agreement

Constructivism   A child-centered view of learning that holds that each child constructs a knowledge of science by themselves

Controlling variables   Science process of controlling the conditions that cause an event to occur

Convergent questions   Questions having a single correct answer

Cooperative learning   Arrangement in which students work in mixed-ability groups and are rewarded on the basis of the success of the group

Corrective feedback   A knowledge of results in which the child is apprised of the "correctness" of the answer and, in the case of incorrect responses, the correct response

Criterion-referenced tests   Testing in which scores are compared to a set performance standard

Cultural deficit models   Explanations for the lack of culturally diverse individuals in careers which presume that children lack academic skills

Cultural pluralism   The acceptance of multiple cultures as equally valid

Culturally diverse students   A reference to "minority" students

Culturally familiar elaborations   Examples of phenomena that are familiar in one culture but that may not be common to all cultures

Culturally transforming   Social reconstructionist view of history that includes culturally diverse individuals, group discoveries, and oral traditions

Curandera   A midwife and herbal healer in the Hispanic community, practitioner of traditional herbal medicine

Declarative knowledge   Knowledge that can be stated

Defined concept   Third level of Gagné's taxonomy of cognitive knowledge

Demonstrations   The act of making evident or proving; an illustration or explanation as of a theory or product by exemplification or practical application

Dependent variable   Responding variable; variable measured to determine changes as a result of changes in the independent variable

Discrepant event   Unexpected natural phenomenon that causes cognitive dissonance in the observer

Discrimination   First level of Gagné's taxonomy of cognitive knowledge

Divergent questions   Questions having no single correct answer

Domains of learning   Fields of action or thought

Educational technology   Instructional systems design approach to curriculum development

Elaborations   Adding and extending meaning by connecting new information to existing knowledge

Epistemology   The division of philosophy that investigates the nature and origin of knowledge

Eurocentric   A European-centered viewpoint; European-centered as opposed to Eastern or Native American practices

Evaluation   Sixth level of Bloom's taxonomy, involves judging the quality of answers

Evaluator   One who makes decisions about student performance and about appropriate teaching strategies

Events of instruction   Gagné's theory of learning that relates phase of instruction to stages of information processing

Expeditor   One who speeds up the progress of, helps along, assists, facilitates

Experimenting Science process that involves identifying and controlling variables

Explanatory feedback A knowledge of results in which the child is apprised of the accuracy of his or her answer, the "correct" answer, and the reasons for that response

Explication Critical exposition and interpretation, as of literary texts; method of literary criticism in which a detailed reading and analysis of a given text in each of its linguistic, compositional, and expressive parts is undertaken

Exploration phase Beginning phase of learning cycle, in which students manipulate materials and ideas; the act of exploring

Expository teaching Teacher-as-lecturer model of teaching

Extraneous variable Introduced or coming from without; not belonging or proper to a thing; external

Extrinsic External; coming from without

Familia groups Extended family group, could include members of the immediate family, neighbors, cousins, and so forth

Feeling tone Motivation factor dependent upon the physical atmosphere of the classroom

Formal debate A formal contest in which the affirmative and negative sides of a proposition are advocated by opposing speakers

Formative evaluation Ungraded testing used before or during instruction to aid in planning and diagnosis

Formulating hypothesis Science process of making a scientific guess

Fotonovela A highly visualized textual material, similiar to a comic book but dealing with an academic topic; also called a *photonovel*

Generative cognitive strategies Embedded learning strategies that enhance learning; using rules to generate surface forms from underlying abstract forms; preverbal, intuitive rules

Geocentric perspective Earth-centered outlook; describes curriculum used in many Native American science programs

Graphing packages Computerized software that generates a graphic representation of knowledge

Gustatory Of or pertaining to the sense of taste

Hierarchy of needs Maslow's model of levels of human needs from physiological requirements to self actualization

Holistic learning Total learning, combining all curriculum areas, used commonly in Native American schools

Home culture A child's belief system, based on country of origin, cultural background, or ethnic group

Home language Language of the child's home or culture

Home learning   Values, attitudes, and beliefs derived from a child's home or home culture

Humanistic pyschology   Branch of psychological thought that stresses the uniqueness of the human condition

Hydroponic   Cultivation of plants in water containing dissolved inorganic nutrients rather than soil

Icon   A picture or symbol used to present a concept or idea

Identifying variables   Science process of identifying causal conditions or effects of the condition

Independent variable   Variable that is changed or manipulated

Inferring   Science process of drawing an inference from data

Instructional map   Embedded graphic device that reports student's location in a software package

Instructional systems design   Systematic design of curriculum based on principles of learning from authors such as Gagné

Instrument interfacing   Connecting devices to computers to record data in real time

Intellectual exceptionality   Reference to special needs children; need may range from handicapping condition to intellectually gifted and talented

Intellectual skills   Skills involved with learning, verbal ability

Interest   Motivational factor that is based on a child's internal curiosity

Internalizing   To incorporate as through learning, socialization, or identification

Intrinsic   Internally motivated

Investigating   Science process that involves finding out about the physical world

Journal writing activity   Assessment device that shows students' knowledge base and awareness of learning

Kinesthetic   Sensation of movement or strain in muscles, tendons, and joints; muscle sense

Kinetic energy   Energy due to motion

Knowledge   First level of Bloom's taxonomy

Knowledge of results   Feedback, or knowledge of correctness of an answer

Learning   Process through which experience causes permanent change in knowledge or behavior

Learning disability   An umbrella concept used to refer to children and adolescents who encounter difficulty with school-related material despite apparently normal intelligence

Lecturer   A member of the faculty of a college or university, usually without rank or tenure

Level of concern Motivation factor in learning dependent upon a student's level of anxiety

Likert instrument A variation of the graphic rating scale; used for attitude evaluation; numerically scored on a 5- to 7-point scale

Long-term memory Permanent store of knowledge

Manipulative materials Realia or real world objects used in concept formation

Mathemagenic models Computer software that is linear in nature and is an electronic drill-and-practice application

Measuring Science process of assigning standard units of mass, volume, temperature, length, etc., to given quantities

Mediated conversations Meanings derived from social discourse

Mediator One who mediates, especially a person who serves as an intermediary to reconcile differences

Metacognition Knowledge about our own thinking processes

Metaphysical Based on speculative or abstract reasoning

Modes of learning Ways of deriving information, such as written words, spoken words, realia, icons, or other visual representations

Motivation Internal state that arouses, directs, and maintains behavior

Multicultural models Curriculum models and materials that assume culture to be of equal value

Multimedia Including or involving the use of several media of communication, entertainment, or expression

Navigator One who explores; a crew member who plots the course of a ship or aircraft or, in a classroom, the course of learning

Need Something required or wanted; a requisite

Negotiate meaning Deriving a meaning for words or concepts through social interactions

Negotiated doing Deriving meaning from interacting in a social group; usually includes the use of manipulative materials

Negotiated meaning Meaning derived from social discourse

Networking A supportive system of sharing information and services among individuals and groups having a common interest

Neurobiology The branch of biology that is concerned with the anatomy and physiology of the nervous system

Neuropsychology The study of the functioning of the human mind

Norm-referenced tests Tests in which scores are compared with the average performance of others

Objectivism Any one of several doctrines holding that all reality is objective and external to the mind and that knowledge is reliably based on observed objects and events

Observing   Science process of using the senses to gain information about the natural world

Olfactory   Of or contributing to the sense of smell

Operant conditioning   Learning in which voluntary behavior is strengthened or weakened by consequences or antecedents; learning in which a response continues to be made because it is reinforced

Operational definition   A working definition specifying a variable by expressing the activities or operations required to measure it

Operational question   A question that may be answered by manipulating materials or conducting an investigation

Operationally defining   Science process of formulating a working definition, or a definition based on usage.

Organizational strategies   Strategies for organizing information

Organizing   To pull or put together into an orderly, functional, structured whole

Peer tutoring   Individual or small group tutoring by students of the same approximate age level

Perception level   First level of psychomotor skills

Physical exceptionality   Handicapping condition involving the use of sight, limbs, etc.

Physiological needs   Food, clothing, and shelter; basic survival needs

Pictorial tests   Testing that uses pictures or icons in questioning

Pipeline theory   An explanation for the lack of minority children and females in science careers

Portfolio   Container of documents that shows proficiency or mastery of subject material

Potential energy   Stored energy, energy due to position

Predicting   Science process that involves foretelling occurrences

Procedural knowledge   Knowledge that can be done

Psychometric   The measurement of psychological variables, such as intelligence, aptitude, and emotional disturbance

Psychomotor domain   Physical ability objectives

Realia   Objects such as coins, tools, etc., used by a teacher to illustrate everyday living

Realism   Inclination toward literal truth and pragmatism

Receiving   Perceiving information

Rehearsal strategies   Repeating words, terms, or phrases over and over until they are encoded into long-term memory

Research team approach   Cooperative learning strategy in which a group of students researches part of a topic

Response   Observable reaction to a stimulus

Retrieval   Process of searching for and finding information in long-term memory

Review sessions   Practicing declarative knowledge, usually in preparation for a test or other measure of long-term memory

Role models   Adults whom children voluntarily emulate

Rule using   Fourth level of Gagné's taxonomy of cognitive knowledge

Scaffolding   Layers of meaning conveyed through photos or drawings, low-level reading material, and higher level reading material

SCALE   Science Concept and Language Experience

Schema   Mental structure, basic structure for organizing information

Schooling   Instruction or training given at school, especially a program of formal education

Science anxiety   Apprehension about the study of science

Scientific method   A systematic way of investigating the physical world

Selective perception   The focusing of attention on certain aspects of experience while ignoring irrelevant or distracting sensations

Self-directed learning   Independent or individual self-initiated learning

Self-referenced tests   Tests that make reference to oneself or one's own experience

Semantic differential scale   A technique for measuring the connotative meaning of concepts by having an individual rate each concept on a series of graduated scales, each scale defined by a pair of polar adjectives such as good-bad or strong-weak

Semantic network   The study of meanings

Sensory stimuli   Stimuli received by skin, eyes, ears, nose, or tongue

Set level   Second level of psychomotor skills

Short-term memory   Working memory, holding a limited amount of information briefly

Simulations   The representation of the behavior or characteristics of one system through the use of another system

Smoothness   In Norman's theory of learning, the stage that describes expert performance

Social interactions   Working, talking together in groups

Social learning theory   Theory that learning social traits occurs through imitation of and identification with other people

Social-emotional exceptionality   Handicapping condition that interferes with one's ability to engage in social interactions

Sociocultural context   Of or pertaining to the combination or interaction of social and cultural elements

Socratic method   The use of questions to develop a latent idea

Stage-setting behaviors   Social behaviors that precede academic work, such as pencil sharpening, calling to friends, etc.; noted by Wilma Longstreet among African-American students

Stage theory   The particular set of schemata that are in a relative state of equilibrium; a phase of intellectual development

Status   Motivation factor in learning dependent upon a child's social status due to country of origin, socioeconomic status, and so forth

Status characteristics   The position of an individual in relation to another

Stimulus   Event that activates behavior

Structural knowledge   Sometimes referred to as problem-solving, higher order thinking skills; incorporates declarative and procedural knowledge

Structuring   To construct, give form or arrangement

Success   The achievement of something desired, planned, or attempted

Summative evaluation   Testing that follows instruction and assesses achievement

Superordinate figure   A significant other or role model in a child's life

Synthesis   Fifth level of Bloom's taxonomy

Tactile   Perceptible to the sense of touch

Talk story   Phenomenon of group construction of a story observed by Kevin Au among Hawaiian American children

Target students   Students with whom the teacher interacts more than others

Task skills   Social skills that involve task performance in a group setting

Task tests   Piagetian-based assessments of students' science process knowledge

Teaching   The work or occupation of teachers; a precept or doctrine

Tuning   Final step in Norman's schemata formation process

Unassimilated   Unintegrated culturally or linguistically into mainstream culture

Unobtrusive measure   Assessment without the conscious knowledge of the observed

Using numbers   Science process that involves manipulation and use of numbers

Using space/time relationships   Science process that involves use of time, distance, etc., relationships

Valuing   Determining or estimating the worth or value of; appraising

Visual   Serving, resulting from, or pertaining to the sense of sight

Wait time   Time allowed for student to process a teacher's question or response

Bibliography

Abraham, M.R., & Renner, J.W. (1986). The sequence of learning cycle activities in high school chemistry. *Journal of Research in Science Teaching, 23*(2), 121–143.

Abruscato, J. (1988). *Teaching Children Science.* Englewood Cliffs, NJ: Prentice Hall.

Adams, D.W. (1990). Fundamental considerations: The deep meaning of Native American schooling, 1880–1900. *Harvard Educational Review, 58*(1), 1–28.

Addison-Wesley. (1993). *Multiculturalism in Mathematics, Science, and Technology.* Menlo Park, CA: author.

Al-Daffa, A.A., & Stroyls, J.J. (1984). *Studies in the Exact Sciences in Medieval Islam.* Dhahran, Saudi Arabia: University of Petroleum and Minerals.

Alic, M. (1986). *Hypatia's Heritage: A History of Women in Science from Antiquity to the Nineteenth Century.* London: Women's Press.

Alifrangis, C. (1990, March). *An Integrated Learning System in an Elementary School: Implementation, Attitudes, and Results.* Paper presented at the International Conference on Technology and Education.

Allen, J.A. (1987). The gunpowder river project: Experiential education in a large public school system. *Journal of Experiential Education, 19*(3), 11–15.

Allen, P.G. (1989). *Spider Woman's Granddaughters: Traditional Tales and Contemporary Writing by Native American Women.* Boston: Beacon.

Allen, W.H. (1960). Audio-visual communication. In C.W. Harris (Ed.), *Encyclopedia of educational research (pp. 115–137).* New York: Macmillan.

Allen, W.H. (1975). Intellectual abilities and instructional media design. *AV Communication Review, 23*(2), 139–167.

American Association for the Advancement of Science. (1990). *The Liberal Art of Science: Agenda for Action.* Washington, DC: author.

American Association of University Women. (1992). *The AAUW Report: How Schools Shortchange Girls.* Washington, DC: American Association of University Women Educational Foundation.

American Chemical Society. (1988). *ChemCon: Chemistry in the Community.* Dubuque, IA: Kendall/Hunt.

American Psychological Association Task Force on Psychology in Education (Aug., 1992). *Learner-Centered Psychological Principles: Guidelines for School Redesign and Reform.* Washington, DC: American Psychological Association.

Anders, P.L., & Lloyd, C.V. (1989). The significance of prior knowledge in the learning of new content-specific instruction. In D. Lapp, J. Flood, & N. Farnan (Eds.), *Content Area Reading and Learning: Instructional Strategies* (pp. 258–271). Englewood Cliffs, NJ: Prentice Hall.

Anderson, C. (1962). *Technology in American Education: 1650–1900* (Report No. OE- 34018). Washington, DC: Office of Education, U.S. Department of Health, Education, and Welfare.

Anderson, K. (1989). Urban coalition encourages minority youth to "Say YES" to math and science. *Black Issues in Higher Education, 5*(2), 6–8.

Anderson, O.R. (1992). Some interrelationships between constructivist models of learning and current neurobiological theory, with implications for science education. *Journal of Research in Science Teaching, 29*(10), 1037–1058.

Anderson, T.H., & Armbruster, B.B. (1986). *The value of taking notes during lectures. Technical Report No. 374.* Cambridge, MA: Bolt, Beranek & Newman, Illinois University, Urbana. Center for the Study of Reading.

Arch, E.C. (1995, April). *The Baldwin Effect: A Basis for Sex Differences in Attitudes toward Technology and Science.* Paper presented at the Annual Meeting of the American Educational Research Association, San Francisco, CA.

Archibald, R.C. (1949). *Outline of the History of Mathematics.* New York: Mathematics Association of America.

Arnold, L.B. (1984). *Four Lives in Science: Women's Education in the Nineteenth Century.* New York: Schocken.

Asimov, I. (1964). *Asimov's Biographical Encyclopedia of Science and Technology: The Living Stories of More than 1000 Great Scientists from the Age of Greece to the Space Age Chronologically Arranged.* Garden City, NY: Doubleday.

Assetto, A.R., & Dowden, E. (1988). Getting a grip on interfacing. *Science Teacher, 55*(6): 65–67.

Atkinson, J.W. (1964). *An Introduction to Motivation.* Princeton, NJ: Van Nostrand.

Atwater, M.M. (1993). Multicultural science education: Assumptions and alternative views. *Science Teacher, 60*(3), 32–37.

Atwood, V.A., & Wilen, W.W. (1991). Wait time and effective social studies instruction: What can research in science education tell us? *Social Education, 55*(3), 179–181.

Au, K.H. (1980). Participation structures in a reading lesson with Hawaiian children: Analysis of a culturally appropriate instructional event. *Anthropology and Education Quarterly, 11*(2), 91–115.

Au, K.H., & Jordan, C. (1977). *A Multidisciplinary Approach to Research in Education: The Kamehameha Early Education Program.* Paper presented to the American Anthropological Association, Houston, TX.

Ausubel, D.P. (1963). *The Psychology of Meaningful Verbal Learning.* New York: Grune & Stratton.

Ausubel, D.P., Novak, J.D., & Hanesian, H. (1978). *Educational Psychology: A Cognitive View,* New York: Werbel and Peck.

Banchoff, T. F. (1990). Dimension. In L.A. Steen (Ed.), *On the Shoulders of Giants* (pp. 11–59). Washington, DC: National Academy.

Bandura, A. (1962). Social learning through imitation. In N.R. Jones (Ed.), *Nebraska Symposium on Motivation.* Lincoln: University of Nebraska Press.

Bandura, A. (1977). *Social Learning Theory.* Englewood Cliffs, NJ: Prentice Hall.

Barba, R.H. (1987). In pursuit of the yeast beast. *Science Teacher, 54*(7): 30–32.

Barba, R., & Cardinale, L. (1991). Are females invisible students: An investigation of teacher-student questioning interactions. *School Science and Mathematics, 91*(7), 306–310.

Barba, R.H. & Rubba, P.A. (1992). A comparison of preservice and in-service earth and space science teachers' general mental abilities, content knowledge, and problem-solving skills. *Journal of Research in Science Teaching, 29*(10), 1037–1058.

Barman, C.R. (1989). The learning cycle: Making it work. *Science Scope, 12*(5), 28–31.

Barnes, L.W., & Barnes, M.B. (1991). Assessment, practically speaking. *Science and Children, 28*(6), 14–15.

Beane, D.A.B. (1990). "Say YES to a youngster's future": A model for home, school, and community partnership. *Journal of Negro Education, 59*(3), 360–374.

Bennett, W.J. (1986). *First Lessons: A Report on Elementary Education in America.* Washington, DC: U.S. Government Printing Office.

Benson, F.C. (1986). *From Straw into Gold.* Santa Rosa, CA: Occasional Publications of the Jesse Peter Memorial Museum.

Bergeron, B. (1995). Temporal issues in the design of virtual learning environments. *Journal of Educational Multimedia and Hypermedia, 4*(2–3), 127–145.

Berlin, D.F. (1990). SMILES. *School Science and Mathematics, 90*(3), 254–257.

Berryman, S. (1983). *Who Will Do Science?* New York: Rockefeller Foundation.

Biehler, R.F., & Snowman, J. (1986). *Psychology Applied to Teaching* (5th ed.). Boston: Houghton Mifflin.

Bierer, L.K., Lien, V.F., & Silberstein, E.P. (1987). *Heath Life Science*. Lexington, MA: D.C. Heath.

Blakely, R.J. (1979). *To Serve the Public Interest: Educational Broadcasting in the United States*. Syracuse: Syracuse University Press.

Blaschke, C.L., & Sweeney, J. (1977). Implementing effective educational technology: Some reflections. *Educational Technology, 17*(1), 13–18.

Bloom, B.S. (1956). *Taxonomy of Educational Objectives. Handbook I. Cognitive Domain*. New York: David McKay.

Bloom, B.S. (1971). Affective consequences of school achievement. In J.H. Block (Ed.), *Mastery Learning: Theory and Practice*. New York: Holt, Rinehart, and Winston.

Bomeli, C.L. (1991). Mathematics and meteorology: Perfect partners. *School Science and Mathematics, 91*(1), 31–33.

Bowman, J. (1996). Technology approaches to teaching ESL students. *Media & Methods, 32*(3), 26–27.

Bracey, G.W. (1982). What the research shows. *Electronic Learning*. Nov/Dec: 51–54.

Bracey, G.W. (1984). *Issues and Problems in Devising a Research Agenda for Special Education and Technology*. Paper presented at Special Education Technology Research and Development Symposium. Washington, DC: Department of Education.

Breslich, E.R. (1936). Integration of secondary school mathematics and science. *School Science and Mathematics, 36*(1), 58–67.

Brinckerhoff, R.E. (1986). *Values in School Science: Some Practical Materials and Suggestions*. Exeter, NH: Phillips Exeter Academy.

Broker, I. (1983). *Night Flying Woman: An Ojibwa Narrative*. St. Paul: Minnesota Historical Society Press.

Brown, A.L., & Palincsar, A.S. (1989). Guided cooperative learning and individual knowledge acquisition. In L.B. Resnick (Ed.), *Knowing, Learning, and Instruction: Essays in Honor of Robert Glaser* (pp. 393–451). Hillsdale, NJ: Erlbaum.

Brown, R., Fournier, J.F., & Moyer, R.H. (1977). A cross-cultural study of Piagetian concrete reasoning and science concepts among rural fifth grade Mexican and Anglo-American students. *Journal of Research in Science Teaching, 14*, 329–334.

Brunig, I.L. (1983). An information processing approach to a theory of instruction. *Educational Communications and Technology Journal, 31*; 91–101.

Burbridge, L.C. (1991). *The Interaction of Race, Gender, and Socioeconomic Status in Education Outcomes*. Wellesley, MA: Center for Research on Women.

Burns, P.C., Roe, B.D., & Ross, E.P. (1984). *Teaching Reading in Today's Elementary Schools*. Boston: Houghton Mifflin.

Burns, R.A. (1985, May). *Information Impact and Factors Affecting Recall*. Paper presented at the Annual National Conference on Teaching Excellence and Conference of Administrators, Austin, TX.

Cajori, F. (1980). *A History of Mathematics*. New York: Chelsea House.

California State Board of Education. (1990). *Science Framework for California Public Schools Kindergarten Through Grade Twelve*. Sacramento, CA: California Department of Education.

Campbell, M. (1982). *Halfbreed*. Lincoln: University of Nebraska Press.

Carin, A.A. (1993). *Teaching Science through Discovery*. New York: Macmillan.

Carnegie Commission of Educational Television. (1967). *Public Television: A Program for Action*. New York: Harper & Row.

Carrier, C.A. (1983). Notetaking research: Implications for the classroom. *Journal of Instructional Development, 6*(3), 19–26.

Carter, D.J., & Wilson, R. (1991). *Tenth Annual Status Report: Minorities in Higher Education.* Washington, DC: American Council on Education, Office of Minorities in Higher Education.

Chambliss, M.J., & Calfee, R.C. (1989). Designing science textbooks to enhance student understanding. *Educational psychologist, 24,* 307–322.

Cheng, L.R.L. (1992, May). *Language Difference vs. Language Disorders: An ESL/EFL Perspective.* Paper presented at the jointly sponsored ESL Symposium (San Diego State University & National Kaohsiung Normal University, R.O.C.), San Diego, CA.

Chittenden, E.A. (1970). Piaget and elementary science, *Science and Children, 8*(4), 9–15.

Chu, G.C., & Schramm, W. (1967). *Learning from Television: What the Research Says.* Washington, DC: National Association of Educational Broadcasters.

Cicourel, A.V. (1974). *Cognitive Sociology.* New York: Free Press.

Clark, M. (1986). Predictors of scientific majors for black and white college students. *Adolescence, 21,* 205–213.

Clarkson, P. C. (1991). *Bilingualism and Mathematics Learning.* Geelong, Victoria, Australia: Deakin University Press.

Clawson, T., Firment, C., & Trower, T. (1981). Test anxiety: Another origin for racial bias in standardized testing. *Measurement and Evaluation in Guidance, 13,* 210–215.

Cobern, W.W. (1991, April). *Contextual Constructivism: The Impact of Culture on the Learning and Teaching of Science.* Paper presented at the Annual Meeting of the National Association for Research in Science Teaching, Lake Geneva, WI.

Cohen, E.G. (1991). *Designing Groupwork: Strategies for the Heterogeneous Classroom.* New York: Teachers College Press.

Cohen, E.G., DeAvila, E.A., Navarette, C., & Lotan, R. (1988). *Finding Out/Descubrimiento Implementation Module.* Stanford, CA: Program for Complex Instruction.

Cohen, E.G., Intili, J.K., & Robbins, S.H. (1979). Task and authority: A sociological view of classroom management. Paper published in *Seventy-eighth Yearbook of the National Society for the Study of Education.* Chicago: The Society.

Cohen, E.G., Knight, L.R., & Kagan, M. (1977). *Interdependence and Management in Bilingual Classrooms.* Final Report. Palo Alto, CA: Stanford University Center for Educational Research at Stanford.

Cohen, E.G., & Lotan, R.A. (1990, July). *Beyond the Workshop: Conditions for First Year Implementation.* Paper presented at International Association for the Study of Cooperation in Education, Baltimore, MD.

Cohen, E.G., & Lotan, R.A. (1991). *Producing Equal-Status Interaction in the Heterogeneous Classroom.* Stanford, CA: Program for Complex Instruction.

Cohen, E.G., Lotan, R.A., & Catanzarite, L. (1990). Treating status problems in the cooperative classroom. In S. Sharan (Ed.), *Cooperative Learning: Theory and Research* (pp. 203–229). New York: Praeger.

Cohen, E.G., Lotan, R.A., & Leechor, C. (1989). Can classrooms learn? *Sociology of Education, 62*(4), 75–94.

Cohen, M. (1984). Exemplary computer use in education. *Sigcue Bulletin, Computer Uses in Education, 18*(1), 16–19.

Cohen, P.A. (1981, April). *Educational Outcomes of Tutoring: A Research Synthesis.* Paper presented at the Annual Meeting of the American Educational Research Association, Los Angeles, CA.

Cohen, V.B. (1983). *A Learner-Based Evaluation of Microcomputer Software.* Paper presented at the annual meeting of the American Educational Research Association, Montreal, Canada.

Cole, M., & Griffin, P. (1987). *Improving Science and Mathematics Education for Minorities and Women: Contextual Factors in Education*. Madison, WI: Wisconsin Center for Education Research.

Collette, A.T., & Chiappetta, E.L. (1989). *Science Instruction in the Middle and Secondary Schools*. Columbus, OH: Merrill.

Collins, A. (1992). Portfolios: Questions for Design. *Science Scope, 15*(6), 25–27.

Combs, A.W., & Avila, D.L. (1985). *Helping Relationships* (3rd. ed.). Boston: Allyn & Bacon.

Comes-Diaz, L. (1984). Content themes in group treatment with Puerto Rican women. *Social Work with Groups, 7*(3), 75–84.

Comfort, K.B. (1992). Missouri's process skills approach. *Science Scope, 15*(6), 56–57.

Connery, M.A. (1990, April). *An Interpretive Study of Target Students and Classroom Interactions*. Paper presented at the Annual Meeting of the National Association for Research in Science Teaching, Atlanta, GA.

Contreras, A., & Lee, O. (1990). Differential treatment of students by middle school science teachers: Unintended cultural bias. *Science Education, 74*(3), 433–444.

Conway, J.K. (1968). Information presentation, information processing, and the sign vehicle. *AV Communication Review, 16*(4), 403–414.

Cortes, C.E. (1986). The education of language minority students: A contextual interaction model. In C.F. Leyba (Ed.), *Beyond Language: Social and Cultural Factors in Schooling Language Minority Children* (pp. 3–33). Los Angeles: Evaluation, Dissemination, and Assessment Center, California State University.

Costantino, G., Malgady, R.G., & Rogler, L.H. (1988). Folk hero modeling therapy for Puerto Rican adolescents. *Journal of Adolescence, 11*(2), 155–165.

Covington, M.V. (1984). The self-worth theory of achievement motivation: Findings and implications. *Elementary School Journal, 85*, 5–20.

Crandall, V.C. (1969). Sex differences in expectancy of intellectual and academic reinforcement. In C.P. Smith (Ed.), *Achievement Related Motives in Children*. New York: Russell Sage Foundation.

Cronnel, B. (1981). *Dialect and Writing: A Review*. Los Alamitos, CA: Southwest Regional Laboratory for Educational Research and Development.

Crow Dog, M. (1990). *Lakota Woman*. New York: Harpers.

Culp, L., & Malone, V. (1992). Peer scores for group work. *Science Scope, 15*(6), 35–36.

Cummins, J. (1979). Linguistic interdependence and the educational development of bilingual children. *Bilingual Education Paper Series. No. 2*. Los Angeles: National Dissemination and Assessment Center.

Cunningham, J.W., Cunningham, P.M., & Arthur, S.V. (1981). *Middle & Secondary School Reading*. New York: Longman.

Czerniak, C., & Chiarelott, L. (1985). Science anxiety among elementary school students: Equity issues. *Journal of Educational Equity and Leadership, 5*, 291–308.

Daintith, J., Mitchell, S., & Tootill, E. (1981). *A Biographical Encyclopedia of Scientists*. New York: Facts on File.

Dale, E. (1946). *Audio-visual Methods in Teaching*. New York: Dryden.

Dansereau, D.F., Collins, K.W., McDonald, B.A., Holley, C.D., Garland, J., Diekhoff, G., & Evans, S.H. (1979). Development and evaluation of a learning strategy training program. *Journal of Educational Psychology, 71*; 64–73.

Dantonio, M., & Beisenherz, P.C. (1991). Don't just demonstrate—Motivate! *Science Teacher, 57*(2), 27–28.

Day, W.F., & Beach, B.R. (1950). *A Survey of the Research Literature Comparing the Visual and Auditory Presentation of Information*. Air Force Technical Report 5921, Contract No. W-33–039–AC-21269. Charlottesville: University of Virginia.

DeAvila, E.A., Duncan, S.E., & Navarrete, C. (1987). *Finding Out/Descubrimiento*. Northvale, NJ: Santillana.

Debus, A.G. (1968). *World Who's Who in Science: A Biographical Dictionary of Notable Scientists from Antiquity to the Present.* Chicago: Marquis.

Definition and Terminology Committee of the Association for Educational Communications and Technology. (1972). The field of educational technology: A statement of definition. *Audiovisual Instruction, 17*(8), 36–43.

DelGiorno, B.J. (1969). *The Research Team Approach (ReTAL): A Structure for Openness.* Fairfield, CT: Fairfield Public Schools.

Deloria, E.C. (1988). *Waterlily.* Lincoln: University of Nebraska Press.

Dembo, M.H. (1988). *Applying Educational Psychology in the Classroom* (3rd ed.). New York: Longman.

Dence, M. (1980). Toward defining the role of CAI: A review. *Educational Technology, 20(*11): 50–54.

Denenberg, S.A. (1988). Semantic network designs for courseware. In D.H. Jonassen (Ed.), *Instructional Designs for Microcomputer Courseware.* Hillsdale, NJ: Lawrence Erlbaum.

DePaolo, T. (1978). *The Popcorn Book.* New York: Holiday House.

Dick, W., & Carey, L. (1985). *The Systematic Design of Instruction.* Glenview, IL: Scott, Foresman.

Dinkheller, A., Gaffney, J., & Vockell, E. (1989). *The Computer in the Mathematics Curriculum.* Santa Cruz, CA: Mitchell.

Docking, R.A. (1978). *Anxiety, Achievement, and Cognitive Incongruence.* Unpublished manuscript, Murdoch University, Murdoch, Western Australia.

Doran, R.L., & Hejaily, N. (1992). Hands-on evaluation: A how-to guide. *Science Scope,15*(6), 9–11.

Dowd, F. (1990). Geography is children's literature, math, science, art and a whole world of activities. *Journal of Geography, 89*(2), 68–73.

Doyle, J. J. (1980). The order of attainment of eight projective groupings: An analysis of Piaget's spatial model. *Journal of Research in Science Teaching, 17*(1), 55–58.

Driver, R., (1989). The construction of scientific knowledge in school classrooms. In R. Millar (Ed.), *Doing Science: Images of Science in Science Education* (pp. 83–106). New York: Falmer.

Driver, R., & Bell, B. (1986). Students' thinking and the learning of science: A constructivist view. *School Science Review, 67*, 443–456.

Driver, R., Guesne, E., & Tiberghien, A. (1985). Children's ideas and the learning of science. In R. Driver, E. Guesne, & A. Tiberghien (Eds.), *Children's Ideas in Science.* (pp. 1–9). Philadelphia: Milton Keynes.

Driver, R. & Oldham, V. (1986). A constructivist approach to curriculum development in science. *Studies in Science Education, 13*, 105–122.

Dubitsky, B. (1986, October). *Implications for Teacher Education of Assuming That Schools of the Future will Have Unlimited Access to Technology.* Seminar paper presented at a Hearing of the National Commission on Excellence in Teacher Education, New York, NY.

Duckworth, E. (1987). *"The Having of Wonderful Ideas" and Other Essays on Teaching and Learning.* New York: Teachers College Press.

Dufresne, R.J., Gerace, W.J., Hardiman, P.T., & Mestre, J.P. (1992). Constraining novices to perform expertlike problem analyses: Effects on schema acquisition. *Journal of the Learning Sciences, 2*(3), 307–331.

Dunn, R. (1995). Comparing three innovative instructional systems. *Emergency Librarian, 23*(1), 9–15.

Dunne, J.J. (1984). *Gaming Approaches in Educational Software: An Analysis of Their Use and Effectiveness.* (ERIC Document ED 253 207).

Dwyer, F.M. (1978). *Strategies for Improving Visual Learning.* State College, PA: Learning Services.

Edwards, D., & Mercer, N. (1987). *Common Learning.* London: Methuen.

Ehindero, O.J. (1980). The influence of two languages of instruction on students' levels of cognitive development and achievement in science. *Journal of Research in Science Teaching, 17*(4), 283–288.

Elementary Grades Task Force. (1992). *It's Elementary! Elementary Grades Task Force Report.* Sacramento, CA: California Department of Education.

Elliott, D. (1987). Scientific illiteracy in elementary school science textbook programmes. *Journal of Curriculum Studies, 19*(1), 73–76.

Entwistle, N., & Duckworth, D. (1977). Choice of science courses in secondary school: Trends and explanation. *Studies in Science Education, 4,* 63–82.

Erdrich, L. (1984). *Love Medicine.* New York: Holt, Rinehart, & Winston.

Erickson, F. (1984). School literacy, reasoning, and civility: An anthropologist's perspective. *Review of Educational Research, 54*(4), 525–546.

Esler, W.K., & Esler, M.K. (1993). *Teaching Elementary Science.* Belmont, CA: Wadsworth.

Eves, H. (1976). *An Introduction to the History of Mathematics.* New York: Holt, Rinehart, & Winston.

Ferrio, J. (1991). *Native American Doctor: The Story of Susan LaFlesche Picotte.* Minneapolis: Carolrhoda Books.

Fiber, H.R. (1987). The influence of microcomputer-based problem-solving activities on the attitudes of general mathematics students toward microcomputers. *Dissertation Abstracts International, 48*/05A:1102.

Fields, S. (1988). Cooperative learning: A strategy for all students. *Science Scope, 12*(3), 12–14.

Filep, R., & Schramm, W. (1970). *A Study of the Impact of Research on Utilization of Media for Educational Purposes Sponsored by NDEA Title VII 1958–1968. Final Report: Overview.* El Segundo, CA: Institute for Educational Development.

Finn, J.D. (1972). The emerging technology of education. In R.J. McBeath (Ed.), *Extending Education through Technology: Selected Writings by James D. Finn.* Washington, DC: Association for Educational Communications and Technology.

Flora, C.B. (1980). Women in Latin American fotonovelas: From Cinderella to Mata Hari. *Women's Studies International Quarterly, 3,* 95–104.

Flory, J. (1978, April). *Visual Literacy: A Vital Skill in the Process of Rhetorical Criticism.* Paper presented at the meeting of the Southern Speech Communication Association, Atlanta, GA. (ERIC Document Reproduction Service No. ED 155 772).

Foley, M.U. (1984). Personal computers in high school general mathematics: Effects on achievement, attitude, and attendance. *Dissertation Abstracts International, 46*/07A: 1859.

Forgan, H.W., & Mangrum, C.T. (1989). *Teaching Content Area Reading Strategies.* Columbus, OH: Merrill.

Fradd, S., & Hallman, C.L. (1983). Implication of psychological and educational assessment and instruction of culturally and linguistically different students. *Learning Disability Quarterly, 6*(4), 468–478.

Freire, P. (1970). Cultural action and conscientization. *Harvard Educational Review, 40*(3), 452–477.

Friend, H. (1985). The effect of science and mathematics integration on selected seventh grade students' attitudes toward and achievement in science. *School Science and Mathematics, 85*(6), 453–461.

Fry, E. (1982). *Writeability.* Paper presented at the Annual Meeting of the International Reading Association, Chicago, IL.

Gaffney, K.E. (1992). Multiple assessment for multiple learning styles. *Science Scope, 15*(6), 54–55.

Gagné, R.M. (1987). *Instructional Technology: Foundations.* Hillsdale, NJ: Lawrence Erlbaum.

Gagné, R.M., Briggs, L.J., & Wager, W.W. (1988). *Principles of Instructional Design* (3rd. ed.). New York: Holt, Rinehart, & Winston.

Gallagher, J.J., & Tobin, K. (1987). Teacher management and student engagement in high school science. *Science Education, 71*(4), 535–555.

Garcia, G.E., & Pearson, P.D. (1990). *Modifying Reading Instruction to Maximize Its Effectiveness for All Students.* Technical Report No. 489. Center for the Study of Reading, Illinois University, Urbana. Cambridge: Bolt, Beranek, & Newman.

Gascoigne, R.M. (1984). *A Historical Catalogue of Scientists and Scientific Books: From the Earliest Times to the Close of the Nineteenth Century.* New York: Garland.

Gay, G. (1988). Designing relevant curricula for diverse students. *Education and Urban Society, 20*(4), 327–340.

Gega, P.C. (1986). *Science in Elementary Education* (5th ed.). New York: Wiley.

Gesshel-Green, H.A. (1987). The effect of interactive microcomputer graphics on student achievement and retention in second year algebra in an academic high school. *Dissertation Abstracts International, 48*/02A: 326.

Gibb, H.H. (1989). A model program for gifted girls in science. *Journal for the Education of the Gifted, 12*(2), 142–155.

Gibson, J.J. (1947). *Motion Picture Testing and Research.* Army Air Forces Psychology Program Research Report No. 7. Washington, DC: U.S. Government Printing Office.

Gilbert, S. E., & Gay, G. (1985). Improving the success in school of poor black children. *Phi Delta Kappan, 10*, 133–137.

Gonzales, N.A. (1989, December). *Searching for Insight by Viewing Mathematics through the Eyes of Hispanic Students.* Paper presented at the Mathematics Science Education Board,"Making Mathematics Work for Minorities" Region VI Workshop, San Antonio, TX.

Gooding, C.T., Kephart, M.M., Swift, P.R., Swift, J.N., & Schell, R.E. (1990, April). *A Comparative Analysis of Target and Nontarget Students.* Paper presented at the Annual Meeting of the National Association for Research in Science Teaching, Atlanta, GA.

Goodman, K. (1970). Behind the eye: What happens to reading. In *Reading Process and Program* (pp. 25–26). Urbana, IL: National Council of Teachers of English.

Gornick, V. (1983). *Women in Science: Portraits from a World in Transition.* New York: Simon & Schuster.

Granger, C.R. (1986). *Restructuring Introductory Biology According to the Learning Cycle Instructional Strategy.* Washington, DC: Fund for the Improvement of Postsecondary Education.

Green, R. (1992). *Women in American Indian Society.* New York: Chelsea House.

Greenberg, P.J. (1932). Competition in children: An experimental study. *American Journal of Psychology, 44*, 221–248.

Greeno, J.G. (1989). Some conjectures about number sense. In J.T. Sowder & B.P. Schappelle (Eds.), *Establishing Foundations for Research on Number Sense and Related Topics: Report of a Conference* (pp. 43–56). (Tech. Rep. of National Science Foundation, Grant No. MDR-8751373). San Diego: San Diego State University, Center for Research in Mathematics and Science Education.

Gumpert, G. (1967). Closed-circuit television in training and education. In A.E. Koenig & R.D. Hill (Eds.), *The Farther Vision: Educational Television Today.* Madison: University of Wisconsin Press.

Hadfield, O.D., Martin, J.V., & Wooden, S. (1992). Mathematics anxiety and learning style of the Navajo middle school student. *School Science and Mathematics, 92*(4), 171–176.

Halpern, D.F., Hansen, C., & Riefer, D. (1990). Analogies as an aid to understanding and memory. *Journal of Educational Psychology, 82(2)*, 298–305.

Hamm, M., & Adams, D. (1991). Portfolio assessment: It's not just for artists anymore. *Science Teacher, 58(5)*, 18–21.

Hannafin, M.J. (1985). Keeping interactive video in perspective. In E. Miller (Ed.), *Educational Media and Technology Yearbook 1985*. Littleton, CO: Libraries Unlimited.

Harding, S. (1991). *Whose Science? Whose Knowledge? Thinking from Women's Lives*. Ithaca, NY: Cornell University Press.

Harlen, W. (1985). Girls and primary-school science education. *Prospects: Quarterly Review of Education, 15*, 553–564.

Harris, G.A. (1985). Consideration in assessing English language performance of Native American children. *Topics in Language Disorders, 5(4)*, 42–52.

Hart, D. (1977). Enlarging the American dream. *American Education, 13(4)*, 10–17.

Haughton, E., & Loeb, A.L. (1965). Symmetry: The case history of a program. *Journal of Research in Science Teaching, 2*, 132–145.

Healy, J.M. (1990). *Endangered Minds: Children's Learning in Today's Culture*. New York: Simon and Schuster.

Heid, M.K. (1988). Resequencing skills and concepts in applied calculus using the computer as a tool. *Journal for Research in Mathematics Education, 19(1)*, 3–25.

Herber, H.L. (1978). *Teaching Reading in Content Areas*. Englewood Cliffs, NJ: Prentice Hall.

Herron, J.D. (1952). Piaget for chemists: Explaining what "good" students cannot understand. *Journal of Chemical Education, 53(3)*, 145–150.

Herzenberg, C.L. (1986). *Women Scientists from Antiquity to the Present: An Index*. West Cornwall, CT: Locust Hill.

Hezel, R.T. (1980). Public broadcasting: Can it teach? *Journal of Communication, 30*, 173–178.

Hill, J.H., & Browner, C. (1982). Gender ambiguity and class stereotyping in the Mexican fotonovela. *Studies in Latin American Popular Culture, 1*, 43–64.

Hill, K.T., & Wigfield, A. (1984). Test anxiety: A major educational problem and what can be done about it. *Elementary School Journal, 85*, 105–126.

Hill, O.W., Pettus, C., & Hedin, B.A. (1990). Three studies of factors affecting the attitudes of blacks and females toward the pursuit of science and science-related careers. *Journal of Research in Science Teaching, 27(4)*, 289–314.

Hinding, A. (1979). *Women's History Sources: A Guide to Archives and Manuscript Collections in the United States*. New York: Bowker.

Hochel, S.S. (1983, November). *A Position Paper on Teaching the Acquisition of the Mainstream Dialect in Kindergarten and Elementary School*. Paper presented at the Annual Meeting of the Speech Communication Association, Washington, DC.

Hockberg, J. (1962). Psychophysics of pictorial perception. *AV Communications Review, 10*: 22–54.

Holford, D.G., & Kempa, R.F. (1970). The effectiveness of stereoscopic viewing in the learning of spatial relationships in structural chemistry. *Journal of Research in Science Teaching, 7*, 265–270.

Horn, M. (1983). Recent Mexican scholarship on comics. *Studies in Latin American Popular Culture, 2*, 208–212.

Howard, A.V. (1951). *Chamber's Dictionary of Scientists*. London: Chambers.

Humphreys, B., Johnson, R.T., & Johnson, D.W. (1982). Effects of cooperative, competitive, and individualistic learning on students' achievement in science class. *Journal of Research in Science Teaching, 19(5)*, 351–356.

Hunter, M. (1982). *Mastery Teaching*. El Segundo, CA: TIP.

Hvitfeldt, C. (1986). Traditional culture, perceptual style, and learning: The classroom behavior of Hmong adults. *Adult Education Quarterly, 36(2)*, 65–77.

Hykle, J.A. (1992, March). *The Effect of Laboratory versus Lecture Science Teaching Methods: A Meta-analysis.* Paper presented at the Annual Meeting of the National Association for Research in Science Teaching, Boston, MA.

Ireland, N.O. (1962). Index to Scientists of the World, from Ancient to Modern Times: Biographies and Portraits. Boston: F.W. Faxon.

Jacobson, W.J., & Bergman, A.B. (1987). *Science for Children: A Book for Teachers* (2nd ed.). Englewood Cliffs, NJ: Prentice-Hall.

Jacques Cattell Press (1986). *American Men and Women of Science: Physical and Biological Sciences* (16th ed.). New York: Bowker.

Johnson, D.W., & Johnson, R.T. (1987). *A Meta-Analysis of Cooperative, Competitive, and Individualistic Goal Structures.* Hillsdale, NJ: Erlbaum.

Johnson, D.W., & Johnson, R.T. (1994). *Learning Together and Alone: Cooperation, Competition, and Individualization.* Englewood Cliffs, NJ: Prentice-Hall.

Johnson, R.T., & Johnson, D.W. (1987). How can we put cooperative learning into practice? *Science Teacher, 54*(6), 46–50.

Johnson, R.T., Johnson, D.W., Scott, L.E., & Ramolae, B.A. (1985). Effects of single-sex and mixed-sex cooperative interaction on science achievement and attitudes and cross-handicap and cross-sex relationships. *Journal of Research in Science Teaching, 22*(3), 207–220.

Jonassen, D.H. (1988). *Instructional Designs for Microcomputer Courseware.* Hillsdale, NJ: Erlbaum.

Kagan, S., Zahn, G.L., Widaman, K.F., Schwarzwald, J., & Tyrrell, G. (1985). Classroom structural bias: Impact of cooperative and competitive classroom structures on cooperative and competitive individuals and groups. In R. Slavin, S. Sharan, S. Kagan, R. Hertz-Lazarowitz, C. Webb, & R. Schmuck (Eds.), *Learning To Cooperate, Cooperating To Learn* (pp. 277–312). New York: Plenum.

Kahle, J.B. (1985). Minority women: Conquering both sexism and racism. In J.B. Kahle (Ed.), *Women in Science* (pp. 102–123). Philadelphia: Falmer.

Kanis, I.B. (1991). Ninth grade lab skills: An assessment. *Science Teacher, 58*(1), 29–33.

Karlin, M., Coffman, T.L., & Walter, G. (1969). On the fading social stereotypes: Studies in three generations of college students. *Journal of Personality and Social Psychology, 13,* 1–16.

Karplus, R. (1974). *Science Curriculum Improvement Study: Teacher's Handbook.* Berkeley, CA: Lawrence Hall of Science.

Karplus, R., et al. (1977). *Science Teaching and the Development of Reasoning.* Berkeley, CA: Lawrence Hall of Science.

Kass-Simon, G. (1962). *Women of Science: Righting the Record.* Bloomington, IN: Indiana University Press.

Keig, P.F. (1992, May). *Construction of Conceptual Understanding in the Multicultural Science Classroom.* Paper presented at "Multicultural Classrooms—A Constructivist Viewpoint" Symposium at San Diego State University, San Diego, CA.

Kessler, C., & Quinn, M.E. (1980). Bilingualism and science problem-solving ability. *Bilingual Education Paper Series, 4,* 1–30.

Kitano, M.K. (1991). A multicultural educational perspective on serving the culturally diverse gifted. *Journal for the Education of the Gifted, 15*(1), 4–19.

Knight, G.P., & Kagan, S. (1977). Acculturation of prosocial and competitive behaviors among second- and third-generation Mexican-American children. *Journal of Cross-Cultural Psychology, 8,* 273–284.

Kohlberg, L. (1980). High school democracy and education for a just society. In R.D. Mosher (Ed.), *Moral Education: A First Generation of Research and Development.* New York: Praeger.

Kolesnik, W.B. (1978). *Motivation: Understanding and Influencing Human Behavior.* Boston: Allyn & Bacon.

Koopmans, M. (1987). Formal school and task familiarity. *Cognition, 27,*109–110.

Koran, J.J., Koran, M.L., & Baker, S. (1980). Differential response cueing and feedback in the acquisition of an inductively presented biological concept. *Journal of Research in Science Teaching, 17*(2), 166– 172.

Koran, M.L. (1972). Varying instructional methods to fit trainee characteristics. *AV Communications Review, 20,* 135–146.

Kracjik, J.S., Simmons, P.E., & Lunetta, V.N. (1986). Improving research on computers in science learning. *Journal of Research in Science Teaching, 23*(5), 465–470.

Kracjik, J.S., Simmons, P.E., & Lunetta, V.N. (1988). A research strategy for the dynamic study of students' concepts and problem-solving strategies using science software. *Journal of Research in Science Teaching, 25*(2), 147–155.

Kahle, J.B. (Ed.). (1985). *Women in Science: A Report from the Field.* Philadelphia: Falmer.

Kass-Simon, G., & Farnes, P. (1990). *Women of Science: Righting the Record.* Bloomington: Indiana University Press.

Kren, S.R., & Huntsberger, J. P. (1977). Should science be used to teach mathematical skills? *Journal of Research in Science Teaching, 14*(6), 557–561.

Krendl, K.A., & Lieberman, D.A. (1988). Computers and learning: A review of recent research. *Journal of Educational Computing Research, 4*(4), 367–389.

Kulik, J.A., Bangert, R.L., & Williams, G.W. (1980). Effects of computer based teaching on secondary school students. *Journal of Educational Psychology, 75*(1), 19–26.

Kurtz, R., & James, R. K. (1975). Implementation of an integrated program of science: A process approach and nuffield mathematics. *School Science and Mathematics, 75*(3), 258–266.

Lapp, D., & Flood, J. (1992). *Teaching Reading to Every Child.* New York: Macmillan.

Lapp, D., Flood, J., & Farnan, N. (1989). *Content Area Reading and Learning.* Englewood Cliffs, NJ: Prentice-Hall.

Lawson, A.E. (1975). Developing formal thought through biology teaching. *American Biology Teacher, 37*(7), 411–420.

Lawson, A.E., Abraham, M.R., & Renner, J.W. (1989). A theory of instruction. *Monographs of the National Association for Research in Science Teaching.* Number 1. New York: Wiley.

Lawson, A.E., & Renner, J.W. (1975). Piagetian theory and biology teaching. *American Biology Teacher, 37*(6), 336–343.

Lazarowitz, R. (1984, October). *The Affective Domain of Junior High School Students in an Audio-Tutorial Biology Setting.* Paper presented at a conference of the International Society for Individualized Instruction, Atlanta, GA.

Lazarus, B.D. (1991). Guided notes, review, and achievement of secondary students with learning disabilities in mainstream content courses. *Education and Treatment of Children, 14*(2), 112–127.

Le Boterf, G. (1984). The challenge of mass education in Nicaragua. *Quaternaire Education, 65/68,* 247–266.

Lee, V.E. (1988). Identifying potential scientists and engineers: An analysis of the high school–college transition. In *Elementary and Secondary Education for Science and Engineering, Grade School to Grad School,* Office of Technology Assessment, U.S. Congress.

Lefkowith, E.F. (1955). *The Validity of Pictorial Tests and Their Interaction with Audio-Visual Teaching Methods.* Technical Report, SDC-269-7-49. Port Washington, NY: Special Devices Center, Office of Naval Research.

Lefley, H.P. (1990). Rehabilitation in mental illness: Insights from other cultures. *Psychosocial Rehabilitation Journal, 14*(1), 5–11.

Lehman, J.R., & McDonald, J.L. (1988). Teachers' Perceptions of the Integration of Mathematics and Science. *School Science and Mathematics, 88*(8), 642–649.

Lesh, R., Landau, M., & Hamilton, E. (1983). Conceptual models and problem-solving research. In R. Lesh & M. Landau (Eds.), *Acquisition of Mathematics Concepts and Processes* (pp. 263–342). New York: Academic.

Levie, W.H., & Dickie, K.E. (1973). The analysis and application of media. In R.M.W. Travers, (Ed.), *Second Handbook of Research on Teaching.* Chicago: Rand McNally.

Levie, W.H., & Levie, D. (1975). Pictorial memory processes. *AV Communication Review, 23*(1), 81–96.

Levine, M.A., & Hanes, M.L. (1976). *Dialect Usage as a Factor in Developmental Language Performance of Primary Grade School Children.* (ERIC Document ED346949).

Lewis, A.C. (1990). Getting unstuck: Curriculum as a tool of reform. *Phi Delta Kappan, 71*(7), 534–538.

Liftig, I.F., Liftig, B., & Eaker, K. (1992). Making assessment work: What teachers should know before they try it. *Science Scope, 15*(6),4–8.

Lipson, A. (1984). *The Concentration Choice Study, 1978–1983.* Boston: Henry A. Murray Research Center.

Lockard, J., Abrams, P.D., & Many, W.A. (1987). *Microcomputers for Educators.* Boston: Little, Brown.

Longstreet, W. (1978). *Aspects of Ethnicity.* New York: Teachers College Press.

Lorsbach, A., & Tobin, K. (1992). Constructivism as a referent for science teaching. *NARST News, 34*(3), 9–11.

Lucas, T., Henze, R., & Donato, R. (1990). Promoting the success of Latino language–minority students: An exploratory study of six high schools. *Harvard Educational Review, 60*(3), 315–340.

Lucker, G., Rosenfield, D., Sikes, J., & Aronson, E. (1976). Performance in the interdependent classroom: A field study. *Journal of Education Psychology, 68*, 588–596.

Lunetta, V.N. (1972). The design and evaluation of a series of computer simulated experiments for use in high school physics. *Dissertation Abstracts International, 33*, 2785A.

Maehr, M. (1978). Sociocultural origins of achievement motivation. In D. Bar-Tal & L. Saxe (Eds.), *Social Psychology of Education: Theory and Practice.* Washington, DC: Hemisphere.

Manoleas, P., & Carrillo, E. (1991). A culturally syntonic approach to the field education of Latino students. *Journal of Social Work Education, 27*(2), 135–144.

Marek, E.A., & Methven, S.B. (1991). Effects of the learning cycle upon student and classroom teacher performance. *Journal of Research in Science Teaching, 28*(1), 41–53.

Marrett, C.B. (1981). *Minority females in high school mathematics and science* (NIE report on the Program on Student Diversity and School Processes). Madison, WI: Wisconsin Center for Education Research.

Marshall, N. (1989). The students: Who are they and how do I reach them? In D. Lapp, J. Flood, & N. Farnan (Eds.), *Content Area Reading and Learning: Instructional Strategies* (pp. 59–72). Englewood Cliffs, NJ: Prentice-Hall.

Martinez, D. I., & Martinez, J.V. (1982). *Aspects of American Hispanic and Indian Involvement in Biomedical Research.* Bethesda, MD: Society for Advancement of Chicanos and Native Americans in Science.

Maslow, A. H. (1962a). *Motivation and Personality.* New York: Harper & Brothers.

Maslow, A. (1962b). *Toward a Psychology of Being.* New York: Van Nostrand.

Mason, C.L., Kahle, J.B., & Gardner, A.L. (1991). Draw-a-scientist test: Future implications. *School Science and Mathematics, 91*(5), 193–198.

Maurer, J.F. (1981). *Concise Dictionary of Scientific Biography.* New York: Scribner's.

Mayer, V.J. (1990). Teaching from a global point of view. *Science Teacher, 57*(1), 47–51.

McBride, J.W., & Silverman, F.L. (1991). Integrating elementary/middle school science and mathematics. *School Science and Mathematics, 91*(7), 285–292.

McClelland, D.C. (1965). Toward a theory of motive acquisition. *American Psychologist, 20,* 321–333.

McCormack, A.J., & Yager, R.E. (1989). A new taxonomy of science education. *Science Teacher, 56*(2), 47–48.

McGarry, T.P. (1986). Integrating learning for young children. *Educational Leadership, 44*(3), 64–66.

McGinnis, J.R. (1992, March). *Science Teacher Decision-Making in Multicultural Classrooms.* Paper presented at the annual meeting of the National Association for Research in Science Teaching, Boston, MA.

McGraw-Hill. (1966). *McGraw-Hill Modern Men of Science (Vols. 1 and 2).* New York: McGraw-Hill.

McGraw-Hill. (1980). *McGraw-Hill Modern Scientists and Engineers.* New York: McGraw-Hill.

McNeil, J.D. (1985). *Curriculum: A Comprehensive Introduction.* Boston: Little, Brown.

Mechling, K.R., & Oliver, D.L. (1983). *Handbook I. Science Teaches Basic Skills.* Washington, DC: National Science Teachers Association.

Melnik, A. (1968). Questions: An instructional-diagnostic tool. *Journal of Reading, 11,* 509.

Melson, D., Joseph, G.G, & Williams, J. (1993). *Multicultural Mathematics.* Oxford: Oxford University Press.

Merrill. (1987). *Focus on Physical Science.* Columbus, OH: Merrill.

Merrill, M.D. (1988). Applying component display theory to the design of courseware. In D.H. Jonassen (Ed.), *Instructional Designs for Microcomputer Courseware.* Hillsdale, NJ: Erlbaum.

Milson, J.L., & Ball, S.E. (1986). Enhancement of learning through integrated science and mathematics. *School Science and Mathematics, 86*(6), 489–493.

Montagu, A. (1965). *The Human Revolution.* New York: World.

Moore, D.M., & Dwyer, F.M. (1995). *Visual Literacy: A Spectrum of Visual Learning.* Englewood Cliffs, NJ: Educational Technology Publications.

Moran, J.B., & Boulter, W. (1992). Step by step scoring. *Science Scope, 15*(6), 46–47.

Mucha, L. (1987). *Attitudinal and achievement effects of mathematics homework games on second grade students and their parents.* (ERIC Document Reproduction Service No. ED 283698).

Mulkey, L.M., & Ellis, R.S. (1990). Social stratification and science education: A longitudinal analysis, 1981–1986, of minorities' integration into the scientific talent pool. *Journal of Research in Science Teaching, 27*(3), 205–217.

Mullis, I.V.S., & Jenkins, L.B. (1988). *The Science Report Card Elements of Risk and Recovery: Trends and Achievement Based on the 1986 National Assessment.* Princeton, NJ: Educational Testing Service.

Nachmias, R., & Linn, M.C. (1987). Evaluations of science laboratory data: The role of computer-presented information. *Journal of Research in Science Teaching, 24*(5), 491–506.

Naisbitt, J. (1982). *Megatrends: Ten New Directions Transforming Our Lives.* New York: Warner.

National Research Council. (1990). *Everybody Counts: A Report to the Nation on the Future of Mathematics Education.* Washington, DC: National Academy.

National Research Council. (1996). *National Science Education Standards.* Washington, DC: National Academy.

National Science Board Commission on Precollege Education in Mathematics, Science, and Technology. (1983). *Educating Americans for the 21st Century.* Washington, DC: National Science Foundation.

National Science Foundation. (1987). *The Science and Engineering Pipeline*. PRA Report 67–2, 3.

National Science Teachers Association Board of Directors. (1991). *An NSTA Position Statement: Multicultural Science Education*. Washington, DC: National Science Teachers Association.

Nijhof W., & Kommers, P. (1985). Cooperation in relation to cognitive controversy. In R. Slavin, S. Sharan, S. Kagan, R. Hertz-Lazarowitz, C. Webb, & R. Schmuck (Eds.), *Learning to Cooperate, Cooperating to Learn* (pp. 126–133). New York: Plenum.

Norman, D.A. (1982). *Models of Human Memory*. New York: Academic Press.

Norman, D., Gentner, S., & Stevens, A.L. (1976). Comments on learning schemata and memory representation. In D. Klahr (Ed.), *Cognition and instruction*. Hillsdale, NJ: Erlbaum.

Nott, L., Reeve, C., & Reeve, R. (1992). Scoring rubrics: An assessment option. *Science Scope, 15*(6), 44–45.

Novak, J. (1991). Clarify with concept maps: A tool for students and teachers alike. *Science Teacher, 58*(7), 45–49.

Odubunmi, O., & Balogun, T.A. (1991). The effect of laboratory and lecture teaching methods on cognitive achievement in integrated science. *Journal of Research in Science Teaching, 28*(3), 213–224.

Ogbu, J.U. (1992). Understanding cultural diversity and learning. *Educational Researcher, 21*(8), 5–14.

Ogilvie, M.B. (1993). *Women in Science: Antiquity through the Nineteenth Century—A Biographical Dictionary with Annotated Bibliography*. Cambridge: MIT.

Okebukola, P.A. (1985). The relative effectiveness of cooperative and competitive interaction techniques in strengthening students' performance in science classes. *Science Education, 69*(4), 501–509.

Okebukola, P.A. (1986). The influence of preferred learning styles on cooperative learning in science. *Science Education, 70*(5), 509–517.

Okebukola, P.A., & Ogunniyi, M.B. (1984). Cooperative, competitive, and individualistic science laboratory interaction patterns—effects of students' achievement and acquisition of practical skills. *Journal of Research in Science Teaching, 21*(9), 875–884.

Okebukola, P.A., & Ogunniyi, M.B. (1986). Effects of teachers' verbal exposition on students' level of class participation and achievement in biology. *Science Education, 70*(1), 45–51.

Olion, L., & Gillis-Olion, M. (1984). Assessing culturally diverse exceptional children. *Early Child Development and Care, 15*, 203–232.

Olsen, J.R., & Bass, V.B. (1982). The application of performance technology in the military, 1960–1980. *Performance and Instruction, 21*(6): 32–36.

Olson, D.R. (1986). The cognitive consequences of literacy. *Canadian Psychology, 27*(2), 109–121.

Olson, D.R., & Torrance, N. (1987). Language, literacy, and mental states. *Discourse Processes, 10*, 157–167.

Oram, R.F. (1986). *Biology Living Systems*. Columbus, OH: Merrill.

Ornstein, A.C., & Hunkins, F.P. (1988). *Curriculum: Foundations, Principles, and Issues*. Englewood Cliffs, NJ: Prentice-Hall.

Ornstein-Galicia, J.L., & Penfield, J. (1981). A problem-solving model for integrating science and language in bilingual/bicultural education. *Bilingual Education Paper Series, 5*, 1–22.

Ortiz, A.A., & Maldonado-Colon, E. (1986). Recognizing learning disabilities in bilingual children: How to lessen inappropriate referrals of language minority students to special education. *Journal of Reading, Writing, and Learning Disabilities International, 2*(1), 43–56.

Ortiz, F.I. (1988). Hispanic-American children's experiences in classrooms: A comparison between Hispanic and non-Hispanic children. In L. Weis. (Ed.), *Class, Race, and Gender in American Education* (pp. 63–85). New York: SUNY Press.

Ostlund, K.L. (1992). Sizing up social skills. *Science Scope, 15*(6), 31–33.

Pallrand, G.J., & Seeber, F. (1984). Spatial ability and achievement in introductory physics. *Journal of Research in Science Teaching, 15*, 507–516.

Pang, V.O. (1988). Ethnic prejudice: Still alive and hurtful. *Harvard Educational Review, 58*(3), 375–379.

Parakh, J.S. (1967). *A Study of Relationships among Teacher Behavior, Pupil Behavior, and Pupil Characteristics in High School Biology Classes: Final Report.* Bellingham: Western Washington State University.

Patchen, M. (1982). *Black-White Contact in Schools: Its Social and Academic Effects.* West LaFayette, IN: Purdue University Press.

Pearson, W., & Bechtel, H.K. (1989). *Blacks, Science, and American Education.* New Brunswick, NJ: Rutgers University Press.

Pedersen, J.E. (1992). The effects of a cooperative controversy, presented as an STS issue, on achievement and anxiety in secondary science. *School Science and Mathematics, 92(7)*, 374–380.

Peper, R.J. & Mayer, R.E. (1986). Generative effects of note-taking during science lectures. *Journal of Educational Psychology, 78*(1), 34–38.

Piaget, J. (1964). Cognitive development in children: Development and learning. *Journal of Research in Science Teaching, 2*, 176–186.

Pitman, M.A. (1989). *Culture Acquisition: A Holistic Approach to Human Learning.* New York: Praeger.

Pizzini, E.L., Bell, S.A., & Shepardson, D.S. (1990). Rethinking thinking in the science classroom. *Science Teacher, 55*(9), 22–25.

Pogge, A.F., & Lunetta, V.N. (1987) Spreadsheets answer "What If . . . ?". *Science Teacher, 54(8)*, 46–49.

Pollard, R.J. (1992, March). *Using Instructional Strategies for Conceptual Change.* Paper presented at the National Association of Research in Science Teaching, Boston, MA.

Premack, D. (1965). *Reinforcement theory.* In D. Levine (Ed.), *Nebraska Symposium on Motivation.* Lincoln: University of Nebraska Press.

Purser, R., & Renner, J. (1983). Results of two tenth-grade biology teaching procedures. *Science Education, 67*(1), 85–98.

Raizen, S.A. (1991). The state of science education. In S.K. Majumdar, L.M. Rosenfeld, P.A. Rubba, E.W. Miller, & R.F. Schmalz (Eds.), *Science Education in the United States: Issues, Crises and Priorities* (pp. 25–45). Phillipsburg, NJ: Pennsylvania Academy of Science.

Rakow, S.J. (1992). Assessment: A driving force. *Science Scope, 15*(6), 3.

Ramirez, M., & Castaneda, A. (1974). *Cognitive Strategy Research: Educational Applications.* New York: Springer-Verlag.

Ramsey, J. (1989). A curriculum framework for community-based STS issue instruction. *Education and Urban Society, 22(1)*, 40–53.

Ramsey, J.M., Hungerford, H.R., & Volk, T.L. (1990). Analyzing the Issues of STS. *Science Teacher, 57*(3), 60–63.

Recsigno, R.C. (1988, October). *Practical Implementation of Educational Technology. The GTE/GTEL Smart Classroom. The Hueneme School District Experience.* Paper presented at the United States/Union of Soviet Socialist Republics Joint Conference on Computers, Education and Children. Moscow, USSR.

Reed, J.S. (1988). *The Enduring Effects of Education.* Chicago: University of Chicago Press.

Reed, M. (1991). Videodiscs help American Indians learn English and study heritage. *T.H.E. (Technological Horizons in Education) Journal, 19*(3), 96–97.

Reed, S.K. (1988). *Cognitive Theory and Applications.* Pacific Grove, CA: Brooks/Cole.

Renner, J.W., & Lawson, A.E. (1973). Promoting intellectual development through science teaching. *Physics Teacher, 6,* 273–276.

Rennert, R.S. (1995). *African American Answer Book: Science & Discovery.* New York: Chelsea House.

Resnick, L.B. (1987). *Education and Learning to Think.* Washington, DC: National Academy.

Rhodes, R.W. (1988). Holistic teaching/learning for Native-American students. *Journal of American-Indian Education, 27*(2), 21–29.

Rhoton, J. (1990). An investigation of science-technology-society education perceptions of secondary science teachers in Tennessee. *School Science and Mathematics, 90*(5), 383–395.

Rigney, J. (1978). Learning strategies: A theoretical perspective. In H.F. O'Neil (Ed.), *Learning Strategies.* New York: Academic.

Riley, J.P. (1986). The effects of teachers' wait-time and knowledge comprehension questioning on science achievement. *Journal of Research in Science Teaching, 23*(4), 335–342.

Roblyer, M.D. (1985). *Measuring the Impact of Computers in Instruction: A Non- technical Review of Research for Educators.* Washington, DC: Association for Educational Data Systems.

Rodriguez, I., & Bethel, L.J. (1983). An inquiry approach to science/language teaching. *Journal of Research in Science Teaching, 20,* 291–296.

Roehler, L.R., & Duffy, G.G. (1989). The content area teacher's instructional role: A cognitive mediational view. In D. Lapp, J. Flood, & N. Farnan (Eds.), *Content Area Reading and Learning: Instructional Strategies* (pp. 115–122). Englewood Cliffs, NJ: Prentice-Hall.

Roessel, R. (1981). *Women in Navajo Society.* Rough Rock, AZ: Navajo Resource Center.

Rogers, C.R. (1983). *Freedom to Learn for the 80's.* Columbus, OH: Merrill.

Ronan, C.A. (1982). *Science: Its History and Development among the World's Cultures.* New York: Hamlyn.

Roschelle, J. (1992). Learning by collaborating: Convergent conceptual change. *Journal of the Learning Sciences, 2*(3), 235–276.

Rosenthal, D.B. (1990). Warming up to STS. *Science Teacher, 54*(9), 28–32.

Roth, W.M. (1990, April). *Collaboration and Constructivism in the Science Classroom.* Paper presented at the annual meeting of the American Educational Research Association, Boston, MA.

Roth, W.M. (1992a). Bridging the gap between school and real life: Toward an integration of science, mathematics, and technology in the context of authentic practice. *School Science and Mathematics, 92*(6), 307–317.

Roth, W.M. (1992b). Dynamic evaluation. *Science Scope, 15*(6), 37–40.

Roth, W.M., & Bowen, M. (1993). The unfolding vee. *Science Scope, 16*(5), 28–32.

Roth, W.M., & Verechaka, G. (1993). Plotting a course with vee maps. *Science and Children, 30*(4), 24–27.

Rowe, M.B. (1974a). Relation of wait-time and rewards to the development of language, logic, and fate control. Part II, Rewards. *Journal of Research in Science Teaching, 11*(4): 291.

Rowe, M.B. (1974b). Wait-time and rewards as instructional variables, their influence on language, logic, and fate control: Part I, Wait-time. *Journal of Research in Science Teaching, 11*(2), 81–91.

Rowe, M.B. (1983). What can science educators teach chemists about teaching chemistry? A symposium: Getting chemistry off the killer course list. *Journal of Chemical Education, 60*(11), 954–956.

Rubalcava, M. (1991). *Locating Transformative Teaching in Multicultural Education.* Unpublished manuscript. University of California–Berkeley, Department of Anthropology, Special Project.

Rubba, P.A., & Anderson, H. (1978). Development of an instrument to assess secondary students' understanding of the nature of scientific knowledge. *Science Education, 62*(4), 449–458.

Rubba, P.A., & Wiesenmayer, R.L. (1991). Integrating STS into school science. In S.K. Majumdar, L.M. Rosenfeld, P.A. Rubba, E.W. Miller, & R.F. Schmalz (Eds.), *Science Education in the United States: Issues, Crises, and Priorities.* Easton, PA: Pennsylvania Academy of Science.

Rubin, R.L., & Norman, J.T. (1989, March–April). *A Comparison of the Effect of a Systematic Modeling Approach and the Learning Cycle Approach on the Achievement of Integrated Science Process Skills of Urban Middle School Students.* Paper presented at the annual meetings of the National Association for Research in Science Teaching, San Francisco, CA.

Rumelhart, D.E., & Ortony, A. (1977). The representation of knowledge in memory. In R.C. Anderson, R.J. Spiro, & W.E. Montague (Eds.), *Schooling and the Acquisition of Knowledge*, Hillsdale, NJ: Erlbaum.

Rutherford, F.J. (1991). Project 2061: An agenda for achieving national scientific literacy. In S.K. Majumdar, L.M. Rosenfeld, P.A. Rubba, E.W. Miller, & R.F. Schmalz (Eds.), *Science Education in the United States: Issues, Crises, and Priorities.* Easton, PA: Pennsylvania Academy of Science.

Rutherford, F.J., & Ahlgren, A. (1988). Rethinking the science curriculum. In R.S. Brandt (Ed.), *Content of the Curriculum: 1988 ASCD Yearbook of the Association for Supervision and Curriculum Development.* New York: Jarboe.

Sadker, M.P., & Sadker, D.M. (1979). *Beyond Pictures and Pronouns: Sexism in Teacher Education Textbooks.* Washington, DC: Women's Educational Equity Act Program of US Department of Health, Education, and Welfare.

Saettler, P. (1968). *A History of Instructional Technology.* New York: McGraw-Hill.

Sammons, V.O. (1990). *Blacks in Science and Medicine.* New York: Hemisphere.

Sarton, G. (1952). *A Guide to the History of Science: A First Guide for the Study of the History of Science, with Introductory Essays on Science and Tradition.* Waltham, MA: Chronica Botanica.

Saunders, W.L. (1992). The constructivist perspective: Implications and teaching strategies for science. *School Science and Mathematics, 92*(3), 136–141.

Saville-Troike, M. (1978). *A Guide to Culture in the Classroom.* Rosslyn, VA: National Clearinghouse for Bilingual Education.

Scarnati, J.T., & Weller, C.J. (1992). The write stuff. *Science and Children, 29*(4), 28–29.

Schallert, D.L., & Rose, N.L. (1989). The role of reading in content area instruction. In D. Lapp, J. Flood, & N. Farnan (Eds.), *Content Area Reading and Learning: Instructional Strategies* (pp. 25–35). Englewood Cliffs, NJ: Prentice-Hall.

Scharmann, L.C., & McLellan, H. (1992). Enhancing science-technology-society (STS) instruction: An examination of teacher goal orientations. *School Science and Mathematics, 92*(5), 249–252.

Schick, F.L., & Schick, R. (1991). *Statistical Handbook on US Hispanics.* Phoenix, AZ: Oryx.

Schimmel, B. J. (1986). *A Meta-Analysis of Feedback to Learners in Computerized and Programmed Instruction.* Paper presented at the annual meeting of the American Educational Research Association, Montreal. (ERIC Document 233 708)

Schimmel, B.J. (1988). Providing meaningful feedback in courseware. In D.H. Jonassen (Ed.), *Instructional Designs for Microcomputer Courseware* (pp. 183–195). Hillsdale, NJ: Erlbaum.

Schlenker, R.M. (1983). The molar concept: A Piagetian-oriented learning cycle. *Journal of College Science Teaching, 12*(6), 431–434.

Science Curriculum Framework and Criteria Committee (1990). *California State Science Framework.* Sacramento, CA: California Department of Education.

Sevenair, J.P., & Carmichael, J.W. (1988). A high school chemistry prep course designed to increase the number of black Americans in science-related careers. *Journal of College Science Teaching, 18*(1), 51–54.

Severin, W. (1967). Another look at cue summation. *AV Communication Review, 15*(3), 233–245.

Seymour, L.A., Padberg, L.F., Bingman, R.M. & Koutrieck, P.G. (1974). A successful inquiry methodology. *American Biology Teacher, 36*(9), 348–353.

Shade, B.J. (1982). Afro-American cognitive style: A variable in school success. *Review of Educational Research, 52*, 219–244.

Shade, D.D. (1979, November) *Microcomputers in Preschool Environments: Answers to Questions, Theoretical Guidance and Future Directions.* Paper presented at the annual meeting of the National Association for the Education of Young Children, Chicago, IL.

Shann, M.H. (1977). Evaluation of an interdisciplinary, problem solving curriculum in elementary science and mathematics, *Science Education, 61*(4), 491–502.

Shapiro, K.R. (1975). An overview of problems encountered in aptitude treatment interaction (ATI) research for instruction. *AV Communications Review, 23*, 227–241.

Shapiro, S.B. (1972). Developing models by "unpacking" confluent education. Occasional Paper No. 12, *Development and Research in Confluent Education.* Santa Barbara: University of California.

Sharan, S. (1985). Cooperative learning and the multiethnic classroom. In R. Slavin, S. Sharan, S. Kagan, R. Hertz-Lazarowitz, C. Webb, & R. Schmuck (Eds.), *Learning to Cooperate, Cooperating to Learn* (pp. 255–276). New York: Plenum.

Shick, J. (1990). Textbook tests. *Science Teacher, 57*(6), 33–39.

Showalter, V. (1974). Program objectives and scientific literacy. *Prism II, 2*(4), 1–3, 6–8.

Shrigley, R.L. (1974). The attitude of preservice teachers toward science. *School Science and Mathematics, 74*, 243–250.

Sieber, J., O'Neil, H., & Tobias, S. (1977). *Anxiety, Learning, and Instruction.* Hillsdale, NJ: Erlbaum.

Sieber, J., O'Neill, J., & Tobias, Sheila (1987). A "Star Wars" objector lays his research on the line. *Educational Record, 68*(1), 14–17.

Silberman, R.G., & Zipp, A.P. (1986). The science and magic of chemistry: A learning cycle laboratory on oxidation-reduction. *Journal of Chemical Education, 63*(12), 1098.

Simpson, E.J. (1972). *The Classification of Educational Objectives: Psychomotor Domain.* Urbana: University of Illinois Press.

Singer, H., & Donlan, D. (1990). *Reading and Learning from Text.* Hillsdale, NJ: Erlbaum.

Singer, H., & Simonsen, S. (1989). Comprehension and instruction in learning from a text. In D. Lapp, J. Flood, & N. Farnan (Eds.), *Content Area Reading and Learning: Instructional Strategies.* (pp. 25–35). Englewood Cliffs, NJ: Prentice-Hall.

Slavin, R.E. (1982). *Cooperative Learning: Student Teams.* Washington, DC: National Educational Association.

Sleeter, C.E., & Grant, C.A. (1987). An analysis of multicultural education in the United States. *Harvard Educational Review, 57*(4), 421–444.

Slesnick, I.L., Balzer, L., McCormack, A.J., Newton, D.E., & Rasmussen, F.A. (1985). *Scott, Foresman Biology.* Glenview, IL: Scott, Foresman.

Sless, D. (1983). Visual literacy: A failed opportunity. *ECTJ, 32*(4), 224–228.

Sloyer, C., & Smith, L.H. (1986). Applied mathematics via student-centered computer graphics. *Journal of Computers in Mathematics and Science Teaching*, Spring, 17–20.

Smith, T.R., & Smith, S.W. (1992). *It's Elementary! Elementary Grades Task Force Report.* Sacramento: California Department of Education.

Smith, W.S. (1983). Science careers in the classroom. *Science and Children, 20*(5), 19–29.

Smith, W.S., Frazier, N.I., Ward, S., & Webb, W. (1983). Early adolescent girls' and boys' learning of a spatial visualization skill—Replications. *Science Education, 67*(2), 239–243.

Solomon, J. (1989). The social construction of school science. In R. Millar (Ed.), *Doing Science: Images of Science in Science Education* (pp. 126–136). New York: Falmer.

Sosa, A.S. (1986). *Valued Youth Partnership Program: Dropout Prevention through Cross-Age Tutoring.* San Antonio, TX: Intercultural Development Research Association.

Souviney, R.J. (1981). *Teaching and Learning Mathematics in the Community Schools of Papua New Guinea,* Indigenous Mathematics Project Working Paper, No. 20, Department of Education, PNG.

Sowder, J.T. (1991, August). *Considerations for Research on Computation: Borrowing from Others.* Paper presented at the Gwinganna Computation Conference, Gold Coast, Australia.

Spitler, H. R. (1889). *The Syntonic Principle, Its Relation to Health and Ocular Problems.* Eaton, OH: College of Syntonic Optometry.

Sprayberry, R.R. (1994). *Using Multimedia to Improve the Aural Proficiency of High School Students of Spanish,* Practicuum Report. Fort Lauderdale, FL: Nova University.

Spring, D. (1950). Awareness of racial differences of preschool children in Hawaii. *Genetic Psychology Monographs, 41*, 214–270.

SRI International & Policy Studies Associates. (1992). *Study of Academic Instruction for Disadvantaged Students: Academic Challenge for the Children of Poverty.* Washington, DC: United States Department of Education.

Stahl, R.J. (1992, March). *Using the Information-Constructivist (IC) Perspective To Guide Curricular and Instructional Decisions toward Attaining Desired Student Outcomes of Science Education.* Paper presented at the annual meeting of the National Association for Research in Science Teaching, Boston, MA.

Stahl, R.J., Hunt, B.S., & Matiya, J.C. (1980). Humanism and behaviorism: Is there really a difference? *Educational Leadership, 38*(3), 230–231.

Stasson, M.F., Kameda, T., Parks, C.D., Zimmerman, S.K., & David, J.H. (1991). Effects of assigned group consensus requirement on group problem solving and group members' learning. *Social Psychology Quarterly, 54*(1), 25–35.

Staver, J.R. (1991). Why is science basic in elementary school? In S.K. Majumdar, L.M. Rosenfeld, P.A. Rubba, E.W. Miller, & R.F. Schmalz (Eds.), *Science Education in the United States: Issues, Crises and Priorities* (pp. 117–126). Easton, PA: Pennsylvania Academy of Sciences.

Steen, E.B. (1971). *Dictionary of Biology.* New York: Barnes & Noble.

Steen, L.A. (1990). *On the Shoulders of Giants: New Approaches to Numeracy.* Washington, DC: National Academy.

Stewart, D.A., & Benson, G. (1988). Dual cultural negligence: The education of Black deaf children. *Journal of Multicultural Counseling and Development, 16*(3), 98–109.

Struik, D.J. (1987). *A Concise History of Mathematics.* New York: Dover.

Superka, D.P., Ahrens, C., Hedstrom, J., Ford, L.J., & Johnson, P.L. (1976). *Values Education Sourcebook.* Boulder, CO: Social Science Education Consortium.

Suzuki, B.H. (1984). Curriculum transformation for multicultural education. *Education and Urban Society, 16*(3), 294–322.

Tanner, L.N., & Lindgren, H.C. (1971). *Classroom Teaching and Learning: A Mental Health Approach.* New York: Holt, Rinehart, & Winston.

Tanner, T. (1987). Environmental education for citizen action. *Science through Science, Technology and Society Reporter*. University Park, PA: The Pennsylvania State University.

Taton, R. (Ed.) (1963). *History of Science: Ancient and Medieval Science from the Beginnings to 1450*. New York: Basic Books.

Taylor, R.P. (1980). *The Computer in the School: Tutor, Tool, Tutee*. New York: Teachers College Press.

Temple, R.K.G. (1986). *China: Land of Discovery*. Wellingborough, UK: Patrick Stephens.

Texley, J., & Wild, A. (Eds.) (1996). *NSTA Pathways to the Science Standards*. Arlington, VA: National Science Teachers Association.

Thompson, C.L., & Shrigley, R.L. (1986). What research says: Revising the Science Attitude Scale. *School Science and Mathematics, 86*(4), 331–343.

Thurgood, D.H., & Weinman, J.M. (1991). *Summary Report 1990: Doctorate Recipients from United States Universities*. Washington, DC: National Academy.

Tippins, D.J., & Dana, N.F. (1992). Culturally relevant alternative assessment. *Science Scope, 15*(6), 50–53.

Tobias, S. (1980). *Paths to Programs for Intervention: Math Anxiety, Math Avoidance, and Reentry Mathematics*. Washington, DC: Institute for the Study of Anxiety in Learning.

Tobias, S. (1990). *They're Not Dumb, They're Different: Stalking the Second Tier*. Tucson, AZ: Research Corporation—A Foundation for the Advancement of Science.

Tobin, K.G. (1984). Effects of extended wait-time on discourse characteristics and achievement in middle school grades. *Journal of Research in Science Teaching, 21*(8), 779.

Tobin, K.G. (1989). Learning in science classrooms. In *Curriculum Development for the Year 2000* (pp. 25–38). Colorado Springs, CO: BSCS.

Tobin, K.G. (1990). Research on science laboratory activities: In pursuit of better questions and answers to improve learning. *School Science and Mathematics, 90*(5), 403–418.

Tobin, K.G., & Capie,W. (1981, March). *Wait-Time and Learning in Science*. Paper presented at the annual meeting of the Association for Educators of Teachers of Science, Washington, DC.

Tobin, K.G., & Gallagher, J.J. (1987). The role of target students in the science classroom. *Journal of Research in Science Teaching, 24*(1), 61–75.

Tobin, K.G., Tippins, D., & Hook, K. (1992, March). *Critical Reform of the Science Curriculum: A Journey from Objectivism to Constructivism*. Paper presented at the annual meeting of the National Association for Research in Science Teaching, Boston, MA.

Total enrollment in institutions of higher education, by race or ethnicity of student and by state and territory: Fall 1988. In *Digest of Educational Statistics, 1990* (p. 201). Washington, DC: National Center for Educational Statistics.

Towell, R. (1991). Innovation and feedback in a self-access learning project in modern languages. *British Journal of Educational Technology, 22*(2), 119–128.

Tyler, F.B., Dhawan, N., & Sinha, Y. (1989). Cultural contributions to constructing locus-of-control attributions. *Genetic, Social, and General Psychology Monographs, 115*(2), 207–220.

United States Department of Commerce (1990). Statistical abstract of the United States. Washington, DC: U.S. Department of Commerce, Economics and Statistics Administration, Bureau of the Census.

United States Department of Education. (1992). *Study of Academic Instruction for Disadvantaged Students: Academic Challenge for the Children of Poverty*. Washington, DC: author.

Useem, E.L. (1990, April). *Social Class and Ability Group Placement in Mathematics in the Transition to Seventh Grade: The Role of Parental Involvement*. Paper presented at the annual meeting of the American Educational Research Association. Boston, MA.

Vacca, R.T., & Vacca, J.L. (1989). *Content Area Reading*. Glenview, IL: Scott Foresman.

Valle, R. (1978a). *The Best of BES—Basic Educational Skills Materials*. Austin TX: Southwest Educational Development Laboratories.

Valle, R. (1978b). The development of a polycultural social policy curriculum from the Latino perspective. In D.G. Norton (Ed.), *The Dual Perspective: Inclusion of Ethnic Minority Content in the Social Work Curriculum* (pp. 58–79). New York: Council on Social Work Education.

Valle, R. (1986). Cross-cultural competence in minority communities: A curriculum implementation strategy. In M.R. Miranda & H.H.L. Kitano (Eds.), *Mental Health Research and Practice in Minority Communities: Development of Culturally Sensitive Training Programs* (pp. 29–49). Rockville, MD: National Institute of Mental Health.

Valle, R. (1989). Cultural and ethnic issues in Alzheimer's disease family research. In E. Light & B.D. Lebowitz (Eds.), *Alzheimer's Disease Treatment and Family Stress: Directions for Research* (pp. 122–153). Rockville, MD: National Institute of Mental Health.

Valle, R. (1990). The Latino/Hispanic family and the elderly: Approaches to cross-cultural curriculum design in the health professions. In U.S. Department of Health & Human Services (Ed.), *Minority Aging: Essential Curricula Content for Selected Health and Allied Health Professions* (pp. 433–452). Washington, DC: U.S. Department of Health & Human Services.

Van Otten, G.A., & Tsutsui, S. (1983). Geocentrism and Indian education. *Journal of American-Indian Education, 22*(2), 23–27.

Van Sertima, I.V. (1986). *Blacks in Science: Ancient and Modern*. New Brunswick, CT: Journal of African Civilizations.

VanTassel-Baska, J., Patton, J., & Prillaman, D. (1989). Disadvantaged gifted learners at-risk for educational attention. *Focus on Exceptional Children, 22*(3), 1–15.

Vargas, E.M., & Alvarez, H.J. (1992). Mapping out students' abilities. *Science Scope, 15*(6), 41–43.

Verhoeven, L.T. (1987). Literacy in a second language context: Teaching immigrant children to read. *Educational Review, 39*(3), 245–261.

Vockell, E., & Schwartz, E. (1988). *The Computer in the Classroom*. Santa Cruz, CA: Mitchell.

Voss, B.E. (1980). Objectives for middle school science. *School Science and Mathematics, 80*(7), 573–576.

Vygotsky, L.S. (1978). *Mind in Society: The Development of Higher Psychological Processes* (M. Cole, V. John-Steiner, S. Scribner, & E. Souberman, Eds.). Cambridge: Harvard University Press.

Wadsworth, B.J. (1978). *Piaget for the Classroom Teacher*. New York: Longman.

Wallace, J. (1986). *Social Interaction within Second Year Groups Doing Practical Science*, Unpublished master's thesis, University of Oxford, Oxford, England.

Ware, N., & Steckler, N. (1983). Choosing a science major: The experience of women and men. *Women's Studies Quarterly, 11*(2), 8–15.

Watson, S.B. (1991). Cooperative learning and group educational modules: Effects on cognitive achievement of high school biology students. *Journal of Research in Science Teaching, 28*(2), 141–146.

Watts, S. (1986). Science education for a multicultural society. In R.K. Arora & C.G. Duncan (Eds.), *Multicultural Education: Towards Good Practice* (pp. 135–160). London: Routledge & Kegan Paul.

Weatherford, J. (1988). *Indian Givers: How the Indians of the Americas Transformed the World*. New York: Fawcett Columbine.

Weiner, B. (1980). The role of affect in rational (attributional) approaches to human motivation. *Educational Researcher, 9*, 4–11.

Weisner, T.S., Gallimore, R., & Jordan, C. (1988). Unpackaging cultural effects on classroom learning: Native Hawaiian peer assistance and child-generated activity. *Anthropology and Education Quarterly, 19*(4), 327–353.

Weiss, I.S. (1987). *Report of the 1985–86 National Survey of Science and Mathematics Education.* National Science Foundation. SPE-8317070. Washington, DC: U.S. Government Printing Office.

Wellesley College Center for Research on Women. (1992). *The AAUW Report: How Schools Shortchange Girls.* Washington, DC: American Association of University Women.

Welton, D.A., & Mallan, J. T. (1992). *Children and Their World: Strategies for Teaching Social Studies.* Boston: Houghton Mifflin.

Wertsch, J.V., & Toma, C. (1991, April). *Discourse and Learning in the Classroom: A Sociocultural Approach.* Presentation made at the University of Georgia Visiting Lecturer Series on Constructivism in Education, Athens, GA.

Wheatley, G.H. (1991). Constructivist perspectives on science and mathematics learning. *Science Education, 75*(1), 9–21.

Williams, H., Fast, J., Berestiansky, J., Turner, C.W., & Debreuil, L. (1979). Designing science lessons to promote cognitive growth. *Science Teacher, 46,* 26–29.

Williams, T.I. (1982). *A Biographical Dictionary of Scientists.* (3rd ed.). New York: Wiley.

Winner, A.A., & Holloway, R.E. (1983). Technology integration for a new curriculum. *Journal of Computers in Mathematics and Science Teaching, 2*(4), 30–35.

Wittrock, M.C. (1978). The cognitive movement in instruction. *Educational Psychologist, 15,* 15–29.

Woerner, J.J., Rivers, R.H., & Vockell, E.L. (1991). *The Computer in the Science Curriculum.* Santa Cruz, CA: Mitchell.

Wolfinger, D.M. (1984). *Teaching Science in the Elementary School: Content, Process, and Attitude.* Boston: Little, Brown.

Woodward, J., & Noell, J. (1991). Science instruction at the secondary level: Implications for students with learning disabilities. *Journal of Learning Disabilities, 24*(5), 277–284.

Woolfolk, A.E. (1993). *Educational Psychology* (5th ed.). Boston: Allyn & Bacon.

Woolfolk, A.E. & McCune-Nicolich, B. (1984, April). *An Empirical Investigation of Training in Time Management: Effects of Special Planning and Self-Monitoring.* Paper presented at the annual meeting of the American Educational Research Association, New Orleans, LA.

Wraga, W.G., & Hlebowitsh, P.S. (1991). STS education and the curriculum field. *School Science and Mathematics, 91*(2), 54–59.

Wright, E.L. (1981). Fifteen simple discrepant events that teach science principles and concepts. *School Science and Mathematics, 81*(7), 575–580.

Yager, R.E. (1987). Assess all five domains of science. *Science Teacher, 54*(7), 33–37.

Yager, R.E. (1990). STS: Thinking over the years. *Science Teacher, 57*(3), 52–55.

Yost, E. (1943). *American Women of Science.* Philadelphia: Lippincott.

Young, S.L. (1990). IDEAS. *Arithmetic Teacher, 38*(2), 24–34.

Zakaluk, B.L., & Samuels, S.J. (Eds.). (1988). *Readability: Its Past, Present, and Future.* Newark, DE: International Reading Association.

Index

Note: Page numbers followed by *t* and *f* indicate tables and figures, respectively.